DRONE CULTURES

BLOOMSBURY STUDIES IN DIGITAL CULTURES

Series Editors
Anthony Mandal and Jenny Kidd

This series responds to a rapidly changing digital world, one which permeates both our everyday lives and the broader philosophical challenges that accrue in its wake. It is inter- and trans-disciplinary, situated at the meeting points of the digital humanities, digital media and cultural studies, and research into digital ethics.

While the series will tackle the "digital humanities" in its broadest sense, its ambition is to broaden focus beyond areas typically associated with the digital humanities to encompass a range of approaches to the digital, whether these be digital humanities, digital media studies or digital arts practice.

Titles in the Series
The Trouble with Big Data, Jennifer Edmond, Nicola Horsley, Jörg Lehmann and Mike Priddy
Hacking in the Humanities, Aaron Mauro
Ambient Stories in Practice and Research, edited by Amy Spencer
Metamodernism and the Postdigital in the Contemporary Novel, Spencer Jordan
Representing the New AI in Film and Television, Graham Allen
Resisting Big Tech, Niels Niessen

Forthcoming Titles
New Directions in Digital Textual Studies,
edited by Christopher Ohge, Kristen Schuster

DRONE CULTURES

From Surveillance and Warfare to Literature and Art

John Muthyala

BLOOMSBURY ACADEMIC
LONDON • NEW YORK • OXFORD • NEW DELHI • SYDNEY

BLOOMSBURY ACADEMIC

Bloomsbury Publishing Plc, 50 Bedford Square, London, WC1B 3DP, UK
Bloomsbury Publishing Inc, 1359 Broadway, New York, NY 10018, USA
Bloomsbury Publishing Ireland, 29 Earlsfort Terrace, Dublin 2, D02 AY28, Ireland

BLOOMSBURY, BLOOMSBURY ACADEMIC and the Diana logo are trademarks of
Bloomsbury Publishing Plc

First published in Great Britain 2026

Copyright © John Muthyala, 2026

John Muthyala has asserted his right under the Copyright, Designs and Patents Act, 1988,
to be identified as Author of this work.

For legal purposes the Acknowledgements on pp. xxiii–xxiv constitute an extension of this
copyright page.

Cover design: Lara Himpelmann
Cover illustration by swillklitch via Adobe Stock

All rights reserved. No part of this publication may be: i) reproduced or transmitted in
any form, electronic or mechanical, including photocopying, recording or by means of
any information storage or retrieval system without prior permission in writing from the
publishers; or ii) used or reproduced in any way for the training, development or operation
of artificial intelligence (AI) technologies, including generative AI technologies. The rights
holders expressly reserve this publication from the text and data mining exception as per
Article 4(3) of the Digital Single Market Directive (EU) 2019/790.

Bloomsbury Publishing Plc does not have any control over, or responsibility for, any
third-party websites referred to or in this book. All internet addresses given in this
book were correct at the time of going to press. The author and publisher regret any
inconvenience caused if addresses have changed or sites have ceased to exist, but can
accept no responsibility for any such changes.

A catalogue record for this book is available from the British Library.

A catalog record for this book is available from the Library of Congress.

ISBN: HB: 978-1-350-53046-1
PB: 978-1-350-53045-4
ePDF: 978-1-350-53047-8
eBook: 978-1-350-53048-5

Series: Bloomsbury Studies in Digital Cultures

Typeset by Newgen KnowledgeWorks Pvt. Ltd., Chennai, India
Printed and bound in Great Britain

For product safety related questions contact productsafety@bloomsbury.com.

To find out more about our authors and books visit www.bloomsbury.com
and sign up for our newsletters.

CONTENTS

List of Figures vi
Preface vii
Acknowledgments xxiii

1 Rise of the Drone: Mobile Eye of Power 1

2 The Global Anarchy of the Surveillant Assemblage 33

3 Biopolitics, Necropolitics, and Ethics in a Drone World 69

4 Drone, Baby, Drone: Techno-Neocolonialism and Postcolonial Mediations in Namwali Serpell's *The Old Drift* 101

5 The New Aesthetic: Post-Digitality, Eversion, and Drone Cultures 135

6 Drone Dispositions in Art and Culture 159

Epilogue 191
Bibliography 201
Index 223

FIGURES

1.1 Global Hawk, NASA 2

1.2 MQ-9 Reaper. Leslie Pratt 3

1.3 MQ-1B Predator. Sabrina Johnson 4

1.4 X-47B on an aircraft carrier. Timothy Walter 7

1.5 Bayraktar TB2, Turkish drone. By Bayhaluk 7

6.1 Islamabad truck art, Pakistan. Baptiste Marcel 168

6.2 Truck art in Pakistan. Riyan Chaudhary 169

6.3 "By the Moonlight," by Mahwish Chisty 170

6.4 "Hellfire Missile" by Mahwish Chisty 171

6.5 Truck wheel art. Murtaza Imran Ali 173

6.6 "Reaper Drone," by Mahwish Chisty 173

PREFACE

How do digital tools, systems, and networks extend, justify, or thwart power and influence in the world? What impact do they have on society, culture, and liberal democracy?

In response to these questions, *Drone Cultures: From Surveillance and Warfare to Literature and Art* makes three core arguments: digital technologies are essential to establishing new forms of dominance through drones and surveillance systems; these forms have significant effects on individuality, privacy, and democracy; and popular culture registers how the various uses of drone technologies raise questions about individual, governmental, and social power.

Why do these questions and arguments matter?

Rise of the Drone Age

After the Euromaidan Uprisings (2013–14) and the Revolution of Dignity (2014) led to civil war in Ukraine, resulting in the ouster of President Viktor Yanukovych, Russia annexed Crimea. A decade of skirmishes between Ukraine and Russia followed, culminating in Russia invading Ukraine in February 2022. To overwhelm Ukraine, Russia sent a few hundred thousand troops into the country, yet, with surprising grit, Ukraine held on, and soon a new phase of conflict began to take shape: drone wars. A month into the conflict, using drones, Ukraine disrupted Russian troops marching in a fifty-mile stretch from Chernobyl to Kyiv. Russia soon emulated Ukraine's use of Turkey's TB-2 drone, by deploying its natively produced Lancet and Orlan-10 and Iran's Shahed-136.[1] Soon, the Ukraine-Russia war began to be described as the "first drone war" and the "first Starlink War."[2]

These are apt characterizations, given that, per *United24Media*, a Ukrainian news feed, there were "over 54,000 drone strikes on Russian targets in December [2024], half using FPV suicide drones."[3] First-Person View (FPV) means viewing through goggles or a headset, not on a small or big screen, what the drone sees, which merges the drone operator's sight with a drone's line of sight. The *New York Times* updated an article on January 1, 2025, about "how suicide drones transformed the front lines in Ukraine," which adds, "Known as first-person-view drones, or FPVs, the weapons have altered the human experience of war and flooded the internet with footage chronicling the desperate last seconds of lives ended by mini aircraft that transmit video of the people they pursue, then smack into them and explode."[4] Intriguingly, the reference to drone videos points to the theatricality of drone warfare, where the widespread production and dissemination of drone-produced images and videos of war conditions and killings become central to warfare.

Another unique feature of this war is Ukraine's (and later, Russia's) attempt to leverage commercial drones to send drone swarms attacking Russian targets. Unlike military drones, small, mini drones bought on the market can be jiggered to take images and video and sent as airborne scouts on reconnaissance missions or turned into kamikaze drones. With Russia adopting a similar approach, the war has become "a window into the future of warfare" as drones have taken center stage in a war between two nation-states.[5] For the first time in military history, two nation-states are using military and repurposed civilian drones to engage in large-scale conflict. The Biden administration approved sending to Ukraine 100 "switchblade" drones, also known as "kamikaze drones" or suicide drones, to help it resist Russian military operations.[6] Ukraine set a target of producing a million small drones per year for military use, which was met in 2024, and Russia has been aiming to manufacture 4,000 drones a day. Both the war belligerents are seeking to produce more than 3 million small drones in 2025.[7] And there is more.

According to a United Nations report published in March 2021 by the Panel of Experts on Libya, in Tripoli, Libya, a lethal autonomous weapons system (LAWS) was used in March 2020 to "attack targets without requiring data connectivity between the operator and the munition."[8] A remarkable development, because the drone was deployed to function autonomously without human piloting or input to identify and attack targets, this event, nevertheless, did not involve taking human life. However, it is the first report of an AI-enabled drone used in conflict-ridden regions. Similarly, Ukraine has been using the Saker company's drones that are loaded with AI software to help identify tanks, munitions, and geo-markers to navigate the terrain, and to identify the location and nature of military groups or armaments. When this information is relayed to drone operators with FPV teams, they can decide to deploy missiles for attack. The Saker Scout is a new development, because "the most radical use of the Saker Scout is to carry out attacks without a human in the loop, finding and hitting targets autonomously."[9]

Drones have also been used to take out a head of state. In August 2018, at a public event, President Nicolás Maduro of Venezuela was subjected (he survived) to two drones exploding over him, an apparent attempt at an assassination.[10] According to a report published in the Joint Intelligence Bulletin, a "DJI Mavic-2, a small quadcopter-type drone, was found carrying a copper wire attached to it by nylon cords in what was believed to be an attempted attack on a power substation in Pennsylvania last year [2020]."[11] Fitting a small commercial, hobby drone with explosives to destroy power grids demonstrates the potential of using drones to destroy critical infrastructure, which can cripple a city for a long time.

On October 16, 2024, the Israel Defense Forces encountered suspects hiding in a building in Rafah. Retreating awhile, "the soldiers withdrew, and a drone flew in to search the room. It found a man with his arm injured and his face covered—Sinwar—who threw a wooden stick at the drone."[12] The person who threw a stick at the drone turned out to be Yahya Sinwar, the mastermind of the deadly October 7, 2023, attack against Israelis by Hamas terrorists. Three days later, it was reported that a drone targeted Israeli Prime Minister Benjamin Netanyahu's house, but failed in its mission.[13]

In November 2024, thousands of drone sightings were reported in New Jersey, particularly close to military centers and President Trump's Bedminster golf resort. In response to a public outcry over the lack of information about the nature and purpose of these drones, the Department of Defense (DoD), the Federal Bureau of Investigation (FBI), the Department of Homeland Security (DHS), and the Federal Aviation Administration (FAA) issued joint statements that the drones were not a national security threat, yet refused to explain their origins and the sudden surge in their sightings.[14] Interestingly, these drones were reported to be large in size, a few feet in height or length, which were characterized as "commercial drones," because they are "sophisticated unmanned vehicles designed for professional use, equipped with specialized technology tailored to various industries. These drones enhance efficiency, precision, and innovation in tasks that were once labor-intensive or hazardous. Commercial drones and unmanned vehicles suit a diverse range of applications including logistics, agriculture, public safety, search and rescue, firefighting, construction, inspection, and mapping."[15] According to the FAA, "there are more than one million drones lawfully registered with the FAA in the United States and there are thousands of commercial, hobbyist and law enforcement drones lawfully in the sky on any given day."[16] These examples, and many more, as we shall study in this book, point to a new world we are living in today: a world of drones.

World of Drones

Unlike the traditional war in which the machinery of combat—troops, tanks, weapons, electronic gadgets, munitions, battleships, fighter jets—is assembled, managed, and deployed, and often visible, this new war is fought secretly and virtually. It's a cheap war. It's an invisible war. It's a war of stealth and silence. Drone wars can take place anytime and anywhere; they redefine notions of normalcy and exception, as they generate constant insecurity by waging perpetual war. In drone warfare, it is difficult to ascertain when a country is at war, and when it is not, when conditions of peace prevail, and when they don't, because the anytime-everywhere matrix enables powerful states to create and manage conditions of emergency on a trans-territorial and biopolitical scale.[17]

Consider what transpired over the past two decades: in Pakistan, under President George W. Bush, there were 48 drone strikes, 116–37 civilian deaths, and 218–326 militant casualties, and under President Obama, there were 353 strikes, 129–62 civilian deaths, and 1,659–2,683 militant casualties.[18] In Yemen, Bush authorized one strike resulting in zero civilian casualties, and six militants killed, while Obama authorized 184 strikes, leading to 89–101 civilians killed, and 973–1,240 militants killed.[19] President Donald Trump continued Obama's aggressive use of drones, by authorizing 112 strikes, among others, in Pakistan and Yemen combined[20] but began scaling them down, which President Biden continued to follow, although his administration went after high-value targets with drone strikes in 2021 in Afghanistan, which also killed ten civilians.[21]

Whereas the locations for these events are outside the United States, the foreign turns out to be intimately connected to the domestic, particularly in the rise of Big Tech, shorthand for the conglomeration of information technology companies exercising inordinate control over the flow of information and data, resulting in extreme politicization of public discourse, free speech restrictions, and compromising people's abilities to engage meaningfully in democratic governance. Such conceptual, legal, and policy difficulties do not absolve America's drone wars, but they clearly point to the immense difficulty in addressing the killing of innocent men, women, and children as the global war on terrorism continues unabated, taking on new configurations in international conflicts.

In June 2013, *The Guardian*, a British newspaper, and *The Washington Post*, an American newspaper, published ex-CIA contractor Edward Snowden's claims that the National Security Agency (NSA) was illegally conducting electronic surveillance on millions of Americans and numerous allies throughout the world. The central figures in this government-business nexus are the White House, NSA, the Justice Department, Facebook, Yahoo, Twitter, YouTube, Google, Skype, AOL, Paltalk, and Apple. The solid evidence-based reporting by newspapers led to their getting the Pulitzer Prize for Public Service; later, reporters Glenn Greenwald and Laura Poitras, journalists for these newspapers, followed up with more material, Greenwald with a book (*No Place to Hide: Edward Snowden, the NSA, and the U.S. Surveillance State*) documenting their interactions with Edward Snowden, and Poitras with a documentary (*Citizenfour*) on Snowden, which won the Academy Award for Best Documentary Feature (2014).

Apparently, the nexus between the state and social media businesses came to a head in 2020, when Twitter suspended the account of the *New York Post* for publishing a story on the laptop of Hunter Biden, son of President Biden, focusing on the former's attempts to monetize his family connections. In January 2021,

Twitter suspended President Trump's account due to the January 6 protests at the Hill. Upon acquiring Twitter in October 2022, Elon Musk shared the company's internal documents regarding suspending newspapers, official accounts, and private accounts with journalists Matt Taibi, Bari Weiss, and Michael Shellenberger, who released reports in late 2022 and early 2023, following their assessment. This activity acquired the nomenclature "The Twitter Files." Reactions to them ranged from confirmation of liberal bias to the right to suppress misinformation, from suspicion of media platforms as vehicles for liberal and Democratic propaganda to justifying filtering or reducing visibility to decrease online bullying.[22] Some facts, however, are indisputable: a national newspaper's story about a presidential candidate's son was suppressed, a sitting president's twitter account was suspended, and government agencies pressured social media companies to suspend posts and tweets, or suspend accounts or downgrade their visibility.

Predictably, political lenses can influence the interpretation of these facts, but the facts themselves are unprecedented, showing the nontransparent workings of the security state with social media and private businesses. When the peoples and institutions involved can act without oversight and public knowledge, people's right to know is compromised, undermining their participation in democratic governance. Despite voicing skepticism at those who view the Twitter Files as irrefutable evidence of suppressing conservative voices, Kenan Malik, writing for *The Guardian*, characterizes the situation well:

> The most worrying issue the Twitter Files have exposed is the level of contact between the social media company and state security organisations. The FBI regularly holds meetings with Twitter executives, pressuring them to take action against "misinformation," even when this amounted to little more than a satirical tweet, and demanding the personal data of users. Twitter, to its credit, often pushed back. Nevertheless, the Twitter Files do show an unhealthy relationship between social media and state security.[23]

Malik's point about the "unhealthy relationship between social media and state security" is borne out well when the Indian government asked Twitter to delete or throttle tweets critical of its response to Covid-19, which, in spring 2021, ravaged many parts of India, killing people in the thousands. India justified its position by pointing to the need to decrease false information or panic, which would undermine Indian sovereignty, a position that many governments have taken to suppress dissenting voices.[24] Even if we grant that in times of emergencies, we might have to trust the government more than others, the problem is that trust in institutions is not automatic nor mandatory; trust must be earned through a record of deep, pervasive engagement with various publics on matters critical to their well-being. There was little evidence showing that the government was doing a top job at curtailing Covid-19's spread or providing medical resources to the most vulnerable. To the contrary, ground realities showed conditions that belied official narratives, making it hard to accept the argument that dissent and satire must be suppressed. As digital media gives more people the wherewithal to engage in what can be called, perhaps generously, "citizen journalism," and, if not that, the opportunity to participate in the digital commons to speak freely and exercise their right to do so, the onus is on the state to practice a politics of accountability and transparency to increase institutional trust and guard from acting illiberally.

From the secret surveillance of American citizens to widespread surveillance through drones on numerous communities in several countries, the power—and resistance to it—of digital technologies to shape official narratives about the actions of the powerful continues unabated. Meanwhile, the costs of war are increasing, with drones yet again playing a key role in demonstrating their normalization in military activities. According to the *Cost of War* project of the Watson Institute for International and Public Affairs, Brown University, since 9/11, the United States spent $8 trillion on the War on Terror, around 900,000 people died, and America's overseas operations in this war have extended into eighty countries. President Biden referenced its report:

> After more than $2 trillion spent in Afghanistan, costs that Brown University researchers estimated would be over $300 million a day for 20 years—yes, the American people should hear this … what have we lost as a consequence, in terms of opportunities? … I refuse to send America's sons and daughters to fight a war that should have ended long ago.[25]

Biden's comments, in fact, extend his predecessor's (President Trump) America First policy that sought to minimize American wars and downgrade ongoing conflicts. In August 2021, as the United States was pulling out of Afghanistan, it launched a drone strike on suspects; tragically, the suspects were innocent people. Ten were killed, including seven children. One of the adults was Zemari Ahmadi, who was working for a California NGO called "Nutrition and Education International."[26] Clearly, international concerns about drone warfare almost a decade ago are as relevant today as they were then.

While militarized drones are changing the modality of war, a civilian, commercial front opened for drones, where they are used as a hobby—for research, for entertainment, for education. It is important to avoid reducing drones to tools for domination, control, or violence. Because, as digital innovations, they have become part of quotidian life, drones are domesticated, so to speak, no longer only tools of war but instruments for expressive, creative activity, vectors for entertainment, and catalysts for innovative education and public safety. As Beryl Pong notes, "drones have become technological woodwork, naturalized as a familiar presence in everyday life."[27]

Drone Art and Culture

In a dark, dangerous terrain, far from home and potentially inhabited by terrorists wanting to harm American troops, a drone, also called "remotely piloted aircraft" or "unmanned aerial vehicle," shoots a beam of light from the heavens. When the heat laser hits the earth, it appears as the "light of God" in night-vision goggles to soldiers on the ground. "It's quite beautiful," says the drone pilot, describing the aesthetic effect of releasing laser heat from a Predator drone to target a potential IED (improvised explosive devise).[28]

This is the account of a drone pilot reminiscing on camera for Omer Fast, who creatively interweaves video testimony into a performative narrative (*5,000 Feet is the Best*) that highlights the challenges of being a drone pilot who, ensconced in urban locations far removed from life-threatening battlefields, wages war against targets thousands of miles away: he sees them, surveils them, hones in on them, kills them. All this is done with the aid of digital and surveillance technologies that connect complicated communication networks, command and control centers, video and image feeds, intelligence analyses, military officials, and politicians working in real-time in locations strewn across the world to assess, interpret, and decide whom to kill, how to kill, and when to kill. Using photo-morphing and layering tools, British media artist James Bridle takes a famous picture of a man standing forlornly in a desert and overlays it with the green-tinged image produced by infrared night glasses that bring into visibility the "light of God" emanating from a hovering drone: a single shaft of purposeful laser light in a desolate landscape of the war against terrorism.[29]

The figures of remotely piloted aircraft or unmanned aerial vehicles—Predator (decommissioned), Reaper, Global Hawk—have become objects d'art for Pakistani-American painter Mahwish Chishty. She produces gauche paintings of drones by drawing on the colors and patterns of truck art, a mainstay of Pakistani road culture.[30] Her intent is to undermine the globally popular idea of drones as military symbols and reinsert them into the public imagination as aesthetic objects worth studying and using for expression and social reflection: drones are artifacts that can be used for war and for beauty, for destruction and for art.

In "Seraph," a dance developed by the Massachusetts Institute of Technology (MIT) and Pilobolus, a famous dance company, the setting is stark and haunting as a dancer clothed only with a dance belt encounters a drone that appears out of nowhere.[31] As they asses each other carefully, step and side-step, twist and extend, hide and glance, slowly but surely, the human being and the drone begin to interact. The dance becomes a meeting of two minds—a machine that is not just a machine and a human that relates to the machine as if it were autonomously intelligent. In this dance, the drone is not a deadly tool of imperial technology that appears out of nowhere, unleashes fury, and recedes into nowhere, but it is a performer, a dancer in an artistically rendered and digitally manipulated theatrical act accompanied by sound, lighting, and music.

In 2016, Dubai hosted the world's first Drone Grand Prix, offering prizes worth a million dollars for drone pilots who could demonstrate their skill of drone racing at high speeds and executing a series of complex movements on a racetrack built specially for drones.[32] In 2019, the Drone Racing League, which holds racing events around the United States, hosted a special event for the Artificial Intelligence Robotic Racing Circuit to hold races for drones equipped with an "AI framework that's capable of racing a drone—without any pre-programming or human intervention," as per Nicholas Horbaczewski, CEO and Founder, Drone Racing League.[33] Denmark hosted an International Drone Show at Odense in May 2024 to showcase new drone technologies and provide international networking events for companies and other groups.[34] In Australia, drones called "Little Ripper Lifesavers" are mounted with AI software that can scan shorelines and coastal waters to spot sharks and activate their megaphone to warn people. Where human sighting and assessing of images were accurate 20 percent to 30 percent of the time, these drones' accuracy rate shot up to 90 percent.[35] Whether for art or for war, for research or for entertainment, for play or for law, drones have opened a new front in the globalization of technologies, the normalization of surveillance cultures, the exercise of imperial domination, and the ideation of war and peace.

What is common to Fast's *5,000 Feet Is the Best*, Bridle's *Light of God*, Chishty's drone paintings, MIT-Pilobolus's dancing drones, the riveting publications of *The Guardian* and *The Washington Post*, the UN Special Rapporteur's reports, the drone wars in Afghanistan, Pakistan, and the Middle East, in Ukraine and Russia, the attacks against heads of state and power grids, the drone life savers in Australia, and the drone racing championships in Dubai is this: drones and surveillance are the new digital technologies for dominance and aesthetics. Drones and surveillance compel a rethinking of spatiotemporal coordinates that help us map national boundaries and locate ourselves in space and history. Drones are not only remotely operated weaponized aircraft but also fascinating new tools that enable us to transcend the limitations of geography and time. They can unleash hellish destruction even as we yearn to play with them and make them do wondrous things. They surveil us even as we find their ability to surveil compelling enough to use their affordances for research, education, and entertainment.

Drones are objects of fear and objects of wonder. They enable us to perform dances, make gauche drone paintings, morph images to produce new ones, renegotiate space and time, and surveil our environments and each other differently. Art and surveillance, technology and beauty, aesthetics and politics collide head-on in the new configurations of power and pleasure that are shaping our economic, military, and social systems of communication and entertainment. In war and in art; in conflict and in literature; in establishing territorial, atmospheric, and naval dominance; and in expressing human aspiration and creativity, the drone has taken center stage. Hence, it is important to examine how drones are transforming war and peace, and how drones are generating global digital cultures that register peoples' attempts to imagine new possibilities for human agency and responsibility.

Digital technologies, which make possible the drone, to extend Edward Said, are "in the world, and hence worldly," and are "always enmeshed in circumstance, time, place, and society."[36] Whatever the vastness of digital corpora, the complexity of coding languages, and the sophistication of algorithmic, robotic logics that compress information in space and time to generate analytics with predictive power, the conception, production, dissemination, and use of the digital are worldly endeavors, a series of innumerable acts and motivations profoundly and inescapably shaped by human interests, local pressures, national trends, and global flows. To engage with the worldliness of the digital is to grasp technological innovation as a social and cultural phenomenon that can rewrite, erase, re-draw, or affirm the histories, cultures, and spaces of many peoples and living things in the world; it is to grasp the digital as affording new ways of conceiving of the world and our being in the world.

The worldliness of the digital links First World concerns with so-called Third World realities, by foregrounding the enduring legacies of colonialism and the struggle for postcolonial provenance. To grasp the nature of drone warfare, we have to understand the material and discursive contexts and practices that have given rise to a new technology whose efficacy and function are inextricably linked to digital systems and cultures: data storage and processing sites, software programming, data cataloging and mining, visualization, cross-platform integration, interfacing analog and digital systems, Geographical Information Systems, high-resolution pixels, processing speeds, nodes and networks, technologies of surveillance, Googlization, digitization, face, voice, eye recognition, genome mapping, fiber optics, automation, predictive analytics, robotics, artificial intelligence, and a host of other forms and activities that integrate information and digital technologies.

To understand the workings of these elements in their atomized manifestations and networked iterations; to conceptualize the logics of interaction that constantly connect them or disperse them or realign them in variable and unpredictable forms and content; to conceive of them as creating large and small networks and systems that generate their own methods and protocols of engaging with natural and human environments, and in ways that question, undermine, or change ideas of authority, intention, privacy, authenticity, individuality, agency, privacy, the real, the virtual, and the human: these are the aims of this book.

Let me stress here a key argument of the book: drones must be grasped at two levels—as tools for creativity, research, and education, and as tools for dominance, destruction, and death. We should understand drones primarily as new technological developments in our digital world, whose impact extends into all spheres of social, economic, cultural, and political life. If this point gains clarity to readers on reading this book, my task would be well executed. The use of drones opens a global theater of war in which the "world is a battlefield";[37] in this global theater, there are endless wars and there is perpetual peace; that is, drone warfare changes traditional meanings of war and peace.

But what is at stake for democracy and justice in a world of drones and global surveillance? How do we imagine our humanity and ethical responsibility to each other and our communities when they are leading us to rethink the nature of peace and war, guilt and innocence, pleasure and pain, life and death: and what makes us human? These are the central concerns of this book, whose chapters are organized thus:

Chapter 1, "Rise of the Drone: Mobile Eye of Power," traces the rise of drone warfare, when the United States began using armed drones tentatively during the Bush presidency, and dramatically accelerated its use in the Obama presidency, which continues into the present. The chapter draws from the United Nations' special committee reports on armed drones to underscore the need for developing international policies to regulate new disruptive digital technologies—drones—harnessed to the state, military, and police. I trace the historical use of remotely operated technologies in warfare right up to the current drones, like the iterations of the Global Hawk, Predator, and Reaper.

I build on the work of Grégory Chamayou, Ole Jensen, Lisa Parks, and Denis Zuev to explain the drone's affordances like dronescapes, volumetric thinking, thermal imaging, and surveillance, sousveillance, and counterveillance. To these concepts, I connect Lauren Alex O'Hagan and Elisa Serafinelli's idea of drone photography leading to new modes of visuality, one that zooms out and zooms in, one that provides users a kind of interactivity that repositions them as people exercising agency, not become entirely subjective and passive in their engagement with the visuals and feeds produced by drones. A key point is that drone aerials do not privilege verticality as inherently prone to dominance. The focus in this section is to explain and connect various theorists' arguments of how drones are changing our sense of geography, visual perception, and sensory affect. The use of drones opens a global theater of war in which the "world is a battlefield";[38] in this global theater, there are endless wars and there is perpetual peace; that is, drone warfare changes traditional meanings of war and peace. All these have a direct bearing on the book's focus on drone warfare and drone cultures.

Chapter 2, "The Global Anarchy of the Surveillant Assemblage," examines how drones and surveillance networks enable nation-states to exercise power and control at scale, both demographic and geographic. This new power normalizes cultures of surveillance in which people are scrutinized based on techniques of data production and data analysis to apprehend, track, or eliminate suspects. The efficacy of drone wars is predicated on the establishment of surveillance systems and data management both within and without national boundaries. Drone warfare produces a state of emergency in which everyone is presumed worthy of being surveilled in anticipation of detecting, apprehending, or disposing off suspects.

I study the risks and dangers of a surveillance society in which dataveillance—production of electronic dossiers, data doubles, data profiles—can lead to absurd situations where the real and the digital generate identity mergers, conflicts, overlaps, and other contradictions with profound consequences for people, justice, and civil society. In a section on ChatGPT and drones, I discuss the growing influence of programs driven by large language models to facilitate drone flights, aerial photography, and task-oriented programming leading to an algorithmic-driven form of war and surveillance. The current public discourse about ChatGPT tends to view it as a new disruptive technology. I show that ChatGPT and other AI-driven programs are enhancements of robotic war models; what ChatGPT does is make AI more pervasive, more functional, more autonomous than before, leading to a point where the ultimate fighting machine becomes a material possibility: a drone that can, on its own, decide over life and death.

Chapter 3, "Biopolitics, Necropolitics, and Ethics in a Drone World," argues that the biopolitical (Michel Foucault) nature of empire today sustains a social order of necropolitics (Achille Mbembe) that thrives on deep, pervasive surveillance of daily life, making it difficult for people to live freely and pursue their dreams, except on terms legitimized by the illiberal state. I demonstrate how drones and surveillance instantiate a new dispensation of dominance—powerful control through digital, light, mobile, shadowy networks, systems, and processes. I revise Foucault, Agamben, and Mbembe's ideas by drawing on the work of Edward Said, Mark Haugaard, and Thomas Lemke. In a digitally saturated world, we must rethink both domination and resistance as having horizontal, interactive practices that can be used to deflect global power and resist invasive drone surveillance. Using the concept of "sousveillance" (Steve Mann, Roger Stahl, Rita Raley, and Sebastian Kaempf), I show how people are seeking to undermine or reverse the authoritative surveillance of the state. In a digitally saturated world, we must rethink both domination and resistance as having horizontal, interactive practices that can be used to deflect global power and resist invasive drone surveillance.

I also analyze Zygmunt Bauman's concept of "adiaphorization," which describes the centering of ethical decisions in nonhuman entities, as a profound ethical problem that must be countered by a relentless insistence on the human-oriented and politically charged nature of AI. Put another way, AI is a product of scientific ingenuity and an intelligence that bears all the hallmarks of human passion, engineering, politics, and cultural aspiration. Much of the resistance to digital innovation takes place in the cultural realm, which I take up in the final chapter of the book, but after first discussing, in the next chapter, how a digitally mediated form of resistance with drones finds a compelling plot in the celebrated Zambian-American writer Namwali Serpell's novel, *The Old Drift*.

Chapter 4, "Drone, Baby, Drone: Techno-Neocolonialism and Postcolonial Mediations," examines Namwali Serpell's *The Old Drift*, a literary text, to demonstrate how, in the context of Zambian colonial and postcolonial histories, the drone becomes a symbol of techno-neocolonialism and, paradoxically, a potent weapon of resistance against it, embodying a unique vision of postcoloniality. Drawing on Frantz Fanon and William E. B. DuBois's ideas of colonial Manicheanism and double consciousness, this chapter explores how error, chance, and contingency determine the geographic, biologic, and gendered dynamics of empire, ideology, and subaltern resistance.

I extend the insights of Kwame Nkrumah, Ella Shohat, Ofunmilayo Arewa, Mirca Madianou, and Bhakti Shringapure to demonstrate how new iterations of colonialist socioeconomic logic in postcoloniality are evident in Zambia's digital networked economy. I develop the idea of techno-neocolonialism as an ensemble of practices concentrating political and economic power within oligarchic groups to use the police, big business, the military, and government entities to forge connections with global and local information technology companies, their allies, affiliates, and beneficiaries, to co-opt or silence popular dissent and protest movements.

The novel dramatizes techno-neocolonialism as the nexus of Information Technology, government agencies, and international businesses that generate conditions of subalternity for peoples deemed as threats or superfluous to the political and economic order sustained by the postcolonial state. To understand the relationship of subaltern resistance to techno-neocolonialism, a resistance that leads to a catastrophic, yet hopeful, ending in the novel, driven in large measure by digitally mediated platforms, underground communications, and automated, remotely controlled drones, I analyze how Frantz Fanon's idea of the Manichean logic of coloniality extends into postcolonial Zambia, and W. E. B. DuBois's "double consciousness" influences the psychology of the main characters, and their interactions with others, Zambian culture, and African history.

Chapter 5, "The New Aesthetic: Drones, Post-digitality, and Eversion," argues against viewing artificial intelligence, surveillance, and drones as primarily negative digital systems and tools. They can be used for aesthetic purposes. They produce a sense of wonder and excitement when human beings remotely operate devices to control space and time. People also use drones to resist established practices for doing business, relating to people, and registering discontent with official culture.

This chapter studies the rise of a new artistic mood called the New Aesthetic (James Bridle, Dave Berry, Justin Hodgson, Katherine Hayles, and Adam Greenfield), explains the New Aesthetic's key features, and examines several examples of art and literature to underscore how they counter the dehumanizing effects of drone wars. I also discuss how the ability to move across locations in a global world impacts our views of drones and drone art. Furthermore, criticisms of the New Aesthetic are examined (deep immersion in the digital; extreme self-reflexivity; insufficient critique of the multiple axes of social power that influence the production, flow, and use of the digital, etc.) because the next chapter applies the concept to study a range of multimedia texts to show the New Aesthetic as a cultural mood produced by digital culture.

Chapter 6, "Drone Dispositions in Art and Culture," takes up the artistic impulse about drones and surveillance, demonstrating how they have become cultural life: people are painting drones and using surveillance games, methods, and tools for entertainment; they are using mixed media to generate new juxtapositions of ideas and symbols; they are singing about them in telefilms in Pashtun Afghani societies; they are making paper or cloth imprints to attract drone operators; they are using drones in live dance performances; they are rewiring it for paint bombing, or graffiti art; and they are making videos of drones. Examples include Mahwish Chishty's gouache drone paintings that draw on popular truck art in Pakistan; the use of drones and the power of surveillance in romance and love in Pashtun music and literature; British artist James Bridle's installation and public performance of drone art that seek to give physical representation to the invisibility of drones and drone wars; and the choreography of a drone dance by Pilobolus, a company in Massachusetts.

The authority of representation (who has the right to creatively represent drones?) and the politics of location (how does geography affect artistic production, circulation, and reception?) have become chief concerns. I argue that we need to develop transnational social and political contexts to better understand these developments, and how to address them, rather than dismissing drones as weapons of war and a danger to humanity or democracy or celebrating them as the latest technological marvel that can lead to social amelioration and scientific advancement.

The *Epilogue* highlights how the global commercialization of armed drones in the global market has led to what Garret Hardin calls the "tragedy of the commons," where each participant, acting out of self-interest, takes a part of the commons until the commons get depleted, leading to intense political and economic struggle. Globalization and digital technologies have changed the terms and forms in which violence has become untethered from state control; today, small groups and individuals can bring down or weaken powerful nation-states or deflect their power through drones.

It is in the global commons, understood as the networked space for open-ended intellectual curiosity, ethical critique, historical understanding, and cross-cultural give-and-take that the generative impulse for liberal democracy will thrive. While reclaiming privacy as a right, we must deliberate ethically and act thoughtfully to increase social awareness and initiate policy changes to reduce the risks of war and invasive surveillance, particularly in a world increasingly caught up with AI.

Notes

1. Paul Lushenko, "Cult of the drone: At the two-year mark, UAVs have changed the face of war in Ukraine—but not its outcomes," *theconversation.com* February 26, 2024, https://theconversation.com/cult-of-the-drone-at-the-two-year-mark-uavs-have-changed-the-face-of-war-in-ukraine-but-not-outcomes-221397
2. Seth Cropsey, "Drone Warfare in Ukraine: Historical Context and Implications for the Future." *hoover.org* March 14, 2024, https://hoover.org/research/drone-warfare-ukraine-historical-context-and-implications-future
3. Vlad Litnarovych, "Ukraine launches over 54,000 drone strikes on Russian targets in December, half using FPV suicide drones," *united24media.com* January 7, 2025, https://united24media.com/latest-news/ukraine-launches-over-54000-drone-strikes-on-russian-targets-in-december-half-using-fpv-suicide-drones-4920
4. C. J. Chivers, "How Suicides Drones Transformed the Front Lines in Ukraine," *nytimes.com* December 31, 2024, https://www.nytimes.com/2024/12/31/magazine/drones-weapons-ukraine-war.html
5. Mark Jacobsen, "Ukraine's Drone Strikes Are a Window into the Future of Warfare." *atlanticcouncil.org* September 14, 2023 https://atlanticcouncil.org/blogs/new-atlanticist/ukraines-drone-strikes-are-a-window-into-the-future-of-warfare/; Marcel Plichta, "Russia's Growing Kamikaze Drone Fleet Tests Ukraine's Limited Air Defenses." *atlanticcouncil.org* May 14, 2024, https://atlanticcouncil.org/blogs/ukrainealert/russias-growing-kamikaze-drone-fleet-tests-ukraines-limited-air-defenses/
6. Macias, Amanda. "U.S. Sends 100 Killer Drones Called Switchblades to Ukraine." *cnbc.com* March 30, 2022, https://cnbc.com/2022/03/30/us-sends-100-killer-drones-called-switchblades-to-ukraine.html
7. Mark Santora et al., "A Thousand Snipers in the Sky: The New War in Ukraine," *ntyimes.com* March 3, 2025, https://www.nytimes.com/interactive/2025/03/03/world/europe/ukraine-russia-war-drones-deaths.html
8. Panel of Experts on Libya, United Nations, "Report Pursuant to Security Council Resolution 1973 (2011)," *documents.un.org* March 8, 2021, accessed January 26, 2025, https://documents.un.org/doc/undoc/gen/n11/268/39/pdf/n1126839.pdf
9. David Hambling, "Ukraine's AI Drones Seek and Attack Russian Forces without Human Oversight." *forbes.com* October 17, 2024, https://forbes.com/sites/davidhambling/2023/10/17/ukraines-ai-drones-seek-and-attack-russian-forces-without-human-oversight/?sh=2e0e6db66da6
10. BBC, "Venezuela President Maduro Survives 'Drone Assassination Attempt.'" *bbc.com* August 5, 2018, https://bbc.com/news/world-latin-america-45073385
11. Miriam McNabb, "Drone Attack on U.S. Power Grid Failed–This Time." *dronelife.com* November 8, 2021, accessed June 10, 2024, https://dronelife.com/2021/11/08/drone-attack-on-u-s-power-grid-failed-this-time/
12. Times of Isreal, "New Details Emerge of Sinwar's Final Moments," *theliveblog* October 17, 2024, https://timesofisrael.com/liveblog_entry/drone-catches-wounded-sinwars-final-moments-before-his-killing-by-idf/
13. Adam Schreck and Samy Magdy, "A Drone Targets the Israeli Prime Minister's House during New Barrages with Hezbollah," *apnews.com* October 19, 2024, https://apnews.com/article/israel-hamas-war-news-10-18-2024-c49911f11a40b7d81b21bc8568ecfe11

14 Todd C. Lopez, "Joint Staff Address Drones over New Jersey Military Installations," *defense.gov* December 14, 2024, https://defense.gov/News/News-Stories/Article/Article/4002374/joint-staff-addresses-drones-over-new-jersey-military-installations/
15 Unmanned Systems Technology, "Commercial Drones," accessed December 31, 2024, https://unmannedsystemstechnology.com/expo/commercial-drones/#
16 Federal Aviation Administration, "DHS, FBI, FAA & DoD Joint Statement on Ongoing Response to Reported Drone Sightings," *faa.gov* December 17, 2024, https://faa.gov/newsroom/dhs-fbi-faa-dod-joint-statement-ongoing-response-reported-drone-sightings
17 The Intercept, "The Drone Papers," *theintercept* accessed October 26, 2024, https://theintercept.com/drone-papers/
18 Newamerica.org. "Drone Strikes: Pakistan." https://newamerica.org/in-depth/americas-counterterrorism-wars/pakistan/
19 Newamerica.org. "Drone Strikes: Yemen." *newamerica.org* https://newamerica.org/in-depth/americas-counterterrorism-wars/us-targeted-killing-program-yemen/
20 Ben Wolfgang, "Trump Outpacing Obama in Drone Strikes; 80 in First Year: Report." *washingtontimes.com* June 7, 2018, https://washingtontimes.com/news/2018/jun/7/donald-trump-outpacing-barack-obama-drone-strikes-/
21 Anna Coren, et al, "US Military Admits It Killed 10 Civilians and Targeted Wrong Vehicle in Kabul Strike," *cnn.com* September 17, 2021, https://cnn.com/2021/09/17/politics/kabul-drone-strike-us-military-intl-hnk/index.html
22 Shannon Bond, "Elon Musk Is Using the Twitter Files to Discredit Foes and Push Conspiracy Theories." *npr.org* December 14, 2022, https://npr.org/2022/12/14/1142666067/elon-musk-is-using-the-twitter-files-to-discredit-foes-and-push-conspiracy-theor; Joan Donavan, "Why the 'Twitter Files' Are Falling Flat," *politico.com* December 15, 2022, https://politico.com/news/magazine/2022/12/15/twitter-files-falling-flat-00073979
23 Kenan Malik, "The Twitter Files Should Disturb Liberal Critics of Elon Musk—and Here's Why," *theguardian.com* January 1, 2023, https://theguardian.com/commentisfree/2023/jan/01/the-twitter-files-should-disturb-liberal-critics-of-elon-musk-and-heres-why
24 BBC, "India Covid: Anger as Twitter Ordered to Remove Critical Virus Posts," *bbc.com* April 26, 2021, https://bbc.com/news/world-asia-56883483; Antonia Noori Farzan, "Amid 'heartbreaking' coronavirus surge in India, government orders Twitter to remove posts critical of response," *washingtonpost.com* April 26, 2021, https://washingtonpost.com/world/2021/04/26/twitter-india-coronavirus/
25 Neta Crawford, "The U.S. Budgetary Costs of the Post-9/11 Wars." *Costs of War.* Watson Institute for International and Public Affairs. September 1, 2021, https://watson.brown.edu/costsofwar/files/cow/imce/papers/2021/Costs%20of%20War_U.S.%20Budgetary%20Costs%20of%20Post-9%2011%20Wars_9.1.21.pdf; "News from Brown," *brown.edu* September 1, 2021, https://brown.edu/news/2021-09-01/costsofwar
26 Charlie Savage, Eric Schmitt, Azmat Khan, Evan Hill, and Christoph Koettl, "Newly Declassified Video Show U.S. Killing of 10 Civilians in Drone Strike." *nyt.com* January 19, 2022, https://nytimes.com/2022/01/19/us/politics/afghanistan-drone-strike-video.html
27 Beryl Pong, "The Art of Drone Warfare," *Journal of War and Culture Studies* 15, no. 4 (2022): 380.
28 Omer Fast, *5,000 Feet Is Best* (Berlin, Germany: Sternberg Press, 2012), 40.

29. James Bridle, "Four Greens." *booktwo.org* November 26, 2012, http://booktwo.org/notebook/four-greens/
30. Josh Harkinson, "Friendly Fire: Drones as Folk Art." *motherjones.com* June 24, 2013, http://motherjones.com/media/2013/06/pakistani-drone-art-mahwish-chishty
31. MIT Computer Science and Artificial Intelligence Laboratory, "'*Seraph*' Featured in Robot Festival." *csail.mit.edu* July 5, 2012, https://csail.mit.edu/news/seraph-featured-robot-film-festival
32. June Javelosa, "The First 'World Drone Prix' Is Being Held in Dubai." *futurism.com* March 11, 2016, https://futurism.com/world-first-world-drone-prix-held-dubai
33. Khari Johnson, "Drone Racing League Launches $2 Million Autonomous Drone Competition," *venturebeat.com* September 5, 2018, https://venturebeat.com/ai/drone-racing-league-launches-2-million-autonomous-drone-competition/
34. International Drone Show, *internationaldroneshow.com* accessed December 31, 2024, https://internationaldroneshow.com/about/
35. Patrick Caughill, "Australia Is Deploying AI Drones to Help Prevent Shark Attacks." *futurism.com* August 8, 2017 https://futurism.com/australia-is-deploying-ai-drones-to-help-prevent-shark-attacks
36. Edward Said, *The World, the Text, and the Critic* (Cambridge: Harvard University Press, 1983), 35.
37. Jeremey Scahill, *Dirty Wars: The World Is a Battlefield* (Nation Books, 2013). It's the subtitle of Scahill's book.
38. Ibid.

ACKNOWLEDGMENTS

A writer. A book.

A one-to-one relationship seems obvious: an individual, by dint of hard work, produces, over time, a book.

But books and writing are rarely about individual effort; they are the fruit of many ideas and support systems. Exploring ideas about drones; finding relevant primary and secondary materials; exchanging half-baked notions and testing theories; writing lousy first, second, and yet more drafts; losing and regaining interest because of encouragement; sorting book and article requests: such acts—big, small, and numerous—profoundly shaped my work on this book.

Therefore, a big thank you to:

My colleagues at the Glickman Library, University of Southern Maine: William Sargent, Zachary Sogluizzo, Jill Piekut Roy, and Noah Burch.

My colleagues in the English Department and university administrators for supporting a sabbatical request.

My students for asking dozens of questions, sharing research, and persistently countering and affirming perspectives.

At Bloomsbury

Ben Doyle's consistent interest and support made the work of writing and revising the manuscript a rewarding experience—thank you, Ben, for shepherding the manuscript through several phases, and for being a wonderful editor. You've always been gracious with extensions, perspectives, and deadlines.

Thanks to the anonymous reviewers, whose reports helped me to rethink core ideas, and to delete chapters and write new ones with better arguments.

With patience and focus, Leigh Collins helped me with manuscript preparation, putting me on track to meet deadlines. Thanks to Rachel Walker, Senior Production Manager, Merlie Nirmal Jackson and Vignesh, NewGen Knowledge Works, for overseeing the production process with focus and patience. Haaris Naqvi's interest in scholarship from a global perspective is much appreciated.

With Gratitude

Thanks to Deborah Nyangulu, Postdoctoral Researcher, Contradiction Studies, University of Bremen, Germany, and Daniel O'Donnell, Professor, Department of English, University of Lethbridge, Canada, who, as editors, published sections of this book as articles in *Research in African Literatures* and *Digital Studies/La Champ Numérique,* respectively. Their wide-ranging interest in digital studies helped me study the drone from interdisciplinary perspectives.

During the early drafting phases, Alan Liu, Distinguished Professor, Department of English, University of California, Santa Barbara, strongly encouraged pursuing the project to call attention to cultural criticism in the digital humanities.

Mahwish Chisty, Associate Professor, Department of Art, University of Massachusetts, generously granted permission to use her outstanding drone art in the book.

Stephen Houser, Director of Academic Technology and Consulting, Bowdoin College, Maine, offered concise language to explain AI and ChatGPT protocols.

Ali Abedi, Vice Provost for Research and Professor of Electrical Engineering, University of Wisconsin-Milwaukee, gave nuanced suggestions to sharpen discussions of AI and ChatGPT.

To Hannah, for putting up with my droning on drones for several years: many thanks for your patience and support.

1 RISE OF THE DRONE: MOBILE EYE OF POWER

What Nicholas Negroponte said in the mid-1990s, "Computing is not about computers anymore. It is about living"—has acquired sharper, deeper, and global resonance.[1] This chapter briefly traces the emergence of remote piloting technologies in military history to the current moment that can be aptly described as the age of the drones, in which new visual cultures produced by drones and surveillance platforms consolidate a trans-planetary regime of sight: it's the mobile eye of power. What it is, and why it matters to democracy, art, and culture, I essay in this chapter.

Rise of the Drone

Balloons for reconnaissance were used by French armies in 1794, during the American Civil War, and in the British Empire between 1884 and 1901. After Wilbur and Orville's first flight in 1903, interest in a plane's potential for remote operations increased.[2] Another early use is noted in Austria's 1849 war against Venice, when it sent balloons with explosives into enemy territory where they could be ignited, although a big difficulty was that sometimes the wind would blow some balloons back into Austrian territories.[3] Early use of unmanned vehicles deigned to deliver force with indirect human control dates back to the First World War when the Navy produced biplanes (Sperry's torpedoes) that could be catapulted or flown over a short distance and to release its munitions.[4] In the Second World War, Operation Anvil produced planes that could be flown for a distance by a pilot who would abandon the plane in mid-flight while it would, with radio-controlled operations, continue towards its target. Guided cruise missiles began to be used in the 1950s, and in the next two decades, unmanned aerial vehicles could be flown to surveil and gather data.⁵ The AQM-34 Firebee, for instance, was used in battle situations in the 1950s and 1960s wars, and its use as an armed drone began in 2002.⁶

Today, with the increase of sophisticated technology, drones are capable of flying higher and faster while carrying powerful arsenals with precise targeting capabilities. Drones "can achieve a variety of military effects, as other air platforms can. They can kill, disable, support fighters on the ground, destroy, harry, hinder, deny access, observe, and track."⁷ There has been a dramatic shift in the use of drones in one decade alone: in 2002, the number of drones in the United States was 167, but by 2011, it shot up to more than an astonishing 7,000,⁸ of which 5 percent are drones with attack capacity.⁹ The Department of Defense (DoD) budget for drones grew from 284 million in FY 2000 to 3.3 billion in FY 2010,¹⁰ a change reflected in the rapid increase in drone inventory: in 2005, 95 percent of aircraft maintained by the DoD were manned vehicles, and by 2012, it dropped to 69 percent, which means a 34 percent increase in drone inventory in less than a decade (10,767 manned, 7,494 unmanned).¹¹ Moving forward ten years, for FY 2021, the DoD allocated $7.5 billion "for a variety of robotic platforms and related technologies … All of the military services and Special Operations Command are pursuing these capabilities, also known as UxV, for the air, ground, maritime surface and subsurface domains."¹² According to Expert Market Research, "The global military robots market attained a value of nearly USD 20804.93 million in 2024. The market is further expected to grow at a CAGR [compound annual growth rate] of 8.10% during the forecast period of 2025–2034 to reach a value of USD 45333.91 million by 2034."¹³ (See Figure 1.1.)

With their bulbous front ends, the Predator, Reaper, and Global Hawk are the iconic symbols of drones: 27 ft. in length and with a wingspan of 55 ft., the Predator can fly for 24 hours at 25,000 ft. and costs $20 million; 36 ft. in length

FIGURE 1.1 Global Hawk, NASA.

FIGURE 1.2 MQ-9 Reaper. Leslie Pratt, Wikimedia Commons.

and with a wingspan of 66 ft., the Reaper can fly for 24 hours at 50,000 ft. and costs $26.8 million; and 48 ft. in length and with a wingspan of 131 ft., the Global Hawk can fly for 28 hours at 60,000 ft. and costs $149.9 million.[14] Other models include Altair, Firescout, I-GNAT, Mariner, Grey Eagle, Raven, Sentinel, Scan Eagle, Wasp III, Prowler II, Puma, Shirke, Predator C Avenger, Switchblade, and Hummingbird.[15] Companies producing drones or drone technology include General Atomics ($2.4 billion contract with the Pentagon between 2000 and 2010); AeroVironment (85 percent of its $300 million revenue since 2001 are from drones); Raytheon (produces the Griffin, a missile like the Hellfire, and got a $40 million deal by 2010); Boeing (given $400 million for X-37B); Northrop Grumman ($218 million in costs for a Global Hawk); and Lockheed Martin ($68.000 for each Hellfire missile).[16] Drones like Switchblade can fire missiles and also plunge toward a target in a mission to kill it. In other words, the drone can become a suicide drone. Research is being conducted to produce technology that will enable drones to be almost fully automatic, requiring little pilot control.[17] (See Figures 1.2 and 1.3.)

The United Nations Takes Notice

In January 2013, the UN Office of the High Commissioner for Human Rights appointed Ben Emmerson as United Nations Special Rapporteur on human

FIGURE 1.3 MQ-1B Predator. Sabrina Johnson, Wikimedia Commons.

rights and counterterrorism, charging him to inquire into the "civilian impact, and human rights implications of the use of drones and other forms of targeted killing for the purpose of counter-terrorism and counter-insurgency."[18] In September 2013, in a presentation to the UN General Assembly, Emmerson noted that the government of Pakistan reported to the Special Rapporteur that drone strikes killed 2,200 people and injured 600, including 400 civilians and 200 "non-combatants." Assessing damage and civilian deaths due to drone strikes requires evaluating various reports and data sets, which is rendered difficult since a "consequence is that the United States has to date failed to reveal its own data on the level of civilian casualties inflicted through the use of remotely piloted aircraft in classified operations conducted in Pakistan and elsewhere, or any information on its methodology for evaluating this."[19] In April 2014, the Human Rights Council passed a resolution encouraging states to meet international human and humanitarian laws when waging asymmetric war, provide detailed information about casualties when they appear to go against international codes, request the High Commissioner for Human Rights to follow the policies of the Human Rights Council in conducting inquiries, and organize a public panel on which representatives from government and civil organizations can participate. The United states voted against the Resolution.[20]

Tempting as it is to view this as a clear instance of imperial hubris and hypocrisy, clearly, the challenges posed by global asymmetrical warfare cannot easily be addressed by existing Human Rights laws, international treaties, and civil agreements—formal and informal. Special Rapporteur Emmerson concurs:

> The ability of drones to loiter and gather intelligence for long periods before a strike, coupled with the use of precision-guided munitions, is therefore a positive advantage from a humanitarian law perspective.[21]

He adds:

> The Special Rapporteur does not use the expression "targeted killing" here, because its meaning and significance differ according to the legal regime applicable in specific factual circumstances. In a situation qualifying as an armed conflict, the adoption of a pre-identified list of individual military targets is not unlawful; if based upon reliable intelligence it is a paradigm application of the principle of distinction. ... The threshold question therefore is not whether a killing is targeted, but whether it takes place within or outside a situation of armed conflict.[22]

Emmerson notes that the United States distinguishes between "international" and "transnational" global conflict situations, linking al Qaeda with the latter, which leads to its refusal to recognize international humanitarian laws based on international, not transnational, models. Another major obstacle to aligning asymmetrical conflict with humanitarian and human rights laws is this: "One consequence is that the United States has to date failed to reveal its own data on the level of civilian casualties inflicted through the use of remotely piloted aircraft in classified operations conducted in Pakistan and elsewhere, or any information on its methodology for evaluating this."[23] Emerson's concerns are visualized well with data in *Out of Sight, Out of Mind*, which presents moving graphics showing US drone strikes in Pakistan between 2004 and 2015, with casualties sorted into militants, suspects, and civilians.[24]

In 2021, the United Nations' Office of Counter Terrorism launched the "Global Counter-Terrorism Programme on Autonomous and Remotely Operated Systems (AROS)" to focus on the "threats posed by drones, UAS, and other AROS."[25] In 2022, drones gained center stage in the Russia-Ukraine war, as both countries began using micro and mid-size drones to attack convoys, supply lines, army and navy stations, and infrastructural areas. "Russia, Ukraine exchange drone, missile attacks," a June 2024 Voice of America article, describes it this way: "Kyiv and Moscow staged dozens of drone and missile attacks overnight, officials said Friday, leaving several wounded in Ukraine and damaging a fuel reservoir site in a Russian border region."[26] It is clear, however, that in the game of nations and empires, the United States is primus inter pares in drone warfare.

Drone Theater of Empire

On May 14, 2013, a drone, X-47B, took off from an aircraft carrier, thus setting a precedent for drone warfare, because it makes mobile the infrastructural needs of maintaining, protecting, and launching drones from areas over which the military can establish control. Without such mobility, the US State and Defense departments have to negotiate often tacit agreements with other countries to set up control centers or launch sites. This development sets "the way for the U.S. to launch unmanned aircraft from just about any place in the world."[27] Designed to operate, in large measure, autonomously, the X-47B reduces the need to be piloted constantly and increases the ease of one individual remotely piloting multiple drones or having the done operate autonomously. Built as a prototype for the Unmanned Combat Air System Demonstration program, the X-47B, having successfully demonstrated its capabilities, was decommissioned to pave the way for a new program called the Carrier-Based Aerial Refueling Research System that produced the MQ-25 Stingray drone.[28] Seeking to push the innovation envelope, the Senate's Committee on Armed Services was asked by military advisors and political leaders to recommend the creation of a drone corps in the US Armed Forces, demonstrating the growing recognition that integrating the drone into several military divisions was necessary. Opposing a new division's creation, General Randy George, Army Chief of Staff, suggested that drones be made "resident in every formation, at every echelon."[29] (See Figure 1.4.)

The efficacy of drone warfare is predicated on the range and quality of the military, technological, and political infrastructure necessary to share intelligence, coordinate missions, and execute them successfully. The "military's secret military,"[30] referred to as US Special Operations Command (SOCOM), set up in 1987, today includes the Green Berets, Rangers, Navy Seals, Air Force Air Commandos, and Marine Corp Special Operations Teams. This unit "carries out the United States' most specialized and secret missions. These include assassinations, counter terrorist raids, long-range reconnaissance, intelligence analysis, foreign troop training, and weapons of mass destruction counter-proliferation operations."[31] Its core cell, Joint Special Operations Command, acts under the President's direct supervision. With 66,000 professionals and a budget of 10.6 million, SOCOM conducts operations in seventy to ninety countries everyday.[32] Countries where SOCOM is or was active include Afghanistan, Bahrain, Belize, Brazil, Bulgaria, Burkina Faso, Dominican Republic, Egypt, Germany, Indonesia, Iran, Iraq, Jordan, Kazakhstan, Kuwait, Kyrgyzstan, Lebanon, Mali, Norway, Oman, Pakistan, Panama, Poland, Qatar, Romania, Saudi Arabia, Senegal, South Korea, Syria, Tajikistan, Thailand, Turkmenistan, United Arab Emirates, Uzbekistan, and Yemen.[33] (See Figure 1.5.)

FIGURE 1.4 X-47B on an aircraft carrier. Timothy Walter, Wikimedia Commons.

FIGURE 1.5 Bayraktar TB2, Turkish drone. By Bayhaluk, Wikimedia Commons.

To maintain, manage, and deploy drones, command and control centers with varying degrees of sophisticated infrastructure and technological capabilities have been sent up in sixty bases all over the world, including in Arizona, Florida, New Mexico, Missouri, New Mexico, Nevada, North Dakota, Ohio, South Dakota, New York, and Texas. The drones, Special Operations Command, and control centers "are the backbone of the new American robotic way of war. They are also the latest development in a long-evolving saga of America power projection abroad; in this case, remote-controlled strikes anywhere on the planet with a minimal foreign 'footprint' and little accountability."[34]

Colin Vanderburg explains well the connection between drone warfare and empire:

> Drones offer the most compact, iconic representation of the new image of warfare that every American administration wants to project: sanitary, sleek, almost post-human ... War—which is never named as such—is not just the domain of the grunt soldier or even the commanding general. More and more it belongs to the expert advisor and trained technician controlling small metal devices from thousands of miles away. Drones have a dual being as both moving, sensing agents and inert, controllable devices: perceiving but passive, mobile but mindless. Any art or politics of drones must engage with this radical abstraction of military violence from its perpetrators, even from places and people.[35]

Abstracted from the grunt and heave of bloody battles, far removed from threats of violence and death, drone warfare inaugurates a new dispensation of empire engaged with new threats to the social order. The use of drones by Presidents Bush, Obama, Trump, and Biden evidence the difficulty of countering threats in a globally networked world in which non-state actors can acquire adequate know-how and mobilize themselves and others to attack nation-states from within and without their boundaries, societies, and institutions, while killing civilians. Drones have compelling advantages over traditional forms of war, avers Micah Zenko in a special report "Reforming US Drone Strike Policies," published by the *Council of Foreign Relations*: large troops and support personnel do not need to be deployed on the battlefield; intelligence can be collected over long periods using digital technologies for surveillance; specific targets can be identified and surveilled; the time to "find-fix-finish" gets highly compressed; if necessary, missile paths can be re-routed several moments before impact to reduce or avoid collateral effects.[36]

Drones "can handle what humans cannot—G forces and speed, tedium and boredom. Among the other 'intrinsic benefits' of drones: they deprive the enemy of human targets; they don't get tired or thirsty or hungry; they are relatively inexpensive; and with the coming of nuclear-powered drones, they offer the possibility of nearly endless above-target operation."[37] Because drones obviate the need for boots on the ground, local public anger or suspicion against foreign occupants radically diminishes.[38] Also, "the public's growing distaste for US casualties and the Pentagon's shrinking share of the budget" lead to the growing use of drones because "the absence or presence of US personnel in a military operation dramatically changes the calculus of war."[39]

New Ethics of Drone Wars

Nevertheless, operating drones involves setting up an intricate infrastructure: agreements have to be made with host countries to set up or use facilities and enter territories; inter-state allowances to cross other countries' airspace and territories have to be tacitly, secretly, or publicly negotiated; provisions to rescue drones or those impacted by them need to be set up; operational bases in neighboring regions or countries have to be maintained; permission to use local or national satellite systems for communication or control of drones have to be obtained.[40] "As a result," comments Zenko, "drones are not just another weapons platform. Instead, they provide the United States with a distinct capability that significantly reduces many of the inherent political, diplomatic, and military risks of targeted killings."[41]

But as Sarah Kreps and John Kaag argue, there is a tendency to conflate technological sophistication with ethical and legal assessment because technology is not neutral but used by human beings: "The ability to undertake more precise, targeted strikes should not be confused with the determination of legal or ethical legitimacy," which raises the question of war and justice.[42] To the two dimensions of just war theory—the justification for war (jus ad bellum) and the rules of engagement during war (jus in bello), philosopher Michael Walzer in *Arguing about War* adds a third, justice after the war (jus post bellum).[43]

A good argument can be made that in drone warfare, the new dispensation of the American empire, all three dimensions are skewed. The United States is engaged in a global hunt for people posing imminent danger to the country and scours the entire world for them without formal intimations or declarations of war; the United States envelopes entire regions and populations and subjects everyone, without distinction, to a surveillance regime to ferret out suspects and kill them; the United States disposes of its targets without consistently verifying the proportionality of the strikes because the targets are chosen by macro-analyzing big data generated by secret digital surveillance.

This conundrum is evident in how the military addresses two important elements of just war theory and international humanitarian law: distinction and proportionality. In contemporary war, the battleground is not far from the city but within the city; combatants do not often distinguish themselves from civilians but in fact try to use them or blend into them; as targets move themselves and their base of operations continuously, civilian aiding of targets can be discontinuous, which makes their value as targets variable in space and time, further complicating the distinction principle. Proportionality requires military goals to be higher in proportion to damaging effects of military operations. Bush's war on terror problematically broadened distinctions between civilian and combatants, while also enlarging the scope of military aims. By contrast, Obama's Overseas

Contingency Operations, while appearing to reduce such scope and enable sharper distinctions, went a step further—they legitimized strikes against contingent operations that have happened or have the potential to happen (K and K20–21). But although it "redu[ces] the risks and costs of war, the use of UAVs and precision weapons may actually encourage more bellicosity and longer wars."[44] Likewise, In Dirty Wars: The World Is a Battlefield, Jeremy Scahill argues:

> In the same way that Afghanistan and Iraq provided a laboratory for training and developing a whole new generation of highly skilled, seasoned special operators, Yemen represented a paradigm that is sure to permeate US national security policy for decades to come. It was under the Bush administration that the United States declared the world a battlefield where any country would be fair game for targeted killings, but it was President Obama who put a bipartisan stamp on this worldview that will almost certainly endure well beyond his time in office.[45]

A major reservation about drone warfare, says Greg Kennedy in "Drones: Legitimacy and Anti-Americanism," is the question of legitimacy, a term often used "in such circumstances interchangeably with concept such as proportional, moral, ethical, lawful, appropriate, reasonable, legal, justifiable, righteous, valid, recognized, and logical." Four issues come to the forefront, namely "who is controlling the weapon system, does the system of control and oversight violate international law governing the use of force; are the drone strikes proportionate acts that provide military effectiveness given the circumstances of the conflict they are being used in; and does their use violate the sovereignty of other nations."[46] The CIA's covert use of drones results in a lack of information and explanation in the public domain, which raises the necessity of forming judicial courts, in addition to Congressional committees, to review the practice. Although drone strikes compared to traditional missile strikes or bombardment are more circumscribed in scope and effect, response to their use has resulted in local state apparatuses, not American bases or personnel only, being targeted. Nation-states also have to cooperate and open up airspaces to allow other countries to use drones, which "can endanger vital strategic relationships."[47]

Endless War/Perpetual Peace

The condition that the drone creates on the ground is what Lisa Parks refers to as "vertical mediation," which is "not only the capacity of drone sensors to detect phenomena on the earth's surface so that it can be rendered as live-video feeds at terminal interfaces, but also to the potential to materially alter or affect the phenomena of the air, spectrum, and/or ground."[48] Drone flights change "the chemical composition of the air," "movements on the ground," and "affect thought and behavior," and through their munitions, they can "turn homes into holes and living into the dead."[49] Parks's point is important because it draws attention to the materiality of drone warfare, whose digital modalities often give it a virtual, onscreen, immersive yet simulated feel, making it seem that drone warfare is essentially a virtual phenomenon. Parks questions this approach persuasively by arguing that "the drone is as much a technology of inscription as it is a technology of sensing or representation."[50]

A major shift on the ground due to vertical mediation is apparent in a redefining of threats, elements that can make war a possibility or inevitability. The criteria of "imminent threat," viability of capturing suspects, and reducing civilian casualties, points out Fred Kaplan in "The World as Free-Fire Zone," are displaced onto a series of actions, locations, and intentions that change the meaning of imminent: that which is imminent has to be dealt with expeditiously, which obviates the need to go through a systematic and thorough process of review to ensure that the strikes are necessary and proportional with limited collateral effects. What all these strictures miss, and deliberately so, Kaplan argues, is one pivotal fact: drone strikes take place outside of war zones. They can happen anywhere the US decides threat is imminent. He writes, "For when we talk about accidental civilian deaths by drones in Pakistan and Yemen, we are talking about countries where the United States is not officially fighting wars. In other words, these are countries where the people killed—and their embittered friends and relatives—didn't know that they were living in a war zone."[51]

When this critical fact is occluded or rendered superfluous in the drive to remove imminent threats, the people living in areas where drones conduct constant surveillance without their knowledge but experience the aftermath of deadly strikes become victims to a protocol of war that robs them of the ability and choice to stay or move from strike zones. In his testimony to the Senate Judiciary Committee, Farea al-Muslimi, a journalist from Yemen, noted that native villagers changed their positive impressions of America due to drone attacks: "When they think of America, they think of the terror they feel from the drones that hover over their heads, ready to fire missiles at any time."[52] Drones breed a culture of fear and dread.

Whereas a key criterion is that suspects must be a threat to the United States, it is not the case that many of the victims of drone strikes can thus be categorized. In fact, the United States has been targeting people deemed as rebels or outlaws or terrorists by the local government. One such instance is the US attack on the Al Shabab group in Somalia, which has been fighting against its government.[53] Another disturbing feature of drone warfare that departs from the frequently asserted principle that the targets are those posing imminent danger to the United States is that "in more and more instances, the targets of drone strikes are low-level militiamen, not terrorist leaders. In a striking number of cases, they are targeted for death even though their identities—their names, ranks, and the scope of their involvement in a terrorist organization—are unknown."[54] All this, says Kaplan, leads to the logical outcome of avoiding the redundancy of gathering information after drone strikes because the necessity to verify has been obviated in the principle by which the strike is justified: imminent danger and suspicious patterns of behavior. As Tom Ferer and Frederic Bernard note, "At this point, the US government appears to regard itself as justified in eliminating not only persons playing significant roles in substantial, hierarchically organized groups like ISIL, Al-Qaeda in the Maghreb, the Haqqani Network and the Shabab in Somalia, but any person associated with such groups even where they pose no immediate threat to US nationals or the nationals of allied states."[55]

Earth as Battlefield

In *The Drone Age: How Drone Technology Will Change War and Peace*, Michael J. Boyle argues that the benefits of drones (low cost, expedient use, focused application) also have the potential to increase drone warfare for the same reasons. This turned out to be true: the early drone wars of the Bush and Obama administration, particularly in its accelerated phase in the latter, moved from targeting Al Qaeda to numerous groups designated as such in the world. Boyle calls this "goal displacement," which describes "the process by which an organization enlarges its ambitions and begins to substitute alternative, sometimes more expansive, goals for the ones that it originally had."[56] Pretty soon, America's drone program went global, as the whole world became subject to the scopic power of the drone.

The preponderance of drone attacks in Afghanistan, Pakistan, Yemen, and Somalia against the Pukhtun, Yemenis, Somalis, and Kurds reveals a postmodern war against tribal groups whose encounter with the modernity of the nation-state is a tale of bloody conflict, observes Akbar Ahmad in *The Thistle and the Drone: How America's War on Terror Became a Global War on Tribal Islam*. The structure of the segmentary lineage system of these tribes includes the belief in a common ancestor, strong sense of independence and equality, territorial privileges accorded by tradition, language, elders as arbiters in conflict mediation, and honor codes. One key reason for Mullah Omar's refusal to give up Osama bin Laden in Kandahar was the risk of tribal shame for not living up to the honor ideal.[57] In response to American pressure, Pakistan's attempt to control Tehrik-e-Taliban in the tribal region of Waziristan led to intense hostilities between the central government and the Taliban militia.[58] Ahmad argues that the tribes' vexed relations with authoritarian state governments and rapid modernization make them particularly vulnerable to religious extremism, and that it is important not to conflate their antipathy toward the state with direct or unproblematic anti-Americanism:

> These societies live in areas administered by central governments whose ability to bomb, kidnap, humiliate, and rape tribal members at will has been enhanced by U.S. financial and military backing in the war on terror. For the tribes, this has been the worst of fates, leaving them emasculated and helpless, with every moral boundary crossed, every social structure attacked. The wholesale breakdown of their tribal system is not unlike the implosion of a galaxy, with fragments shooting off in unpredictable directions.[59]

These useful insights are strong caveats to restrict drone strikes and help the United States maintain a reasonable distance between itself and the oppressive state. These insights can be further strengthened by acknowledging the fact that the religion binding all these tribes is Islam. To interpret this as an inherent flaw of the religion would not only be misleading but also historically and experientially false; however, more attention should be paid to how religious discourse, myths, traditions, and practices also become the basis for anti-state, anti-American, and anti-modern resistance whose forms are often vicious and targets random, leading to deeply repressive societies. This further complicates the notion that US drones are targeting threats to America and that such threats are imminent. In addition, by bracketing off these regions from contemporary geospatial processes, Ahmad's focus on tribal Islam cannot account for the dense networks of extremism spanning many parts of the world, and linking urban settings and, in some cases, highly developed centers of the Western world.

Many of the terrorists, including the 9/11 attackers and the Boston Marathon bombers of May 2013, were living in Europe and America as students, immigrants, or would-be immigrants. These factors also play a pivotal role: a disoriented experience with modernity, embodied materially in America's economic and political relationships with the Middle East and Palestine, and symbolically in a ubiquitous global American culture; and an apocalyptic vision of redemption grounded in religious belief and practice, in which the self finds ultimate fulfillment in yielding its life for a noble cause. To say, as Ahmad does, that religious ideas and meanings are tangential to extremism would be to obscure a powerful element that is woven into the larger fabric of orientations shaping extremist worldviews. Nevertheless, there is little doubt that particular tribal groups are bearing the brunt of drone attacks and civilian casualties are not fully acknowledged, thus leaving this new form of conflict to be waged in the shadows without adequate accountability.

Becoming cognizant of drone warfare as a new form of empire that centers US hegemony is difficult because we are generally accustomed to the inside-outside frame of the nation. With such a frame, we turn events outside the United States into a remote happenstance, events that are part of a war or national security effort to contain threats beyond national boundaries to ensure peace inside national boundaries. We are here and they are there. We are inside America, and war is taking place outside America. The inside/outside divide, notwithstanding the porousness and liquidity of globalization, continues to shape our views of the world and our societies. And for good reason: it would be a mistake to think that notions of inside and outside do not matter or are fanciful fictions. What does matter is ascribing to them a natural state, a character of being, an essence rooted in immutable truth, history, and location. Often, what takes place outside the boundaries of the nation is informed by what occurs within its boundaries. Our life within the boundaries of the nation state is influenced, in some measure, through knowledge and impact of the world outside. It is not sheer coincidence that in the post-Cold War era, the rise of surveillance society in America is coincident with a dramatic escalation of commercial drone use and drone warfare. In the same decade that thousands of terrorists and civilians are killed by drone strikes outside America, we see a concerted effort by the government to establish a regime of constant surveillance on citizens and inhabitants inside America.

These two developments are linked. More to the point, they are networked—unevenly, fragmentarily, nodularly. American foreign policy is linked to domestic policy, a dynamic that Amy Kaplan encapsulates as the "anarchy of empire" to suggest the interconnections—often irregular, indirect, but nonetheless forceful, influential—between the world outside the United States and the world inside the United States.[60] It's the anarchy of empire in the sense that there is no evenly distributed diffusion of power from a stable center but a crisscrossed circuit of power, domination, and influence whose flows make the center dependent on the periphery, and its domestic politics influence and be influenced by events and forces outside the country. The foreign and the domestic, the inside and the outside, feed and blur into each other. But are drone wars distant wars? Are they wars whose remoteness can be confidently assumed because their technological assemblage offers remote operability and invisibility and knowability to the drone pilots? How far can distance as radical benefit be assumed?

Second Drone Age

One challenge we face in addressing this new phenomenon of war is distance—physical and psychological distance. Not a single drone, to date, has been fired upon by a foreign state on American soil and taken life. At least not yet. Drone warfare is something taking place far way, in Afghanistan, Pakistan, Yemen, and Somali. These are so-called Third World countries. But with rapid technological development has come new global dynamics that have ushered us into what James Rogers calls "the second drone age," which has new features: the "global proliferation of weaponized drones" and "non-Western cases of drone adoption (and deployment)."[61] In the 2020–22 Tigray War in Ethiopia, Prime Minister Abiy Ahmed "altered his regime's fortune by deploying armed drone from the UAE (Wing Loong IIs), Turkey (TB2s), and Iran (Mohajer-06s) against the Tigray Rebels."[62] Whereas earlier around 113 countries had a "military drone programme (an increase from 60 in 2010), there are now an estimated 65 non-state groups that have weaponized drones."[63] The Houthi Rebels, actively supported by Iran, are able to use Iranian-supplied drones (Qassef-2K; Samad-3) to attack those deemed threats to Iran and to the group. Such groups are able to "evade technology control regimes, become resilient against embargos, and create robust supply chains that will facilitate their mastering of the air."[64]

Two other elements can be added to the features defining the second phase of drone wars, to extend Marc R. DeVore's insight: "1) the centrality of attrition rates and cost factors; and 2) the importance of rapid adaptation cycles over exquisitely engineered weapons."[65] Calling the Ukraine-Russia war the "first drone war," DeVore suggests that drones like Bayraktar TB-2 (used by Ukraine) and Forpost and Orion (used by Russia) are low altitude aircraft that can fly short distances and hover for moderate periods. Despite an early lead using the Bayraktar TB-2 against Russia, Ukraine was soon struggling to counter Russia's quick adaptive response, which included interfering with datalinks and deploying air-defense missiles, leading to several drone losses. Russian drones would meet a similar fate because Ukraine figured out counter drone measures to effectively stymie them. This stalemate of sorts led to two developments: harnessing the DIY (do-it-yourself) cultural sensibility to encourage people to buy small commercial or hobby drones, and leveraging "the widespread availability of mechanical and electronic components for building drones" so to make it "easier for designers to modify swiftly drone designs."[66] Due to geopolitical pressures comprising the supply chain necessary for rapidly producing the TB-2 (its transponder is produced by the Swedish company, Garmin), Turkey began locally producing drone parts to decrease "reliance on Western components."[67] Small drones could be re-fitted with munitions and locally produced GPS systems to carry out specific tasks; moreover, these drones would be for one-time use (as in Kamikaze drones) or would incur very low cost loses upon being shot down or disabled, turning them into disposable drones.

Such a shift in military attitude toward acquiring lethal weapons, like small drones, and a willingness to encourage civilians to obtain and redesign hobby or commercial drones for weaponized uses soon produced a startling result: "The larger drones—Bayraktars, Forposts and Orions—all experienced a similar life-cycle, going from being heralded as 'game-changing' weapons to finding themselves withdrawn from frontline service."[68] Such developments are distinct features of societies in which digital technologies gain widespread use; indeed, the notion of DIY is parlance for everyday digital culture in which people learn about an astonishing range of topics and interact with strangers from around the world for a dizzying variety of purposes. We have entered the first and second ages of the drone because of the rise of digital societies and the globalization of all things digital. These five developments—widespread use of drones in the world; increase of drone use in the Global South; growing acquisition of armed drones by non-state entities; encouraging civilian populations to use their skills to obtain commercial drones; supporting adaptive responses to redesign small hobby drones for modest military tasks—define the second drone age.

Volumetric Thinking/Drone Imaginaries

But what exactly makes the drone a unique technology? What kind of visuality does it generate, and how can that visuality be interpreted, by whom and where? What makes this new mode of seeing amenable to projecting power globally? Does the verticality of drone sight perpetuate traditional power dynamics, or does it recalibrate them? It is to these questions that I turn now to set the context for the next chapter on surveillance.

Ole Jensen points out that "the existing cartographies and visual imaginaries within history, geography, and many other disciplines have historically been tied to so-called 'flat projections' and two-dimensional visualizations."[69] The drone introduces "volumetric thinking" that involves viewing space and land in three dimensions (height, breadth, length). The drone view is not static but dynamic, because the drone can move up, down, and sideways to render the world in movement: the drone captures reality, or what is out there, in terms of its own ability to move across space and time, which generates visuals that require visual literacy, a mode of interpretation. To quote Jensen: "Drone visuals are thus not just 'top down imagery' but rather (potentially) complex, visual and volumetric representations rendering the three-dimensionality of the world comprehensible."[70] Thus, drones produce a new "public technological imaginary" that invites viewers to relate to a deeper, wider, volumetric world to make sense of that world and to make sense of one's relationship or position in view of that world, thereby engendering another kind of epistemology.[71] This epistemology's "power lies in combining eye-level and the aerial level in order to understand the materiality of place, the volume of space, and its inhabitants."[72]

Crucial to Jensen's formulation is that the drone is leading to a rethinking of our environments through a volumetric revisualization of space and geography that is at once dynamic and deep, that moves and changes perception by moving. A futuristic speculation is inevitable here, because, as drone technologies become sophisticated and ubiquitous, our drone imaginaries will start to shape our material world building, because what we visualize in order to create or build is thoroughly saturated with drone eyes: the worlds we create are the ones that drones will shape our minds to create, because we will start to think and imagine with the drone technological imaginary.

Adding another angle to the drone imaginary, in "Rethinking Verticality through top-down views in drone hobbyist photography," Lauren Alex O'Hagan and Elisa Serafinelli first point to traditional notions of verticality that were endowed with omnivoyance, the ability of the eye to project unassailable power. In drone hobbyist works, they argue, drone imaginaries take on a new range of meanings and activities. Using drones to chart their geographic dispossession, indigenous communities in Guatemala began to produce an alternate drone geography "that challenges dispossession and unsettles new and dominant vertical orders ... visibility is reclaimed as a form of resistance to top-down governmental surveillance and the idea of asymmetrical observation is decentralized."[73] Drone visuals are created as art for public viewing and interaction, when, for instance, drone images of oyster farms in Jersey are shared on social media, inviting peoples to guess the "real" elements of the visuals. Because dronescapes of oyster farms resemble musical notations and bars, the drone image presents reality as "a form of abstract art, a puzzle that must be deciphered."[74] Similarly, the salt ponds in Arusha, Tanzania, when viewed with the drone's eye, seem to become huge coloring boards filled with pleasant pastel brushes of color, accentuated by the neighboring material structures whose strict contours give the now colorful salt ponds for evaporation a brighter hue.

With "a deliberate focus on mundane features of the environment," a dronescape, note O'Hagan and Serafinelli, "transforms them into something extraordinary. Here, banal items, such as windmills, cargo boxes and rooftops, remain geographically contextualized and are, therefore, more clearly identifiable and easier to interpret, yet they acquire an aesthetic beauty."[75] Drone images of greenhouses in Chelyabinsk, Russia, show them in symmetrically arranged units whose rooftops are regular, aligned, and connected, giving an aura of visual texture, to make up an ordered whole that fills that landscape. The third feature of dronescapes is playful mapping through emplacement, which locates the subject of the drone's camera within its surroundings in order to bring out contrasts and textures. Similarly, "performative cartography" can also become manifest in the "ability to pinpoint symbolic features of the landscape."[76]

The fourth feature is the dronie, which is a selfie with a drone. Whereas in the selfie, the self is the main focus, with the surroundings contextualizing the self's location, the dronie does not register the individual or unique feature of the self but turns it into an integral part of a broader landscape or material setting. Here, "as a modality of self-making rather than a potential form of privacy invasion," the aerial vertical view of the drone resists the quick association of dominance with verticality, instead evoking quotidian acts of self-making as drawing out the circumstantial materiality or setting of the dronie to blend with the self.[77] Put another way, the self in the dronie turns space into a "social actor through the use of ascending cinematic views, clever framing and color/textural contrasts."[78]

Adding a transhistorical perspective to their study of drone visuals, O'Hagan and Serafinelli point to Julius Neubronner's experiment in 1903 that involved attaching cameras to pigeons to take aerial photographs. With "two lenses and a pneumatic system," the camera would be "activated by inflating the left chamber and as the air slowly escaped from the capillary at the bottom, the piston moved back towards the left triggering the exposure. This happened every 90–120s, which meant that thirty photos could be taken on 3 x 6 cm negatives during a 1-h flight."[79] The pigeon images, like their drone counterparts a century later, offer vertical views, but they "make landscapes feel more tactile than visual because angle is distorted and increased attention is paid to the textures of the landscape, which produces views that are distinct from those we perceive from ground level."[80] These images "defamiliarize the familiar" as they "enhance visual experiences of nature, weather, and landscapes through tricks of light and shadows."[81] A crucial difference between the pigeon and the drone images is that where dronies tend to have individuals or groups pose, the pigeon camera takes pictures at odd angles, due to bird flight, and of moments occurring or people behaving naturally, unaware of a pigeon camera. The mundanity of pigeon images is greater than in drone images.

In Ole Jensen, Lauren Alex O'Hagan, and Elisa Serafinelli's analyses, we see that the drone's uses do not accord with verticality as inherently hierarchical or unidirectional; instead, volumetric drone imagery changes the natural world into artistic abstract forms, emplaces things in locations to draw out contrasts, brings out the textured patterns or styles of buildings, enables us to view the mundane differently, as having aesthetic forms that cannot be apprehended at eye-level, and situates the self within the drone's scopic view to blend the self into its surroundings.

Because drones move up and down and sideways, they afford new ways to zoom in on generally difficult to see phenomena, or zoom out to bring something into focus or dronescape land and people. It must be noted that drone images or visuals can also refer to moving images and sound captured in pixels and data bytes, giving drone visuality a multimodal substance.

When these drone affordances are deployed for non-civilian uses, what obtains? Does it change the drone epistemology of technological imaginary? Why does war turn into endless manhunting, peace into an emergency state requiring large-scale, invasive surveillance of peoples? Put another way, how does the drone become a mobile eye of power, an eye that subsumes all it sees into a data domain constructed for computational calculation and algorithmic analysis? What kind of empire emerges in the age of the drone? These questions lead us to theorize the drone as a weapon of war.

Theorizing the Drone

In *A Theory of the Drone*, Grégorie Chamayou highlights principles that give institutional character and social power to drones: "persistent surveillance or permanent watch; totalization of perspective or synoptic viewing; creating an archive or film of everyone's life; data fusion; schematization of forms of life; detection of anomalies and preemptive anticipation."[82] "Persistent surveillance" is about the consistent focus of the drone gaze.[83] It is always watching, not episodically, but persistently. "Totalization of perspective or synoptic viewing" becomes possible when the images from multiple cameras are aggregated "in real time into a single overall view that could be seen in detail when necessary," giving a comprehensive, holistic idea of the surveilled.[84] "Creating an archive or film of everyone's life" requires storing digital content and retrieving them, as needed, including disseminating them across varied networks and platforms for analysis and integration into other data.[85] Here, "everyone's life would become retrospectively researchable."[86] "Data fusion" describes the process of gathering information via diverse modalities (audio, images, moving images, text) and fusing them to be stored, indexed, and shared across the distribution network. "Schematization of forms of life" involves scrutinizing images or data feeds to detect patterns of behavior. It is "identification that is not individual but generic."[87] "Detection of anomalies and preemptive anticipation" refers to sorting through data to trace unusual patterns or occurrences so that they could be expected to occur again, which makes it "possible both to predict the future and to change the course of it by taking preemptive action."[88]

Like Chamayou, Mark Andrejevic argues that the drone marks new ways to understand a world becoming saturated with sensing technologies. The drone, thus, embodies the logic of "droning," which is to "extend the reach, scale, and scope of the senses," to "saturate the times and spaces being monitored," and to "allow for automated response," because "the subtraction of the human element from the decision loop follows naturally from the automation of data processing."[89] Because it generates information overload, "drone logic only individualizes through the lens of the aggregate," since "it is not interested in individuals per se, but only in the patterns of influence that emerge from upstream data collection and downstream targeting."[90] Acting on these principles, the drone develops and legitimates certain ways of seeing the world, the terrain, its peoples, and topographies. To see like the drone is to engage with the world as an epistemological exercise of generating knowledge about future threats that can or must be negated. The processes require surveillance on a massive and consistent scale. Geography and time are linked differently in drone warfare, because what happens where, when, and how become predicates for constructing knowledge and securing the subject who becomes a target for elimination or control.

When I say that geography and time are linked differently in drone warfare, I mean that the world picture created by the drone's field of vision, a field produced by the logic of droning, becomes the terrain on which violence will be directed anytime. Chamayou puts it well: "A single decade has seen the establishment of an unconventional form of state violence that combines the disparate characteristics of warfare and policing without really corresponding to either, find conceptual and practical unity in the notion of a militarized manhunt."[91] In the early phase of its war with Russia, Ukraine, for instance, publicly sought, in digital media, people to provide "hobbyist drones one day into the war and has continued to lean on civil society to source these tools."[92]

As Kerry Chávez and Ori Swed observe, "modern warfare is blurring the boundaries between military and civilian domains in ways that scholars, policymakers, and modern warfighters must flex to master."[93] As is clear by now, drone wars can take place anytime, anywhere as they produce constant insecurity to wage perpetual war. In drone warfare, war becomes peace, peace becomes war, because the drone generates conditions of emergency and exception on a trans-territorial, biopolitical scale.

Such complex and pervasive impact is possible because of what Katherine Maurer argues is the "scopic regime of military drone operations."[94] which are realized by "the drone's optical configuration, its specific mode of image perception, and its visual execution of violence."[95] To turn warfare from a risky-to-both-warring-parties activity into sophisticated man-hunting in a global arena in which the hunter is unreachable and invisible while the hunted gains identity through extreme visibility, drone warfare is executed along "three scopic dimensions" that include "hypervisibility, visual immersion, and invisibility."[96] Maurer's focus on hypervisibility is the same as Chamayou and O'Hagan and Serafinelli's point that the drone gaze is synoptic and persistent, because it creates a comprehensive world picture by stitching together massive data bytes of disparate video and image feeds due to constant surveillance.

The second dimension of the drone's scopic regime is visual immersion, which Maurer explains as a paradoxical condition: despite the drone pilots and the surveilled being separated by immense distance, geographic distance leads to psychological nearness, because the drone's gaze is "a highly immersive one, drawing them [drone operators] very close into the world of the potential targets."[97] The third dimension is the drone's and its operators' invisibility, which alters the jus in bello stipulation, the rights or terms of engagement in war, because in the drone age, the hunted is made visible through persistent surveillance, while the hunter is invisible, beyond the reach of the hunted. These changed conditions of warfare "trigger fundamental changes on how we interpret military action, heroism, and courage."[98] Maurer's point about new notions of heroism at play also has a gendered aspect. Ideas of sacrifice, bravery, and heroism are often masculine in rhetoric and symbology, yet devoid of the potential for harm to the drone pilots.

Maurer moves this a step further, arguing that the drone's panoptic scopic power is different from the English philosopher Jeremy Bentham's panoptic tower.

Surveillance and the Panopticon

Conceived by Bentham in 1791 as a structure to house and manage prisoners, the Panopticon's architecture includes a central tower overlooking a semi-circular range of numerous cells and blocks for the inmates. It enabled the watcher to potentially watch any cell at any time without the inmate's knowledge. The possibility of being watched thus dramatically increased the probability of being watched, resulting in an internalization of being watched. Bentham's panopticon effected prisoner reform through a psychological shift turning the external mode of forced surveillance into an internal mode of self-surveillance leading to reformed behavior. Untethered to the imperative of disciplining the watched, the drone's panoptic vision turns the prisoner into a hunted subject, who must be continually on the run because the panopticon in the drone age does not have a specific architecture and geographic locale; instead, it is shapeless and boundless.

This architecture embodies a dynamic of visibility and invisibility, with the guards or surveillers easily monitoring any of the cells without at the same time being watched by the inmates, a dynamic that Michel Foucault in the late twentieth century characterized as paradigmatic of the mechanisms of discipline and control in the modern Enlightenment, especially because the fear of being watched any time also led to an internalization of surveillance as the inmates self-monitored their behavior.

This was a rational organization at its efficient best. It was functional, detailed, organized, and efficient. It enabled the effective exercise of power through a regime of visibility that subjected the inmates to an order of daily surveillance. Foucault says, "There is no need for arms, physical violence, material constraints, Just a gaze. An inspecting gaze, a gaze which each individual under its weight will end by interiorizing to the point that he is his own overseer, each individual thus exercising this surveillance over, and against, himself. A superb formula: power exercised continuously and for what turns out to be a minimal cost."[99]

One example of how surveillance acquires official power by obscuring its invasive tendencies is explained by Charlene D. Elliot in "Kid-Visible: Childhood Obesity, Body Surveillance, and the Techniques of Care" in which she examines a report on childhood obesity released by the House of Commons Standing Committees on Health in Canada. To contain growing obesity rates among children, the study not only surveilled the eating habits of children but also generated information about, according to the report Elliot cites, "biometric measurements, including body-mass index, waist-to-hip ration, and abdominal circumference" and in measuring these over time, the study also gained information about other activities that influenced or contextualized these factors like before and after school activities and lifestyles. This meant submitting to a form of surveillance that encompassed a wide spectrum of personal activities, which was justified and submitted to by parents and children because "surveillance [was] embraced solely as a technique of care and, as such, [was] beyond reproach."[100] More problematically, it is the visible body, not the healthy body, that becomes the object of surveillance and whose generated knowledge can lead to misguided public policy.

The intersection of state surveillance and public safety is examined in "Public Vigilance Campaigns and Participatory Surveillance" by Mike Larsen and Justin Piché, who point out the subtle ways in which an individual is turned into a "vigilant citizen" by official communiques urging people to keep an eye, watch out for, and report any behavior or objects that seem not normal or unusual. In the post-9/11 era, public safety has become intimately linked to national security, and as terrorists continually seek to strike, destroy, or harm people or property in unexpected ways, the State's reliance on general or "participatory surveillance" gains urgency.

But as Larsen and Piché contend, such practices can just as easily reify stereotypical behaviors and biases as everyone is left to determine the bounds of normalcy. It does not mean that surveillance ought not to be practiced by the state at all to contain or forestall such threats, as that would be irresponsible. The reluctance of the government to provide clear criteria to determine normal and unusual items or behavior can just as easily be criticized for occluding and stereotyping people officially. This is why their point about the eventual incorporation of people into official narratives of identity and belonging through participatory surveillance—that finds public legitimacy in the rhetoric of safety and security—needs further amplification: "Perhaps of greater importance is the capacity of vigilance campaigns to embed or implicate members of the public in dominant narratives about terrorism and to govern them according to an official ideology of (in) security."[101] This presents us with a challenge—do we eschew any kind of surveillance? If so, how can terror threats be addressed? But if we continue with such campaigns, how can these risks be avoided or minimized? Is the panopticon not only inevitable but necessary?

Beyond the Panopticon: The Watchman in Pieces

Foucault's insightful analyses of Bentham's panopticon turned it into a reigning paradigm in surveillance discourse. Many critiques of Foucault and his use of Bentham have been made and reformulations proposed—"superpanopticon," "electronic panopticon," "post-panopticon," "omnicon," "ban-opticon," "global panopticon," "panspectron," "myoptic panopticon," "fractal panopticon," "industrial panopticon," "urban panopticon," "pedagopticon," "polyopticon," "synopticon," "panoptic discourse," "social panopticism," "cybernetic panopticism," and "neo-panopticon."[102] Kevin D. Haggerty stages a full-length critique in "Tear down the walls: on demolishing the panopticon": "The panopticon is oppressive ... analysts have excluded or neglected a host of other key qualities and processes of surveillance that fall outside of the panoptic framework," and, as such, it has become "over-extended to domains where it seems ill-suited, and important attributes of surveillance that cannot be neatly subsumed under the 'panoptic' rubric have been neglected."[103]

Launching a comprehensive critique of Foucauldian and postmodern-inspired interpretations of Bentham's Panopticon, and "with an eye towards retheorizing the basic mechanisms of surveillance itself," David Rosen and Aaron Santesso, in *The Watchman in Pieces: Surveillance, Literature, and Liberal Personhood*, argue that surveillance is given such systemic and discursive status that it becomes "omnipresent and omniscient," thus making resistance and subversion difficult.[104] Foucault sees "the most distinctive spatial feature of the panopticon—the central position of the inspector and peripheral, sequestered aspect of the prisoners-as irredeemably oppressive, a physical embodiment of the way State power traps the individual within limiting discourses."[105] Although Foucault acknowledges moments of resistance, to Rosen and Santesso, the disciplinary apparatus still overdetermines them. Moreover, Foucault sees the Panopticon as disciplining the body and the mind as prisoners internalize the watchman's surveillant gaze and modify their behavior in accordance with official expectations regardless of the actual physical presence of the watchman or his penetrating gaze. To "read Bentham as a prophet of 'internalization' and the modern surveillance State is anachronistic" because he was "never as sanguine as his modern readers about the process of internalization itself,"[106] a view that gains clarity when we recognize that Bentham's architectural system was devised as an alternative to brutal and inhumane penitentiary practices. In the Panopticon, the inhabitants were secure, given food, clothing, and spaces to exist, which underscores the fact that Bentham's "intentions are explicitly philanthropic."[107]

Rosen and Santesso contend that Bentham did not consider the Panopticon to be so powerful because his views about surveillance and personhood ascribe characteristics to individual identity that Foucault does not: the separation of the personal self from the social self; the multiplicity of roles that individuals play in various situations; the self as not reducible to an unchanging essence but emerging in everyday negotiations as people perform numerous roles in accordance with their wishes, habits, traditions, and others' expectations. The more the panopticon gazes, the greater the chances of performance and the greater the inability for surveillance to realize its aims of knowing, managing, and controlling its subjects.

And, "as a result, the more individual behavior is perceived as performance, the greater the social anxiety about authenticity."[108]

Bentham, these critics say, "suggests that prisoners wear masks when observed," since "constant surveillance," he reasons, "may well encourage sullenness and recalcitrance rather than an understanding of or accepting of the rules."[109] Class differences also complicate panoptic power since different individuals respond differently to such surveillance. What Rosen and Santesso point to in that surveillance is shot through with a paradoxical logic: it seeks control and knowledge, but the more it seeks them through certain forms and practices, the more it ends up creating a performative culture in which individuals and groups put up a show of being surveilled. The more surveillance succeeds, the greater the risk of its failing.

Another important contribution of Rosen and Santesso is the literary nature of surveillance practices: the millions of images, voice bits, phone calls, sounds, videos, emails, chats, and movements that end up as big data to be crunched for analysis must be turned into a meaningful act in order to be understood or made amenable for surveillance. In short, it is narrative that becomes the key vector by which surveillance generates aims and purposes of human activity out of big data. The surveiller and the surveilled have some power to construct narratives; therefore, the Watchman is in pieces.

Hence, treating the information surveillance systems garner through credit cards or at gaming resorts or casinos is not the same as other forms (one might add police, governmental, military) of surveillance. Rosen and Santesso contend, "The watchman lies in pieces. Though the sharing of personal information between systems is, and will likely continue to be, a source of concern for lawmakers, the natural competition between systems is inescapable—and will often, again, be to the individual's benefit."[110]

But at times, it appears that in countering the extreme Foucauldian views of surveillance that privileges the system over the individual, these critics, at times, tend to privilege the individual, if not over the system but at least on par with it. It is evident here: "As we observed in our introduction, the interaction between a system and the individual comes down finally to a war of narratives—and on the whole, the advantage lies with the latter, who is able to create his or her own story line, which the system must try to anticipate."[111] But the system or the government or another entity can, unlike most individuals, exert pressure and influence and stop, thwart, delay, revise, or alter the activities and desires of the surveilled, which might mean qualifying or bracketing off individual and collective agency.

Undoubtedly, the drone gaze (or the drone panopticon or the drone vision) aspires toward a persistent, totalizing view of the world, or whatever it wishes to bring into focus, by generating hypervisibility of the surveilled. Tempting, as it is, to ascribe to this view an omnivoyant power, Max Liljefors argues in "Omnivoyance and Blindness" that drone vision also ends up producing different types of blindness. The more it seeks to see and comprehend through its panoptic gaze, the more it also blinds itself to the gaps that inevitably arise that turn sight into blindness. He identifies three forms of blindness: transformation of the life world into a performance to benefit the surveillant gaze; the production of information into oceans of data needing to be processed; and translating the machine view into the human view to understand and act on the knowledge generated by the drone gaze. Liljefors describes as "technovision" a new visuality that produces three forms of blindness: "Imaging technologies like those implemented in drone surveillance, biometrics, and visual artificial intelligence are at the center of this transformation of war. I shall refer to such technologies here simple as "technovision." Technovision increasingly penetrates both military and civilian contexts, contributing to the blurring of the line between those contexts"[112] It is important to underscore that technovision emerges at the intersection of surveillance, biometrics, and AI.

Droneopticon

Where omnivoyance seeks to see and create the seen world in terms of its line or circles of vision, technovision creates conditions in which the constant dread of being watched leads to people acting as if they are not being watched, as if they do not need to be watched, thus performing what the surveillance wishes to avoid. This view of blindness has been made by critiques of Michel Foucault's explication of Bentham's panopticon, because his account of its efficacy does not address how the surveilled can perform behaviors that subvert the purpose of surveillance, which Liljefors characterizes as a form of blindness.

The first form of blindness happens due to an overload of data generated by technovision. The high density of data is reduced by "frame rate or pixel resolution" to smoothen the process of data acquisition and distribution without breaking or slowing the distribution system. Still, the analytical work falling beyond the scope of individual examiners, the assessment of data can be parceled out to several analysts, which inevitably engenders diverse interpretations of data. Lilejefors writes, "All these kinds of negotiation about the capacity and limitations of technovision are forms of systemic friction. Friction, which is an unavoidable part of all systems that include machines of humans, constitutes the first level of blindness."[113]

Another type of blindness emerges when the computational analysis of data must be interpreted by human analysts and drone pilots. Neither smooth nor easy as a process, the interpretive activity necessary to translate a kind of algorithmically examined content into one generated through the application of human skill and proclivity process is not smooth or easy. It means that "the operator is then in the position of a translator between the system of visual artificial intelligence and the realm of human language."[114] Soon enough, as "intelligence becomes more adept and increasingly complex, it is reasonable to expect a divide to grow between the machine and the human mind."[115] Highlighting another feature of blindness, in *The Vision Machine*, Paul Virilio calls the "automation of perception" the "synthetic vision," because not only does the machine collect, aggregate, and sort data, but interprets it algorithmically, to assess its meanings and implications—a task earlier executed by humans.[116]

The challenge here is twofold: the difficulty in reconciling or translating data from the machine to the human, and the simultaneous reliance on the machine to interpret data that makes the human subject views it as fact, a condition Virilio points to as "paradoxical facticity."[117] The facts generated by the vison machine involves "the relative fusion/confusion of the factual (or operational, if you prefer) and the virtual: the ascendancy of the 'reality effect' over a reality principle already largely contested elsewhere, particularly in physics."[118] In the age of the drone where visuality is a product of vision machine, the epistemological question—how do we know whether the drone data is true and reliable and factual?—becomes a gnawing enigma, because the real gets subsumed by the effect of the real through technovision. The risk can be subtle, says Liljefors, as computational analysis acquires a status of pure objectivity, thus superior in value, and becomes the norm by which the human mind develops its behavior. Increasingly, machine vision will supplant or lead human vision.[119]

The third type of blindness occurs when the Global Information Grid, an initiative of the US Department of Defense, organizes a structure for global surveillance: there is a "terrestrial layer of ground-based operators, a tactical layer of low-altitude aircraft, a layer of high-altitude aircraft, and an outer, satellite-based layer within global reach," which together create an "infosphere."[120] In this structure, there is no central space providing the most complete picture of the world; there is no privileged position of the watcher who can control and deploy the information and act on it. Rather, we have a "distributed, net-centric structure of the GIG" in which multiple points of access are provided to several people to use GIG's data or content, which means that "omnivoyant power is not incarnated in the single figure of a central observer but is instead excarnated, made fleshless and abstract."[121]

Liljefors discerningly notes that, since the global infosphere loses perspective, it becomes "aperspectival" (Byung-Chul Han's description), because the "net-centric macrosystems of surveillance ... have abandoned the visual-spatial paradigm of the central perspective."[122] The wide-ranging impact of such global surveillance practices and systems is that the surveilled can end up acting to please the surveillant, thus not revealing true intentions or behaviors, while the surveillant also starts acting as a surveilled subject because there is no guarantee that the watcher is also not being watched. The whole of society becomes infused with "a general paranoiac frame of mind."[123] With their astonishing sophisticated ability to be operated remotely or act autonomously, while persistently subjecting whole cities and regions to surveillance, drones are creating new conditions of sociality that undermine democratic and free living. To better understand the benefits, risks, and problems of drone warfare and its growing use as the preferred system for extending dominance, we must understand the challenges to civil rights and liberties in societies where various forms of surveillance are practiced. Drone warfare is not taking place outside the boundaries of the United States but within; it's a different kind of warfare: it seeks to subject millions of Americans to surveillance by a state that justifies it as necessary for law and order to thwart, contain, or prevent terrorism against America and Americans within and without the country's borders.

Thus far we discussed the rise of drones, their uses across the world, and the sociopolitical implications of their uses, particularly as they manifest new forms of domination and control by powerful nation-states. Drones become lethal not only because they can be armed but because they are inextricable from surveillance platforms that allow them to perform their deadly work. Without surveillance, drones, armed or otherwise, are useless. Drones have to see, and see constantly, and generate trillions of bytes of digital data that must be sorted, typologized, analyzed, distributed, and turned into actionable intelligence to turn the silent drone hovering miles above in the sky into a fearsome predator that can destroy peoples, buildings, and terrain with a precision hitherto unavailable in military technologies. The link between drones and surveillance, between remote capacity and the all-seeing surveillant eye, between data generation and identity formation, between war and peace, must be examined. And that is what I take up in the next chapter.

Notes

1. Nicholas P. Negroponte, *Being Digital* (New York: Vintage Books, 1996), 6.
2. "Unmanned Aerial Vehicle," *Britannica.com* https://britannica.com/technology/military-aircraft/Bombers
3. Sarah E. Kreps, *Drones: What Everyone Needs to Know* (Oxford: Oxford University Press, 2016), 9.
4. Precursors to this and the Wright Brothers's first flight in 1903 include William Samuel Henson's sketched designs for aircraft in the 1830s, John Stringfellow's plane powered by steam and tested indoors in 1848, Alphonse Penaud's use of rubber strands to launch airplane models in the 1870s, and Samuel Pierpont Langley's airplane powered by steam and two propellers, which catapulted from a boat in 1896 (John Villasenor, "Observations from Above: Unmanned Aircraft Systems and Privacy," *Harvard Journal of Law and Public Privacy* 36, no. 2 (2013): 458–517.
5. John Sifton, "A Brief History of Drones." *The Nation* February 7, 2012, http://thenation.com/article/166124/brief-history-drones).

6   Jeremiah Gertler, "U.S Aerial Unmanned Systems." *Congressional Research Service*, U.S. Department of State. January 3, 2012.
7   Jacqueline L. Hazelton, "Drones: What Are They Good For?" *Parameters* 42, no. 4 (2013): 30.
8   International Human Rights and Conflict Resolution Clinic, Stanford Law School, and Global Justice Clinic, NYU School of Law, "Living under Drones: Death, Injury, Trauma to Civilians from US Drone Practices in Pakistan." *livingunderdrones.org* September, 2012, 8, https://law.stanford.edu/wpcontent/uploads/sites/default/files/organization/149662/doc/slspublic/Stanford-NYU-LIVING-UNDER-DRONES.pdf
9   Micah Zenko, "Reforming US Drone Strike Policies." *Council on Foreign Relations*. Special Report Number 65. January, 2013, 3.
10 Jeremiah Gertler, "Summary" in "U.S Aerial Unmanned Systems."
11 Ibid., 9.
12 Jon Harper, "Pentagon Gets $7.5 Billion for Unmanned Systems," *nationaldefensemagazine.org* May 27, 2021, https://nationaldefensemagazine.org/articles/2021/5/27/pentagon-gets-$7-5-billion-for-unmanned-systems
13 Expert Market Research, "Global Military Robots Market Outlook," *expertmarketresearch.com* 2022, https://expertmarketresearch.com/reports/military-robots-market
14 Gertler, 31. These are costs for Systems, not single aircraft, since a System involves other units like control operation centers, maintenance crew and pilots, and data point management in communication links.
15 Medea Benjamin. *Drone Warfare* (New York: Verso, 2013), 34–58; "Media Center: Unmanned Aerial Systems," *AeroVironment.com*, accessed December 31, 2024, https://avinc.com/media_center
16 Benjamin, *Drone Warfare*, 35–58.
17 Ibid., 31, 47.
18 United Nations Human Rights Office, "UN Counter-Terrorism Expert to Launch Inquiry into the Civilian Impact of Drones and Other Forms of Targeted Killing." *Office of the High Commissioner for Human Rights*. January 22, 2013, http://ohchr.org/EN/NewsEvents/Pages/DisplayNews.aspx?NewsID=12943&LangID=E
19 Ben Emmerson, "Promotion and Protection of Human Rights and Fundamental Freedoms While Countering Terrorism." Report to the UN General Assembly. *Office of the High Commissioner for Human Rights*. A/68/389, September 18, 2013, 8, 13. 8.
20 United Nations Human Rights Office, "Resolution Adopted by the Human Rights Council." *Office of the High Commissioner for Human Rights* A/HRC/RES/25/22, April 15, 2014, 2–3.
21 Emmerson, "Promotion and Protection," 7.
22 Ibid., 6.
23 Ibid., 13.
24 *Out of Sight, Out of Mind* http://drones.pitchinteractive.com/
25 Office of Counter Terrorism, "Global Counter-Terrorism Programme on Autonomous and Remotely Operated Systems (AROS)," United Nations, accessed January 3, 2025, https://un.org/counterterrorism/autonomous-and-remotely-operated-systems
26 Agence France-Presse, "Russia, Ukraine Exchange Drone, Missile Attacks," *voanews.com* June 14, 2024, https://voanews.com/a/russia-ukraine-exchange-drone-missile-attacks/7655741.html

27. Brock Vergakis, "US Launches Drone from Aircraft Carrier," *pekintimes* May 15, 2013, https://pekintimes.com/story/news/2013/05/15/us-launches-drone-from-aircraft/47071520007/
28. Chris Littlechild, "Why the U.S. Navy Decommissioned The Incredible X-47B Stealth Drone. *slashgear.com* April 29, 2023, https://slashgear.com/1272081/why-the-u-s-navy-decommissioned-the-incredible-x-47b-stealth-drone /
29. Quoted in John Ferrari, "Unleashing Innovation: The Case for a Drone Operator Branch in the US Army." *breakingdefense.com* June 3, 2024, https://breakingdefense.com/2024/06/unleashing-innovation-the-case-for-a-drone-operator-branch-in-the-us-army/
30. Nick Turse, *The Changing Face of Empire: Special Ops. Drones, Spies, Proxy Fighters, Secret Bases, and Cyberwarfare* (Chicago: Haymarket Books, 2012), 12.
31. Turse, 12.
32. Walter Pincus, "Special Operations Wins in 2014 budget" *Washington Post* April 11, 2013, Accessed June 4, 2013, http://articles.washingtonpost.com/2013-04-11/world/38448541_1_mcraven-socom-special-forces); Stew Magnuson, "Changes in the Horizon For Special Operations Command as Force Grows," *nationaldefensemagazine.org* May 2012 https://nationaldefensemagazine.org/articles/2012/5/1/2012may-changes-on-the-horizon-for-special-operations-comm and-as-force-grows
33. Turse, 15–16.
34. Ibid., 22.
35. Colin Vanderburg, "Drone Art," *Dissent* (2016) https://dissentmagazine.org/article/drone-art-astro-noise-laura-poitras
36. Zenko, 6.
37. Alan W. Dowd, "Drone Wars: Risks and Warning." *Parameters* 42 (4)/43 (1), Spring (2013): 7.
38. Tom Farer and Frederic Bernard, "Killing by Drone: Towards Uneasy Reconciliation with the Values of a Liberal State," *Human Rights Quarterly* 38 (2016): 138.
39. Dowd, 8. 12.
40. Benjamin, 67–8; Zenko 7.
41. Zenko, 7–8.
42. Sarah Kreps and John Kaag, "The Use of Unmanned Aerial Vehicles in Contemporary Conflict: A Legal and Ethical Analysis," *palgrave-journals.com/polity* 44 (2012):17.
43. Michael Walzer, *Arguing about War* (New Haven: Yale University Press, 2004), xiii.
44. Kreps and Kang, 23.
45. Jeremy Scahill, *Dirty Wars: The World Is a Battlefield* (New York: Nation Books, 2013), 468.
46. Greg Kennedy, "Drones: Legitimacy and Anti-Americanism." *Parameters* 42 (4)/43 (1), 2013: 26–7.
47. Kennedy, 27.
48. Lisa Parks, "Drones, Vertical Mediation, and the Targeted Class." *Feminist Studies*. 42. 1 (2016): 232.
49. Ibid.
50. Ibid.

51 Fred Kaplan, "The World as Free Fire Zone," *MIT Technology Review*, June 7, 2013 https://technologyreview.com/2013/06/07/177754/the-world-as-free-fire-zone/
52 Quoted in Fred Kaplan.
53 Medea Benjamin, 132.
54 Fred Kaplan, ibid.
55 Tom Farer and Frederic Bernard, "Killing by Drone: Towards Uneasy Reconclization with the Values of a Liberal State," *Human Rights Quarterly* 38 (2016): 129.
56 Michael J. Boyle. *The Drone Age: How Drone Technology Will Change War and Peace* (Oxford University Press, 2020), 20.
57 Albar Ahmed, *The Thistle and the Drone: How America's War on Terror Became a Global War on Tribal Islam* (Washington, DC: Brookings Institution Press, 2013), 19–22.
58 Ahmed, 70.
59 Ibid., 4.
60 Amy Kaplan, *The Anarchy of Empire* (Cambridge, MA: Harvard University Press), 2002.
61 James Rogers, "The Second Drone Age: Defining War in the 2020s." *Defense and Security Analysis* 39, no. 2 (2023): 256.
62 Ibid., 256.
63 Ibid., 257.
64 Ibid.
65 Marc R. DeVore, "'No End of a Lesson': Observations from the First High-Intensity Drone War." *Defense & Security Analysis* 39, no. 2 (2023): 262.
66 DeVore, 264.
67 Stephen Witt, "The Weapon of Influence," *New Yorker*, May 16, 2022, 26.
68 DeVore, 264.
69 Ole Jensen, "Thinking with the Drone–Visual Lessons in Aerial and Volumetric Thinking." *Visual Studies* 35, no. 5 (2020): 424.
70 Ibid., 426.
71 Ibid., 423.
72 Ibid., 421.
73 Lauren Alex O'Hagan and Elisa Serafinelli, "Rethinking Verticality through Top-down Views in Drone Hobbyist Photography," *Visual Studies* (2023): 3.
74 Ibid., 4.
75 Ibid., 6.
76 Ibid., 9.
77 Ibid., 10.
78 Ibid., 12.
79 Lauren Alex O'Hagan and Elisa Serafinelli, "Transhistoricizing the Drone: A Comparative Visual Semiotic Analysis of Pigeon and Domestic Drone Photography." *Photography and Culture* 15, no. 4 (2022): 331.
80 Ibid., 334.
81 Ibid., 336.
82 Grégorie Chamayou, *A Theory of the Drone* (New York: The New Press, 2015), 38–42.
83 Ibid., 38.
84 Ibid.
85 Ibid., 39–40.

86 Ibid., 41.
87 Ibid., 42.
88 Ibid., 43.
89 Mark Andrejevic, "Theorizing Drones and Droning Theory," *Drones and Unmanned Aerial Systems: Legal and Social Implications for Security and Surveillance*. Edited by Aleš Završnik (Switzerland: Springer, 2016), 23.
90 Ibid., 35.
91 Chamayou, 32.
92 Kerry Chávez and Ori Swed, "Emulating Underdogs: Tactical Drones in the Russia-Ukraine War." *Contemporary Security Policy* 44, no. 2 (2023): 598.
93 Kerry Chávez and Ori Swed, 594.
94 Kathrin Maurer, "Visual Power: The Scopic Regime of Military Drone Operations." *Media, War, and Conflict* 10, no. 2 (2018): 141.
95 Ibid., 142.
96 Ibid., 143.
97 Ibid., 146.
98 Ibid., 148.
99 Michel Foucault, *Power/Knowledge*. Edited by Colin Gordon. Trans. by Colin Jordan, Leo Marshall, John Mepham, and Kate Soper (New York: Pantheon Books, 1972), 155.
100 Carlene D. Elliot, "Kid-Visible: Childhood Obesity, Body Surveillance, and the Techniques of Care." *Surveillance: Power, Problems, and Politics*. Edited by Sean P. Hier and Josh Greenberg (Toronto: UBC Press, 2009), 44.
101 Mike Larsen and Justin Piché. "Public Vigilance Campaigns and Participatory Surveillance after 11 September 2001," *Surveillance: Power, Problems, and Politics*. Edited by Sean P. Hier and Josh Greenberg (Toronto: UBC Press, 2009), 196.
102 Kevin D. Haggerty, "Tear Down the Walls: On Demolishing the Panopticon," *Theorizing Surveillance: The Panopticon and Beyond*. Edited by David Lyon (Portland, OR: Willan, 2006), 26.
103 Haggerty, "Tear Down," 23.
104 Rosen and Santesso, *The Watchman in Pieces*, 7, 103.
105 Ibid., 102.
106 Ibid., 56, 103.
107 Ibid., 103.
108 Ibid., 57.
109 Ibid., 103.
110 Ibid., 247.
111 Rosen and Santesso, *The Watchman in Pieces*, 247.
112 Max Liljefors, "Omnivoyance and Blindness." *War and Algorithm*. Edited by Howard Caygill, Allen Feldman, and Sara Kendall (New York: Rowman and Littlefield, 2019), 128.
113 Ibid., 132.
114 Ibid., 138.
115 Ibid., 139.
116 Paul Virilio, *The Vision Machine* (Bloomington: Indiana University Press, 1994), 59–62.
117 Ibid., 60.
118 Ibid.

119 Ibid., 146.
120 Ibid., 147.
121 Ibid.
122 Ibid. Liljefors mentions Byung-Chul Han.
123 Ibid., 148.

2 THE GLOBAL ANARCHY OF THE SURVEILLANT ASSEMBLAGE

Drones and surveillance networks are deeply intertwined; they establish new modalities for nation-states to exercise power and control at scale, both demographic and geographic; new cultures of surveillance are normalized, in which people are scrutinized based on techniques of data production and data analysis to apprehend, track, or eliminate suspects. That is why, as I will show in this chapter, the drone eye of power embodies a global surveillant assemblage as a drone-enabled form of biopolitics. I demonstrate how drones and surveillance instantiate a new dispensation of dominance through the surveillant assemblage—powerful control through digital, light, mobile, shadowy networks, systems, and digital dossiers. I first theorize drone surveillance to study the generation of biopolitical power in a drone world, and the ethical challenges that we must confront. To show that we have crossed the threshold of automated warfare, I end the chapter with comments on the role of Artificial Intelligence (AI) and ChatGPT in drone warfare.

Boundless Empire

At the heart of surveillance regime are digital technologies. By attempting to control the Internet, the government seeks to access and control nonbusiness or work-related aspects of our lives. The Internet is where we think and communicate, store ideas and images; it is where we converse and interact with others; it is where our notions of education, home, belonging, family, morality, politics, ethics, and professional work are constructed and negotiated. It is a space where we play out our attempts to understand our humanity—who we are, what we are, how we are, why we are—and the eco-systems we inhabit and shape. As Glenn Greenwald puts in *No Place to Hide*, the Internet is "the epicenter of our world, the place where virtually everything is done … It is where we develop and express our very personality and sense of self."[1]

This is why surveillance of the Internet strikes at the root of individuality and identity, and allowing "surveillance to take root on the Internet would mean subjecting virtually all forms of human interaction, planning, and even thought itself to comprehensive state examination."[2] The benevolent state morphs into the Security State as it arrogates immense power to itself, its leaders and apparatchiks, both within its corridors of power and in the terrain of public culture. Whenever ideas and thoughts are formed that question this form of control, the surveillance state seeks to change the "Internet into a tool of repression, threating to produce the most extreme and oppressive weapon of state intrusion human history has ever seen."[3] The government will start "suppressing dissent and mandating compliance."[4]

Drone warfare depends on surveilling peoples in other lands, and the surveillance state surveils people in the very country from which the state emerges. The rationale for surveillance is to contain terrorism outside and within the country's borders, an idea grounded in the ideological and material horrors of 9/11. Yet, for all their public moralizing about preparing the nation for war and spying on suspects, the four US administrations since 2001 ratcheted up surveillance beyond the purview of democratic institutions and laws. When administrations constantly assure peoples that they have nothing to worry about regarding state intrusion of their lives, it is because they leave them no place to hide—they take from them the right to privacy and the freedoms of personal expression and association that come from privacy.

Anarchy of Surveillance

In June 2013 *The Guardian*, a British newspaper, published reports about America's surveillance practices, and in the same month, with the help of journalists Glen Greenwald and Laura Poitras, Edward Joseph Snowden, former systems specialist at the Defense Intelligence Agency and Booz Allen Hamilton employee contracted to work in the National Security Agency in Hawaii, announced in a video broadcast from Hong Kong that he was the leaker of classified information; soon, the US government was charging him with espionage. Since the 1917 Espionage Act and prior to 2010, only three people were charged for leaking classified information; nevertheless, the Obama administration charged eight people, including Snowden, for espionage.[5] Snowden's revelations show a massive program launched and maintained by the United States and its allies to secretly collect electronic data on people in America and other countries.

The scope and depth of this surveillance are stunning: it is vast, secret, and powerful. The program PRISM collects email and phone information directly from service providers such as Microsoft, Google, Yahoo!, Facebook, PalTalk, YouTube, Skype, AOL, and Apple; programs like BLARNEY, FAIRVIEW, OAKSTAR, and STORMBREW tap fiber-optic cables across the Pacific, linking Asia to the United States, and across the Atlantic, linking Europe and Africa to the United States. and gather electronic information flowing into the United States. These programs "exploit the fact that the vast majority of the world's Internet traffic at some point flows through the US communications infrastructure—a residual by-product of the central role that the United States had played in developing the network."[6] Through the program *Dishfire*, the NSA collects 200 million text messages from around the world each day.[7] It has the "capacity to reach roughly 75% of all U.S. Internet traffic in the hunt for foreign intelligence, including a wide array of communications by foreigners and Americans," which includes some content of emails and phone conversations.[8] In one month alone in 2013, the NSA collected, through a program named BOUNDLESS INFORMANT, 3 billion phone and email data flowing in and out of the United States, and in one month, it reviewed "97 billion emails and 124 billion phone calls from around the world."[9]

The program also surveilled countries including Germany, Brazil, India, France, Norway, Spain, Italy, the Netherlands Norway, and Denmark. The United States has partnered with Britain, Canada, Australia, and New Zealand to develop such networked surveillance systems.[10] There is no doubt that the NSA's aim is global in scope: it seeks to "sniff it all," partner it all," explore it all," process it all," "collect it all," and "know it all."[11] Using X-KEYSCORE, the NSA is able to easily collect information from Facebook and chat logs and Twitter, for example, and generate records beyond forty-one billion data events. This program also allows surveillers to access browsing history, search entries, saved elements, and so on, making its spying reach invasive and comprehensive.[12]

The Obama administration offered two counter perspectives: the post-9/11 era where the need to prevent terrorism has increased, and the presence of judicial oversight to prevent abuses of information collected by NSA. But the arguments were weak and misleading. The NSA targeted German Chancellor Angela Merkel's cell phone, and the electronic communications of Brazilian President Dilma Rouseff, and Mexican candidate for President (during elections) Enrique Pena Nieto.[13] The government engaged in "economic espionage" by electronically surveilling Petrobas, the big Brazilian oil company, other companies in Mexico and Venezuela, and the Ministry of Mines and Energy in Brazil.[14] Also, when the NSA secretly got access to the UN Secretary General's notes before he met with the President, and another time, when she was US Ambassador to the UN, Susan Rice asked the NSA to tap into the electronic conversations on UN members who were planning sanctions against Iran. The administration also set up digital spying systems in numerous diplomatic offices and embassies in the United States and the world.[15]

Between 2005 and 2011, the Foreign Intelligence Surveillance Court (FISC) received hundreds of requests from the NSA to collect the business electronic data of people in the United States. Although it narrowed the focus of a few, the court did not reject a single request.[16] Between 2018 and 2020, the United States conducted military or intelligence activities in eighty-four countries. The operations include "air and drone strikes, on-the-ground combat, so-called Section 127e programs in which the U.S. special operations forces plan and control partners force missions, military exercises in preparation for or as part of counterterrorism missions, and operations to train and assist foreign forces."[17] The Bush, Obama, Trump, and Biden administrations have all supervised such activities to strengthen American global dominance.

The role of Snowden in this political drama is not beyond critique, but such is the case with whistleblowing that persuading the organization one works for and persuading others to re-examine policies and practices come at enormous personal risk and death threats. Snowden is no exception. Even as calls for his formal prosecution and pardon continue unabated across the political spectrum, what cannot be overlooked is the deep culpability of government officials, particularly US presidential administrations, which often issued misleading and false information to subvert democracy. What the evidence shows is this fact: empire—American empire. It's in full operation as it actively harnesses digital technologies to bring the domain of electronic activity under its control by engaging in invasive, often illegal, scrutiny. The relationship between the digital and empire is well stated by Greenwald:

> Ultimately, beyond diplomatic manipulation and economic gain, a system of ubiquitous spying allows the United States to maintain its grip on the world. When the United States is able to know everything that everyone is doing, saying, thinking, and planning—its own citizens, foreign populations, international corporations, other government leaders—its power over those factions is maximized ... It is the ultimate imbalance, permitting the most dangerous of all human conditions: the exercise of limitless power with no transparency or accountability.[18]

What is really at stake when the security state becomes a surveillance state? Why should it matter to give up our rights for the state to protect us? Is all this nothing but merely data? Do we not have an embodied existence that transcends the power of Big Data generated by the state? In short, why worry too much about drone warfare, since it is taking place elsewhere, and the surveillance regime, since it is trying to keep us safe? To answer these questions, we first need a conceptual and historical grasp of surveillance.

Visibility/Invisibility: Power Politics

In *Surveillance Studies: An Overview*, David Lyon defines surveillance as "the focused, systematic and routine attention to personal details for purposes of influence, management, protection or direction."[19] Treating surveillance as a uniquely modern phenomenon is a mistake, since "surveillance is as old as human history and has always been ambiguous. It starts with anyone 'watching over' others for some purpose, whether caring for children or supervising workers or registering citizens."[20] David Rosen and Aaron Santesso view surveillance as "the monitoring of human activities for the purposes of anticipating or influencing future events."[21] Similarly, Roger A. Clarke "explicitly reject[s] the notion that surveillance is, of itself, evil or undesirable; its nature must be understood, and society must decide the circumstances in which it should be used, and the safeguards that should be applied to it."[22] To Kevin D. Haggerty, "surveillance involves monitoring people or things typically as the basis for some form of social intervention. In the past half century, surveillance has emerged as the dominant organizing practice of later modernity and is prompting widespread chances across assorted social domains."[23]

He adds that surveillance is not inherently problematic but an "inevitable attribute of knowledge-production ... while one can generate knowledge without engaging in surveillance—through introspection or dialogue, for instance, surveillance is nearly always a component of a knowledge-generation process."[24] When cholera spread rampantly in mid-nineteenth century England, physician John Snow systematically analyzed, or more appropriately surveilled, city maps, water pumps, drainage and sewage systems, and river flows, concluding that seepage of sewage into the Thames led to soiled water consumption at home. After persuading city officials to redirect sewerage water away from the river, cholera dropped rapidly.

In other instances, like Nazi Germany in the twentieth century, the use of complex organizational methods led to a highly efficient bureaucracy that used surveillance technologies to round up and perpetuate horrendous atrocities on the Jews and minorities. In both examples, surveillance is prevalent, but its imbrication into power and politics changes its role and impact in society. "These dramatically different examples of the uses of the state infrastructure of population surveillance," says Haggerty, "highlight the point that surveillance is neither inevitably good nor inevitably bad; rather, it is a generalized technology that can be used for a host of different government projects."[25]

Modernity as Surveillance

Lyon, Rosen, Santesso, Clarke, and Haggerty rightly caution against viewing surveillance as uniformly nefarious, criminal, injurious activity, because "the garnering of personal data by institutions frequently facilitates entitlement, efficiency, convenience or security. The fact that it may have sinister or suspect sides does not negate this."[26] In *Surveillance and Identity: Discourse, Subjectivity, and the State*, David Barnard-Wills points out, "Far from just being an activity associated with policing or intelligence agencies, any social process which functions through the gathering and processing of information can be understood to have a surveillant dimension. Surveillance is therefore linked to processes of the production and use of knowledge" and as such it "is a fundamental social and political activity."[27] Because the use of information technology today permeates many aspects of social life that involve "exclusion, inclusion, judgment, suspicion, the allocation of resource, decision-making, moral assessment, crime, statecraft and warfare ... it is important to avoid the danger of technological determinism, in which a change in social life is directly read off from the capacities of technological innovation, or to assume that technologies emerge unaffected by their social milieu."[28]

One danger is that "identity produced and attributed by surveillance is taken by institutions as more reliable than any account of themselves that any individual might be able to give."[29] Barnard-Wills cautions against this view, because data and language, in and around which surveillance is practiced and apprehended as knowledge, form discourses that create and authenticate particular subject positions (notion of self, particular orientations, social norms, and discursive practices). This implicates surveillance in relationships of power, because social meanings are generated, codified, and used through structures and processes of governmentality.

Lyon suggests that instead of viewing surveillance as a contemporary problem specific to developed societies or the First World, studying how surveillance evolved, continues, stops, or changes will help us understand the unique features of the present. The military organized soldiers, trained them, and executed war plans that required identifying, numbering, and classifying all personnel. Establishing and maintaining rigid hierarchies and codes of discipline, and distinguishing between friends and enemies, evident in the military even today, could be done only with the tools of surveillance. Ancient empires and city states maintained detailed censuses to tax and conscript people. Differentiating among natives, aliens—documented and undocumented—and visitors requires collecting personal and social data.

Such surveillance enhances the ability of the state to provide relief and voting rights, and also targets individuals and groups to deny rights and deprive them of property and life. Workplaces are also everyday sites of surveillance as various kinds of activity are monitored, tabulated, and reevaluated to increase productivity and streamline work. Developing policies and practices to contain or enhance public health is also a prerogative that the state exercises through organizing and maintaining personal data and information about natural environments. Surveillance at work also means the ability to discipline and control workers and organizations, with extreme forms resulting in the erosion of the worker as a contributing individual leading to a system whose values lie in its ability to absorb and expel workers. The police also use surveillance not only to apprehend suspects but also to maintain law and order.

Peace is not a natural condition without norms or laws but a state that is produced through the observance of certain explicit and implied rules and practices. Business often seek and maintain consumer information to assess market value, product liability, and trend prediction. Providing customers with an array of choices or products geared to satisfy specific tastes and likes continues to be an organizing work principle for business big and small.[30]

As a modern phenomenon, surveillance has five elements: rationalization (standardization of processes and "reason" as opposed to "tradition, emotion, or common-sense knowledge" becomes the "guide to social, political and economic life"); technology (use of tools and practices to increase surveillance and rationalization); sorting (to separates people into types or groups);' knowledgeability (the degree to which those subjected to surveillance are aware and engage with it); and urgency (the risks involved in slowing or stopping surveillance in times of mass threats).[31] But in the shift from the modern to the postmodern present, what transformations are evident?

Surveillance in Liquid Modernity

In *Liquid Modernity*, Zygmunt Bauman characterizes the present as marking the shift from heavy modernity to light modernity. In heavy modernity, space and time were deeply connected: those with the ability to explore and conquer space and maintain it over time amassed immense power. In heavy modernity, empire was obtained through the use of steamships, gunboats, planes, guns, bombs, compasses, maps, and swords—and in economics, through massive manufacturing plants, Fordist production lines, and time-bound activities—to bring the natural world and its inhabitants under the domain of order, stability, and predictability.[32] Like Bauman, Lyon explains modern surveillance "as an outgrowth of capitalist enterprises, bureaucratic organization, the nation-state, a machine-like technology and the development of new kinds of solidarity involving less 'trust' or at least different kinds of trust."[33] These distinctions can be best viewed as points of departure and exploration, rather than as clear markers separating historical periods.

To Bauman, as the agent of heavy modernity, the Panopticon symbolizes and materializes a certain practice and form of power as both the inmates (society in general) and the surveillants (those in power or with access to power) interact within delimited territory and time. But Bauman argues that we are living in a post-Panopticon age because all territories are mapped and time has shrunk, and social life can be managed without the surveillants and the surveilled being unduly limited by time and space.[34] In *Machine Vision: How Algorithms Are Changing the Way We See the World*, Jill Walker Rettberg argues that computer visuality, or the visuals created by the digital eye of the computer, is a "machine vision" that affords us a way to look at the world by seeing it in certain ways. Rettberg explains machine vision "as the registration, analysis and representation of visual information by machines and algorithms. Machine vision technologies register visual information and store it as data that can be processed computationally."[35] Vision technologies—or the instruments we use to see, enhance human sight, or imagine a setting visually—do not have objective features that help us see the world imagistically.

Rather, since "we don't fully control the technologies we use, and the technologies don't fully control us," we must examine the "assemblages we choose to enter into (or that are thrust upon us)" so that we can "untangle how technologies work in specific contexts."[36] Three relevant issues can be drawn out from Rettberg's formulation: the social embeddedness of technologies' rises and uses; information obtained through the machine vision requires computational processing to become meaningful data; the relationships created among technologies and a range of socioeconomic and political spheres and peoples produce "assemblages" that we select or are selected for us by others, often, in the context of this book's focus on drones, by the state and powerful non-state entities. The next chapter details the limitations of machine vision; here, let's examine the idea of assemblages.

The Surveillant Assemblage

In *Dialogues*, Gilles Deleuze explains the concept of the assemblage:

> What is an assemblage? It is a multiplicity which is made up of many heterogeneous terms and which establishes liaisons, relations between them, across ages, sexes and reigns–different natures. Thus, the assemblage's only unity is that of co-functioning: it is a symbiosis, a "sympathy." It is never filiations which are important, but alliances, alloys; these are not successions, lines of descent, but contagions, epidemics, the wind. Magicians are well aware

of this. An animal is defined less by its genus, its species, its organs, and its functions, than by the assemblages into which it enters.[37]

In "What is an Assemblage?" Thomas Nail points out that when the French term "agencement" is rendered in English as "assemblage," meaning is not borne across languages well. Agencement is about ordering or laying out things and structures, while assemblage is about connecting or putting things together. Because, as Nail says, "a layout or arrangement is not the same thing as a unity or simple coming together ... While an assemblage is a gathering of things together into unities, an agencement is an arrangement or layout of heterogenous elements."[38] Here, two terms acquire specific meanings: unity shifts to multiplicity and essence to events. He adds, "Assemblages are more like machines, defined solely by their external relations of composition, mixture, and aggregation. In other words, an assemblage is a multiplicity, neither a part nor a whole. If the elements of an assemblage are defined only by their external relations, then it is possible that they can be added, subtracted, and recombined with one another ad infinitum without ever creating or destroying an organic unity."[39]

Instead of focusing on the essential substance of a thing, as if such elemental possession were possible, Deleuze and Guattari, as Nail sees it, move from essence to event, by stressing the "how? where? when? from what viewpoint?"[40] Assemblages have three common features: the "abstract machine," the "concrete assemblage," and the "personae."[41] A few more comments about the terms are in order here, because, as I will soon show, the drone's surveillant assemblage takes on new dimensions. The abstract machine refers to "the network of specific external relations that holds the elements together ... The condition of an assemblage is abstract because it is not a thing or object that exists in the world, but rather something that lays out a set of relations wherein concrete elements and agencies appears."[42]

When the abstract machine is embodied in concrete forms, we have the concrete assemblage that arranges specific elements in certain groupings or orderings to realize particular objectives. The third feature describes "personae," who are "the mobile operators that connect the concrete elements together according to their abstract relations. In other words, personae do not transcend the assemblage but are immanent to it."[43] These features are common to the four types of assemblages examined by Deleuze and Guattari: "the territorial, state, capitalist, and nomadic."[44]

In *Assemblage Theory*, Manuel DeLanda explains features common to all assemblages, as he interprets Deleuze and Guattari's concepts: the assemblage "has a fully contingent historical identity, and each of them is therefore an individual entity: an individual person, an individual community, an individual organization, an individual city";[45] an assemblage is "composed of heterogenous components";[46] an assemblage can "become parts of larger assemblages"; an assemblage "emerge[s] from the interaction between their parts."[47]

In using Deleuze and Guattari's concept of the assemblage to examine drone warfare, we can draw on Nail and DeLanda's interlocutions to detail the emergence of a new assemblage in the digital world: the surveillant assemblage. It is an ordering and joining together of heterogenous elements to surveil, gather, store, and process data, using machine learning and deep learning, to sort, typecast, build digital profiles, assess threats, and eliminate them. The abstract machine of this assemblage involves the political and juridical protocols to exercise power globally through digital technologies; the concrete elements include the drone, its wireless and remote operational capabilities, its drone eye, the data obtained through surveillance, and the ensemble of distribution mechanisms and analytics that generate targeting policies and decision-making processes to contain, delay, or destroy whatever is deemed harmful to the security state.

Regarding personae, which Nail noted as the third common element to assemblages, we have the drone operators, data analysts, intelligence specialists, military leaders, and politicians who become part of the assemblage depending on its fluid operations across the globe. In the next chapter, I discuss the biopolitical and necropolitical nature of drone warfare to draw out its perplexing ethical challenges for us to consider. Here, I will explain how the surveillant assemblage operates to produce data, information, and knowledge about the world through the drone eye that generates a unique type of visuality to make sense of all that is surveilled and to exercise dominance.

The Digital Surveillant Assemblage

Kevin Haggerty and Richard Ericson take the critique of the panopticon a step further in proposing a new paradigm called "surveillant assemblage." This is not to replace the panopticon but to foreground profound changes in society that the panopticon metaphor does not adequately capture. The proliferation of non-state agencies engaged in surveillance, the greater participation and involvement in surveillance processes by the public, the intense compression of space and time due to globalization, and the manifold uses to which surveillance is put distinguish the panoptic from the surveillant assemblage. Surveillance as a flowing process or one that negotiates with the flow of information and data that are produced through a surveillance of ideas, things, and people in migration means that mobility becomes a crucial dimension of the politics of visibility. They write, "This assemblage operates by abstracting human bodies from their territorial settings and separating them into a series of discrete flows. These flows are then reassembled into distinct 'data doubles' which can be scrutinized and targeted for intervention. In the process, we are witnessing a rhizomatic leveling of the hierarchy of surveillance, such that groups which were previously exempt from routine surveillance are now increasingly being monitored."[48]

The body here becomes disembodied but does not replace the corporeal body but acts as its "data double." The data about the body is gathered by disassembling it into its many constituent parts and in practices and behaviors associated with them and reassembling it virtually. "The body," they note, "is itself, then, an assemblage comprised of myriad component parts and processes which are broken down for purposes of observation."[49] This kind of surveillance "brings into the visual register a host of heretofore opaque flows of auditory, scent, chemical, visual, ultraviolent and informational stimuli."[50]

A problem with such a data doubles produced through surveillant assemblages is that ensuring the difference between the embodied and the virtual becomes less important as they become a "form of pragmatics: differentiated according to how useful they are in allowing institutions to make discriminations among populations."[51] They develop a life of their own, and their value and utility depend on particular convergences of individuals, groups, or agencies whose interests overlap temporarily to meet certain ends. This complicates notions of identity, power, and agency as the politics of surveillance extends beyond the principle of distinction separating the material from virtual and into the domain of sorting, stopping, thwarting, occluding, and withdrawing: visibility becomes a terrain of and for the political.

Drawing from Gilles Deleuze and Félix Gautari's notion of the rhizome used to describe temporary processes, Haggerty and Ericson contend that the surveillance assemblage operates like a rhizome and is structured like a rhizome. A plant whose stem grows roots horizontally, and under the surface—rhizomatically—the rhizome has nodes, breaks, non-linear patterns, and irregular reproducibility. Like the rhizome, metaphorically, the surveillant assemblage "comprise[s] use discrete flows of an essentially limitless range of other phenomena such as people, signs, chemical, knowledge, and institutions. To dig beneath the surface stability of any entity is to encounter a host of different phenomena and processes working in concert" as "flows exist prior to any particular assemblage, and are fixed temporarily and spatially by the assemblage."[52] Such rhizomatic surveillance does not abolish hierarchies but makes them uneven and flat, even as it enhances its capabilities by adding on to or changing its codes and fields of operations.

Sean P. Hier and Josh Greenberg, while agreeing with Haggerty, argue that in countering Foucault's overemphasis on the panopticon's gaze infusing all social practices, the assemblage tends to relativize surveillance systems in their plurality. The use of the rhizome metaphor adequately captures the flow of information and surveillant power across rhizomatic networks, but in different points and at various times, these flows are arrested or made use of "at nodal points along rhizomes in the assemblage and in the context of existing institutional relations of power and control. The lack of analytical care to centers of appropriation leads them [Haggerty and Ericson], however unintentionally, to relativize, or at least to under-theorize, asymmetrical surveillant applications."[53]

Heir and Greenberg propose "visibility, as a field of cultural action [that] is conditioned by aesthetics (relations of perception) and politics (relations of power)."[54] In this respect, their ideas give conceptual clarity to Rosen and Santesso's point about the performative self under surveillance by underscoring visibility as a field for strategy and subversion. They write, "In the surveillant assemblage, that is, where innumerable data flows bring about the "disappearance of disappearance" in the context of ubiquitous social monitoring, it is in fact appearance (virtual or embodied) that becomes normal, unmarked, unnoticed, and banal." This raises questions that go beyond privacy and visibility, the spiritual inviolable self and the public persona: "Why are certain groups of people more visible than others at certain moments in time? In what contexts does visibility work against democratic participation in social institutions? What is worth being seen under different government regimes? How is visibility (the ordinary/normal) intrinsic to invisibility and super-visibility (the extraordinary/abnormal)? What does the visible minority tell us about the invisible and super-visible majority at specific historical moments?"[55]

To Haggerty and Ericson, Hier and Greenberg's "disappearance of disappearance" leads not to total visibility but to a striated visibility where particular forms of visibility are tied to benefits like "credit card rating, computer services, or rapid movement through customs" and so on.[56] Their point about privacy is worth underscoring: "Privacy is now less a line in the sand beyond which transgression is not permitted, than a shifting space of negotiation where privacy is traded for products, better services or special deals."[57] Hier and Greenberg extend this further to connect power and politics to the surveillant assemblage as surveillance becomes imbricated in the exercise of domination and control. Their questions open the concept of surveillance and the practice of surveillance to "thresholds of visibility," a range of discursive and material manifestations and practices that modulate the seen and unseen, which need to be apprehended synchronically and diachronically.[58]

Digital Dossiers and Dataveillance

Surveillance, argues Daniel J. Solove in *The Digital Person: Technology and Privacy in the Information Age*, leads to the creation of "digital dossiers" that are "collection[s] of detailed data about an individual ... data is digitized into binary numerical form, which enables computers to store and manipulate it with unprecedented efficiency."[59] Three types of information flows are embodied in digital surveillance: data flowing among private firms; data flowing from government controlled or owned entities to private ones, which construct dossiers based on such information; and data flowing from the private companies to the local and national government agencies. As he says, "the increase in digital dossiers has thus resulted in an elaborate lattice of information networking, where information is being stored, analyzed, and used in ways that have profound implications for society."[60]

Roger A. Clarke in "Information Technology and Dataveillance" coins the term "dataveillance" to characterize a new modality of surveillance enhanced by the growth of digital technologies: "Dataveillance is the systematic use of personal data systems in the investigation or monitoring of the actions or communications of one or more persons."[61] It can take many forms including screening, front-end verification, front-end audit, and file analysis. The initial process of relatively simple verification for a transaction, claim, permission, application, or some such activity is screening. Front-end verification involves consulting more than one database that may or may not be part of the same unit performing the surveillance.

Front-end audit is more expansive than front-end verification as it covers multiple data bases in many organizations whose aims and roles may be different. A drive stopped for a traffic infraction can be surveilled through multiple databases for other traffic violations and non-traffic violations also, like outstanding liens or arrest warrants not related to the event initiating the surveillance. File analysis is done irrespective of already detected anomalies; it is set in motion as a regularized process, often automated, to assess the smooth functioning of systems of verification and surveillance and check past and current processes or interactions.

Front-end audit and file analysis are forms of mass, not personal, surveillance, because it "is concerned with groups of people and involves a generalized suspicion that some as yet unidentified members of the group may be of interest. Its purposes are to identify individuals who may be worth subjecting to personal surveillance, and to constrain the group's behavior."[62] Clarke's comprehensive explanations of the problems with dataveillance are worth considering in full in their effects on individuals and groups. Individuals subjected to dataveillance have to face the effects of "wrong identification, low data quality, acontextual use of data, low quality decisions, lack of subject knowledge of data flows, lack of subject consent to data flows, blacklisting, denial of redemption." The effects of mass surveillance on individuals include "arbitrariness, acontextual data merger, complexity and incomprehensibility of data, witch hunts, ex ante discrimination and guilt prediction, selective advertising, inversion of the onus of proof, covert operations, unknown accusations and accusers, denial of due process."[63]

The effects on society can be pernicious as it leads to a "prevailing climate of suspicion, adversarial relationships, focus of law enforcement on easily detectable and provable offenses, inequitable application of law, decreased respect for the law, reduction in the meaningfulness of individual actions, reduction in self-reliance and self-determination, stultification of originality, increased tendency to opt out of the official level of society, weakening of society's moral fiber and cohesion, destabilization of the strategic balance of power, repressive potential for a totalitarian government."[64] Such surveillance is banal as it is woven into the fabric of everyday life saturated with information technologies.

Between Big Brother and Joseph K

As Solove points out, dataveillance requires us to rethink traditional notions of privacy. The paradigm of Big Brother does matter, and it is hardly the case that we are seeing the replacement of one paradigm of surveillance by another. In dataveillance, we see an odd comingling of the two paradigms best exemplified in Orwell's Big Brother and Franz Kafka's Joseph K. Big Brother seeks domination—all parts of human interaction and living are subjected to another seeing eye, another standard. It "demands complete obedience from its citizens and controls all aspects of their lives. It constructs the language, rewrites the history, purges its critics, indoctrinates the population, burns the books, and obliteratres all disagreeable relics from the past." This results in the formation of a "terrifying totalitarian state" as everyone's life is made amenable to being watched on the screen by somebody else, an Other power.[65]

Big Brother embodies the panoptic drive for power. Solove notes that with dataveillance, we have some aspects of Big Brother but there are differences, since most of the data is not collected by a unitary powerful agency with the single desire to erase, suppress, and penalize, but by business and companies to ascertain product information, consumer tastes and behavior, and by governmental agencies to improve bureaucratic management, which means that "it is a story about a group of different actors with different purposes attempting to thrive in an increasingly information-based society."[66]

Many of us today live with varying degrees of comfort with the knowledge that some information about us—workplace, gender, profession, and so on—is already public. The "secrecy paradigm" invests too much in privacy, but "this does not mean that avoiding disclosure is the sum and substance of our interest in privacy."[67] But the risks for human dignity in a society of dataveillance is dramatized in the predicament of Kafka's Joseph K in *The Trial* as he veers from being arrested to becoming an indifferent object of police attention, from being subjected to the vagaries of institutional incompetence to losing his life for reasons that elude understanding both to himself and to those exerting their power on him. *The Trial* "depicts an indifferent bureaucracy, where individuals are pawns, not knowing what is happening, having no say or ability to exercise meaningful control over the process."[68]

Dataveillance leaves us positioned as Joseph K, because digital dossiers are constructed about ourselves without our knowledge, input, and ability to control the uses of those dossiers. These are "unauthorized biographies about us, the complete content of which we often do not get to see."[69] The categories used to construct such dossiers are formal, abstract, and codified. They will doubtlessly yield useful information, but the partial nature of such dossiers does not prevent their being used as authoritative pieces of information about us by information systems and human users to evaluate, control, or otherwise subject us to judgment. Our inability to contribute and interact with data purposefully is compromised because "certain uses of databases foster a state of powerlessness and vulnerability created by people's lack of any meaningful form of participation in the collection and use of their personal information."[70] This is further problematic because "the process of information collection in America is clandestine, duplicitous, and unfair."[71] Also, "the problem is not simply a lack of individual control over information, but a situation where nobody is exercising meaningful control over the information."[72] We are subjected to capricious evaluations of our identities and lives, which often leave us powerless, confused, and without clear means to seek redress or rectification.

A key reason why resistance to surveillance is difficult to generate, through individual or collective choice, is that the technique for surveillance involves technology and people interacting constantly. Lyon is right in cautioning us not to conceive of surveillance primarily as a social and political aberration, something that happens occasionally, since watching over something or someone, keeping tabs, collecting information, sorting types or cataloging, and maintaining or archiving records have immense social benefits. The problem in the present is that new technologies change the nature of these processes as they transform the risks for people, and the fields of business, education, health care, politics, entertainment, and notions of trust and intimacy, including social ways of engaging with presence and absence. The protocols of these transformations emerge not as the results of official edicts by the powerful or government but in and through everyday patterns of thinking, interacting, and living.

Toward the Ban-Opticon

Dataveillance in this context is best apprehended as "meticulous rituals of power," asserts William G. Staples in *Everyday Surveillance*. It is meticulous because they are "microtechniques of social monitoring" and " 'small' procedures and technique that are precisely and thoroughly exercised"; they are "ritualistic because they are faithfully repeated and are often quickly accepted and routinely practiced with little questions"; and they exude "power because they are intended to discipline people into acting in ways that others have deemed to be lawful or have defined as appropriate or simple 'normal.' "[73] Such procedures and rituals, "no matter how small or seemingly trivial, have their own significance, for they define a certain mode of political investment in the body. That is, meticulous rituals of power are the concrete ways in which our bodily lives are shaped, manipulated, and controlled by public and private organizations and by the people who have authority over us."[74]

Deviance and abnormality now encompass a wide range of attitudes and behaviors that lead to monitoring eating and sleeping habits, reading news, patterns of buying and selling, the details of people with whom we interact, and so on. This results in the construction of social problems like "promiscuity," teenage pregnancy," "lifestyles," "substance abuse," "attention deficit disorders," or "troublesome individuals."[75] When modern techniques are harnessed to the power of computing and dataveillance, it leads to the growth of a "society increasingly lacking in personal privacy, individual trust, or viable pubic life that supports and maintains democratic values and practices."[76] The ability for social control increases exponentially, and the lines between outside imposition of and inside support for surveillance begin blurring as each becomes constitutive of the other. When people trade privacy for social stability, personal information for better services, and constant monitoring for security, is it a good bargain?

No, argues Neil Richards, because "surveillance by government and private actors threatens intellectual privacy and chills the exercise of vital civil liberties," and "surveillance affects the power balance between individuals and those who are watching, increasing the rise of persuasion, blackmail, and other harmful uses of sensitive information by others."[77] Offering "intellectual privacy" as a conceptual and experiential principle to counter surveillance culture, Richards notes that "new ideas often develop best away from the intense scrutiny of public exposure."[78] The civil rights of association and expression will be compromised, as well as each person's right to expect privacy when thinking, associating, or communicating. "Intellectual diversity and eccentric individuality" will be stifled in a surveillance society.[79] This aspect of intellectual surveillance is further strengthened when its merits are linked directly to the functioning of democracy.

Experientially, because "free minds are the foundation of a free society," which is a "normative claim," the surveillance of the daily activities of people makes it less likely that those surveilled will explore new ideas, seek other perspectives, think out of the box, and behave differently. Therefore, "surveillance thus menaces our society's foundational commitments to intellectual diversity and eccentric individuality."[80] In a democracy, the pressure for "self-censorship" increases drastically as people generally end up going with the flow when faced with prospect of being surveilled. In addition, the protection for free speech has historically meant "err[ing] on the side of caution," meaning that "errors in the adjudication of free speech cases tend to allow unlawful speech rather than engage in mistaken censorship."[81] In the public commons, free speech can lead to mistakes and abuses, but it is a risk worth taking and protecting to ensure the fullest and freest exercise of expression and deliberation "even if society must endure some of that speech's undesirable consequences."[82] Both arguments, I think, are strong in questioning the current public and media tendency to make a bargain with the state to yield liberty and privacy of thought, association, and movement in exchange for security.

This is by no means a clear case of security for privacy, because we must recognize that it's not just the government seeking personal information but businesses and other entities to whom people voluntarily give information, a practice that makes surveillance different from that of Big Brother, the Panopticon, or the courts of Joseph K. The worldwide increase in terrorism also requires monitoring of people in motion to ensure safety of person and property. Post-Panopticon power is modulated in material elements even as it becomes invisible and transversal. It runs in and through heterogeneous networks immanent to contemporary life. Power resides in compressing space and time while managing the dynamics of visibility and invisibility for both the surveilled and the surveillants. In a global world where millions of people move as migrants, exiles, and refuges, and where money, commodities, and power are just as mobile, practices of surveillance and control are structured around what Dieder Bigo calls the "ban-opticon," a term that describes the protocols necessary to manage unease in everyday life.

The ban-opticon has discourses, juridical practices, administrative measures, and architectural spaces that form networks within which information and knowledge are produced and managed in order to contain the threat of internal and external instability: airports, airline authorities, immigration and custom officials, various intelligence agencies, border patrols, police personnel, state and national policies, international criminal courts and intelligence networks, politicians and political apparatuses all work, however unevenly, to manage "the governmentality of unease beyond the State."[83]

Bigo further observes, "The central question relevant to defining security is thus to know who is authorized or to whom is delegated the symbolic power to designate exactly what the threats are … That is to say that the agents of the field fight for the authority to impose their definition of who and what inspires fear."[84] This changes the notion of imminent threat or imminent attack. Physical proximity to the potential targets or space cannot be the main criterion when networks of support to carry out violence against peoples and property can be established and sustained in systems both material and virtual across space and time. But in dealing with such new configurations of power and influence, the government's response has been to institutionalize the drone's ban-opticon where the locus of threat is not the individual or accomplice but groups of people moving in and out of constantly changing territorial zones, and assumed to have the potential to become imminent threats. Complicating matters further today is Artificial Intelligence. As Philip L. Frana and Michael J. Klein note in *Encyclopedia of Artificial Intelligence*, "Artificial Intelligence is fueling the reinvention of ourselves in a new computational universe."[85]

AI and Drones

Ajay Lele points to these areas as critical for AI application: "predictive maintenance," involving figuring out the most opportune time to repair, recharge, and renew; "target identification and tracking" used to locate and follow suspects and targets; "military simulation and training" where complex wargames can be simulated in protected environments; "autonomous weapons systems" that can function with little to no human engagement; cybersecurity used to safeguard networks and protocols; and "intelligence analysis" to sort big data for anomalies and signature conduct.[86] Examining the integration of computers into military technologies and cultures in *War in the Age of Intelligent Machines,* Manuel DeLanda begins with the PROWLER, a "small terrestrial armed vehicle" that can "maneuver around a battlefield and distinguish friends from enemies."[87] The aspiration, however, goes beyond a robotic vehicle that can blend "advisory and executive capabilities," meaning a robot that would not only assist humans in war but also take decisions independent of humans to engage in warfare.[88]

In the Second World War, tracking functions were added to military arsenal to follow and forecast where an aircraft might be at a point in time; fifty years later, at the end of the twentieth century, "BRAVE 3000, a jet-powered drone" flying at 400 mph was capable of identifying "the position of enemy radar installations" and by tracking the "radar signal," the drone could destroy the signal-emitting device.[89] DeLanda presages a time when "information-processing technology" would realize "the military commander's dream of a battlefield without human soldiers a reality."[90] He adds, "The development of Artificial Intelligence has allowed the military to begin the mechanization of the task of bringing patterns to the surface. To get humans out of the decision-making process, computers will have to learn "to see" and "to understand language."[91] Two elements are critical to DeLanda: "machine vision" and "machine translation."[92]

AI, then, will acquire the ability to see as a machine, collect and tabulate data, analyze images (and today, multimodal content) in specific computer languages, and interpret and generate meaningful analyses of the gathered information. When these two functions can be executed automatically, we move from assistive technologies endowed with machine intelligence capable of independently executing a series of tasks to robotic warriors endowed with Artificial Intelligence capable of thinking and acting like human beings. In 2021, the Strategic Futures Group of the National Intelligence Council published a report titled "Global Trends: The Future of the Battlefield." The report notes, "As autonomous technology progresses, some countries may not be concerned about having humans in the loop of firing decisions.

As a result, it is possible that by 2040—and despite the associated ethical and legal challenges to their use—truly autonomous, lethal weapons could roam the battlefield and make their own targeting and engagement decisions."[93] Writing in 2021 for National Public Radio (NPR), Joe Hernandez notes that the United Nations mentioned instances in Libya in March 2020 of armed drones acting autonomously to pursue targets, "but the report [UN report] does not say explicitly that the LAWS [lethal autonomous weapons systems] killed anyone."[94] That both the report about autonomous drone uses and the caution about their inevitable use in combat appear in 2021 show that AI in drone warfare is not literary fiction but our present. As Gwenola Ricordeau says, "The deployment of LAWS could dramatically change warfare as previously gunpowder and nuclear weapons did. It would end the distinction between combatants and weapons, and complicate the delimitation of battlefields."[95] Before moving further, an excursus into AI and ChatGPT is necessary here so that we can examine why it matters to drone warfare and understand how ethics gains urgency.

Artificial Intelligence

In 1950, the British mathematician and computer scientist Alan Turing speculated in "Computing Machinery and Intelligence" that, in what has come to be called the "Turing Test," when we are unable to distinguish between a computer and a person when they respond to questions we pose, a new type of intelligence emerges—one produced by machines. It is not natural, born biologically, but is created to convincingly simulate human processes of interaction.[96] "AI," says Will Douglass Heaven in the *Massachusetts Institute of Technology Review*, "is a catchall term for a set of technologies that make computers do things that are thought to require intelligence when done by people."[97] Paul Burgess in *AI and the Rule of Law* points out that because "a computer is, fundamentally, a calculation machine," AI "can be taken to include any machine that acts intelligently–as a machine that can make correct decisions in a given circumstance."[98]

In *Encyclopedia of Artificial Intelligence: The Past, Present, and Future of AI*, Philip F. Frana and Michael J. Klein offer this definition of Artificial Intelligence,[99] a concept proffered by John McCarthy, a mathematician, who led the Dartmouth Summer Research Project on the topic in 1956: "More broadly, artificial intelligence describes real or imagined efforts to simulate cognition and creativity. The term distinguishes machine and code from the natural intelligence of animals and people. But artificial intelligence (AI) researchers often view the brain as a natural computer and the mind as a human-made computer program."[100]

Since then, AI has seen the return of connectionism added to symbolic representation, creating two central research methodologies. Per Britannica, connectionism "developed out of attempts to understand how the human brain works at the neural level and, in particular, how people learn and remember."[101]

The idea is that a neuron "in the brain is a simple digital processor and the brain as a whole is a form of computing machine."[102] The symbolic method takes a formalist approach to "replicate intelligence by analyzing cognition independent of the biological structure of the brain."[103]

To these two can be added machine learning and deep learning. Machine learning (ML) aims "to detect and characterize complex patterns in large datasets."[104] It can be applied to symbolic AI data, but it should be noted that all neural networks involve machine learning, but not all machine learning involves neural networks. Algorithms for machine learning execute discretization, which changes "continuous equations, functions, model, and variables into discrete equations, functions, and so forth for digital computers";[105] feature engineering involves selecting, extracting, and possibly transforming data to demarcate the less from the more important or relevant elements, and reducing error rates. ML algorithms "learn patterns from large data sets and independently find the solution to a specific problem without explicitly programming each case beforehand."[106] Because algorithms are designed to work differently, they characterize data differently; some detect linear forms, others non-linear ones. In ML, algorithms "make a prediction or classification," "an error function evaluates the predication of the model," and "weights are adjusted to reduce" discrepancies, thereby generating a human-like type of learning, where inputs, variables, and weights are algorithmically analyzed iteratively, with each iteration refining learning by adjusting weights, hence the descriptor "learning" to describe the machine's (algorithmic or computerized) work.[107]

Paul Scharre points out three types of machine learning: supervised learning, unsupervised learning, and reinforcement learning. In supervised learning, "an algorithm is trained on labeled data" and, for instance, when an image is labeled, AI "learns to associate the image with the label."[108] In unsupervised learning, AI is "trained on unlabeled data and the algorithm learns patterns in the data" as evident in large language models like GPT-2 and GPT-3.[109] ChatGPT, it must be noted, trains on a mix of supervised and unsupervised data. In reinforcement learning, an "algorithm learns by interacting with its environment and gets rewards for certain behaviors," as in "getting dieback for actions that rack up a higher score" when game playing.[110]

Critical to AI is data. There can be no good, efficient, or sophisticated AI without reliable and extensive data. It is data in all its iterations that powers AI. Data used to train an algorithm to perform specific tasks is not fungible, because the same data will not make the algorithm perform other tasks beyond what the data allows it to learn, which is called the problem of "distributional shift." Data cannot be distributed because when a "model is trained on one set of data and then presented with data that is different (shifted) from the training data," it will not perform well unless the model can adapt to data shifts; we have not reached the point of sophistication in AI to make its training in one kind of data to make it perform beyond the data's parameters.[111] Hence, Scharre says that "'distributional shift failures' point toward the broader problem of the inability of AI systems to generalize what they have learn," unlike humans who have an extraordinary capacity to do so.[112]

Deep learning (DL), a form of Machine learning with large numbers of layers, by contrast, and a subtle one at that, works with both labeled and unlabeled datasets, particularly with unstructured data, and generates discretization, modeling, and labeling of data. DL requires more computational power and hardware resources, and, of course, more time, whereas ML (in general, not the DL subset) works by and large with labeled datasets, and "is more dependent on human intervention to learn."[113] DL is a sub-domain in neural learning-based ML, involving the gleaning of information from multiple layers, often "stacked" or "hidden."[114] True to all neural networks, every neuron in the program is linked to other neurons, creating a neural network in which processed information enables the neural network to function, with neurons exhibiting common or unique functions.

We must bear in mind, Paul Burgess cautions, that an algorithm does not mean AI, that when a computer uses an algorithm, it does not therefore mean AI. He offers this definition: "An algorithm is a finite and organized sequence of defined instructions that is used to perform a calculation or function or to solve a problem."[115] An algorithm can, for instance, be designed for a basic task as taking in inputs and producing certain outputs. Far from being "intelligence," such small or large-scale algorithmic operations cannot simulate cognition of any sort. What tips algorithms into the realm of intelligence is machine learning, which "relates to the design and use of an algorithm that automatically alters the way in which it works in order to improve output. Crucially, this means that performance can be improved *without* this being specifically programmed."[116]

By designing complex algorithms to function in sophisticated neural networks and using extraordinarily large datasets, we end up with AI, the simulation of human-like cognitive activity. Machine learning and deep learning find robust expression in a recent innovation—ChatGPT—that is already affecting business, information and entertainment industries, higher education, and culture. More to the point, as a unique form of AI, ChatGPT is also affecting drone warfare. Let me explain the terms and discuss its relevance to drones and surveillance.

ChatGPT and Drones

GPT stands for Generative Pre-trained Transformer. It is generative because it "generates text"; it is "pre-trained," because it is trained on "a vast body of text" for training; and it is a "transformer," because it sets up "different weights (significance) to different parts of the input."[117] The GPT series are "large language models"

(LLMs) in that "a language model is a probability distribution over a given piece of text–a mathematical function that describes how probable it is that a particular word will occur. A large language model is simply a language model that uses a large amount of text."[118]

ChatGPT is an interactive chat-based application or service making use of LLMs and "was developed through a two-phase process involving unsupervised pre-training followed by supervised fine-tuning."[119] Using techniques like "language modeling and masked language modeling," in the first phase, the model develops a "comprehensive understanding of the structure of natural language and the complex interrelationships between words and sentences."[120] In the second phase, the focus is on "fine-turning various downstream tasks such as text-completion, question-answering, and dialogue generation," and also "data preparation, architecture modification, and parameter optimization."[121] In the pre-processing phase, activities include following a "sequence of procedures comprising tokenization, subword encoding, and data cleaning."[122]

The major innovation of the GPT series of models is the use of a network architecture know as a transformer. Transformers are a neural network architecture that moves beyond "sequence to sequence challenges" to "extended challenges" or "extended sequences."[123] Furthermore, transformers have a "self-attention mechanism to weigh the relative importance of different parts in the input," which enables it to "process sequential data effectively."[124] The "middle layer of the transformer contains [an] encoder and a decoder," with the encoder abstracting input features and the decoder using those features to predict or generate new content.[125]

Stephen Wolfram's definition of ChatGPT is simple and clear: "The first thing to explain is that what ChatGPT is always fundamentally trying to do is produce a 'reasonable continuation' of whatever text it's got so far, where by 'reasonable' we mean 'what one might expect someone to write after seeing what people have written on billions of pages of webpages, etc.'"[126] Whatever ChatGPT does is predicated on the data it's trained on and the algorithms designed to create and operate a neural network in which data is constantly, in response to prompts and dataset changes, encoded and decoded. Because datasets are not lying around for the taking, the nature, scope, and integrity of data source are pivotal, a point we must bear in mind because drone surveillance generates data about the surveilled. How and why it does determines the nature, scope, and integrity (viable for computation) of the collected data, which means that drone surveillance is always enmeshed in the political and economic calculations that seek to justify surveillance.

Per Open AI, ChatGPT models are trained on "three primary sources of information: (1) information that is publicly available on the internet, (2) information that we license from third parties, and (3) information that our users or our human trainers provide."[127] ChatGPT-3, for instance, has been trained on datasets provided by Common Crawl, WebText2, Books1, Books2, Wikipedia, and so on. Common Crawl has "petabytes of data collected over 8 years of web crawling" and includes "raw web page data, metadata extracts and text extracts with light filtering."[128] WebText2 has "web pages from all outbound Reddit links from posts with 3+upvotes."[129] Books1 and Books2 "are two internet-based books corpora," and Wikipedia's corpus comprises its "pages in the English language."[130]

In February 2023, the Autonomous Systems and Robotics Group of Microsoft announced that it had "extended the capabilities of ChatGPT to robotics" including drones, because ChatGPT is a new paradigm for digital innovation.[131] The established model has engineers who "translate the tasks' requirements into code of the system."[132] To "correct the robot's behaviors," the "engineer sits in the loop" to "write new codes."[133] But ChatGPT enables a "user to sit on the loop, providing high-level feedback to the large language model (LLM) while monitoring the robot's performance."[134] Upon connecting a drone to ChatGPT, the research group began prompting the program to produce and execute code to make the drone inspect a bookshelf, fly zig-zag, take a selfie, and, in a simulated environment, fly up to a wind turbine and systematically check each blade and return with the data. The ChatGPT-enabled drone was able to detect objects in space and avoid them while charting a flight path. Not a pre-programmed robot, the drone became a technological tool simulating human-like perception and action. This brings us to a critical element: the datasets on which ChatGPT is trained.

In "ChatGPT Isn't Magic," Tama Leaver and Suzanne Srdarov argue, "Generally, these tools are thought to get better by absorbing ever greater amounts of data, with most AI companies acknowledging that scraping the web in form has been part of the training data harvesting for their AI tools. Not knowing what data have been used makes it almost impossible to know which perspectives, presumptions and biases are baked into these tools."[135]

AI Impacts Drone Warfare

The US Air Force announced, in April 2024, a contract with Anduril and General Atomics to build Collaborative Combat Aircraft (CCA), as part of the Next Generation Air Dominance (NGAD) program for fighter jets. These CCAs include small uncrewed drones that sync with piloted fighter jets to provide enhanced aerial support for covert and bombing operations. The pilot phase's objective is to produce 200 NGADs and 1,000 CCAs.[136] The initiative takes a "system-of-systems approach with the next-generation fighter aircraft, weapons, sensors, networking and battle management systems to maintain air superiority in the coming decades."[137] Designed to operate as loyal wingmen, these drones "will utilize cutting-edge AI-driven autonomous software to enable seamless and effective collaboration and augment the performance of manned combat aircraft by providing comprehensive situational awareness, greater lethality, and improved survivability in highly contested environments."[138] As the Ukraine-Russia war drags on, Ukraine has become a fertile ground for drone innovation. In April 2024, a company called Swarmer held a demonstration of "drones that use artificial intelligence to work together as a coordinated swarm."[139] One or multiple pilots can control swarms of drones, dramatically increasing air dominance.

Also, AI-enabled drones are having a geographical effect because they are creating "buffer zones" as broad as 20 kilometers between Ukraine and Russia, as it's in those zones that the drones' remote control capacities extend over limited distances.[140] Such drones, Paul Scharre notes, "have all of the components needed to build fully autonomous weapons that can go out over the battlefield, find their own targets and then all on their own attack those targets without any further human intervention. And that raises very challenging legal, and moral and ethical questions about human control over the use of force of war."[141]

What Scharre and many others have worried about is coming true: in January 2022, the Congressional Research Office released a report titled "Joint All-Domain Command and Control: Background and Issues for Congress," in which AI plays a critical role. JADC2 refers to the Department of Defense's "concept to connect sensors from all of the military services—Air Force, Army, Marine Corps, Navy, and Space Force—into a single network."[142] Whereas the plan seeks to streamline the flow of information and enhance intelligence gathering, distribution, analysis, and operational use, the integration of AI becomes necessary because the information produced and examined exceeds the collective human capacity of military personnel.

Consequently, "JADC2 envisions providing a cloud-like environment for the joint force to share intelligence, surveillance, and reconnaissance data, transmitting across many communications networks, to enable faster decision-making. JADC2 intends to enable commanders make better decisions by collecting data from numerous sensors, processing the data using artificial intelligence algorithms to identify targets, then recommending the optimal weapon—both kinetic and nonkinetic (e.g., cyber or electronic weapons)—to engage the target."[143]

A similar Department of Defense imitative is Project Convergence, which is "designed around five core elements—soldiers, weapons systems, command and control, information, and terrain."[144] The goal is to "conduct experiments with technology, equipment, and solicit soldier feedback throughout the year, culminating in an annual exercise or demonstration."[145] One of the goals was to test autonomous and AI-enabled systems. A test conducted in 2020 successfully modeled a networked system that used satellite imagery to identify targets in the air and on the ground. The Joint Base Lewis McChord, Washington, "processed" the target, and the Yuma Proving Ground in Arizona was activated to "engage the target."[146] The operation took around 20 seconds. The test demonstrated the successful integration of AI in multiple systems and at varied levels in Project

Convergence. Such developments, observes Michael T. Klare, presage a world in which "AI-powered systems ["robot generals"] could be deployed to deliver combat orders to American soldiers, dictating where, when, and how they kill enemy troops or take fire from their opponents. In some scenarios, robot decision-makers could even end up exercising control over America's atomic weapons, potentially allowing them to ignite a nuclear war resulting in humanity's demise."[147]

In 2023, the Government Accountability Office issued a report on "drone swarms technologies" that can "coordinate at least three and up to thousands of drones to perform missions cooperatively with limited needed for human attention and control."[148] Drone swarms can use any of the three networks of command and control: centralized (controlled by humans); decentralized semi-autonomous (specific drones in a swarm linked to each other and given occasional human input); and decentralized fully autonomous (a swarm that can sense, move, collect information, and surveil on its own).

Drone swarms draw on "swarm intelligence," which is the "collective behavior observed in decentralized, self-organized systems" where "each of the agents follows simple rules but through interactions, the swarm exhibits emergent intelligence beyond the capabilities of the individual parts."[149] Based on the behavior patterns of ants, insects, and birds, such intelligence enables the swarm to self-correct and realign without human intervention when some of the drones malfunction or fail. Because the swarm can reorganize on its own autonomously by functioning as a swarm, it reduces risk and human interaction, enabling it to carry out its mission effectively. "Modern swarms," observes Aja Melville, "integrate artificial intelligence (AI) and machine learning (ML) to navigate obstacle like GPS jamming, radio signal interference, and adverse environmental conditions, maintaining synchronized operations."[150] The United States, for instance, is investing heavily in the Replicator Program that can "deploy thousands of inexpensive, autonomous drones by August 2025," because "swarms provide unapparelled situational awareness and agility in real-time. They can overwhelm defense, penetrate adversaries' networks, and execute missions with a combination of stealth and brute force, all while maintaining a high tolerance for attrition."[151]

This example of AI-enabled drones seems like the stuff of science fiction, but the question for us is the extent to which "fiction" is becoming reality. I've highlighted several developments in AI-enabled technologies in the military to show that AI is here to stay, that AI is disrupting how wars are imagined and fought, and that AI and drone assemblages are becoming increasingly interconnected. Right away, ethical questions emerge because "as U.S. forces introduce more artificial intelligence technologies into their decision-making apparatus, distinctions among the dimensions begin to blur. For example, the 'who' and 'how' begin to look similar, particularly as computers or algorithms make recommendation to commanders, who may not understand the information or the process that produced the recommendation."[152]

It leads to ethical befuddlement because it's unclear "how much commanders can trust AI and how well human operators will need to understand why the AI system recommends a particular action."[153] Here, trusting AI becomes a challenge because human subjects still have to understand how AI works, how the drone's surveillant assemblage, for instance, works, because we have not yet reached technological singularity: the threshold of development when AI transcends the human race's cognitive abilities to acquire a superintelligence that can act on its own.

We are, as these developments show, on the cusp of an "Oppenheimer Moment" in the drone age.[154] What these drones produce as data, images, charts maps, visuals, and multimodal information are new forms of representing the world around us, of far-flung regions, natural terrain, the oceans, space, and built habitations. The more we use digital media—here drones and their surveillant assemblages—to see, map, coordinate, and control the world before us, the more we will start sensing the world as a machine senses the world. As algorithms direct these machines to function as they do, algorithms will also transform our understanding of and behaviors in space and time. This leads us to governmentality and the politics of bio-power—two features of contemporary surveillance that are essential to understand the risks and dangers of drones and the new arts of empire.

Governmentality and Civil Society

In Governmentality: Power and Rule in Modern Society, Mitchell Dean describes government as "any more or less calculated and rational activity, undertaken by a multiplicity of authorities and agencies, employing a variety of techniques and forms of knowledge, that seeks to shape conduct by working through our desires, aspirations, interests and beliefs, for definite but shifting ends and with a diverse set of relatively unpredictable consequences, effects and outcomes."[155] The concept takes form in "Western European societies in the 'early modern period' when the art of government of the state becomes a distinct activity, and when the forms of knowledge and techniques of the human and social sciences becomes integral to it."[156] Since liberalism's sites of operation and contestation involved the "economy, security, law and society," surveillance becomes a technology for social and political organization and management.[157]

Four features of modern governmentality come into play, suggests Michel Foucault: civil society, instrumental rationality, population management, and social intervention. Civil society is a dimension of social life that lies outside the state but creates and is created by the state; it is the enactment site for the role that the state can or ought to play in society when the monarchy and the church are either absent, become supplementary or complementary governance institutions, or are superseded by the state. But to discharge its obligations to the body politic to which it owes its power and existence, the state embarks on governance practices whose forms and content are determined by scientific rationality.

When its policies are weakly supported by or lack such science, they can be viewed as illegal or ineffectual, which can create the specter of illegitimacy. In modern society, which birthed the individual in the sense of creating new forms of interiority and individuality, the rise of the self as having a unique or separate station that can be unaffected by society saw a concomitant development of the rise of scientific technology, one that could grasp society in two registers—as an aggregation of individuals (the process of individuation becomes paramount) and as a social entity to be governed (individuals become massified into populations). This governmentality based on reason, observation, individuation, and aggregation into populations facilitated interventions to control, discipline, manage, or administer public health, hygiene, birth and mortality, economics, education, security, and the many spheres of social life.[158]

Here we see a different exercise of power, one that goes beyond the individual or society and the sovereign, prince, or head. Foucault's example is worth following as it explicates the subtle shifts from pre-modern to modern forms of governmentality and power. The stipulation not to steal or kill means that its transgression would result in some punishment. The exercise of such power happens where "everything is framed by, on the one hand, a series of supervisions, checks, inspections, and varied controls to identify whether or not he is going to steal, and so on. And then, on the other hand, at the other end, punishment will not just be the spectacular, definitive moment of the hanging, fine, or banishment, but a practice like incarceration with a series of exercises and a work of transformation on the guilty person in the form of what we call penitentiary techniques: obligatory work, moralization, correction, and so forth."[159]

Foucault's modern governmentality changes in the digital age, where the Internet, the computer, software, and a plethora of digital devices offer boundless connectivity spanning continents, involving billions of people, and facilitating the flow of communication, knowledge, finances, and radiating the juridico-political across the world. Points out Alexander Galloway in *Protocol: How Control Exists after Decentralization*, the regnant system of organization in the digital age is the distribution system (multiple nodes and hubs acting in concert), decentralized system (few core nodes and hierarchical points), and centralized system (core hubs radiating connections and power outward). Stressing only the triumphalist, grassroots, organic, populist, progressive, and democratic impulses galvanized by the digital network mischaracterizes the network's organization that is based on protocol. Generally thought to mean etiquette, convention, command, or practice, protocol takes on new meaning in the digital age: "A computer protocol is a set of recommendations and rules that outline specific technical standards";[160] "Now, protocols refer specifically to standards governing the implementation of specific technologies";[161] "Viewed as a whole, protocol is a distributed management system that allows control to exist within a heterogenous material milieu."[162]

The network is a vast agglomeration of computers across the world that interact with each other, one possible only when the coding languages in which they interact embody specific logics; absent the logics, there will be little to no interaction, and the network and Internet as we know will cease to function. Galloway notes that "TCP [transmission control protocol) and IP (internet protocol) are the leading protocols for the actual transmission of data from one computer to another over the network."[163] Because these protocols are organized to transmit information (digital data), "any computer on the network can talk to any other computer, resulting in a nonhierarchical, peer-to-peer relationships."[164]

Another "machinic technology" is DNS (Domain Name System), which is a "large decentralized database that maps network addresses to network names."[165] By connecting domain names to IP addresses (each connected computer has a unique IP address), DNS enables multiple servers to decode, connect, and transmit serves and devices. The main argument Galloway makes is this: "Ironically, then, nearly all Web traffic must submit to a hierarchical structure (DNS) to gain access to the anarchic and radically horizontal structure of the Internet … this contradictory logic is rampant throughout the apparatus of control."[166] When we connect Foucault's modern governmentality to Galloways post-modern protocol, we end up dealing with a fundamental "contradictory logic" of digital networks.

When the state seeks to control digital flows, it can activate or leverage the hierarchical systems, themselves fused or embedded in material hardware, to change protocol: alter the rules that make networked interaction possible, and direct the effects as desired, and soon, a whole region, populace, or county will be without the Internet. Blacked out. Wiped out. Galloway's insight is critical because it helps us understand the nature of the surveillant assemblage, since governance and civil society in the digital age must involve direct, deep engagement with the ideologies that enable and legitimize protocol, and a direct, deep interaction with protocol as the governing logic of distribution systems.

In the network society of protocol, the surveillant assemblage generates what Antoinette Rouvroy and Thomas Berns call "algorithmic governmentality":

> Algorithmic governmentality produces no subjectification. It circumvents and avoids reflexive human subjects … without ever asking them to themselves describe what they are or what they could become. The moment of reflexivity, critique, and recalcitrance necessary for subjectification to form seems to constantly become more complicated or to be postponed.[167]

Rouvroy further elaborates that this mode of governmentality is "based on the algorithmic processing of big data sets rather than on politics, law, and social norms. Digitisation becomes a sort of quantification of political issues that is achieved through algorithms," since "the mass processing of data is about taming uncertainty."[168]

As surveillance generates data about people, a growing disjunction grows between information at the level of the individual and information generated by profiling people, which involves, as we saw earlier with Solove and Clark, dataveillance and digital dossiers leading to profiles. In this mode of governmentality, people often give up information voluntarily; with consent comes millions of peoples' data; with profiling comes distancing between individuals and profiles, creating challenges of correspondence and correlation. Soon, if we can extend Rouvroy, the reflexive, critical subjectivity embodied with agency becomes subordinated to creating a new algorithmic subjectivity whose behaviors, habits, and desires become amenable for greater control; it's made pliable for acting on impulses, not on informed choices, because the global surveillant assemblage is now in the business of managing life itself, the bios.

Things get complicated when identification, prevention, and modifying behavior are directed at the social body, of whole populations. A key aim is to undermine, reduce, or eliminate risk; the goal is to think in advance and trigger the protocol to ensure a way of life deemed acceptable by the state or governing entity. The management of life, of the bios, necessarily means comprehensive surveillance of peoples and their habitations, as statistical aggregates, correlations, and exceptions to the norm are identified as subjects for elimination, reduction, or modification. All this leads us to biopolitics (Michel Foucault) and necropolitics (Achille Mbembe) in a surveillance society that exercises state power through the logic of exception (Giorgio Agamben), which is what I take up in the next chapter.

Notes

1. Glenn Greenwald, *No Place to Hide: Edward Snowden, the N.S.A. and the U.S Surveillance State* (New York: Metropolitan Books, 2014), 5–6.
2. Ibid., 6.
3. Ibid.
4. Ibid., 4.
5. Elizabeth Shell and Vanessa Dennis, "11 'Leakers' Charged with Espionage." *pbsnewshour* August 21, 2013, http://pbs.org/newshour/spc/multimedia/espionage/
6. Glen Greenwald, *No Place to Hide*, 107–10.
7. James Ball, "NSA Collects Millions of Text Messages Daily in 'Untargeted' Global Sweep." *theguardian.com* January 16, 2014, http://theguardian.com/world/2014/jan/16/nsa-collects-millions-text-messages-daily-untargeted-global-sweep
8. Sibohan Gorman and Jennifer Valentino-Devries, "New Details Show Broader NSA Surveillance Reach." *wsj.com* August 20, 2013, http://online.wsj.com/news/articles/SB10001424127887324108204579022874091732470
9. Greenwald, 92.

10 Ibid., 91–2.
11 Ibid., 97.
12 Ibid., 159.
13 Ibid., 139.
14 Ibid., 134–5.
15 Ibid., 143–6.
16 Ibid., 129.
17 Stephanie Savell, "United States Counterterrorism Operations 2018–2020." Costs of War. watson.brown.edu Watson Institute for International and Public Affairs. Brown University, 2021, https://watson.brown.edu/costsofwar/files/cow/imce/papers/2021/US%20Counterterrorism%20Operations%202018-2020%2C%20Costs%20of%20War.pdf
18 Greenwald, *No Place to Hide*, 169.
19 David Lyon, *Surveillance Studies: An Overview* (Polity: 2007), 14.
20 Ibid., 74.
21 David Rosen and Aaron Santesso. *The Watchman in Pieces: Surveillance, Literature, and Liberal Personhood* (New Haven: Yale University Press, 2013), 10.
22 Roger A. Clarke, "Information Technology and Dataveillance." *Communications of the ACM* 31, no. 5 (1988): 498–99.
23 Kevin D. Haggerty, "Foreword: Surveillance and Political Problems." *Surveillance: Power, Problems, and Politics*. Edited by Sean P. Hier and Josh Greenberg (Toronto: UBC Press, 2009), ix.
24 Ibid., "Foreword," xi–xii.
25 Ibid., "Foreword," xv.
26 Lyon, *Surveillance Studies*, 162.
27 David Barnard-Wills, *Surveillance and Identity: Discourse, Subjectivity and the State* (Burlington, VT: Ashgate, 2012), 2.
28 Ibid., 4.
29 Ibid., 3.
30 Lyon, *Surveillance Studies*, 27–44.
31 Ibid., 6–7.
32 Zygmunt Bauman, *Liquid Modernity* (Malden, MA: Polity Press, 2000), 10–11.
33 Lyon, *Surveillance Studies*, 51.
34 Bauman, *Liquid Modernity*, 10–11; 113–19.
35 Jill Walker Rettberg, *Machine Vision: How Algorithms Are Changing the Way We See the World* (UK, Polity Press, 2023), 3.
36 Ibid., 11.
37 Gilles Deleuze and Claire Parnet, *Dialogues*. Trans. by Hugh Tomlinson and Barbara Habberjam (New York: The Anthlone Press, 1977), 69. Deluze and Félix Guattari discuss this concept in other writings, including *A Thousand Plateaus: Capitalism and Schizophrenia*. Trans. by Brian Massumi (Minneapolis: University of Minnesota Press, 1987).
38 Thomas Nail, "What Is an Assemblage?" *SubStance* 46, no. 1 (2017): 22.
39 Ibid., 23.
40 Ibid., 24.
41 Ibid.
42 Ibid.
43 Ibid., 27.
44 Ibid., 28.

45 Manuel DeLanda, *Assemblage Theory* (Edinburgh: Edinburgh University Press, 2016), 19.
46 Ibid., 20.
47 Ibid., 21.
48 Kevin D. Haggerty and Richard Ericson. "The Surveillant Assemblage." *The Surveillance Studies Reader*. Edited by Sean P. Hier and Joshua Greenberg (New York: Open University Press, 2007), 104.
49 Ibid., 109.
50 Ibid., 108.
51 Ibid., 110.
52 Haggerty and Ericson, "The Surveillant Assemblage," 106.
53 Sean P. Hier and Josh Greenberg, eds. "The Politics of Surveillance." *Surveillance: Power, Problems, and Politics* (Toronto: UBC Press, 2009), 22.
54 Ibid., 24.
55 Ibid., 25.
56 Haggerty and Ericson, "The Surveillant Assemblage," 111.
57 Ibid.
58 Hier and Greenberg, "The Politics," 25.
59 Daniel J. Solove, *The Digital Person: Technology and Privacy in the Information Age* (New York: New York University Press, 2004), 1–2.
60 Ibid., 3.
61 Roger A. Clarke, "Information Technology and Dataveillance." *Communications of the ACM* 31, no. 5 (1988): 499.
62 Ibid., 503.
63 Ibid., 505.
64 Ibid.
65 Solove, *The Digital Person*, 29.
66 Ibid., 34.
67 Ibid., 43.
68 Ibid., 38.
69 Ibid., 46.
70 Ibid., 48.
71 Ibid., 51.
72 Ibid., 53.
73 William G. Staples, *Everyday Surveillance: Vigilance and Visibility in Postmodern Life* (New York: Rowman and Littlefield Publishers, Inc., 2000), 3.
74 Ibid., 153.
75 Ibid., 6.
76 Ibid., 153.
77 Neil M. Richards, "The Dangers of Surveillance." *Harvard Law Review* 126, no. 7 (2013): 1945.
78 Ibid., 1946.
79 Ibid., 1948.
80 Ibid.
81 Ibid., 1949.
82 Ibid., 1950.
83 Didier Bigo, "Globalized-In-Security," *Translation, Biopolitics, Colonial Difference*. Edited by Naoki Sakai and Jon Solomon (Hong Kong: Hong Kong University Press, 2006), 110.

84 Bigo, "Globalized-In-Security," 125–6.
85 Philip F. Frana and Michael J. Klein. *Encyclopedia of Artificial Intelligence: The Past, Present, and Future of AI* (California: ABC-CLIO, 2021), xiv.
86 Ajay Lele, "Defense Applications of Artificial Intelligence," *Artificial Intelligence, Ethics and the Future of Warfare*. Edited by Kaushik Roy (Taylor and Francis, 2024): 73.
87 Manuel De Landa, *War in the Age of Intelligent Machines* (New York: Zone Books, 1991), 1.
88 Ibid., 1.
89 Ibid., 128.
90 Ibid., 129.
91 Ibid., 192.
92 Ibid., 193.
93 Strategic Futures Group, *Global Trends: The Future of the Battlefield*. National Intelligence Council. 2021, 6, https://dni.gov/files/images/globalTrends/GT2040/NIC-2021-02493--Future-of-the-Battlefield--Unsourced--14May21.pdf#page=6
94 Joe Hernandez, "A Military Drone with a Mind of Its Own Was Used in Combat, U.N. says."*npr.org* June 1, 2021, https://npr.org/2021/06/01/1002196245/a-u-n-report-suggests-libya-saw-the-first-battlefield-killing-by-an-autonomous-d
95 Gwenola Ricordeau, "Lethal Autonomous Weapons Systems," *Encyclopedia of Artificial Intelligence: The Past, Present, and Future of AI*. Edited by Philip F. Frana and Michael J. Klein (California: ABC-CLIO, 2021), 208.
96 Amanda K. O'Keefe, "Turing, Alan (1912–1954)," *Encyclopedia of Artificial Intelligence: The Past, Present, and Future of AI*. Edited by Philip F. Frana and Michael J. Klein (California: ABC-CLIO, 2021), 327. Also see Lawrence Livermore Laboratory, "The Birth of Artificial Intelligence (AI) Research," *st.llnl.gov* https://st.llnl.gov/news/look-back/birth-artificial-intelligence-ai-research
97 Will Douglass Heaven, "What Is AI?" *MIT Technology Review*, July 10, 2024, https://technologyreview.com/2024/07/10/1094475/what-is-artificial-intelligence-ai-definitiveguide/?truid=&utm_source=the_algorithm&utm_medium=email&utm_campaign=the_algorithm.unpaid.engagement&utm_content=07-15-2024
98 Paul Burgess, *AI and the Rule of Law: The Necessary Evolution of a Concept* (New York: Bloomsbury, 2024), 8–9.
99 Enamul Haque, *The Ultimate Modern Guide to Artificial Intelligence* (London: Enel Publications, 2020), 9–21.
100 Philip F. Frana and Michael J. Klein. *Encyclopedia of Artificial Intelligence: The Past, Present, and Future of AI* (California: ABC-CLIO, 2021), xi.
101 Britannica, "Connectionism," *brittanica.com*, July 16, 2024, https://britannica.com/technology/connectionism-artificial-intelligence
102 Britannica, "Connectionism."
103 Britannica, "Methods and Goals in AI," *brittanica.com*, January 27, 2025, https://britannica.com/technology/top-down-approach
104 Jason H. Moore, "Automated Machine Learning," *Encyclopedia of Artificial Intelligence: The Past, Present, and Future of AI*. Edited by Philip F. Frana and Michael J, Klein (California: ABC-CLIO, 2021), 20.
105 Ibid., 20.
106 Enamul Haque, *The Ultimate Modern Guide to Artificial Intelligence* (London, Enel Publications, 2020), 34.

107 IBM, "What Is Machine Learning (ML)?" *ibm.com* accessed January 27, 2025 https://.ibm.com/topics/machine-learning
108 Paul Scharre, *Four Battlegrounds: Power in the Age of Artificial Intelligence* (NY: W.W. Norton and Company, 2023), 232.
109 Ibid.
110 Ibid.
111 Ibid., 233.
112 Ibid.
113 IMB, "What Is Machine Learning (ML)?"
114 Jeffrey Andrew and Thorne Lupker, "Deep Learning," *Encyclopedia of Artificial Intelligence: The Past, Present, and Future of AI*. Edited by Philip F. Frana and Michael J, Klein (California: ABC-CLIO, 2021), 112.
115 Burgess, *AI and the Rule of Law*, 51.
116 Ibid., 52, emphasis in original.
117 Guy Hart-Davis, *Killer ChatGPT Prompts* (New Jersey: John Wiley and Sons, 2023), vi.
118 Ibid.
119 Konstantinos I. Roumeliotis and Nikolaos D. Tselikas, "ChatGPT and Open-AI Models: A Preliminary Review" *Future Internet* 15, no. 6: 192, 2023, https://doi.org/10.3390/fi15060192
120 Ibid.
121 Ibid.
122 Ibid.
123 Govind Kumar, Introduction to ChatGPT and Open AI (PACKT Publishing, 2023. Film). https://video.alexanderstreet.com/watch/introduction-to-chatgpt-and-openai.
124 Ibid.
125 Ibid.
126 Stephen Wolfram, *What Is ChatGPT Doing ... and Why Does It Work?* (Wolfram Media, 2023), 1.
127 OpenAI, "How ChatGPT and Our Language Models Are Developed." *openai.com*, accessed July 26, 2024, https://help.openai.com/en/articles/7842364-how-chatgpt-and-our-language-models-are-developed
128 Kindra Cooper, "OpenAI GPT-3: Everything You Need to Know [Updated]." *springboard.com* September 27, 2023, https://www.springboard.com/blog/data-science/machine-learning-gpt-3-open-ai/
129 Ibid.
130 Ibid.
131 Autonomous Systems and Robotics Group, "ChatGPT for Robotics: Design Principles and Model Abilities," *microsoft*, February 20, 2023, https://microsoft.com/en-us/research/group/autonomous-systems-group-robotics/articles/chatgpt-for-robotics/
132 Ibid.
133 Ibid.
134 Ibid.
135 Tama Leaver and Suzanne Srdarov, "ChatGPT Isn't Magic: The Hype and Hypocrisy of Generative Artificial Intelligence (AI) Rhetoric." *M/C Journal* 26, no. 5, 2023, https://doi.org/10.5204/mcj.3004

136　Airforce Technology, "Next Generation Air Dominance Programme," *airforce-technolology.com* March 8, 2024, https://airforce-technology.com/projects/next-generation-air-dominance-programme-us/?cf-view

137　Airforce Technology, "Collaborative Combat Aircraft (CCA), USA," *airforce-technology.com* June 21, 2024, https://airforce-technology.com/projects/collaborative-combat-aircraft-cca-usa/?cf-view; Institute for Defense and Government Advancements, "Air Force Awards Contracts for Collaborative Combat Aircraft Development," *idga.com* April 25, 2024, https://idga.org/aviation/articles/air-force-awards-contracts-for-collaborative-combat-aircraft-program

138　Ibid.

139　Gian Volpicelli, Veronika Melkozerova, and Laura Kayali, "'Our Oppenheimer moment'–In Ukraine, the robot wards have already begun," *politico.com* May 16, 2024, https://politico.eu/article/robots-coming-ukraine-testing-ground-ai-artificial-intelligence-powered-combat-war-russia/

140　Ibid.

141　PBS News Weekend, "How Militaries Are Using Artificial Intelligence on and off the Battlefield," *pbs.org* July 9, 1013, https://pbs.org/newshour/show/how-militaries-are-using-artificial-intelligence-on-and-off-the-battlefield

142　John R. Hoehn, "Joint All-Domain Command and Control (JADC2)," *Congressional Research Office*, *sgp.fas.org* January 21, 2022, 1.

143　Ibid., 2.

144　Department of Defense, "The Army's Project Convergence," *Congressional Research Office*, June 2, 2022, https://crsreports.congress.gov/product/pdf/IF/IF11654/6

145　Ibid.

146　Ibid.

147　Michael T. Klar, "The Future of AI Is War," *thenation.com*, July 17, 2023, https://thenation.com/article/world/artificial-intelligence-us-military/

148　Government Accountability Office, "Drone Swarm Technologies," GAO: Science, Technology Assessment, and Analytics, September 2023, https://gao.gov/assets/gao-23-106930.pdf

149　Sentient Digital, Inc., "Military Drone Swarm Intelligence Explained," *sdi.ai* 2024, https://sdi.ai/blog/military-drone-swarm-intelligence-explained/

150　Aja Melville, "Drone Wars: Developments in Drone Swarm Technology," Defense Security and Monitor *dsm.forecasinternational.com* January 21, 2025, https://dsm.forecastinternational.com/2025/01/21/drone-wars-developments-in-drone-swarm-technology/

151　Ibid.

152　Hoehn, "Joint All-Domain Command and Control (JADC2)," 4.

153　Ibid.

154　Volpicelli, Melkozerova, and Kayali, "Our Oppenheimer moment." Julius Robert Oppenheimer supervised the production of the world's first nuclear bomb at the Los Alamos Laboratory in New Mexico between 1943 and 1945. On July 16, 1945, the Trinity Test, the code for the bomb experiment in the Manhattan Project was successful. On August 6, 1945, the United States dropped Little Boy on Hiroshima, and on August 9, 1945, it dropped Fat Man on Nagasaki, resulting in horrendous destruction and the death of a quarter million people.

155　Mitchell Dean, *Governmentality: Power and rule in Modern Society*. E-bookCentral ProQuest, University of Southern Maine (Thousand Oaks, CA: SAGE Publications, 1999), 18.

156 Ibid., 28.
157 Ibid., 134.
158 Michel Foucault, *Security, Territory, Population: Lectures at the Collége de France, 1977–78* (New York: Palgrave Macmillan, 2007), 353–9.
159 Ibid., 4.
160 Alexander Galloway, *Protocol: How Control Exists after Decentralization* (MIT, 2004), 6.
161 Ibid., 7.
162 Ibid., 8.
163 Ibid.
164 Ibid.
165 Ibid., 8–9.
166 Ibid., 9.
167 Antoinette Rouvroy and Thomas Berns, "Algorithmic Governmentality and Prospects of Emancipation," *Réseaux* 177 (2013): x.
168 Antoinette Rouvroy. "Algorithmic Governmentality and the Death of Politics," interview by *Green European Journal, greeneuropeanjournal.eu* March 27, 2020, 1.

3 BIOPOLITICS, NECROPOLITICS, AND ETHICS IN A DRONE WORLD

Drone warfare is a type of biopolitics that raises important questions about privacy, innocence, sovereignty, and freedom. Drawing from Michel Foucault, Giorgio Agamben, and Achille Mbembe's theories of biopolitics and necropolitics, I examine the deep entanglement of technologies with the production of scientific knowledge about peoples and the natural world. I show how the effective management of vast populations through perpetual, invasive surveillance reduces them to living a bare life.

I will show that the drone's Gorgon Stare manifests a biopolitical drive that, when unimpeded, creates necropolitical conditions in which bare life becomes the sine qua non for the establishment of the security state. The ethical conundrum in a necropolitical world takes us to Zygmunt Bauman's notion of adiaphorization, where ethical thinking and practice assumed to be embodied in complex digital systems, not human subjects and human agency, raise the question of ethics in a world of drones. The chapter ends with Steve Mann's idea of sousveillance, as a mode of resistance to surveillance, which can, I argue, open social and institutional spaces for progressive change and accountability, leading us to equiveillance, a negotiation of power between the twin poles of surveillance and sousveillance.

The Biopolitical Imperium

Biopolitics, Foucault contends, refers to "control over relations between the human race, or human beings, insofar as they are a species, insofar as they are living beings, and their environment, the milieu in which they live. This includes the direct effects of the geographical, climatic, or hydrographic environment ... biopolitics will derive its knowledge from, and define its power's field of intervention, in terms of the birth rate, the mortality rate, various biological disabilities, and the effects of the environment."[1] This power does not replace the individual in favor of the populace but produces its discriminating effects across the species or social or political body. Foucault explicates, "It is therefore not a matter of taking the individual at the level of individuality but, on the contrary, of using overall mechanisms and acting in such a way as to achieve overall states of equilibrium or regularity; it is, in a word, a matter of taking control of life and the biological process of man-as-species and of ensuring that they are not disciplined, but regularized."[2]

Biopower seeks to manage all of life or bring the multitude of the living under the domain of governmentality—to administer, take charge, manage, sort, distribute, and maintain life. It is this biopolitical impulse that gains incredible computational and surveillant power today. And for drones to be effective, a surveillant assemblage equipped with various panoptic gazes of power is necessary. To be sure, they form the ideological, material, and discursive armature for drone warfare—for empire in the twenty-first century. To understand how sovereign power finds biopolitical expression, we need to follow Giorgio Agamben's analysis of states of exception and bare life.

States of Exception

Drawing on Greek political discourse, in *Home Sacer: Sovereign Power and Bare Life*, Giorgio Agamben explains the meaning of "homo sacer," using Michel Foucault as an interlocutor to examine the term's relevance to modern and postmodern notions of sovereignty. To the Greeks, zoē and bios mean life but carry different meanings. Zoē "expressed the simple fact of living common to all living beings (animals, men, or gods)," whereas bios "indicated the form or way of living proper to an individual or a group."[3] Furthermore, zoē means bare life, or existence in its basic, essential modality, an instance or embodiment of life *as life*. It also means natural or familial life distinct from the polis; we can also consider the gendered meaning of zoē as situated in domestic spheres, and the polis as the male site for politics. Whereas life as reproduction is relegated to the oikos, bios is the sphere for intentional human activity designed to produce and sustain certain forms of living. Zoē, "the simple fact of living" and reproducing, contrasts with bios, "the politically qualified life."[4]

Agamben quotes Michel Foucault who, in *The History of Sexuality*, argues that modernity marks the phase when "natural life begins to be included in the mechanisms and calculations of Sate power, and politics turns into *biopolitics*."[5] To

Foucault, classical man is "a living animal with the additional capacity for political existence," while "modern man is an animal whose politics calls his existence as a living being into question."[6] To connect zoē to bios in the contemporary age, Agamben goes further, arguing that Foucault's biopolitics needs revising.

That homo sacer "*may be killed and yet not sacrificed*" means that the subject of bare life must be considered in multiple ways.[7] Religious discourse positions homo sacer as the subject with the potential to muddy or contaminate the individual or collective body; political discourse positions homo sacer as the subject for expulsion from the polis. For homo sacer, there is no ritualized process leading to sacrifice; the subject cannot stand in or symbolically or materially embody pleasure, innocence, or guilt. Homo sacer is a marked subject, who can, not must, be killed without expulsion or punishment. As such, bare life becomes a zone of juridico-political and ethical indeterminacy *in the service of power*. It is the connection to power, to sovereignty, that we must pay attention to understand how Agamben extends Foucault's biopolitics.

Having subsumed zoē into bios, and subjecting it to state power, biopower does not necessarily erase zoē, the social space of bare life; instead, the crucial dynamic of contemporary biopolitics is the subsumption of all life into state calculations to produce—on the state's terms—a new bios for zoē, i.e., bare life takes different forms in response to diverse sociocultural and political systems. And it is the state's ability to exempt itself from the laws governing society that gives the state the power and ability to generate and manage bare life. Agamben writes, "This is modern democracy's strength and, at the same time, its inner contradiction: modern democracy does not abolish sacred life but rather shatters it and disseminates it into every individual body, making it into what is at stake in political conflict."[8]

And Foucault writes, "It is no longer a matter of bringing death into play in the field of sovereignty, but of distributing the living in the domain of value and utility. Such a power has to qualify, measure, appraise, and hierarchize, rather than display itself in its murderous splendor."[9] Hence, as zoē and bios "enter into a zone of irreducible indistinction … the production of a biopolitical body is the original activity of the sovereign power."[10] That is why, he contends, "the fundamental activity of sovereign power is the production of bare life as originary political element and as threshold of articulation between nature and culture, *zoē and bios*."[11]

Bare life is not a universal constant but a condition shaped by geography, ideology, politics, and power. This is where we can connect Agamben and Foucault to Achille Mbembe, whose "necropolitics" describes the creation of "death worlds," which are "new and unique forms of social existence in which vast populations are subjected to living conditions that confer upon them the status of the living dead."[12] Neither living nor dead, but the living dead; neither fully excluded nor fully included in the polis but living a bare life in an indeterminate zone where necropower empowers people to kill without punishment, and proscribes ritualistic significance to sacrifice. Mbembe locates necropolitics as the dark underside of Western modernity, but with a difference: it is not an other reality or realm beyond Western geography, empire, and discourse but a constitutive element that enhances and constricts the demos to find its social fulfillment in the polis by actively exercising necropower to grow capital, expand territories, control populations, and dominate the natural and lived environment. Roger Stahl and Sebastian Kaempf's observation about the drone's biopolitical power is apt: "Although commonly called a weapon, the drone is first and foremost a way of seeing, of distributing the gaze of the state over vast territory, from the Mexican-American border to the Peshawar Province."[13] To understand how, let's follow Mbembe's argument, albeit briefly, to shed light on the topic at hand: drone warfare as a form of biopolitics.

Drone Warfare as Biopolitics

Traditionally, the West's entry into modernity is shaped by two major shifts: democratic systems and the primacy of Reason to order social relations, and the containing of animality to forge a new humanity that directs powerful instincts for social good. The psychic and cultural dimension of these shifts means the growth of an individualized self and its ability to affirm freedom. But Western modernity also simultaneously unleashed capitalism's force by combining it with a colonial mandate. Global trade routes were discovered and policed; the rise of transnational circuits for the exchange of goods, peoples, food, and commodities required massive labor forces whose formation and use meant the forced apprehension and relocation of millions of people across continents. As Mbembe points out, "From their origins, modern democracies have always evinced their tolerance for a certain political violence, including illegal forms of it. They have integrated forms of brutality into their culture, forms borne by a range of private institutions acting on top of the state, whether irregular forces, militias, or other paramilitary or corporatist formations."[14]

In *Necropolitics, Racialization, and Global Capitalism*, Marina Grižinić and Šefik Tatlić delineate the geographic contours of the material exercise of necropolitics, arguing that where, by and large, Foucault's biopolitics described Western and First World or advanced capitalist societies, Mbembe extends that to show how Western biopolitical operations consolidated the West's imperium by creating zones for the living dead across the world. Grižinić and Tatlić note, "This means making surplus value from a double from of death: death from *real* massive impoverishment, and a *symbolical* death from capital interventions in the social, political, and imaginary."[15] Bios becomes "forms-of-life or life-as-style," as it is "the only thing that matters in the First Capitalist World (global capitalism)."[16] They further add, "Necropolitics is connected to the concept of necrocapitalism, that is, contemporary capitalism, which organizes its form of capital accumulation around dispossession and the subjugation of life to the power of death."[17]

Grižnić argues that by subjecting life to the logic of instrumentalization, the state ensures the financialization of life by subjecting it to productive forces that control and extract labor and surplus value to benefit the few: "In neoliberal capitalism, the entire society has been transformed into *one big investment sector* that provides new opportunities for the incessant capitalisation of capital in order to make surplus value."[18]

Taking the slave trade as a prime example (others include apartheid, indenture servitude, settler colonies, non-settler colonies), we see how necropower influenced slavery as a social and economic institution: the slave loses personal rights, familial connections, and political standing. Mbembe observes, "This triple loss is identical with absolute domination, natal alienation, and social death (expulsion from humanity altogether)." It is why "slave life, in many ways, is a form of death-in-life."[19] Necropolitics is and was manifest in other ways, as in the Middle East where contending groups seek access and control of particular regions in Palestine, in the townships of South Africa where segregation is spatially delineated, in indentured servitude, in settler and non-settler colonies, in complex colonial administrative systems, and in innovative technologies used to extract and process natural resources to further imperial interests and concentrate wealth and capital in the West.

As Christine Rosen says in *The Extinction of Human Experience: Being Human in a Disembodied World*, "Areas of life that used to be off limits for technological mediation and manipulation are now saturated by it. And we are changed."[20] Shoshana Zuboff argues in *The Age of Surveillance Capitalism: The Fight for a Human Future at the New Frontier of Power*, "Surveillance capitalism unilaterally claims human experience as free raw material for translation into behavioral data. Although some of these data are applied to produce or service improvement, the rest are declared as proprietary *behavioral surplus*, fed into advanced manufacturing processes known as 'machine intelligence,' and fabricated into *prediction products* that anticipate what you will do now, soon, or later."[21] Zuboff's formulation can be extended to necropolitics in drone warfare, particularly for the first point made in the citation above—"human experiences" become "free raw material for translation into behavioral data."

Whether countries in the Global South are also capitalizing on this data by selling or using products designed to shape peoples' behaviors needs examination. The security state justifies collecting data about the surveilled by declaring a state of exception that suspends the rules, while exempting itself from the rules, to create a safe space for the people. When drone warfare becomes adjunct to turning surveillance zones into areas for financial gain, then the security state morphs into a global machine expressly designed to colonize all living things by extracting from them information for capitalist production without their consent: a profoundly dehumanizing condition that leads to a bios for the living dead. I am not arguing that this is true of drone warfare per se, as sui generis, but that the surveillant assemblage of the drone and the surveillant assemblage of global capitalism can work in tandem, simultaneously, with direct, indirect, or no coordination. It can be reasonably argued that where surveillance capitalism is more acute in countries with advanced or pervasive digital technologies, drone surveillance uncovers a North-South divide in which the South is brought under the domain of the North.

Problematizing Biopolitics

Let me, at this point, sort out a few conceptual difficulties about biopolitics, because it is essential to developing the argument that the drone's scopic regime as biopolitics reinscribes—while innovatively modulating—an acquisitive, dominating drive to create the living dead. To Agamben, the move from zoē to bios suggests that it is the cultivated, civilizing social and individual body that gains legitimacy in joining the bios. But, he argues, this view is misguided, because historically, it was not the socialized or cultivated subject around which the discourse of inherent rights emerged, but it was the bare body, one shorn of culture; it was the corpus as such, the mere fact of having bodily embodiment, that was the sine qua non for a new juridical order to emerge. Agamben cites the 1679 *habeas corpus* writ in English, which required "the physical presence of a person before a court of justice."[22] He goes on, "It is not the free man and his statures and prerogatives, nor even simply homo, but rather corpus that is the new subject of politics. And democracy is born precisely as the assertion and presentation of this 'body': *habeas corpus ad subjiciendum*, 'you will have to have a body to show.'"[23]

The modern rupture in Western jurisprudence is described well by Agamben, as he persuasively argues that it is bare life that must be brought forth (the body must be produced in court) for justice to gain legitimacy. It is why Agamben characterizes biopower in the post-panopticon era as a radical break in Western political and legal history: bios is no longer needed for the law to exercise its power. Zoē, the body made visible to the court, is endowed with inherent value and the right to be heard, the right to ask for recompense, and the right to contest the accusation. But as we shall see, in the post-panopticon, all these are up for grabs because the drone relentlessly produces a visuality of the surveilled to lay it bare, to remove all privacy. The drone's biopower is predicated on surveilling bios to reduce it to bare life, such that preemptive measures are deployed to destroy those deemed as threats to the imperium.

But before going further, we must attend to the perplexing questions posed by Roberto Esposito in "The Enigma of Biopolitics"—how we do know if zoē "is an absolutely natural life?"[24] Was there such a thing as natural life without any technological attempt to sustain itself? He adds, "That is because, contrary to the underlying presupposition of Anglo-Saxon biopolitics, something like a definable and identifiable human nature doesn't exist as such, independent from the meaning that culture and therefore history have, over the course of time, imprinted on it."[25] Esposito foregrounds zoē and bios as having a dialectical relationship, leaving either unable to exist in isolation or bring the other into being without also changing itself in the process.

Where Foucault highlights Western modernity's rupture as it moves from a society of discipline to a society of control, and where Agamben locates zoē as the prerequisite for modern jurisprudence to affirm the rights of Man (of all human beings as human beings, first and foremost), Esposito shifts the focus to the historical contingencies always at play in any exercise of biopower. This is where Mbembe's necropolitics gains sharpness because it demonstrates that the West's experience of modernity had a dark underside of dispossession and domination not only for peoples within the so-called West but also for those outside its geographies, those races and peoples in outposts and colonies. Mbembe's views map well onto those offered by Walter Mignolo who, in *Local Histories/Global Designs*, argues, "there is no modernity without coloniality and that coloniality is constitutive, and not derivative, of modernity."[26] Esposito goes on to solidify his argument: "Life as such doesn't belong either to the order of nature or to that of history. It cannot be simply ontologized, nor completely historicized, but is inscribed in the moving margin of their intersection and their tension."[27]

Similarly, Thomas Lemke in "A Zone of Indistinction" sharpens Agamben's conception of biopolitics by making these strong points: focusing heavily on "repression, reproduction and reduction," Agamben does not consider the "relational, decentralized and productive aspect of power"[28]; in the present moment, it is not the state exercising greater power but society itself taking on the "capacity and competence of decision-making ... beyond authoritarianism and medical paternalism"[29]; biopower is now "exercised through a multiplicity of agencies" that are "loosely associated with the formal organs of the state"[30]; the conditions of marginalization often ascribed to Third World societies are taking root in modern or Western societies. Like Lemke, Ajana points out that "seduction, self-monitoring, pre-emptive interventions, anticipatory preventions and so forth are all features enacted within the various practice of biopolitics and coherent with the state of technicism that characterizes contemporary societies."[31]

Lemke nicely qualifies Agamben, and Foucault, by extension, focusing on the diffusive effects of power and their contingent, thus historical, causes. His views align with Rosen and Santesso's about how the centripetal dynamics of networked societies create spaces in which surveillance is upended, underscoring the fluid nature of power. In their sequel to *Empire*, Michael Hardt and Antonio Negri in *Multitude: War and Democracy in the Age of Empire* (2004) describe multitude as "an internally different, multiple social subject whose constitution and action is based not on identity or unity (or, much less, indifference) but what it has in common."[32] As global capitalism subsumes the multitude, it also generates a social capital embodying shared experiences or conditions, because "it tends to mobilize what it shares in common and what it produces in common against the imperial power of global capital."[33] Because I discuss this view in detail in the fifth chapter on drone art and culture, I briefly note it here to highlight biopolitics as containing within itself the seeds of its own transgression. Let us circle back to Grižnić and Taltić to connect biopolitics and necropolitics to the new mode of digital, semi-robotic warfare: armed drones. In Mbembe's theories of necropolitics, Grižnić and Taltić see continuities in Western global domination in the history of global capitalism in that necropolitics revises biopolitics to reveal "the geopolitical demarcation of world zones that are based on the mobilization of the war machine."[34]

New Dispensation of Empire

Applying Agamben, Foucault, Mbembe, and Lemke's ideas to study the profound ethical, political, and socio-cultural shifts inaugurated by drone warfare, we can say that a new dispensation of Empire has become manifest: Empire suspends laws of war and peace. Empire exempts itself from its own laws. Empire envelops zoē and bios into new configurations of preferred life. Empire manages the production of bare life. We must examine what kind of "war machine" is effectuating this new phase of Empire, which requires us to study the imbrication of digital technologies with the surveillant assemblage.

Today, power flows along and inside panoptic systems, and global movements of peoples and goods, and their patterns of coming, staying, or leaving are codified in the ban-opticon with its own *dispositif* or apparatuses. As national and global surveillance produces data, and data doubles become digital dossiers whose social, personal, and governmental use is determined by the norms of dataveillance, all communications, emails, telephone calls, messaging, texts, tweets, audio or visual, or graphic interface and interactions are sucked into a mammoth datacenter so that the field of social operations for civil and non-civil society becomes safe and secure. Yet, a state of exception is produced that enables the state or imperial entity to create death worlds out of a geographically circumscribed bios in which whole groups or races of people are subjected to the drone's scopic regime to turn them into the living dead, as people whose entire lives are made amenable to a profoundly invasive surveillance produced by the drone's scopic vision.

As Jill Rettberg perceptively notes, the algorithmic gaze of machine vision, here embodied in drone surveillance, as I am arguing, "does not see us in the way we want to be seen or that it does not see us at all."[35] Often, in the Global South, peoples surveilled by the drone are laid bare, uncovered, their lives made visible in ways they cannot control, see, or know. The surveillant assemblage can turn their life worlds inside out for algorithmic calculation to extract meaning from the data generated through surveillance. It is the bringing forth, of laying bare, the lives of peoples as a people, their whole habitus, as it were, that enables drone surveillance to acquire its deceptively unsettling power. Whereas in the seventeenth century, it was the corpus, the body as body, that was needed for the law to exercise authority, today, that body is no longer the individual or even an aggregate of individuals but a whole race or group of people subjected to persistent surveillance in ways that strip them of all, not some, privacy and dignity, with neither their knowledge nor consent.

In these instances, we see a long-lasting process for social and economic ordering in which some peoples are absorbed into the bios of the polis, others relegated to zoē, to bare life. The biopolitical operations that produce geographic and social spaces in which particular populations are reduced to bare life demonstrate the enduring power of necropolitics, where the impulse to kill but not murder, to stifle but not annihilate, to suppress but not extinguish becomes the norm. And thus, sovereignty holds democratic sway, as bare life multiplies in death worlds.

The Gorgon Stare: Every Breath You Take/ I'll Be Watching You

Consider the Gorgon Stare: with twelve cameras, the MQ-9 Reaper can surveil an area of 4 kilometers and produce images and video feeds that can be differentially accessed and analyzed by people separated in space and time.[36] A drone with ARGUS-IS (Autonomous Real-Time Ground Ubiquitous Surveillance-Imaging Systems) takes this further: it can cover 15 square miles and send video feed to sixty-five windows, each capable of focusing continuously on a moving target or one location.[37] In 2005 during the Bush presidency, the Force Application and Launch Continental United States Program (Falcon) was designed to release remote-controlled spacecraft that could fly close to five times faster than the speed of sound, at 100,000 feet, and with 1,000 pounds of armaments and supplies. The aim of the program, in the words of John E. Pike, of GlobalSecuirty.org, is to "crush someone anywhere in world on 30 minutes' notice with no need for a nearby air base."[38] "Surveillance, a technology of racial sorting and subjugation," writes Jennifer Rhee, "structures drone technology and its dehumanizing tendencies."[39] Drone surveillance establishes a "regime of figuration, a way of seeing and, therefore, a modality of thought," argues Nathan K. Hensley.[40]

The Gorgon Stare, ARGUS, and Falcon are designed to bring all things within their scopic purview and enable America to establish global strike capacity. They seek and probe and trace and map the daily activities of several groups of people, including women and children, without their knowledge. In *Drone: Remote Control Warfare*, Hugh Gusterson observes, "As the drones gaze unblinkingly from above, there can be voyeuristic pleasure in watching the Other. In fact, it is hard to imagine a more voyeuristic technology than the drone."[41] Some of them would turn out to be terrorists or actively aiding them, but not all. But to catch the few, the Gorgon Stare compels all whom it watches to lose privacy and dignity. To apprehend the few, the Gorgon Stare requires all whom it sees to demonstrate their innocence. It is helpful here to differentiate the biopolitics of drones from other forms of biopolitics because the concept, as we have seen earlier, cannot be applied uniformly across history; instead, we need to draw out where and how the term designates the imbrication of sovereignty, politics, and biology to produce states of exception to dominate or manage life, whether individual, collective, racial, or multitudinous.

In 2020, as Coronavirus began its global ravage, dramatically increasing sickness and mortality rates, leading governments to enact radical measures that shut down business, religious meetings, educational institutions, indeed, all social, economic, and cultural activity, leading people to lock themselves indoors and distance themselves from everyone, Agamben wrote a series of posts arguing that the global pandemic enables governments to enact a biopolitics of fear and control. In February 2020, in a piece titled "The Invention of an Epidemic," Agamben notes that the virus was more like the influenza virus, which did not justify draconian lockdowns: "It is almost as if with terrorism exhausted as a cause for exception measures, the invention of an epidemic offered the ideal pretext for scaling them up beyond any limitation."[42] A month later, responding to predictable outrage, Agamben clarified:

> The first thing the wave of panic that's paralyzed the country has clearly shown is that our society no longer believes in anything but naked life. It is evident that Italians are prepared to sacrifice practically everything–normal living conditions, social relations, work, even friendships and religious or political beliefs–to avoid the danger of falling ill. The naked life, and the fear of losing it, is not something that brings as a democracy men and women together, but something that blinds and separates them… The dead–our dead–have no right to a funeral and it's not clear what happens to the corpses of our loved ones.[43]

Agamben means here that life has "been reduced to a purely biological condition."[44] Later, in "Reflections," he wonders if the virus did not impose new restrictions but catalyzed existing social conditions, because "the ease with which an entire society has acquiesced to feeling itself plague-stricken" suggests that the "plague was already there."[45] The global pandemic, as Agamben sees it, demonstrated that the biopolitical imperative was not emanating from a panopticon center but was diffused throughout society. People had internalized the state's rule of exception, leading them to distance themselves from other people to hang on to life, to *life as bare life*, to live and breathe, and stay alive. Even the protocols of death and burial, crucial to affirming our humanity, diverse as they are, were suspended. This is what Agamben stresses in saying that life in the pandemic age turned into bare life with the consent of the governed, some handwringing, notwithstanding.

Responding to Agamben, the French philosopher Jean-Luc Nancy points out in February 2020 that while the influenza had vaccines, the coronavirus didn't, and that "technical interconnections of all kinds" were "becoming the rule."[46] He adds, "An entire civilization is in question, there is no doubt about it. There is a sort of viral exception—biological, computer-scientific, cultural—which is pandemic."[47] Roberto Esposito, the Italian philosopher, responding to Nancy and Agamben, says that "to talk of risks to democracy in this case" is an "exaggeration to say the least," because "we should try to separate levels and distinguish between long-running processes and recent events."[48] There was a "breakdown of public authorities," not a turn toward a "dramatic totalitarian grip."[49]

These debates shed light on how biopolitics, as a concept and process, is flexible, provided we are attuned to historical contingencies and cultural differences. Granted, these three philosophers were, like us all, writing when the world was struggling to understand and deal with the Coronavirus, which gives their views, despite any attempt on their part to sound authoritative and data-informed, a tentative, insightful tone. There are three issues that we can highlight from their responses: the biopolitical state of exception and its rule-making propensity have thoroughly diffused into society; the suspension of bios to sustain zoé is to ensure civilizational continuity; the turn to create bare life, to exist as such in the pandemic, required people to submit entirely to the state, as the latter generated data and shared information, however contestable and partial, with the public.

What I am trying to tease out here is that these biopolitical features do not map neatly on to the armed drone's biopolitical drive. Some critical transformational features are apparent in drone warfare—the Gorgon Stare is biopolitical in two ways: it moves beyond the individual to surveil people as a totality, a mass of subjects made amenable to the scopic, panoramic gaze of the drone, and it seeks to manage and regularize life. The Gorgon Stare seeks to manage all of life, to bring the multitude of the living under the domain of governmentality—to administer, to take charge, to manage, to sort, to distribute, to maintain life. It is this biopolitical impulse that gains incredible computational and surveillant power in the age of drones and the cultures of surveillance they engender.

As Lindsay C. Clark and Christian Enemark point out, the drone is a "camera-equipped instrument of war" that has "the potential for someone not only to be killed from afar but also to be closely observed."[50] The drone is "equipped with a satellite-linked video-camera" with "the capacity to reveal to its operator the prosaic humanity of a targeted individual."[51] The drone facilitates "prolonged observation of a targeted individual's prosaic humanity."[52] They go on to add, arguing for a care ethics in drone warfare, "Constantly watching the ordinariness of a particular person's life being lived can sometimes eventually produce a feeling of 'knowing' that person."[53] Sustained observation that uncovers the "prosaic humanity" of the surveillance is only possible when the drone eye deploys the Gorgon Stare: consistent, totalizing, invasive, data-generating surveillance.

Where Clark and Enemark focus on the individual, the Gorgon Stare submits dozens, hundreds, or thousands of peoples to constant, invasive surveillance. Here we see the biopolitical drive becoming necropolitical because the everydayness, the prosaicness, of human lives is subjected to algorithmic logics that generate, through the drone's surveillance assemblage, a data feed of the surveilled; that data feed, as we have seen in the previous chapter, is made amenable to AI programs like machine learning and deep learning to generate meaning out of large data sets; the predictive analytics made possible through the surveillant assemblage lead to target isolation and target elimination.

The Gorgon Stare is necropolitical, because the drone instantiates a new structure of biopolitical power that seeks invasive domination through constant, secret surveillance of a space, its peoples, and its inhabitants. Sabeen Ahmed puts it well: "No longer merely a campaign of identification and detention, the logic of prevention coupled with ever-increasing global panopticism relies on the creation of threatening spaces in which to localize future acts of terror. The immediate consequence is that these spaces of threat have become transformed into spaces of death, in which inhabitants no longer possess any sense of habitual or self-certainty, living therein, as, effectively, walking corpses."[54]

Whereas during the pandemic, people were subjected to the state's directives to cease normal political and sociocultural interaction, here, there is no such imperative; to the contrary, the surveillant drone wants people to act as they do every day; it does not want them to fear it and change their behaviors; it wants them to lead normal lives because it is the normality of their lives that enables the drone to generate data about their lives without their knowledge and consent, and, as we have seen, translate that data into digital doubles and dossiers to align with algorithmic logics to bring out patterns, outliers, concentrations, pockets, and, ultimately, subjects turned into targets for elimination.

It is within the drone's optic field of operations that guilt is assumed and innocence a burden to be proven. The terror of the drone is not only that it takes life without notice and with blinding speed, or that it comes from nowhere and recedes into nowhere, or that it hums its presence and withdraws into thin air whenever it chooses. It is much more than that—it adjudicates life on a daily basis of surveillance that considers everyone suspicious, leaving little room for innocence to become the norm and guilt an aberration. This is the terrifying nature of the Drone: it is a predator on the prowl not only for those intending to cause harm but also for those who, in some situations, cannot speak, establish, or convey their innocence.

National security is the legal and moral justification to construct and deploy a leviathan-like surveillant assemblage, whose circuits of dataflow and nodules of appropriation render individual and social privacy less as zones of life needing protection from others' scrutiny, but as social values to be traded for benefits, including gaining access, receiving information, obtaining interactivity, and so on. Such acts and practices come freighted with social meanings, and, thus, they cannot escape the politics of power in the arts of empire.

Ethics in a Time of Endless War

In *Arguing about War*, Michal Walzer explains that terrorists often take the easy route to effect social change. Lasting revolutionary change that does not lead repeat injustice and violence takes time. It involves building and sustaining difficult coalitions and engaging in mass demonstrations, strikes, sit-ins, and using several other non-violent means of pressure and persuasion. Terrorists tend to downplay the value of such strategies and launch strikes that produce fear and random brutality. Ironically, in waging a war against terrorists, America has built and consolidated a surveillance regime whose efficacy and extensive fields of scrutiny are the preconditions for drone wars. In subjecting hundreds and thousands of peoples to the Gorgon Stare, a technology whose powers amplify with inventions, the fight against terrorism produces affects disturbingly similar or analogous to those unleashed by unprincipled social actors. Walzer writes, "This, then, is the peculiar evil of terrorism—not only the killing of innocent people but also the intrusion of fear into everyday life, the violation of private purposes, the insecurity of public spaces, the endless coerciveness of precaution."[55]

Roger Clarke's warnings that mass surveillance through data increases "arbitrariness," "witch hunts," "inversion of the onus of proof," "climate of suspicion," "repressive potential for a totalitarian government" are critical.[56] A good example of how these risks have become military tactics in drone warfare is the "signature strike," a strategy for increasing domination through dataveillance where nuances and specificities are subsumed into behavioral types, correlative data doubles, and predictive analysis.

In May 2012, *The New York Times* reported that "according to several administration officials," the policy "in effect counts all military-age males in a strike zone as combatants ... unless there is explicit intelligence posthumously proving them innocent."[57] This policy goes beyond surveilling and identifying individual terrorists to targeting groups of people engaged in suspicious activity.

In "Drone is Obama's Weapon of Choice," Peter Bergen points out, "These are drone attacks based on patterns of merely suspicious activity by a group of men, rather than the identification of a particular individual militant."[58] Such a broad categorization reduces the need for gathering reliable intelligence based on close, extended observation and evidence in favor of a guilt-by-association logic that dramatically increases the risk of targeting innocent people, or those whose culpability does not deserve the ultimate punishment of death.

The psychosocial impact of drone strikes includes fear and paranoia among helpers and official rescue personnel who retrieve the dead, rescue the living, and care for the injured. Because the blasts from the strikes often burn bodies, dismember them, or sometimes simply incinerate them, the process of identifying victims means gathering whatever body parts can be found and handing them to friends and relatives of the victims. In villages where the Jirga is conducted—public hearings and discussions to resolve disputes by the *maliks* (local elders) and *khassadars* (local police forces overseen by *maliks*)—due to drone strikes that killed dozens of attendees, some of whom were the Taliban who were present at the meeting to resolve local disputes, there is growing fear and anger about drone attacks that target militants but more often than not result in the loss of innocent life.[59]

Because of the "double tap" strategy of striking targets twice or more, rescuers often hesitate to rush to aid the injured, fearing becoming targets and losing their lives, thus depriving the injured, especially the innocent, of timely medical attention.[60] Strikes that destroy places housing targets also sometimes destroy surrounding houses, leaving individuals and families helpless and destitute. Because medical expenses are high, many of the injured do not get adequate care or take loans they simply cannot afford but need if only to stay alive or avoid becoming severely handicapped. It is common for witnesses to drone strikes to exhibit "anticipatory anxiety" caused by the fear of impending strikes anytime and from anywhere.[61] Terror, anxiety, and fear of becoming victims of drones generate post-traumatic disorders among those living in places hit by drones, or witnesses to the devastating impact of drone missiles. In some instances, parents and families are pulling children from school awhile, or refusing to send them, fearing that when groups of children get together, they could easily become drone targets. Similarly, practices of mourning and burying the dead, which happen in public gatherings, are observed with trepidation because it increases the likelihood of drone attacks on groups.[62]

Drone Materialities

Sites of drone killings or crashes give visibility to the power and infrastructural systems that facilitate drone wars. As Lisa Parks argues, in terms of infrastructure, for instance, using Google Earth, we can discern how drones deal with "geology, physics, energy, and weather" through "earthmoving, importation, construction, installation, and maintenance" to build large air strips and hangars, which become the "staging ground for drone campaigns and vertical maneuvers."[63] In terms of the forensic, places where drones kill or crash become material signs that make visible the invisible structure of drone warfare. The bodies of killed and the injured vivify the violence inflicted, and the debris reveals the type of drone, materials used in its construction, technological systems, and so on.[64] In terms of the perceptual, drones and the surveillance regimes they establish produce "spectral suspects," whose identities are established not by epidermal and other discernable features but through infrared contouring of heat-emitting entities (like the human body), which can be appear black or white, based on a given set of technological settings. Spectral suspects are "visualizations of temperature data that take on the biophysical contours of the human body while its surface appearance remains invisible and its identity unknown."[65]

But here, since identities are not known, "seeing according to temperature turns everyone into a potential suspect or target and has the effect of 'normalizing' surveillance since all bodies appear similar beneath its gaze."[66] It is why other assessment and verifications of threat and identity come into play, like signature strikes and double tap, including computational approaches like maintaining data repositories, metadata analysis, data dossiers, data doubles, and dataveillance. To grasp human behavior as part of a network of actions and patterns, drone surveillance facilitates a distant reading of human collectivities, a macroanalysis of information flows to ascertain suspicious activity and spectral suspects in order to contain or eliminate them preemptively.

Explains Colin Vanderburg, "Drones collect visual signals, detect heat and moisture, and record radiation, space, and sound. Like the roving, collecting "camera eye" of the early twentieth century, the drone eye acts as a visual idiom for its time and place. But even more than the camera eye—whose mimetic precision itself carried a degree of menace—the drone eye's view is also a threat. Every datum it takes in contributes a tiny piece to a vast project of tangled annihilation. Today, American power sees the world through a beady sensor."[67] Through this sensor takes place what Peter Asard calls "bureaucratized killing," because it "involves self-conscious processes and efforts at rationalization—at both the individual and organizational levels to make the processes more efficient, more accurate, and more manageable—it is most appropriate to approach this subject as a form of killing that has an elaborate and intentional bureaucratized structure as well as a psychological dimension."[68]

But the more vivid its data generation, the greater the risk, counter intuitively, of acting in haste; as Michael J. Boyle contends, "vivid drone imagery of a potential incursion could exaggerate the cognitive, affective, or phycological biases that decisionmakers already have. For example such imagery may heighten their sense of urgency, exacerbate pathologies in the decision-making process, or truncate their deliberations by forcing a response too quickly."[69] Boyle underscores the risk in drone wars increasing, not decreasing, because of their unique affordance in conducting nontraditional warfare. The concept of "war" needs to be reconsidered, in that while traditional war decreases in the drone age, nontraditional war soon becomes the norm. What remains constant is war.

Gendering Drone Warfare

Opening another angle to view this phenomenon, in *Gender and Drone Warfare: A Hauntological Perspective*, Lindsay Clark argues that "narratives of masculinity and femininity are reflected in discourses of military technologies."[70] Clark goes further stating that "military technologies simultaneously destabilize and (re) inscribe military masculinity (and femininity)."[71] Because drone warfare generates physical and psychical distance from the battlefield, heroism, risk, and sacrifice on the battlefield are valued more than whatever drone crews experience in drone cockpits. Traditional warfare becomes masculinized as the real and true, whereas drone pilots become feminized because they can fight wars in conditions that either simulate home or enable them to continue the lives they lead at home, unlike the true warriors who must leave home to fight the enemy elsewhere.

Building on the work of Lauren B. Wilcox, Heather Roff, and Sumita Kunashankaran, Clark points to the dialectical dynamic in drone warfare that masculinizes certain traits in drone crews and in the drone technologies themselves. Completely removed from the physical conditions of the battlefield, drones embody a mind that is also freed from the limitations of the human body. Where the masculine value of total objectivity gains technological embodiment, the body, traditionally associated with the feminine, is transcended, turning the drone into a hypermasculine apparatus. Similarly, because the drone stares to surveil without blinking, as it is technologically wired to do, its gaze is produced through an overcoming of the physical to become an extremely efficient surveillance tool. The drone eye, with and through which drone crews view the world, also makes it more difficult to empathize with the surveilled, to become mindful of the larger purposes of war, not the specific tactic of surveilling and eliminating targets as if the latter is an end in itself, and drone crews are unaccountable to anyone but themselves, if at all.[72]

The gendering of drone warfare highlights yet again the cultural turn required in digital studies to connect the human activity of warfare with the scientific preoccupation with technological innovation. Clark's focus on gender and drones helpfully shifts the attention to drone crews and drones as machines, which supplements the focus on the impact of the drone elsewhere, beyond US territories or the regions housing drone bases. The ethical complications of drones and surveillance, thus, require a sustained inquiry into the gendering of drone warfare and its layered geographies of inside and outside zones in which to wage war.

Algorithmic Fog of Drone Warfare

Ethical considerations also come into play when drone surveillance turns into algorithmic insight. As we have seen, AI's generative protocols in drone warfare must have predictive analytics: identifying patterns to forecast potential suspects, events, movements, gatherings, threats. But the enormous data obtained through surveillance does not, in and of itself, set the terms of efficient algorithmic assessments, because AI works best only with reliable data. Citing a study showing algorithmic bias in facial and demographic recognition software, which had false positives and false negatives, William Crumpler, writing for the Center for Strategic and International Studies, notes that while algorithms are getting better at reducing bias or error frequencies, "the most important factor in reducing bias appears to be the selection of training data used to build algorithmic models."[73] Such training can lead to bias being "eliminated entirely with the right algorithms and development processes."[74]

Two ethical problems immediately crop up in the context of drone warfare: collecting data that represents a populace is less about demographic or gender inclusivity and more about identifying, locating, constricting, and eliminating; the data-gathering protocols of drone surveillance do not have the consent of the surveilled. These problems demonstrate that drone warfare has a biopolitical impetus driven by a necropolitics that creates conditions of exemption for perpetual war. Addressing these ethical challenges leads us not to fine-tuning algorithmic neural networks but to the political and economic reasons legitimizing drone warfare. Affirming the human in the age of drone warfare requires that we avoid fetishizing technology embodied in drones, surveillant assemblages, and AI.

There is a tendency, point out Sarah Kreps and John Kaag, to conflate technological sophistication with ethical and legal assessment, because technology is not neutral but used by human beings: "The ability to undertake more precise, targeted strikes should not be confused with the determination of legal or ethical legitimacy," which raises the question of war and justice.[75] Fred Kaplan underscores a key fact: drone strikes take place outside of war zones. They can happen anywhere the US decides threat is imminent. He writes, "For when we talk about accidental civilian deaths by drones in Pakistan and Yemen, we are talking about countries where the United States is not officially fighting wars. In other words, these are countries where the people killed—and their embittered friends and relatives— didn't know that they were living in a war zone."[76]

But such is the amorphous nature of drone war that it is easy to declare the absence of war even when one country's missiles devastate another country's military sites and command centers, however illiberal that country is. The United States launched more than 145 drone attacks to weaken Muammar Qaddafi's regime in Libya, but the Obama administration refrained from characterizing such use of military force in a foreign country as war.[77] The phrase "fog of war" generally describes the cloudiness of perspective and vision that seeps into the consciousness of combatants and military planners in the course of war. They lose sight of objectives and immediate surroundings. Uncertainty and ambiguity replace focus and ethical clarity.

But in the new digital war of drones and cyberspace, the entire field of operations seems designed to produce the fog of war: doubt, uncertainty, slippage, double-movements, visibility, and invisibility. On the face of it, this appears to be wise military strategy in an age of globalization where enemies merge into shadows and take their targets randomly and brutally. But it can also be said that this fog of war is carefully produced to compel visibility of the surveilled while obscuring the culpability of the surveillants. It produces a state of emergency in which the visibility of others that it generates is inversely proportional to the invisibility with which the planners, decision makers, beneficiaries, and visionaries of robotic war cloak themselves.

In the fog of drone war, accountability of those "operating the levers of power on which the fate of the less volatile partners in the relationships depends can at any moment escape beyond reach—into sheer inaccessibility."[78] There is too much blurring of distinctions among the terrorist, the suspect, the sympathizer, the aider, the civilian, the rescuer, the bystander, the protestor, and all those innocent people who get caught up in a vicious war not of their making. It is no longer one state waging war against another state or a state against non-state actors. It has morphed into something else—the logic of bartering, this for that, a quid pro quo is the operational principle of negotiation. The drones kill not just the ones planning to or attack America or its citizens, but others like the Haqqani group in Afghanistan, which often sides with the Taliban; the Lakshar I Jhangvi that comprises Sunnis who target Shias; and the Taliban in Pakistan who eagerly wage war against Pakistan.[79]

Yet, US drones strikes have killed scores of mid-to-low ranking members of these groups, although they are not implicated in planning attacks against the United States. These are the shadowlands of drone warfare where responsibility, law, and policy are inexplicable. In the dataveillance culture of modernity, doubt is perpetual, clarity is in abeyance, and accountability lies in big data. But it is also a culture in which death is as certain as birth. These are the shadowlands where those with the power to determine threats and control the complex, robotic systems to manage life and condemn the living to death will find it easy to exempt themselves from accountability. The coarsening of the ethical imagination is a deadly casualty of drone wars. It is not because the twenty-first century somehow spawned a more vicious evil in human beings but because human interaction with digital technology and information and communication systems is creating a process that Bauman refers to as "adiaphorization" "in which systems and processes become split off from any other consideration of morality ... surveillance streamlines the process of doing things at a distance, of separating a person from the consequences of action."[80]

Adiaphorization in the Digital Age

In *Postmodern Ethics*, Bauman elaborates its meaning: "(The term "adiaphoron" belongs to the language of ecclesia; it meant originally a belief or a custom declared by the Church indifferent—neither merit nor sin—and hence requiring no stand, no official endorsement or prohibition): neither good nor evil, measurable against technical (purpose-oriented or procedural) but not against moral criteria."[81] As pilots and information and intelligence analysts navigate the distance that is compressed and expanded through digital technologies in the virtual and material systems that enable surveillance and disposition of lethal force through drones, another distance emerges—between the agent of action and its recipient, the Other. As this dynamic unfolds, ethics is replaced by or made commensurate with data and technology. Meriting neither "endorsement nor prohibition," the loss of innocent life is adiaphorized as its value is assessed in relation to the internal workings of dataveillence and surveillance systems, program effectiveness, operational readiness, and interpreting and decoding data.

The ethical challenges of drone warfare get further complicated as AI integration with surveillance platforms and armed drones moves apace. Roboticists are considering using complex algorithms that can make the drone perform like humans as it can use an "'ethical adapter' that can generate a sense of compassion when faced with the prospect of lethal force."[82] It will have an "after-action-reflection" feature helping it change its response to threats by improving on past performance, even as another feature of the adapter will help it learn the emotion of guilt, which can make the fully automated armed drone refrain from killing or be more judicious in killing, by approximating or, perhaps, bettering, human behavior.[83]

As P. W. Singer points out in *Wired for War: The Robotics Revolution and Conflict in the 21st Century*, "these weapons don't just create greater physical distance, but also a different sort of psychological distance and disconnection."[84] Constant interaction or immersion in virtual environments encourages the propensity to craft digital characters or virtual personas to play out fictive plots or assume other identities. This creates a psychological distance between the multiple selves, and the consequences of these personas as they act and think digitally or within robotically enhanced systems are located outside the moral horizon of the game players, leading to a disavowing of one's personal responsibility and social accountability.

As drone technology moves further into robotics and automation, and as surveillance systems inundate us with information, minimizing our ability to assess and understand, it increases our reliance on algorithmic data mining and metadata to determine choices of life and death but with one pivotal difference—the agency for ethical contemplation and decision-making shifts onto data, image, and video feeds, tags and meta data, computational readings and simulated environments; that is, it "exonerate[s] the operator of the moral guilt that would haunt him were he fully and truly in charge of selecting the convicts for execution; and, more importantly still, to reassure the operator in advance that if a mistake happens, it won't be blamed on his immorality. If 'innocent people' are killed, it is a technical fault, not a moral failure or a sin—and, judging from the statue books, most certainly not a crime."[85]

In April 2014, the United State Government Accountability Office released a report titled "Air Force: Actions Needed to Strengthen Unmanned Aerial System Pilots, which identified several stressors for drone pilots, whose number increased dramatically in just five years, from 400 pilots in 2008 to 1,350 pilots in 2013. These pilots, who are on-station, that is, deployed not in battlefields outside the United States but working in command and control centers across the United States often report difficulties in balancing work and family life: their work-weeks often exceed fifty hours; they have to maintain secrecy of work from family and friends; they constantly rotate shifts; and they have to move from virtual battlefields to everyday social and cultural life on a daily basis.[86] These pilots spend innumerable hours poring over video and image feeds to surveil and asses possible threats and deploy missiles, if necessary. And their surveillance is profoundly invasive as they watch for hours on end: children playing about, people going to the bathroom for bathing or ablutions, animals and people loitering about. Their work is monotonous and oriented to computer screens and shifting images.[87]

Some also discern the different nature of courage and honor in drone wars and battlefield situations, as when one pilot, after unleashing a drone missile, kept struggling with the ease that accompanied his act, which was in stark contrast to the struggle of soldiers on the ground, to whom his aircraft was giving cover and intelligence.[88] Recently, in an article titled "Remote Warfare with Intimate Consequences" published in *Mental Health Journal*, Seth Davin Norrholm et al. note, "The potential psychological consequences of this type of military occupational specialty can include symptoms of depression, anxiety, and posttraumatic stress disorder (PTSD) as well as moral injury, mental exhaustion or burnout, and disturbed sleep."[89] What Bauman describes as the risk of adiaphorization, which evacuates individual agency from the drone's surveillant assemblage and its capacity and charge to inflict violence, can be seen to have what can be called the drone unconscious, the often unexpressed fear, loathing, doubt, and trauma that drone operators are prone to experience. Acknowledging the nature and power of the drone unconscious is key to developing mechanisms to forestall or decrease their crippling power. It can include diffusing the work of drone pilots by involving several actors in the operational protocol of conducting flight, stability, intelligence gathering, targeting, and eliminating.[90] Here, instead of abstracting ethics from the drone assemblage, we can embed it within the assemblage.

Sousveillance: Creating Agency and Countering Power

Another way to counter the power of surveillance, mediated or not via drones, is sousveillance, a term offered by Steve Mann, who describes it as a reversal of the surveillant gaze. Whereas "sur-veillance denotes a God's eye view from on high," its "inverse, called sous-veillance (French for 'to watch from below'), explores what happens when cameras move from lamp posts and ceilings down to eye level."[91] Sousveillance can be both hierarchical, where people watch the ones in authority doing the watching (police, businesses, public places), and "personal sousveillance," which is about "human-centered recording of personal experience."[92] As an intentional response to surveillance, "sousveillance focuses on enhancing the ability of people to access and collect data about their surveillance and to neutralize surveillance."[93] This includes people using visual or audio devices to record buildings or proceedings; recording the acts of the police; taking satellite imagery of the instruments of surveillance and distributing them on mass or public channels to decrease secrecy, and so on.[94]

Put another way, sousveillance is about watching the watchers, because it involves creating "equiveillance," a term Mann explains as "shifting this equilibrium between surveillance and sousveillance with inverse/reverse accountability/recountability/continuality of continuous sur/sousveillance."[95] British artist James Bridle creates equiveillance by mixing GIS-informed images of drone sites and drones in different parts of the world and using social media to disseminate the information, albeit with an eye toward artistic sensibility. By using available digital systems and digital platforms (images from satellites and social media) to make what the security state (government) seeks to conceal from the public, Bridle engages in sousveillance. What makes his work artistic, in a way, is the attention to form and detail, because he does not take images in whatever form they are produced and put them in circulation, but selectively chooses and frames them to evoke the drone's affordances of zooming out and zooming in. Interestingly enough, Bridle's project, which has seventy-eight images, is aptly titled "Watching the Watchers."[96]

Similarly, in *The Good Drone: How Social Movements Democratize Surveillance*, Austin Choi-Fitzpatrick argues that we can:

> find new tools for nonviolent digital disruption that radically increase the state's cost of monitoring and repression, retaining the moral high ground ensured by nonviolent tactics. This is as relevant to people on the ground reacting to the state's use of drones for targeted killings as it is to the use of drones by disenfranchised communities monitoring states and corporate actors. Drones put increased power into the hands of the powerful. But they also level the playing field for those traditionally excluded from power—thereby opening new horizons for political struggle.[97]

Focusing primarily on small drones, Choi-Fitzpatrick points to their use by people to protest state policies or actions, draw public awareness to effect change, bring people together around shared interests to promote justice. While not all such drone uses can be viewed as sousveillance, certain kinds of uses merit that description. For instance, where the police or security agencies use cameras to monitor crowds or people, small drones can be used to document crowds or individual behavior to counter official narratives about them. Crucially, here, the technology of documenting, archiving, and retrieving for dissemination is afforded to people through drones, thus creating the conditions for democratic sousveillance, or, rather, creating what Mann calls "equiveillance" to alter or disturb the power dynamics of surveillance, not always or necessarily directed toward the stoppage or destruction of tools used for oppressive surveillance.[98]

Such disturbance of official gazes, protocols, and networks is what Rita Raley in *Tactical Media* describes as new media activism whose tactics are not about wholescale revolution, a taking down of institutions deemed to commit oppression, but about creating glitches and stoppages; sousveillance, by extension, if we frame it in Raley's terms, is about initiating a "micropolitics of disruption, intervention, and education."[99] It is about "the temporary creation of a situation in which signs, messages, and narratives [in this context surveillance] are set into play and critical thinking become possible," because as sousveillance makes surveillance's hidden or overt practices public, official power becomes amenable to scrutiny and, hopefully, accountability.[100]

I must add here that sousveillance by itself does not produce policy or practice changes; contesting or disturbing power structures can mean penalties, deplatforming, lawfare, reputational harm, and a host of other things. The critical element in sousveillance is that it's a grounds-up effort by people desirous of maintaining a healthy balance between security and freedom, the state's right to know and the individual's right to privacy. In the example of people using small drones to document crowds or police behavior with crowds, we see surveillance cultures being undermined, limited, or thwarted through drone use by non-state actors, because the surveillers realize they are under surveillance by people who are not in their control.

Roger Stahl and Sebastian Kaempf's revision in "Sousveilling the 'Global War on Terror'" of Mann's notion of sousveillance is helpful here. Where Mann's sousveillance demonstrates the power of unidirectional and bidirectional surveillance and sousveillance, Stahl and Kaempf extend that to "the performative dimension of sousveillance by attending to its sites of struggle, particularly where alternative and counter-performances work to disrupt and dislodge official regimes of truth."[101] Resistances to surveillance can be situated in what they call the "theater of surveillance" because "the function of the panopticon is not necessarily surveillance per se but the performative presentation of a 'theater of surveillance' that functions regardless of whether exact accounting mechanisms even exist."[102] Stahl and Kaempf point to how surveillance and sousveillance produce performances of how the state's surveillant gaze seeks to normalize itself by making it appear natural and safe; how surveillance evokes affective responses that go beyond rational analyses; how sousveillance can include not secret dismantling of security cameras, for instance, but public performances of dismantling and defacing them; how resistance to surveillance lead to theaters of surveillance where people on the street or in public places are urged to view themselves as subjects targeted by a drone and of places being monitored by the state's drone; sousveillance can turn into a data-driven app that offers uses notifications of drone strikes and GIS visualizations of strike locations, which are accessible in mobile devices like smartphones. We should note here that in many of these theaters of souveillance, people "tinkered, in other words, with the very tools that made the drone war"[103] (349).

Such sousveillance can instantiate ethical thinking and action in public arenas by ordinary people using drones to not only watch the watchers but to scramble what the watchers do with what is watched: creating counternarratives using drones to question or expose the agendas of official characterizations of the same event, people, or person. Another way sousveillance can enable ethics to gain prominence, making it move from theoretical reflection to practical application, is when the drone creates machine vision to generate the algorithmic gaze; there is a possibility of reorienting that gaze through an ethic of care grounded in feminist discourse.

Algorithmic Gaze and the Feminist Ethic of Care

Speaking of the algorithmic gaze of the computerized machine as the scope drive to manage social life, Jill Walker Rettberg, in *Machine Vision*, points out three features of surveillance that can, far from providing security, erode social trust. As more people lose trust in social institutions, they become vulnerable to the capitalistic dynamic that sells security cameras to assuage fears. Assuming that cameras provide objective accounts of reality, people tend to push municipalities and national governments to inundate social spaces with security cameras. But because they are part of assemblages, as we have seen in the previous chapter, what is seen, what is visualized, must be interpreted in terms of the assemblage that generated it. Machine vision tends to normalize patterns. She says, "The remarkable rapid increase in surveillance technology in US communities is a response, at least in part, to a loss of trust in community and institutions and the fear that comes with that broken trust."[104]

Rettberg adds that "machine learning has a normalizing effect. It builds a model of the most common patterns in a dataset to make meaningful predictions or inferences, It produces stereotype, not defamiliarizations."[105] Surveillance, produced through machine vision, exacerbates bias; the data used to train AI programs itself needs critical examination because the algorithms extend the unevenness of the data; for instance, where data is gathered primarily from one demographic to create an AI-driven face-recognition technology, the outcome is that the technology will normalize the features of that demographic, "not outliers and details."[106] The affective dimensions also come into play because emotions and affects are culturally specific, making the algorithmic gaze less reliable to generate visual information embodying nuanced cultural differences and diverse human emotions, even when localized in one region of the human body—the face. Put another way, the algorithmic gaze can just as easily misread as read whatever it is seeing.

To avoid such misreading, Lindsay C. Clark and Christian Enemark, in "Drone Warriors, Revealed Humanity and a Feminist Ethics of Care," argue for complimenting the abstract principles of jus in bello with care ethics that locates surveilled subjects in the familiar networks of which they are a part and playing social roles as fathers, mothers, caregivers, providers, etc. Clark and Enemark insightfully note that drone warfare "presents a peculiar moral challenge for that operator."[107] Drone operators are "arguably better positioned than any other kind of warrior in history to observe the features of particular relationships among the people who inhabit prospective drone strikes."[108] Drone warfare is peculiar because drones are remote-killing war machines that enact their killing abilities through close personal surveillance. Instead of denying or marginalizing the intimate visual proximity that the drone eye affords, we can train drone operators and intelligence analysts to examine the impact of drone strokes on the social networks of the targeted individuals, which includes other peoples who will face deprivation or incur excessive rehabilitation costs. Assessing efficiency and cost-benefit calculations, while necessary, must also incorporate a "moral reasoning" that can "account for the way a drone's powerful video-camera reveals a prospective target's humanity as manifested in unique human relationships."[109]

One risk in this approach is that terrorists, would-be terrorists, suspects, and every person, whether surveilled or not, lead social lives. To prioritize the quotidian nature of their lives does not mean that those seeking to cause harm to others will stop doing so. They can be good fathers, providers, caregivers, mothers, sisters, brothers, or children, etc., while also actively planning to aid or abet killing others or destroying infrastructure. The care ethic complements abstract moral reasoning by expanding our understanding of the socially enmeshed nature of human life, here, of those surveilled; however, in some circumstances, the ethics of care must also consider broader assessments of threats, harm, destruction, and death wrought by state and non-state actors, and the preventive measures that should be exercised. The benefits of integrating a feminist ethic of care with *jus ad bellum*, *jus in bello*, and *jus post bellum* cannot be gainsaid: we must, as individuals and social and political collectives, develop and support a culture of ethical care to decrease adiaphorization in drone warfare.

Where the feminist ethic of care prioritizes the affective situatedness of the body (the body as flesh and blood, affirming human experience as embodied in social relations and biological organicity, the ethical turn toward the human in an AI-driven age of drone warfare gains clarity in Simone Natale's *Deceptive Media: Artificial Intelligence and Social Life after the Turing Test*." AI, Natale argues, is deceptive: it simulates human behaviors and thought, but it cannot, at least not yet, exist on its own. Focusing on AI as a technological development gaining extraordinary intelligence as an autonomous or semi-autonomous process is misleading. AI emerges only in relation to human beings, in relation to human intelligence and activity. Arguing that "deception is as central to AI's functioning as the circuits, software, and data that make it run," Natale says that we must examine "the ways computing technologies draw on specific aspects of users' perception and psychology in order to create the illusion of AI."[110] The evolution of AI is a history of "exploit[ing] the limits and affordances of our perception and intellect."[111]

Resisting Banal Deception

Natalie offers "banal deception" as a term that explains "the deceptive mechanisms and practices that are embedded in media technologies and contribute to their integration into everyday life."[112] Such integration has five features: (1) banal deception has an "everyday and ordinary character"[113]; (2) it offers "functionality" to users by offering some value to them like "playful interaction and emotional reward"[114]; (3) it has an "obliviousness" that is "taken for granted and not questioned"[115]; (4) it has "low definition," making voice assistants, for instance, function as blank slates (of sorts) onto which human users can project their fancies, unlike robots with advance AI, which are highly defined, giving them concrete presence, voice, and functionality[116]; (5) it is not the result of user interaction only but is "programmed by designers and users" who "construct a model or image of the expected user" to develop AI.[117]

These five features of banal deception map well on to drones: in the first two decades of the twenty-first century, drones, which gained public attention as weapons of war, have acquired an everyday character due to their functional uses in numerous spheres of human activity beyond war-making. We are taking for granted that because drone warfare's global spread is inevitable, we must adapt to it, not resist it. Our challenge today is that even as we become accustomed to drones as everyday objects in our lives, we must guard against that fact by not blunting our critical ability to examine drones in their manifestations as a surveillant assemblage that protects and extends state power, invasive surveillance, and unaccountable exercise of governmental and socio-political power. Drone wars happen for reasons that human collectivities create.

As drones gain AI affordances, we must continually question the human motivations that lead to the creation and use of such drones, rather than letting the marvelous nature of human ingenuity, and the delights obtained through digital technologies, assume an autochthonous intelligence with no trace of human activity. Put another way, the autonomous, highly complex, sophisticated drone that can apparently (or will soon be able to) act on its own to take life and death decisions tells us more about ourselves and the kind of worlds that we wish to create than we care to admit. Writ large on the global canvas on which drone warfare paints a posthuman future of robotic war, if we can use an art analogy, is the human subject: we, the people.

When these drones are attacking others about whom we do not hear, and of whom we do not know much, we still must reckon with one key fact—these wars are waged in our name. They bear the insignia of America. It would be a mistake to think of surveillance and drones as something that happens outside the United States, as activities engaged in by the military to protect the homeland, and to enhance American leadership in the global fight against terrorism. The panoptic analogy would mean that surveillant power is diffused from a US center to various peripheries spread across the world. Governmentality produces information, establishes structures for data collection, processing, and analysis about people, some of whom are eagerly planning, aiding, or abetting terrorist attacks against America or its allies, and decisions to contain, thwart, incapacitate, or kill radiate from an inside center to an outside periphery. Conceiving of drone warfare and national security in this way obscures the changes wrought by information technology, international relations, long and short distance population migration of millions, rise of capitalism across the world, and the globalization of ideas, cultures, and commodities.

Said otherwise, this view cannot account for the condition of globality in which drone warfare has become major military strategy and national defenses strategy. Haggerty and Ericson's "surveillant assemblage" is more helpful in detailing the transversal, uneven nature of numerous actors and institutions and their forms of surveillance that generate knowledge, information, and data about citizens and inhabitants within the United States and those interacting with them. The rhizomatic forms and techniques of the surveillant assemblage are designed to deal with the unpredictable forces of globalization. This, notes Christopher Dandeker in *Surveillance, Power, and Modernity: Bureaucracy and Discipline from 1700 to the Present Day*, is not a recent development but an enhancement of modern sovereignty, because "the distinctive features of the nation-state derive from an emergent division between external and internal relations together with a corresponding specialization of bureaucratized military power on the one hand and police surveillance on the other."[118]

Drone warfare relies heavily on the kind of police surveillance normally associated with domestic or internally driven national law and order but with a difference: the surveillant assemblage is not confined to national territories or regions administered or controlled by states but comprises multiple centers and states, layers of bureaucracy, points of appropriation, international data mining systems, nodular decision-making, feedback looping—all of which occur in the manifold networks of information and communication linking the military, the police, public and private businesses, and organizations. Empire's surveillance encompasses the domestic and the foreign, and it includes the foreign in touch with or attempting to interact or impact not only the domestic but also the foreign interacting with the non-domestic or foreign entities.

A compelling example of the infrastructural and politico-juridical contours and contents of Empire's rhizomatic and panoptic surveillance is the way *The Guardian*, a well-known newspaper in Britain, was subjected to harsh investigations by the British government. In the aftermath of the Snowden revelations published by *The Guardian*'s journalists or in its papers, the paper reported that it was forced to destroy the computer hard drives purportedly containing classified information: "Under the watchful gaze of two technicians from the British government spy agency GCHQ, the journalists took angle-grinders and drills to the internal components, rendering them useless and the information on them obliterated ... The bizarre episode in the basement of the *Guardian*'s London HQ was the climax of Downing Street's fraught interactions with the Guardian in the wake of Snowden's leak – the biggest in the history of western intelligence."[119] But when governments destroy the fourth estate's (the press) infrastructure to prevent it from holding them accountable, the right of the people to be informed of their government's activities, and question and dissent from its official narratives, is thoroughly compromised.

Adipahorization, dataveillance, digital dossiers, government pressure on newspapers, constant surveillance to create the good society, the psychological and cultural impact of surveillance on people and drone pilots, the misleading and false information given by government officials to the public and news media, and the continuing drone operations and drone strikes in several parts of the world show that digital technologies are fundamentally reshaping contemporary war and peace. In the next chapter, we will study the operations of techno-neocolonialism in Africa, particularly in Zambia, and the subaltern resistance it generates in acclaimed novelist Namwali Serpell's *The Old Drift*. Africa, it turns out, is ground zero for the future of freedom and democracy in the age of the drone.

Notes

1. Michel Foucault, *Society Must Be Defended: Lectures at the Collége de France, 1975–76* (New York: Picador, 2003), 245.
2. Foucault, *Society Must Be Defended*, 246–7.
3. Giorgioa Agamben, *Home Sacer: Sovereign Power and Bare Life*. Trans. by Daniel Heller-Roazen (California: Stanford University Press, California, 1998), 1.
4. Ibid., 2.
5. Ibid., 3.
6. Qtd. in Agamben, *Homo Sacer*, 3.
7. Agamben, *Homo Sacer*, emphasis in original, 9.
8. Ibid., 124.
9. Michel Foucault, "Right of Death and Power Over Life." *Foucault Reader*. Edited by Paul Rabinow (New York: Pantheon Books, 1984), 266.
10. Agamben, *Homo Sacer*, 6–9.
11. Ibid., emphasis in original, 181.
12. Achille Mbembe, *Necropolitics* (Durham: Duke University Press, Durham, 2019), 92.
13. Roger Stahl and Sebastian Kaempf, "Sousveilling the 'Global War on Terror,'" *Australian Journal of International Affairs*, 73, no. 4 (2019): 346.
14. Achille Mbembe, *Necropolitics*, 16–17.
15. Marina Grižinić and Šefik Tatlić. *Necropolitics, Racialization, and Global Capitalism: Historicization of Biopolitics and Forensics of Politics, Art, and Life* (New York: Lexington Books, 2014), 31, emphasis in original.
16. Ibid., 32.
17. Ibid., 34.
18. Marina Grižnić, "What Is the Aesthetics of Necropolitics?" *The Aesthetics of Necropolitics*. Edited by Natasha Lushetich. Academic Search Complete, Ebook Central (London: Rowman and Littlefield, 2018), emphasis in original, 28.
19. Mbembe, *Necropolitics*, 75.
20. Christine Rosen, *The Extinction of Human Experience: Being Human in a Disembodied World* (New York: W.W. Norton, 2024), 16.
21. Shoshana Zuboff, *The Age of Surveillance Capitalism: The Fight for a Human Future at the New Frontier of Power* (New York: Hachette Book Group, Perseus Books, 2019), 8.

22 Giorgio Agamben, "The Politicization of Life," *Biopolitics: A Reader*. Edited by Timothy Campbell and Adam Sitze (Duke University Press, 2013), 148.
23 Ibid., "The Politicization of Life," 149, emphasis in original.
24 Roberto Esposito, "The Enigma of Biopolitics," *Biopolitics: A Reader*. Edited by Timothy Campbell and Adam Sitze (Duke University Press, 2013), 352.
25 Ibid., 366.
26 Walter Mignolo, "Preface to the 2012 Edition," *Local Histories/Global Designs: Coloniality, Subaltern Knowledges, and Border Thinking* (Princeton University Press, 2012), ix.
27 Esposito, 368.
28 Thomas Lemke, "A Zone of Indistinction: A Critique of Giorgio Agamben's Concept of Biopolotics." *Outlines* 1 (2005): 9.
29 Ibid., 9.
30 Ibid.
31 Btihaj Ajana, "Surveillance and Biopolitics." *Electronic Journal of Sociology* (2005): 7.
32 Michael Hardt and Antonio Negri, *Multitude: War and Democracy in the Age of Empire* (New York: Penguin Press, 2004), 100.
33 Hardt and Negri, *Multitude*, 101.
34 Grižinić and Tatlić. *Necropolitics, Racialization, and Global Capitalism*, 32.
35 Rettberg, 142.
36 Noah Shachtman, "Air Force to Unleash 'Gorgon Stare' on Squirting Insurgents," *Wired* February 19, 2009, https://wired.com/2009/02/gorgon-stare/
37 David Hambling, "Special Forces Gigapixel Flying Spy See All," *Wired* February 12, 2009, https://wired.com/2009/02/gigapixel-flyin/
38 Walter Pincus, "Pentagon Has Far-Reaching Defense Spacecraft in Works," *Washington Post*. March 16, 2005, http://washingtonpost.com/wp-dyn/articles/A38272-2005Mar15.html
39 Jennifer Rhee, *The Robotic Imaginary: The Human and the Price of Dehumanized Labor* (Minneapolis: University of Minnesota Pres, 2018), 164.
40 Nathan Hensley, "Drone Form: Mediation at the End of Empire," *Novel: A Forum on Fiction* 51, no. 2 (2018): 229.
41 Hugh Gusterson, *Drone: Remote Control Warfare* (Cambridge, MA: MIT Press, 2016), 62.
42 Giorgio Agamben, "The Invention of an Epidemic," *European Journal of Psychoanalysis* February 2020, https://journal-psychoanalysis.eu/articles/coronavirus-and-philosophers/
43 Agamben, "Clarifications," March 2020, https://journal-psychoanalysis.eu/articles/coronavirus-and-philosophers/
44 Ibid.
45 Agamben, "Reflections," March 2020, https://journal-psychoanalysis.eu/articles/reflections-on-the-plague/
46 Jean-Luc Nancy, "A Viral Exception," *Coronavirus, Psychoanalysis, and Philosophy; Conversations on Pandemics, Politics, and Society*. Edited by Fernando Castrillón and Thomas Marchevesky (London: Routledge, 2021), 27.
47 Ibid.
48 Roberto Esposito, "Cured to the Bitter End," *Coronavirus, Psychoanalysis, and Philosophy; Conversations on Pandemics, Politics, and Society*. Edited by Fernando Castrillón and Thomas Marchevesky (London: Routledge, 2021), 28.
49 Ibid., 29.

50   Lindsay C. Clark and Christian Enemark, "Drone Warriors, Revealed Humanity, and a Feminist Ethics of Car," *Ethics of Drone Strikes: Restraining Remote-Control Killing* (Edinburgh: Edinburgh Scholarship Online, 2022), 144. https://doi.org/10.3366/edinburgh/9781474483575.003.0008
51   Ibid. 130.
52   Ibid. 131.
53   Ibid. 134.
54   Sabeen Ahmed, "From Threat to Walking Corpse: Spatial Disruption and the Phenomenology of 'Living under Drones.'" *Theory & Event* 21, no. 2 (2018): 401.
55   Walzer, *Arguing about War*, 51.
56   Roger Clarke, "Information Technology and Dataveillance," 505.
57   Jo Becker and Scott Shane, "A Measure of Change: Secret 'Kill List' Proves A Test of Obama's Principles and Will." *nytimes.com* May 29, 2012, http://nytimes.com/2012/05/29/world/obamas-leadership-in-war-on-al-qaeda.html?pagewanted=1&_r=2&pagewanted=all&#p[TMATMA]
58   Peter Bergen, "Drone Is Obama's Weapon of Choice," *CNN Opinion*. September 19. 2012, http://cnn.com/2012/09/05/opinion/bergen-obama-drone/index.html
59   Stanford Law School, International Human Rights and Conflict Resolution Clinic at Stanford Law School and Global Justice Clinic at NYU School of Law, "Living under Drones: Death, Injury and Trauma to Civilians from US Drones Practices in Pakistan (2012) in: 23–24. https://law.stanford.edu/publications/living-under-drones-death-injury-and-trauma-to-civilians-from-us-drone-practices-in-pakistan/
60   Ibid., 74.
61   Ibid., 81.
62   Ibid., 89.
63   Lisa Parks, "Vertical Mediation," *Life in the Age of Drone Warfare*. Edited by Lisa Parks, and Caren Kaplan, 134–57 (Durham: Duke University Press, 2017).
64   Ibid., 51–152.
65   Ibid., 145.
66   Ibid.
67   Colin Vanderburg, "Drone Art," *Dissent* (2016), https://dissentmagazine.org/article/drone-art-astro-noise-laura-poitras
68   Peter Asard, "The Labor of Ssurveillance and Bureaucratized Killing: New Subjectivities of Military Drone Operators," *Life in the Age of Drone Warfare*. Edited by Lisa Parks and Caren Kaplan (Durham: Duke University Press, 2017), 284.
69   Matthew J. Boyle, "Correspondence: Debating Drone Proliferation," *International Security* 42, no. 3 (2017): 179.
70   Lindsay C. Clark, *Gender and Drone Warfare: A Hauntological Perspective* (London: Routledge, 2019), 39.
71   Ibid., 18,
72   Ibid., 45–7.
73   William Crumpler, "The Problem of Bias in Facial Recognition," *Center for Strategic and International Studies*, csis.org, May 1, 2020, https://csis.org/blogs/strategic-technologies-blog/problem-bias-facial-recognition
74   Ibid.
75   Sarah Kreps and John Kaag, "The Use of Unmanned Aerial Vehicles in Contemporary Conflict: A Legal and Ethical Analysis." *Polity* 44 (2012): 17.
76   Fred Kaplan, "The World as Free Fire Zone." *MIT Technology Review* June 7, 2013. https://technologyreview.com/2013/06/07/177754/the-world-as-free-fire-zone/

77   Benjamin, *Drone Warfare,* 69.
78   Bauman, *Liquid*, 11.
79   Jonathan S. Landay "Obama's Drone War Kills 'Others,' Not Just al Qaida Leaders," *mcclatchydc.com* April 9, 2013, https://mcclatchydc.com/news/nation-world/world/article24747826.html
80   David Lyon, "Introduction," *Liquid Surveillance: A Conversation* (Malden, MA: Polity Press, Kindle Version, 2013), 6.
81   Zygmunt Bauman, *Postmodern Ethics* (Cambridge, MA: Blackwell, 1993), 125.
82   Sarah E. Kreps, *Drones: What Everyone Needs to Know* (Oxford: Oxford University Press, 2016), 154.
83   Ibid.
84   Peter W. Singer, *Wired for War: The Robotic Revolution and Conflict in the 21st Century* (New York: Penguin Press, 2009), 396.
85   Zygmunt Bauman, and David Lyon. *Liquid Surveillance: A Conversation* (Malden, MA: Polity Press, Kindle version, 2013), 88.
86   "Air Force: Actions Needed to Strengthen Unamanned Aerial System Pilots," *United States Government Accountability Office*, April 2014: 23–5.
87   Elijah Solomon Hurwitz, "Drone Pilots: 'Overworked, Underpaid, Bored.'" *motherjones.com* June 18, 2013, http://motherjones.com/politics/2013/06/drone-pilots-reaper-photo-essay
88   Mark Bowden, "The Killing Machines: How to Think about Drones." *theatlantic.com* August 13, 2013, http://theatlantic.com/magazine/archive/2013/09/the-killing-machines-how-to-think-about-drones/309434/?single_page=true
89   Seth Davin Norrholm, Jessica L. Maples-Keller, Barbara O. Rothbaum, and Chad C. Tossell, "Remote Warfare with Intimate Consequences: Psychological Stress in Service Member and Veteran Remotely-Piloted Aircraft (RPA) Personnel," *Journal of Mental Health and Clinical Psychology*, mentalhealthjournal.org, December 21, 2023, https://mentalhealthjournal.org/articles/remote-warfare-with-intimate-consequences-psychological-stress-in-service-member-and-veteran-remotely-piloted-aircraft-rpa-personnel.html#:~:text=The%20potential%20psychological%20consequences%20of,or%20burnout%2C%20and%20disturbed%20sleep; Rajiv Kumar Saini, MSVK Raju, and Amit Chail, "Cry in the Sky" Psychological Impact on Drone Operators," *Industrial Psychiatry Journal* 30 (1), October 22, 2021, https://pmc.ncbi.nlm.nih.gov/articles/PMC8611566/
90   Ibid.
91   Steve Mann, "Sousveillance: Inverse Surveillance in Multimedia Imaging," *Multimedia '04: Proceedings of the 12th Annual ACM International Conference on Multimedia*," October 10, 2004, 620.
92   Ibid.
93   Steve Mann, Jason Nolan, and Barry Wellman, "Sousveillance: Inventing and Using Wearable Computing Devices for Data Collection in Surveillance Environments," *Surveillance and Society* 1, no. 3 (2003): 333.
94   Ibid.
95   Mann, "Sousveillance: Inverse Surveillance," 620.
96   James Bridle, "Watching the Watchers," *jamesbridle.com*, accessed January 27, 2025, https://jamesbridle.com/works/watching-the-watchers
97   Austin Choi-Fitzpatrick, "Resist!: Resisting Technology and the Technology of Resistance," *The Good Drone: How Social Movements Democratize Surveillance*,

thegooddrone.mitpress.mitedu, MIT Press, 2022, https://thegooddrone.mitpress.mit.edu/pub/ttjs9hf3/release/1
98 Mann, "Sousveillance: Inverse Surveillance," 620.
99 Rita Raley, *Tactical Media* (Minneapolis: University of Minnesota Press, 2009), 1.
100 Ibid., 6.
101 Stahl and Kaempf, 337.
102 Ibid., 341.
103 Ibid., 349.
104 Jill Walker Rettberg, *Machine Vision: How Algorithms Are Changing the Way We See the World* (Cambridge: Polity Press, 2023), 85–6.
105 Ibid., 118.
106 Ibid., 122.
107 Clark and Enemark, 131.
108 Ibid., 133.
109 Ibid., 135.
110 Simone Natale, *Deceptive Media: Artificial intelligence and Social Life after the Turing Test* (New York: Oxford University Press, 2021), 2.
111 Ibid., 5
112 Ibid., 7.
113 Ibid.
114 Ibid., 8.
115 Ibid.
116 Ibid., 9.
117 Ibid.
118 Christopher Dandeker, *Surveillance, Power, and Modernity: Bureaucracy and the Discipline from 1700 to the Present Day* (New York: St. Martin's Press, 1990), 66.
119 Luke Harding, "Footage Released of Guardian Editors Destroying Snowden Hard Drives." *theguardian.com* January 31, 2014, http://theguardian.com/uk-news/2014/jan/31/footage-released-guardian-editors-snowden-hard-drives-gchq

4 DRONE, BABY, DRONE: TECHNO-NEOCOLONIALISM AND POSTCOLONIAL MEDIATIONS IN NAMWALI SERPELL'S *THE OLD DRIFT*

Post-colonialism. Postcolonialism. Two terms. One with a hyphen, the other without. Namwali Serpell's novel *The Old Drift* (2019) hovers between the two terms, and more: it moves restlessly between and across them, foregrounding the ambivalence of Zambian nationalism, the contingent, chance-prone interactions between the natural world and human habitation, the impact of Information Technology globalization on national governance, the rise of techno-neocolonialism, and the struggle for subaltern self-determination in Zambia. But what do the terms mean? How does *The Old Drift* embody such restless movements, and why?[1]

Generally, the hyphenated term points to the disruption of colonial time, a set of events marking the shift from colonial governance to indigenous rule; the term without a hyphen draws attention to the sociocultural transformations necessary for decolonizing colonial society.[2] Postcolonialism describes the material conditions, which today include the production of global capital, labor, and power, and thus calls into focus neocolonialism.[3] Whereas the post in postcolonial marks a political break, the post in postcolonial describes "alternative times, histories and casualties" that are necessary "to deal with complexities that cannot be served under the single rubric 'post-colonialism.'"[4] Drawing attention to the specificity of European and Indian literary and philosophical genealogies in shaping Postcolonialism as a field of study, some scholars question treating temporal breaks as coterminous with epistemological and sociological breaks, finding

Postcolonial Studies and Theory partially relevant to the study of Africa.[5] Some have found the hesitation to historicize postcolonialism's emergence in the Global North to be naïve, including the field's focus on subjectivity, culture, and obtuse jargon.[6] To others, the postcolonial is concerned not only with delimiting the extension of colonial time but also negating it, undermining it, and transforming it, which involves understanding and resisting how colonial mentalities and social institutions persist in postcolonial time, and how transforming them involves rethinking the provenance of coloniality in the age of globalization and information.[7]

Important as these arguments are, my aim is not to interrogate the field or its relevance to African Studies and Africa but to highlight the range of meanings the terms evoke, and their analytical flexibility to understand the continuities and discontinuities, the overlaps and disjunctions, of coloniality, postcoloniality, globalization, and Information Technology, in order to study *The Old Drift*. The novel ends with catastrophic scenes of a dam break, flooding, devastation, and loss caused by microdrones that use forbidden internet servers and platforms to jam sluice gates; yet, the novel also gestures toward new possibilities for living and cooperative endeavor. In this chapter, I argue that to understand the nature of such digitally mediated subaltern resistance, we must examine the rise of techno-neocolonialism in Zambia: its ongoing, uneven integration into a global field of sociopolitical and economic networks, its histories of nation-formation, its postcolonial challenges of governance, and its negotiation of the digital in the everyday lives of its peoples.

Writing not long after Ghana gained independence, and when many African countries were in the throes of obtaining self-rule, Kwame Nkrumah in *Neo-Colonialism: The Last Stage of Imperialism* cautions about the rise of new modes of domination that build artfully on earlier, colonial modes. He writes, "The essence of neo-colonialism is that the state which is subject to it is, in theory, independent and has all the outward trappings of international sovereignty. In reality its economic system and thus its political policy is directed from outside."[8] He adds that the "mechanisms of neo-colonialism are subtle and varied. They operate not only in the economic field, but also in the political, religious, ideological and cultural spheres."[9] Nkrumah particularly underscores how companies outside Africa set up pan-African alliances with non-Africans in powerful positions; they maintain high interest rates, while the "invisible trade" of financial loans and aid packages requires African governments to collect and hand over data, give exclusive rights of operations, and provide access to mineral-rich sites.[10] Along similar lines, Ella Shohat says that the "'neo-colonial,' like the 'post-colonial' also suggests continuities and discontinuities, but its emphasis is on the new modes and forms of the old colonialist practices, not a 'beyond.'"[11]

Tracing these continuities and discontinuities in the digital age, Ofunmilayo Arewa argues that the impact of Information Technologies on Africa continues colonial legacies in new guises, since "the colonial era overhang, which is pervasive," is "exacerbated" and "limits potential digital developments."[12] Internationally, the Global South continues primarily serving the needs and interests of the Global North, where technological innovation presumably originates, and whose export and implementation in Africa continues a relationship of dependency. David Pilling sums up noting that since "the economic template established by Europeans has proved difficult to shift ... the perennial puzzle of African development in the postcolonial era has been how to break the mould—how to extract Africa from its history of extraction."[13] Similarly, examining humanitarian initiatives that use digital technologies to collect, analyze, and reuse data about the peoples they serve, Mirca Madianou argues that "datafication increasingly serves the logic of efficiency and audit rather than the imperative of humanitarian reform and participation," where "the risks of [digital] experimentation are outsourced to some of the most fragile environments in the world with value extracted for the benefit of stakeholders including private entrepreneurs and large companies."[14] When such dynamics influence humanitarianism, Bhakti Shringarpure posits that cultural and ideological cooptation become endemic. Peoples at a far remove (geographically, culturally, and politically) from sites of suffering become individual entrepreneurs, whose use of digital technologies normalizes a "Digital Savior Complex that foregrounds and reinforces existing colonial hierarchies between the savior and the saved."[15] Hence, techno-neocolonialism describes how such dynamics are possible because of, not despite, deep connections between entries and groups outside *and* inside the country. In the postcolonial state, it is elites and native power players who manage its institutions, but in terms of identity and agency, there is a discernable shift from colonial powers and foreigners to the indigenous.

Moreover, as Arewa points out, the lack of governance transparency in many African countries compounds public corruption, further marginalizing many groups of peoples. Geared primarily to serve interests external to Africa of the majorly Western-based IT companies, IT is not adapted to local needs. Rather, it is integrated in ways that perpetuate weak indigenous or local participation, making Africa the site for extractive labor, inconducive to generating a skilled workforce that can shape the digital economy for mutual benefit. Instead, by and large in Africa, we see the "exclusion and marginalization" of people when states are "undertaking law and policy."[16]

Drawing from Nkrumah, Shohat, Arewa, Madianou, and Shringapure's points about economic networks using African labor and resources often at the expense of governance transparency, accountability, and equitable distribution of gains, in this paper I discuss how new iterations of colonialist socioeconomic logics in postcoloniality are evident in Zambia's negotiation of the networked economy of the digital age. I argue that the novel dramatizes techno-neocolonialism as the nexus of Information Technology, government agencies, and international businesses that generates conditions of subalternity for peoples deemed as threats or superfluous to the political and economic order sustained by the postcolonial state. Techno-neocolonialism concentrates political and economic power within oligarchic groups that use the police, big business, the military, and government entities to forge close connections with global and local Information Technology companies, their allies, affiliates, and beneficiaries, to co-opt or silence popular dissent and protest movements.

To understand the relationship of subaltern resistance to techno-neocolonialism, a resistance that leads to a catastrophic, yet hopeful, ending in the novel, driven in large measure by digitally mediated platforms, underground communications, and automated, remotely controlled drones, we need to study the entwinning of the novel's themes and forms, namely, how Frantz Fanon's idea of the Manichean logic of coloniality extends into postcolonial Zambia, and W. E. B. DuBois's "double consciousness" influences the psychology of the main characters, and their interactions with others, Zambian culture, and African history. *The Old Drift* embodies Namwali Serpell's ideas of colonialism and postcolonialism as unstable descriptors requiring an imaginative retelling of Zambian national history, an alternate centering of marginalized figures, and an assessing of the politics of dissent and revolution in a society saturated with digital technologies. Thus, to understand the climactic events that end the novel, we must examine how its multilayered narratives explore the paradoxes of coloniality and postcoloniality, the gendered nature of double consciousness that shapes character interactions, and the pervasive digital culture of contemporary Zambia that influences the nature of and possibilities of subaltern resistance.

Coloniality/Postcoloniality

The Old Drift begins in colonial time and continues into a postcolonial future. It weaves African macrohistories with Zambian microhistories: in 1855, David Livingstone, the Scottish missionary explores Zambia and tracks the Zambezi River; in 1903, Percy M. Clark journeys into North-Western Rhodesia to join the Old Drift, a colonial settlement; North-eastern Rhodesia merges with North-western Rhodesia to become Northern Rhodesia, a British protectorate in the 1920s; Cecil Rhodes and the British South Africa Company become the British Empire's representatives; Italy extends its empire into Africa; Sir Stewart Gore-Browne creates Shiwa Ngandu, as a model estate; in the 1950s, Alice Lenshina Mulenga leads the Lumpa Church; in the next decade the church clashes with Kenneth Kaunda's United National Independence Party, resulting in several hundred church members dying; Italian companies build the Kariba Dam in the late 1950s; in 1964, Zambia becomes an independent country, with Kenneth David Kaunda as President; in the 1960s, Edward Mukuka Nkoloso sets up the Zambia

National Academy of Science, Space Research, and Philosophy, and cadet Matha Mwamba becomes its iconic star; AIDS ravages Zambia in the 1990s; international efforts for a vaccine ensue; China becomes an economic presence in the late 1990s; with the rise of the Internet, social media and online technologies acquire rapid social and governmental use in Zambia; in the novel, Digital-All Beads and drones are used for research and surveillance; the SOTP protests at Kalingalinga; the subalterns use microdrones to jam the sluice gates of the Kariba Dam, leading to its implosion; a flood overwhelms the region; a new post postcolonial entity comes into existence, Lusaka, a city-state, with Kalingalinga as its capital.

These historical and fictional events and peoples become not a picturesque backdrop against which the novel narrates its stories; rather, they provide psychological and intellectual fodder for various character interactions, particularly their modes of self-fashioning. In their interactions and self-perceptions, the novel's African, Indian, British, and Italian families marked by racial, ethnic, linguistic, historical, and geographical difference—foreground Zambian colonial and postcolonial history as a cross-cultural, cross-racial, and trans-geographical phenomenon. Annah Omune Sidigu's characterization of the novel as a "triumphant and tragic retelling of the country's birth and a sage forecast of what the future might hold for Zambia" underlines how the novel's revision of colonial history becomes a postcolonial act of imaginative contestation. It is this imaginative contestation, which involves both a revisiting of colonial historical settings and a revising of colonial values and practices that endows *The Old Drift* with its author's unique approach to postcolonialism.

Decolonization and the Law of the Flaw

Drawing from his experience as a psychiatrist during the French-Algerian War (1954–1962), Frantz Fanon in *The Wretched of the Earth* (1963) argues that because colonialism is founded on physical and psychological violence, decolonization necessarily involves physical and psychological force. Fanon places violence at the heart of decolonization: "Decolonization, which sets out to change the order of the world, is, obviously, a program of complete disorder" (36);[17] because "decolonization is quite simply the replacing of a certain 'species' of men by another 'species' of men ... decolonization is always a violent phenomenon"[18] (35). The colonized peoples are dislocated, fenced in, brutalized, enslaved, and robbed of their histories, cultures, and languages. "The colonial world," observes Fanon, "is a Manichean world."[19] Colonialism organizes society into cultural, political, economic, and geographic binaries. "The colonial world is a world cut into two. The dividing line, the frontiers are shown by barracks and police stations ... It is obvious here that the agents of government speak the language of pure force."[20]

Jean-Paul Sartre writes in his Preface, "Violence in the colonies does not only have for its aim the keeping of these enslaved men at arm's length; it seems to dehumanize them. Everything will be done to wipe out their traditions, to substitute our language for theirs and to destroy their culture without giving them ours. Sheer physical fatigue will stupefy them ... the result, neither man nor animal, is the native."[21] Consequently, Fanon argues, "On the logical plane, the Manicheanism of the settler produces a Manicheanism of the native. To the history of the 'absolute evil of the native,' the theory of the 'absolute evil of the settler' replies."[22] Thus, violence becomes a mode of liberation, a force to galvanize national consciousness. About Zambia, specifically, Andrew Sardanis observes, "The towns were divided into European areas, African areas and Indian areas; they had separate housing, shopping, schools, churches and all other social activities," which echoes Fanon's notion of Manichean exclusivity.[23]

The Old Drift acknowledges the Manichean nature of Zambian coloniality but, nevertheless, refrains from privileging it as the primary lens for forging anti-colonial resistance. In this context, it is worth noting that Serpell views *The Old Drift* as a Zambian novel, concerned primarily with Zambian history and society, although her own life of migration and relocation in the Global North, or United States, positions her in the group of writers outside Africa writing about Africa.[24] Serpell comments, "I could say that, first, this is not a Zambian-American novel. This is a Zambian novel ... I am sort of in the middle. I'm a mixed-race Zambian, I'm very nomadic in my family, and my novel is very much about cultural syncretism, about the missing and mingling of cultures."[25] About her multiracial heritage, Serpell says, "I wanted to subvert expectations of what it means to be African. So the idea of 'being Zambian' gets contested at various points in the novel ... to be Zambian is a very complicated term, one I wanted to throw into contestation."[26]

The discursive space between the insider position of the novel and the outsider position of the writer generates a liminality that, to Serpell, marks the space of colonial and postcolonial border crossings; in these spaces colonial binaries lose their self-evident nature, showing that the boundaries of their Manichean politics frequently overlap, complicating ideas of origin, authenticity, identity, and representation. Moreover, to Serpell, for all of colonialism's ideological animus and Enlightenment-based rationality, the role of accidents and chance in the give and take of ordinary interactions that make up human life has just as much power to determine the course of empires and nations.

The "mosquito asides," short sections in italicized prose interspaced throughout the novel and functioning as a dramatic device in the manner of a Greek chorus, give us a panoramic view of African history. Sprinkled with onomatopoetic expressions, proverb-like statements, mockery, and satire, the asides, in which the mosquitoes acquire characterological standing, dive into the archives of African cultural history to introduce chapters, plots, characters, ideologies, dramatic settings, historical events, and speculative philosophy. The mosquitoes signify the deep relationships of human beings and the natural environment; they symbolize the power of place and its myriad natural spaces in which plant, insect, and animal life influence and are in turn influenced by human life. In the first of these asides and in the first chapter of the novel, we see contingency and happenstance shaping the future of global empires.

Agency, Chance, Contingency

It is 1903, and the explorer Percy M. Clark carves his name on a baobab tree. He is looking for the Old Drift, a settler community a few miles from Victoria Falls, also called Mosi-oa-Tunya, "The Smoke That Thunders," in Kololo, or the Lozi language of Zambia. Clark narrates an event that takes place in a hotel dining room. Stricken with fever, yet eager to socialize in the hotel bar, Clark picks up random conversations and observes Pietro Gavuzzi, from Piedmont, Northwestern Italy, amble into the room with his British wife, Ada, and their five-year-old daughter, Lina. As a prank, Clark grabs Gavuzzi's hat, only to realize his palm gets filled with both the hat and Gavuzzi's hair, eliciting a shocked reaction from the prankster. As Ada lunges forward to her husband, Lina "shriek[s] with fury," striking a native who walks by with a tray, turning him into a person who "was never right in the head again. He be[comes] an imbecile, forever smiling at the daisies."[27]

Ordinary as this event might seem, it sets the conceptual framework for Serpell's views on colonial power and postcolonial resistance. The people involved are from Britain, Italy, and Zambia, interacting in the bar of a dingy hotel room at the Old Drift. The juvenile, drink-fueled banter and prank foreground the contingency of the colonial encounter. Whereas Clark and Gavuzzi's interaction is comic, Lina's action is accidental, devoid of premeditation and colonial impulse. That it takes place during the early phases of European colonial adventurism in Africa cannot be gainsaid. However, ascribing causality to mundane activities in colonial society overprivileges premeditation and rationality. What follows in the rest of the novel is the intergenerational saga of three families, whose members hail from Zambia, Britain, Italy, and India, and each of whom has a different understanding of empire and its discontents, each showing diverse inclinations for empire, imperial power, economic despoil, social advancement, anti-colonial violence, and civil disobedience.

Highlighting this specific instance in the novel, Serpell observes, "This sort of thing happens throughout the novel. Everyone's responsibility for any particular complication is always mitigated. Agency emerges in relation rather than as something we each possess deep inside of us (like 'I did something wrong'). It's very rare in the novel where someone actively does something wrong to someone else. Most of the time, there's some set of contingencies that draw people into some kind of collision."[28] Serpell's ideas of colonial and postcolonial contingency and relationality are manifest as a novelistic device that enables the narrator, the author, and the characters to envision counterfactual histories. In key sections of the novel, the characters engage in creating imagined doubles; they speculate on adopting other personas, which are not only designed to empathize with them but to view their own specific conditions with other eyes. It is a form of what W. E. B. Du Bois called "double consciousness," which is "a peculiar sensation ... this sense of always looking at one's self through the eyes of others, of measuring one's soul by the tape of a world that looks on in amused contempt and pity"[29].

But in *The Old Drift*, double consciousness is initiated through the novel's authorial voice and by the characters themselves, not to evaluate their thoughts or actions according to external prescriptions only, which does happen, but to reflect on their and others' material and psychosocial conditions, and to read against the grain of their interpretations, and their notions of national, familial, and individual history. These moments in the novel presage the final climax at the end when Joseph, Jacob, and Naila foment a public protest that includes jamming the Kariba Dam gates with microdrones, resulting in a cataclysmic fallout for the peoples—Lusaka, and Zambia.

Floods, dam breaks, miscalculation, swerving, error, chance, fever, contingency, mosquito bites, misunderstandings, disorientation, biodiversity, and ecoregions all shape human endeavors, just as much as ideology, science, and rationality. In *The Old Drift*, colonialism and its resistances have complex dimensions, and they are manifest in motivated acts of control and violent exploitation, and in quotidian interactions among colonizers and the colonized in specific bioregions where natural flows, climatic conditions, and the flora and fauna profoundly shape the trajectory of colonialism, conditions of postcoloniality, and modalities for subaltern resistance. *The Old Drift*'s impetus to rewrite Zambian history involves generating a postcolonial diffusionist historical fiction in which Zambian national history is freighted with double consciousness: the search for origins leads to diffusion, to many other points of reference that haunt national icons and myths. Notwithstanding the novel's sharp critique of David Livingstone's role as a foreign explorer bringing civilization to Africa, it does not cancel him or, in a Manichean gesture of revision, replace him with a Zambian icon, or view him through the single lens of anti-colonialist ideology.

Founding Narratives / Ambivalent Legacies

The first mosquito aside of the novel begins with David Livingstone's entry into Africa, and his naming of Mosi-oa-Tunya, "The Smoke Which Thunders," as Victoria Falls, in honor of the Queen. Decades later, at the turn of the century,

Cecil Rhodes and his British South Africa Company would extend imperial economic interests for natural resources in Rhodesia, which would become Zambia and Zimbabwe. Livingstone's death due to malaria, his burial in Zambia, and the transportation of his remains by his close African associates along a long, torturous path back to the coast, and eventually to England, as a gesture of honoring the explorer and missionary, becomes an important event in shaping the reach and import of the British Empire, and, more to the point, its cultural meanings, often varied and contradictory, extending into the next two centuries.[30]

Despite a dismal record of native conversion, Livingstone's dual focus on spreading Christianity with commercial enterprise often meant undermining both British and Arab slave trading. To Livingstone, opposing slavery ideologically was not enough; undermining its commercial stakes by setting up alternate commercial activity would lead to greater self-sufficiency, thus making slavery as an economic institution less rewarding, less viable: "If Christian missionaries and Christian merchants can remain in the interior of the continent, the slave trader will be driven out of the market."[31] That in 2020, of Zambia's 17.4 million population, 95.5 percent are Christians speaks to the enduring legacy of European missionary reach.[32] Ted Olsen points out, "Like Livingstone, these missionaries didn't consider themselves only preachers of the World. They founded institutions like hospital and industrial training centers. They also established schools, which educated generations of Zambians—including Kenneth Kaunda, who became the country's first president in 1965."[33] In the contemporary moment, "the sheer diversity of churches suggests that, far from a singular evangelical movement coming to dominate Zambian theological practice and political culture, this proliferation reflects the fecundity of religious belief and the relative pluralism of views regarding the appropriate relationship between religious belief and political culture."[34]

The infusion of modernity in Zambia is inextricably bound up with colonialism. While a vicious colonial ideology cognized the natives as the Other without reason and feeling, what comes across here is a notion of civilization that is about literacy and the application of rationality to social organization, which is modernity's central enterprise.[35] Colonial and postcolonial Zambia are the products of a deep entwining of modernity, Christian missions, and European Empire.

A strictly Manichean paradigm that overturns the legacy of European Christian missions in Zambia will necessarily mean rejecting Zambia as it emerged and currently exists, socially, politically, and historically. The novel's mosquitoes recognize this well, because they caution that where there is the desire to seek an authentic or pure "origin, you find a vast babble which is also a silence: a chasm of smoke, thundering. Blind mouth!"[36] The metaphor packs the punch of contradiction: the plurality of babble when contracted into singularity to claim origin leads to silence. What matters is to understand and negotiate Zambia's "chasm of smoke, thundering," its entangled history, and intercontinental drift of colonial and postcolonial energies.

Livingstone's death due to malaria, a mosquito-borne disease, underscores the power of the natural world to interfere with human initiatives. And to be sure, this story is narrated by the mosquitoes, whose choral interruptions and asides frame the entire novel. This passage emphasizes it well:

> Men never believe chance can wreak great consequence. Yet the story of this place is full of such slips. Error, n., from the Latin errare: to stray or to veer or to wander ... Neither Oriental nor Occidental, but accidental is this nation ... Where you sought an origin, you find a vast babble which is also a silence: a chasm of smoke, thundering. Blind mouth![37]

Citing the mosquito aside, Serpell comments, "So the mosquitoes talk about the etymology of 'error.' It's 'to stray' or 'to wander.' So error as this kind of overarching principle is being investigated and explored through the way the characters interact with each other over time. Zambia comes into being as an accidental nation and is following this—they call it 'the law of the flaw,' which is the tendency to swerve away from a straight and narrow path and to be in this constant state of drift."[38]

Decades later, in the middle of the following century, Livingstone's legacy drifts; it meanders into colonial Zambian society, transformed into a new register in the rise of Edward Mukuka Nkoloso, an anti-colonial leader. Nkoloso's, at times, outlandish scientific experiments betray not what might initially seem to be a capacity for mixing up sound projects with half-baked prototypes but rather a tenacious postcolonial hope that colonized peoples are capable of rationality and scientific vision. Nkoloso dreams of nothing less than beating Russia and United States to the punch, by sending Zambian Afronauts to the moon. At the height of the space race in the 1960s, Nkoloso set up the National Academy of Science, Space Research and Philosophy, to train young Zambians for space exploration. On the internet are videos with archival footage showing his training programs and snippets of interviews, where his responses to questions about science, technology, and Zambian education sound like a mix of sincerity, comedy, and parody.

But *The Old Drift* shows another side of Nkoloso: one possessed of magnetic charisma; one recruited to fight for the British in the Second World War; one who becomes a teacher; one who seeks to reopen a school shut down by the authorities; one who fights for labor rights and multiracial schools; one who becomes president of a district of the African National Congress. For standing up against settler and native tribal collaborators, Nkoloso was arrested and allegedly suffered extreme physical punishment, resulting in odd public behavior periodically. He also gained the attention and favor of a rising politician, Kenneth David Kaunda, who would go on to become independent Zambia's first president in 1964. The attack against

Lilian Margaret Brown in 1960, resulting in her death, was partly the result of activists and educators involved with Nkoloso. The space program functioned as a cover to enable Nkoloso and other Zambian anti-colonial agitators to provide aid to rebel groups in neighboring colonized regions. According to reliable sources, the penchant he developed later in life for extravagant claims and projects were likely the result of suffering imprisonment and torture.[39]

Nkoloso's commitment to the space program and abiding interest in the cadets' success include teaching Matha Mwamba "how to drive a car, fix an engine, and put together a circuit board with a handful of wires and an old battery."[40] When Nkoloso speaks to local and foreign reporters, who respond with curiosity and amusement, Matha sees something else: "[She] had heard all this before, the way Ba Nkoloso blended together science and fable, African technology and Western philosophy. It confused others, but she had learned to see the world through his double vision. It was as natural to her now as the air through which she was swinging."[41] Eschewing the desire to replace the one with the other, the mosquitoes connect Nkoloso to Livingstone: "If Livingstone was our white father, Nkoloso was our black prince—Bemba royalty they say. Equally smart, just as possessed, abrim with the will to explore … There is no way to tell, but as flyers ourselves, we claim him as one of our own. Makuka Nkoloso, the ultimate bug—needler of conventions and rules."[42]

Matha and the mosquitoes understand that Nkoloso's "double vision" is about educating the new generation, inspiring them to become self-reliant, to take their place in Zambian society as leaders and scientists. It is, also, a social and institutional space for activists and political leaders to spur anti-colonial rebellion within Africa. Nkoloso, like Livingstone, is a figure of doubleness generating a multifocal vision of colonial history and postcolonial culture where the binaries of colonizer and colonized cannot erase the profoundly transformative processes of give-and-take between Africa and Britain, between Africa and the world. In the postcolonial vision of *The Old Drift*, contesting empire does not come in the postcolonial period *after* independence; instead, empire's contradictions and paradoxes continue, in different political and cultural registers, in postcoloniality.

Nation, Gender, Postcoloniality

The doubleness of history and identity takes a different turn in the life of Matha Mwamba, the star Afronaut. In a long passage in the novel, we see Matha experience a moment of dissociation from herself, in which she reimagines the events affecting her. In this moment, her reimagination takes the form not of an alternate possibility, or another perspective, but as a reversal of a life-defining act. The passage reads thus:

She dreamed of a messy mass of blood slipping back inside her with a suction sound. A thick cord ravelled into tight loops. A baby clambered up feet first, bestowing weight and tightness to her belly. Her swollen breasts ebbed, their milky tide receded. Tears travelled up her cheek, trickling into her eye ducts. There was a gradual, deep unwrenching. Then streams of pleasure surged together, imploding with a swallowing action. She hiccupped a moan as sperm sprang back into a penis, which withdrew from her and deflated. A pair of hands left her cheek. A pair of lips drew away. Matha saw him clearly. Godfrey. Those lips as plump as her tomatoes, the keloid on his neck as thin-skinned, his tightcurled lashes like the tendrils on their stems. "Comrade," he whispered and vanished into the dark.[43]

The baby she had delivered is Sylvia; the father is Godfrey Mwango, her fellow cadet, a star like her in the space program. However, this moment happens after Matha learns that Sylvia has been kidnapped by her Aunt Grace who "had more than once thought about rescuing the child."[44] Because Matha has a sexual encounter with Godfrey, a fellow cadet, and becomes pregnant, she crosses two social strictures: the gendered expectation that a woman like her should not be sexually active, and that her pregnancy meant losing her status as the star cadet in the space program. Matha is shunned by her family. Fearful, distraught, and helpless, Matha yields to her sorrow, earning a reputation as the Crying Woman of Kalingalinga. Aunt Grace views Matha's emotional breakdown as postpartum depression, thinking it is "excessive and premature."[45] Matha becomes part of The Weepers, women who gather together and moan publicly and privately together. Their travails include "a philandering husband. A stillborn baby. An abusive brother. But Mrs. Zulu did not care to hear why the women were sad and they did not dare share. As if they were a neverending funeral, they just gathered together to sit in the yard outside Matha's home and cry all day long, their sobs beating through the air."[46] So intense is their humiliation that the women "did not dare share," because sharing would invite further opprobrium; the pressure to maintain silence means becoming overcome with feelings of loss and hopelessness, and generating loud lamentations, a form of non-textual, affective communication among themselves and with others.

What Matha's family, friends, and community members fail to understand about the consequences of transgressing social norms as a woman is that some of them are deeply invested in sustaining the norms Martha crosses. For instance, "To her father, Matha's pregnancy meant that her prospects for marriage and employment, not to mention life on heaven and earth, were ruined … He had already slotted the news about her into an old story. The story went like this: no matter who the world shifts to accommodate her, this kind of woman finds a way to disturb the peace. This kind of woman is the *nganga* that sits at the top of the stream, kicking her feet to make it roil."[47] Making matters worse is her hero Nkoloso's response to her pregnancy, wherein he chastises her: "'You? Here?' he laughed bitterly. 'This is revolutionary business, Matha. Serious business. Not for girls who cannot keep their ... ' He broke off."[48] Shunned by her family and driven into poverty, Matha finds Nkoloso's words particularly depressing, as "she felt like she was hearing his real voice for the very first time. She divined the store of disappointment inside it, like a cave hidden by a waterfall."[49]

Lying semi-clothed on mats, readying to give birth, on hearing others calling her and the baby inside her witches, Matha feels "as hollow as this empty room, her thought eddying around like smoke."[50] Learning about her daughter's disappearance elicits, to Matha's dismay, feelings of relief, not anxiety: "Sylvia had always been a reminder of everything that Matha had lost. Every day, she woke up, felt her daughter's small squirming body beside her, remembered, and despaired ... when she found the girl missing, there had been another feeling—a flash of relief that, for once, there was no skin pressed up against hers."[51]

Succeeding in Nkoloso's ambitious space program means adhering to gender expectations. Despite impregnating Matha, Godfrey irresponsibly shuns her, leaving her to face her future alone. The contrast between Matha's pursuit of education and innovative social endeavors and her mother Bernadette's relentless pursuit of social justice by supporting Nkoloso's anti-colonial activism is striking, because both pay a heavy price: Matha is left socially and familially abandoned, while Bernadette is arrested and dies in prison. The fact of her mother's untimely demise rattles Matha, because "as a girl, Matha had always seen her mother as an ideal woman—the fury, the industry, the permanent sense of grievance. *This world is not enough* ... But when her mother had clawed at the fence, Matha had grabbed her fingers with pride, clutching the fervor there."[52]

The reality of gender imbalances in Zambian colonial and postcolonial society, and the power of gender ideology to shape professional prospects at tremendous personal and psychological cost, are not lost on Matha, as she recognizes that a core part of her existence as a Zambian is to be a woman: "Matha had never considered that being female would thwart her so, that it would be a hurdle she had to jump every time she wanted to learn something: to read a book, shout the answers, to make a bomb, to love a man, to fight for freedom."[53] Decades later, such enduring concerns led to the formation of the Zambia National Women's Lobby Group (ZNWLG) and the Zambia Women Writers' Association (ZWWA). In 2001, ZNWLG set up the Women in Politics Forum, which met at the Mulungushi International Conference, where they publicly affirmed the Zambia Women's Manifesto, which sought to increase women's participation and representation in various political institutions.[54]

While such political activism is vital for women's empowerment, the psychological effects of a gendered double consciousness become evident when Matha reimagines in a dream her baby's delivery and conception. The dream directly reverses biological and psychological moments. Here we see a sharp instance of DuBois' double consciousness manifest its logical conclusion of radical self-alienation. She experiences "that dawning shock that comes when you look at yourself and see a person you might have pitied."[55] Matha views herself as others view her, as if she has to develop an alter ego, another self, another persona that can constantly check her real self, in order to play by gendered norms. Anti-colonial activism comes freighted with gender ideologies, continuing the marginalization of some women in postcolonial Zambia.

Micro Politics of Self-Fashioning

But to Sylvia, Matha Mwamba's daughter, growing up away from her mother, and into a teen and a young adult comes at personal cost; she drops out of school, takes up with a stranger who becomes a friend, Loveness, and from her learns to walk the night streets to lure customers for her body. As a young woman, Sylvia, desperate to eke out her own life, submits to Mr. Mwape's seduction, which is complicated by the fact that he is her Aunt Cookie's friend. Oddly, as a child, Sylvia, at her aunt's behest, calls Mr. Mwape "daddy," though out of casual formality than anything else. With her artful ways, and often drawing from her own experience of being abused as a girl by her uncle, Loveness becomes a shrewd, calculating woman who teaches Sylvia the arts of the street trade, albeit with strong reservations about not compromising their dream of attaining a middle-class lifestyle. Often mistaking her friend's caveats for jealousy, Sylvia ends up befriending a Danish-Dutchman, who beds her. As the man exerts himself on her, Sylvia closes her eyes, imagining an alternate situation: "When he finally put his thing inside her, it hurt but not as much as Loveness had said it would. Sylvia turned her head away from his astringent breath, wondering whether sex had been painful for Loveness when her uncle had first 'started' her. She closed her eyes and tried to picture the big fat man bouncing on top of the skinny title girl – Loveness before she was Loveness."[56]

But this seemingly empathetic gesture by Sylvia to imagine what her friend Loveness experienced in being used by her uncle is also driven by Sylvia's misguided jealousy that Loveness was not helping her become successful in their secret trade. As the man pushes himself off her body, having exhausted himself on her, they both light up cigarettes. Sylvia at this point moves a step further, from empathy to temporarily adopting her friend's identity: "She felt a double feeling: she missed her friend and she hated her friend."[57] When the man asks Sylvia her name, she says "Loveness," making complete her adoption of another persona—that of her close friend—to make sense of her own desperate attempts at self-sufficiency, glamor, and identity. That the women later end up setting up salon, whose business picks up well, testifies to their ability to make their patrons support them.

In this instance, Sylvia's double consciousness involves attempting to experience Loveness's life as a suave, successful professional of the trade. Such is her desperation to advance socially in the profession they have chosen that when Sylvia experiences for the first time a sexual encounter with an ideal patron, she feels let down. Sexual pleasure, if "sweetness" can be interpreted thus, comes as if her body has an afterthought following the act, because "the exact center of her body was ringing with a stinging, smarting sweetness."[58] Her excessive preoccupation with becoming like Loveness makes Sylvia lose her own standing as a person. The obsessive desire to emulate her friend turns into an ambivalent emotion of affection and hatred. Where DuBois' double consciousness had a distinct racial dimension, here we see a deeply gendered experience of self-alienation through adopting other personas, to gain professional status in the ancient trade for pleasure that men have long established as a masculine normative.

National Histories / Subaltern Narratives

The multifocal historical vision of Zambian coloniality and postcoloniality that we see in the Livingstone-Nkoloso juxtaposition, the gendering of double consciousness in Matha's pursuit of national pride through space exploration, and Sylvia's mode of self-fashioning through self-objectification lead us to a central concern of *The Old Drift*: revisioning Zambian colonial history by foregrounding geographical difference, ideological fracturing, idiosyncratic agency, unpredictable happenstance, and contingent macro politics. To question the nation is to foreground its constructedness, to give voice to that which is marginalized, to give expression to that which is suppressed. Put another way, the novel's postcolonial rewriting of Zambian colonial history brings to the fore subaltern subjects, those left outside the national narrative, those deemed uneasy subjects to be accommodated into the national imaginary.

Zambia's emergence as a nation-state is the product of a troubled history. Its official motto "One Zambia, One Nation" is less an accurate signifier of a stable, homogenous national community finding full expression in a new nation; rather, it is a socially constructed narrative to develop temporal and spatial coherence; it is, to use Homi Bhabha's formulation, "the nation as a narrative strategy— and an apparatus of power," whose attempt to create a common culture is often marked by an ambivalence that cannot fully erase that which is left out of the national narrative.[59] It is this excess, this superfluousness of the nation, that the novel's revisionary retelling seeks to foreground, an effort also evident in the scholarly revisions of Zambian history. Under the British as two entities, North-Eastern Rhodesia and Barotziland-North-Western Rhodesia (the latter a part of Cecil Rhode's British South Africa Company, the BSAC) joined to form Northern

Rhodesia in 1911. In 1924, the BSAC relinquished territorial control to the British colonial office. Decades later, in 1953, a new entity called the Federation of Rhodesia and Nyasaland was created, which included Nyasaland, Northern and Southern Rhodesia. In 1964, out of this group emerged modern-day Zambia, with Nyasaland becoming Malawi, an independent country, later a republic. For the next few decades, Zambia faced secessionist pressures from the region of Barotseland, whose Lozi peoples had a pre-colonial kingdom, was a separate British protectorate, and was facing economic marginalization in the new Zambian nation-state. As early as 1979, the nexus of the state, businesses, and parastatals (private or semi-private entities serving the needs of the state) formed a new, elite social class more interested in globalizing Zambian economy and society.[60]

Moreover, revisionary histories are bringing to light other iconic figures like Harry Nkumbula, whose work with Kenneth Kaunda not only led to extensive organizing for the independence struggle but also resulted in Kaunda's breaking way from the Nkumbula-led Northern Rhodesian African National Congress to form the Zambian African National Congress (ZANC); such developments shed light on rivalries around region, ethnicity, and policy goals among African nationalists, which risk being subsumed by nationalist and, at times, party-led propogandist, discourses of organic unity.[61] The tense relations between the Capricorn African Society and other groups like the ZANC involved differences in emphasis on inter-racial solidarities and political strategies. The relations between the Tonga and Bemba peoples, large ethnic groups among more than seventy other tribes, show rivalries over tribal boundaries and national representation.[62] We see paradoxical attitudes to nationalist struggles in how, for instance, Kalonga Gawa Undi X, of the Chewa peoples of Eastern Zambia, responded to the African National Congress (ANC) and the Zambia African National Congress (ZANC), which presaged the United National Independence Party (UNIP. Concerned about the erasure of local, tribal independence under nationalist parties, the chief countered the autocracy and, at times, dismissiveness of African independence leaders; eventually, after several negotiations, he led the ANC, the ZANC, and UNIP.[63] The Capricorn African Society (1949-63), posits Bizeck Jube Phiri, played a significant role in the struggle for Zambian liberalism; despite being led by a white majority, the organization "was a genuine agent for the propagation of multiracial party politics," while seeking European investments and Western economic and political for Zambian adaptation.[64] These developments continue generating political ruptures and social divisions in postcolonial Zambia.

When the mosquitoes say in their first aside, also a preface to the novel, "Neither Oriental nor Occidental, but accidental is this nation,"[65] they underscore the developmental, fragmentary nature of Zambia's emergence as a colonial entity and postcolonial republic. As Miles Larmer et al. point out, "Zambia is, more than most African nation-states, an entity that was imagined and constructed from without. Northern Rhodesia represented the colonial leftovers from the

European scramble, its borders defined by prior and more sought-after claims to the territories to its south, east, west and north."[66] Central to postcolonial Zambia, then, was the national effort to cultivate and sustain the new republic's official motto, "One Zambia, One Nation." Right from the beginning of the novel, Zambia as a unified nation with a unitary history becomes suspect, which later develops into a pungent critique of the Zambian's state's neocolonial measures to apply twenty-first-century technologies to undemocratically surveil and manage its population. This leads us to consider the rise of digital culture in Zambia.

Zambia and the Rise of Digital Culture

Born in the late 1990s, the three protagonists—Naila, Joseph, and Jacob—grow up in the Internet age. As young adults, they, like many in Zambia, the novel's Zambia, that is, are constantly exposed to global music, culture, and ideas; they develop a cosmopolitan sensibility attuned to cross-cultural and cross-racial relationships. A school dropout learning to find his way in the world, Jacob joins Solo and Pepa, orphans, to rummage through discarded heaps of electronic trash and, through creative enterprise, run an underground urban economy to barter and sell antiques, hand me downs, and improvised machines.

Such is Jacob's natural ingenuity that by teaching himself the basis of electrical engineering shortcuts online and, with his grandmother's help, Matha, he builds a drone helicopter, the Moskeetoze. His technical reputation catching the eye of the General in charge of the Lusaka City Airport where he runs a secret economy by surreptitiously pilfering freight from planes, Jacob's drone technology transfers, under duress, to the General. But initial plans change, as "they were more interested in surveillance drone than delivery drones now."[67] Not long thereafter, Naila, Joseph, and Jacob organize protests against the government. There are four issues that need explication here: the impact of the Internet; the AIDS crisis in Zambia; the entrepreneurial spirts of digital culture that bends hierarchies and institutional systems; and the nature of subaltern resistance in the contingent modality of the hive, the swarm, which dramatizes Serpell's views on agency and power in postcolonial Zambia.

The rise of the Internet in the 1990s led to an explosion of information and communication across the world, with the result that three decades later, almost all sectors of human life are being radically reconfigured. Space and time have compressed dramatically, as social media technologies enable the production and circulation of information in various modalities. Global figures for October 2024 show 5.52 billion internet users, and in 2022 show 3.96 billion active on social media.[68] In 2019, figures show that Facebook had 2.4 billion users, while YouTube and WhatsApp each had 1 billion users. From zero mobile service subscriptions in

1980, Zambia registered, in 2013, 10.40 million subscriptions, a remarkable growth in the use of mobile devices and internet use.[69] A major difference between North American and African countries in internet use is mobile services and devices:

> Due to low infrastructure and financial restraints, many emerging digital markets skipped the desktop internet phase entirely and moved straight onto mobile internet via smartphone and tablet devices. India is a prime example of a market with a significant mobile-first online population. Other countries with a significant share of mobile internet traffic include Nigeria, Ghana and Kenya. In most African markets, mobile accounts for more than half the web traffic. By contrast, mobile only makes up around 48 percent of online traffic in the United States.[70]

As Esteban Ortiz-Ospina observes, "Social media has changed the world. The rapid and vast adoption of these technologies is changing how we find partners, how we access information from the news, and how we organize to demand political change."[71] It is in these contexts that the millennial generation of *The Old Drift*, those born at the turn of the millennium marked by the rise of the Internet, is used to Digit-All Beads; functioning like mobile devices, akin to smart phones, they can be implanted in fingers. The Beads are used by the government to send information about voting, credit cards, payments, including communicating with government officials.

Techno-Neocolonialism and Subaltern Resistance

The microdrone that Jacob and Matha design and prototype is the product of technological breakthroughs whose pioneering days included military innovation from the middle of the nineteenth century, to the First and Second World Wars, and later, after 9/11, in the US-Iraq War. Drones, known as UAVs (Unmanned Aerial Vehicles), can be operated remotely by pilots stationed thousands of miles away. When equipped with live ammunition, armed drones can become lethal weapons of war. Due to their sophisticated capacity, reliability, and design, the Global Hawk, the Predator, and the Reaper have become global symbols of warfare in the twenty-first century.[72]

Out of Sight, Out of Mind presents a visually arresting interactive presentation about drones as predatory military technologies.[73] It showcases drone strikes in Pakistan from 2004–15 that caused more than 3,000 casualties, including innocent men, women, and children; that it was during President Barack Obama's presidency that drone warfare was finessed underscores the irony of symbolic diversity and the material and political effects of power. Of late, Africa has become a crucial node in the drone warfare network, as the United States, in partnership with Niger, is setting up a vast drone base in Agadez, Niger. Air Base 201 is "the largest construction project that Air Force engineers had ever undertaken," costing $110 million; it involves building, on 2,200 acres, "a runway more than 6,800 feet long and 150 feet wide," particularly for the MQ-9 Reaper drone and large C-17 cargo aircraft. The goal is to "turn Air Base 201 completely over to the Nigerien military," which shows the close partnerships of American and Nigerien governments to establish a drone base with Pan-African capability, the other drone base, smaller than Niger's, being located in East Africa in Djibouti.[74]

Not often taken seriously is the use of drones by non-state actors, or violent non-state actors (VNSA). There are fifty-seven groups spread across the world who can be categorized as VNSAs, some of whom use drones, because, note Kerry Chávez and Ori Swed, "civilian UAVs are cheap, largely unregulated, and user-friendly, making them feasible for terrorist groups. In fact, because of these traits even advanced militaries have begun deploying civilian drones for tactical missions at the platoon level. As a result, VNSAs have, are, and increasingly will use commercial and hobbyist drones for propaganda; intelligence, surveillance, and reconnaissance (ISR); command and control; and weaponized attacks."[75] In *The Old Drift*, the use of non-militarized drones by activists has to be contextualized, not dismissed as the actions of a terror-inducing group hell-bent on killing people indiscriminately.

When, in the novel, the General takes Jacob's drone designs and uses them to create a swarm of microdrones with which to forcefully overwhelm and puncture people's skin to vaccinate them, when they gather to protest government highhandedness, we see complex military technology used by police departments and the military against their own people within their country. The hunt for global terrorists with armed drones transforms into the management of citizens and inhabitants of a town, city, and country for governments to exercise their power. Crucial to the efficacy of drones is surveillance. Without the ability to generate images and video feeds of what the drone cameras see, the technology loses its lethality. Put another way, the General's use of microdrones for forceful vaccination necessitates constant surveillance of the people; the surveillant gaze of the drone is an extension of the state's seemingly benevolent eye. The more it sees, the more it seeks to intrude in the private affairs of peoples.[76]

What makes armed drones formidable technologies is their conjoining multiple digitally operable systems: hardware and software for remote, semi-autonomous ability to take off, hover, and land in various, especially hard to reach, spaces; the ability to carry lasers, guns, and short and long-range missiles; and the cameras, lenses, and gyroscopes needed to surveil an area or people by producing millions of bytes of information that can be endlessly visualized in loops, distributed and digitally scanned.

While there are certain benefits to drone warfare, like less reliance on troops on the ground, less logistical support to set up infrastructure outside the country to support armed forces, and so on, it cannot be gainsaid that drone warfare is fundamentally changing notions of war and peace. With drones, a nation can be officially not at war, yet for years lob missiles into another country's territory, while justifying such acts in the name of maintaining peace.[77] Endless war becomes de facto. Peace is continually produced in a perpetual state of emergency. Governments concentrate power. Big Tech, lobbyists, aviation companies, defense contractors, military generals, and politicians form formal and informal networks to further their interests, often to the detriment of the peoples they represent, and those who give them power over their lives. Moreover, the vexed relations between the state and civil society further undermine governance, generating mistrust among the people, because "the state had been known to use underhanded methods to reconquer the political arena and criminalize dissent, as if control of a country's government was a birthright for the ruling elites."[78]

In the novel, the Digit-All Bead program is controlled by the government, whose interest in generating and collecting user data is not subject to checks and institutional reviews. The beading system is so invasive, observes Naila, that people cannot "deactivate them" because "it's the perfect system to monitor us, to force compliance," leading Jacob to note that the miners in the Copperbelt, to resist intrusion, had no choice but to lob off their fingertips where the beads are implanted.[79] Such a fusion of the human body with digital technology radically alters the relationship between the state and the people: democratic resistance is possible only through bodily disfigurement, not only protests, sit-ins, civil disobedience, and so on. Such a substantive realignment of social power is possible because, as Thomas Streinz notes, the rhetoric of creative technological innovation obscures the need to ask questions about the ethics and politics of information technologies. Indiscriminate data collection becomes the norm against which rights and responsibilities are accorded, and law and policy are written and implemented. This is "the power to datafy," which is "another dimension of data inequality," says Streinz, especially when the distribution and assessment of data is non-transparent and inaccessible to the people.[80] As an intelligence analyst of the National Geospatial-Intelligence Agency comments, "We're soon moving to a point where we think, essentially, every part of the planet will be imaged on a daily basis. As so we also then look at all that data coming in, and we struggle, and we think about the opportunity, though, with how to handle all of that data."[81] When technology is fetishized, the ethics of its social, economic, and political uses become secondary to innovation, which takes a life and logic of its own. Left unclear is who determines how the data is handled; the who and the how, let alone the what, of such indiscriminate, fetishistic datafying requires the scrutiny of public policy and law, and by extension, civil society.

Put another way, the techno-neocolonial state turns some of its peoples into subalterns. A comment on the use of the term "subaltern" here is in order. In the context of nationalist historiography, peoples left out of the national narrative, deliberately or inadvertently, become subaltern, which, to Subaltern Studies scholar Ranajit Guha, describes a position, not only an identity, that is created in the boundaries between social classes: groups that are foreign to the country but have dominant influence; groups that are dominant but indigenous; and groups that are powerful at local and national sectors. Taking issue with this taxonomy, Gayatri Spivak argues against the assumed homogeneity of the subaltern, where there are "many ambiguities and contradictions in attitudes and alliances, especially among the lower strata" and those who are not the elites.[82] My aim now is not to delve into the history of Subaltern Studies or sift through scholarly discourse to figure out the best definition of the subaltern for this essay. Instead, I wish to draw on Guha and Spivak by connecting their ideas, themselves adapted from the Italian thinker Antonio Gramsci's writings on the subaltern, which he continued to elaborate and refine over several years. For this discussion, I will pick up two ideas from Gramsci that will help in showing the nature of subalternity in postcolonial, contemporary Zambia.

"The history of subaltern social groups," observes Gramsci, "is necessarily fragmented and episodic" … subaltern classes are subject to the initiatives of the dominant class, even when they rebel; they are in a state of anxious defense" because the subaltern is not a stable, abstract identity.[83] Gramsci goes on to underscore the close connections between the state and civil society, and its economic sectors. Changes in the "sphere of economic production" generate new or realigned class formations; these groups will seek to influence majority or government policies; dominant groups will develop strategies to "maintain the consent of the subaltern social groups and to keep them under control"; subaltern groups will make specific demands of dominant groups; new social formations emerge yet largely within parameters set by dominant groups; subaltern groups seek full autonomy, in order to establish a new state.[84] Here, Gramsci lays out several phases that may or may not develop in tandem or chronologically. Rather, he adumbrates interactions between the state and civil society and the social realignments that generally come about due to shifts in economic practices; to Gramsci, the relationship of the dominant to subordinated groups is a matter of economics, culture, and politics. Marcus Green points out, "Gramsci insists that political society and civil society are not two separate spheres: they comprise an organized unity, for they are both elements of modern society."[85]

Civil society here extends across three domains of social life: the associational, the good society, and the public sphere, to extend Michael Edwards's three-dimensional model. Apart from the state and market's domains is the associational life, marked by diverse voluntary associations that people form for different purposes, and which come into existence or disappear periodically. The good society is "an image of civil society as a desirable social order or self-image of modernity defined in normative terms;[86] action in the social arena, when not in congruence with civil society, risks becoming silenced or sidelined. The public sphere seeks to realize the shared norms and goals made possible through democratic deliberation in the commons: "The concept of a 'public'—a whole polity that cares about the common good and has the capacity to deliberate about it democratically—is central to civil society"[87]. Edwards's position that "there is no need to treat the civil society debate as a zero-sum game in which one model is accepted to the exclusion of the others" aligns neatly with Gramsci's views on the formation of subalternity;[88] to him, these three domains function in relation to each other; they derive power or legitimacy insofar as the acts and processes get embedded in other domains, a dynamic whose specific contours are delineated by contingent social forces.

That means the formation of subaltern groups and the nature of their demands emerge in the complex interplay of social, political, and economic forces that generate conditions of subalternity.[89] This Gramscian insight helps us examine how the rise of digital culture in Zambia produces certain forms of subalternation that spurs people to use social media to mobilize mass protest movements against domination. Hence, to raise the question of the subaltern is to raise the question of state power—its dispersions, its concentrations, its effects, its mechanisms, and its operations.

In *The Old Drift*, in terms of the rise of techno-neocolonialism, the subalterns are differentiated groups of people subjected to nondemocratic, top-down impositions of public policy that enables the use of digital technologies for invasive data gathering, spying, and large-scale surveillance to stifle dissent, identify resisting parties, and monopolize access to a host of social services mediated through digital platforms like Digit-All Beads. They are, as we learn in the novel, the "*inactive*: the loiterers, the shitters, the unemployed—the idlers who jam the circulation of money and goods and information."[90] Techno-neocolonialism in this context describes the nexus of government agencies, Information Technology companies, political parties, and the police that generates and manages relationships of domination over peoples considered threats to the sociopolitical order maintained by the state. It is through technology, its platforms, devices, and satellite services that are embedded in Zambian local and international economic and political networks, that dissenters, and the public at large, are silenced or punished, their freedoms curtailed. As we see in the novel, the Zambian postcolonial state actively produces subaltern spaces for deceptive manipulation and influence. It is for this reason that Jacob, Joseph, and Naila plan to disrupt AFRINET and tap into other Wi-Fi systems and make Digit-All Beads lose temporary functionality.

In the novel, President Kalulu's despotic attempts to concentrate power in his office lead him to round up protesters, arrest dissidents, close newspaper offices, bring frivolous charges against opponents, and engage in nepotism—all which exacerbate tensions in the populace. When Digit-All objects to his policies, the president peremptorily shuts down AFRINET, the country's internet provider, crippling the company and program for a week, and forcing new taxes on voice-over-internet-protocol (VOIP) communications. The government seeks to partner with Chinese, American, and European entities to develop vaccines and medicines to stem Zambia's AIDS epidemic. Zambia was one of the sub-Saharan countries severely affected by the AIDS epidemic. Detected in the late 1980s in the country, by 2016 around 1.2 million people had HIV, with close to 21,000 people dying from it in that year alone.[91] The gendered impact of AIDS shows that "women are disproportionately affected due to several factors including gender imbalances in all spheres of life and Gender Based Violence."[92] In the novel, Dr. Lionel Banda's research to find a vaccine leads him to partner with other researchers to find the "Lusaka patient," one who displays immunity while fully exposed to the virus. They find one from the "shadiest corners of Zambian society," which meant "it was indisputable: they had revolutionized the hunt for the virus vaccine."[93]

But as the doctor's son Joseph realizes, his father gets the virus, and so do his mother, Sylvia, his stepmother, Selina, and his brother, Farai. Frustrated that his relatives, especially his grandmother, are prone to glossing over these harsh truths, Joseph asks himself, "Did she actually think he had contracted The Virus, passed it on to a wife and a son, divorced, remarried, and then stopped fucking around? Did she not realize that sex was what had killed him?"[94]. The stark difference between such a naïve response and Matha's Mwamba's treatment for having a child before marriage and losing opportunities for personal and professional advancement shows that societal norms significantly shape the uneven spread of the pandemic, often positioning women, and those from the rural areas, at a disadvantage. Such contradictions show a dynamic of neglect that further affirms people's mistrust of the state and its functionaries.

When Jacob, Naila, and Joseph argue over Zambia's economic interaction with other countries, Jacob blurts out, "The Chinese fucked us ... They stole our work and then they took the credit for it," to which Joseph replies, "Why you frikkin racist, men? It's bigger than 'the Chinese. It's the Consortium," a reference to US-China political and economic partnerships.[95] But their immediate concern is that the government had taken Joseph's Virus research and, in partnership with foreign companies, was "giving out free beta vaccines for the Virus ... They should just say black version. They're testing it on us."[96] Such criticism of the government and China can be viewed in the broad context of Sino-Zambian initiatives. Over the last three decades, there has been a dramatic increase in Chinese and Indian investments in Zambian copper mines, agriculture, banking, and public sector. While poverty rates decreased largely due to such initiatives, the quality of life has not necessarily improved, in that the nature of the jobs lead to a cycle of low-paying employment, and weak labor laws. Moreover, the state-backed interest loans to Chinese companies undermine local Zambian companies that cannot avail of the same financial support. A challenge for Zambia is to decrease the risk of becoming a weak node in a global economy, a country whose resources and peoples end up being positioned in dependency relationships with other countries, leaving it more vulnerable to disruptions in the global order.[97]

These new nexi for power politics have become "an accelerated and newer version of imperialism,"[98] an Electronic Empire that "is not particularly locatable or containable, but it nevertheless has effects that can be discerned. It does not easily align with watchwords, or adjectival buzzwords, of what is called the world economy and cannot as such be integrated, total, systematized, synchronized, compatible, balanced, or complete."[99]

As public anger mounts, the three young leaders initiate a public protest event called SOTP (Sum of the Parts, or state of the Planet). To forestall them, the government freezes Digit-All temporarily, halting communications among the people, who soon feel "the well of that fierce, quivering vibration. A dark immensity lowered" ... Not smoke, microdrones ... A dozen twinges, a hundred, a thousand, each no more panful than a normal mosquito bite. The swarm ... had landed upon the crowd and begun to puncture them."[100] Simply put, the government successfully uses drone technologies and the Internet to implement a massive vaccination program with or without the consent of the people, an act the protestors view as neocolonialism. In the final sections of the novel, SOTP attempts a second attempt at public protest with a difference: jamming public infrastructure, the Kariba Dam, temporarily, to force the government to negotiate. Notwithstanding internal arguments about the negative impact on the populace, the young leaders settle for a strategic short-term public difficulty to obtain long-term democracy.

Drone, Baby, Drone: Postcolonial Mediations

Jacob's designing another set of microdrones foregrounds both a theme and novelistic device in the novel: the role of error; the impact of the natural world on human habitation; and the inspirational legacy of Edward Nkoloso. Just as the mosquitoes regularly gives us a philosophical and quasi-omniscient view of the grand scheme of things, colonial and postcolonial, they also provide to Jacob a model to design a drone that can, like the insects, use subterfuge to go around official security and technology protocols, and halt the function of a necessary public utility. Because "drones had turned out to be the most nefarious tech of all," Jacob and his group decide to use Bluetooth technology to circumvent governmental control by creating "virtual private networks ... and string a chain of communication from drone to drone to reach air towers outside the borders and tap into Wi-Fi from one of the seven countries that surround Zambia."[101] We learn earlier that in creating his Moskeetoze prototype, Jacob studies the wings and body of the mosquito, particularly its "built-in web of nerves, veins, and arteries" that "carry blood energy." It seems that "the workings of animal biology seemed to mirror the workings of human society."[102] For his innovation, Jacobs replaces "blood with fuel, nerves with circuits, and the tiny hairs with antennae that would brush the planes of the world and send Wi-Fi signals to the cloud—and to other microdrones ... It would be a swarm that ate itself once in a while to stay afloat."[103] In the mosquito aside that follows the previous citation, we learn that white colonizers were more susceptible to being ravaged by malaria, caused by mosquitoes, than Black Africans.

A key lesson was to draw from the contingency of natural effects to develop subaltern subterfuge, like the mosquito and its ability to collaborate in murmuration. Their plan of jamming the gates of the Kariba Dam ends up dramatizing the novel's preoccupations: the role of nature and chance in directing, deflecting, or destroying human endeavor, and the deep contradictions of culture, nation, history, identity, and agency in influencing our being in the world. The use of microdrones to jam Kariba can be viewed as a political gesture that takes the very tools of state oppression and violence—internet, surveillance technologies, Digit-All Beads, smart phones, drones—to register discontent, to express dissent, and to demand change.

A corollary development in global culture, generally, is the overlapping of the political with the poetic in the use of drones. Artists like Mahwish Chisty, James Briddle, and Addie Wagenknecht, and sites like Notabugsplat and Murmaration, a Festival of Drone Culture demonstrate the extensive range of creative and critical work emanating from different parts of the world.[104] That these three protagonists, in the final plot of the novel, choose to use microdrones to deactivate dam gates, cut internet services, disrupt Digit-All Beads, and use communication networks to generate public dissent against the government demonstrates the cultural and political contradictions generated in the digital age.

However, such a gesture of subaltern resistance is not devoid of micropolitics and, more to the point, a reinscription of neocolonial mentality. As Jacob, Naila, and Joseph plan their subterfuge, Mai, who often enraptures them with "philosophical treatises on the nature of colonialism," cautions them whether they "warned the peepo."[105] Joseph, in particular, worries about how their actions risk perpetuating techno-neocolonialism: "It always just harms the people it's supposed to help. We're shutting down a dam that provides electricity of millions. Mai is right. We should send out a warning now."[106] Naila and Jacob respond that because they—now are the ones acting on behalf of the subalterns—know that any negative effect would be temporary, presumably on account of their excellent plan, about the need to warn the public about the loss of electricity caused by their jamming the dam gates. Ironically, and tellingly, the subaltern leaders lapse into the conundrum that Gayatri Spivak notes is endemic to those seeking to foreground subaltern presences: the elites/intellectuals know what the subalterns want; the leaders will give them what they need; they know the true reality of the subalterns. These tendencies, Spivak astutely points out, construct certain subalterns as Other to effect social change on terms that do not grow organically from within subaltern groups.[107] As Jacob, Naila, and Joseph accord to themselves the right to speak and act on behalf of the subalterns without preparing them for the potentially life-changing impact of their dam-jamming plan, we can, extending Spivak, "glimpse the track of ideology,"[108] which introduces a new subordinate relationship between them and those whose interests they seek to represent.

Nonetheless, we see a new social mode of dissent and resistance emerge, whose modalities are digital, user-generated, multimodal, and distributive. Changing Stop signs by blocking off words or symbols yields new terms or abbreviations, or even a new nomenclature. STOP becomes SOTP (Sum of the Parts). By hacking Digit-All Beads, the organizers send messages to thousands of users with details for a public meeting; the messages also direct people to a website with s SOTP domain, and a response form inviting individual participation. Such an "infiltration of the capitalistic circuits" involving hacking public utilities and official signage generates popular unrest, leading to a massive gathering.[109]

Evident here is a fundamental shift in Zambia society, as it becomes a networked society, which Yochai Benkler defines as "a particular historical moment when computer-mediated networks and communications have come (a) to play a particularly large role, and (b) to realign in ferly substantive ways the organization of production, power, and meaning making in contemporary society, relative to how similar aspects of social life were organized in the preceding century or earlier."[110] In the novel, we see how the networked society produces what Darin Barney et al. refer to as the "participatory condition the digital age," which is the "degree and extent to which the everyday social, economic, cultural, and political activities that comprise simply being the world have been thematized and organized around the priority of participation as such."[111]

It is the nature of digitality, of the networked society, to generate paradoxes of power and resistance; that is, digital technologies have a "double-edged quality" which is the "hallmark of so many technological innovations today."[112] Despite being caught off guard and getting confused by the popular uprising, the government of Lusaka carries off a bold plan of cooptation: instead of preventing the people from gathering or jamming their Beads, it sends swarms of microdrones carrying a vaccine payload and successfully injects thousands of people. Such a public display of forced state power not surprisingly creates a backlash. Soon, Naila, Joseph, and Jacob, and their friends, plot a counter move: using the tools of oppression, the microdrones, as the tools of resistance. They program a swarm of micro drones to seek transmitters hidden, by them, in the sluice gates; on contact, the gates jam, but not temporarily, as they anticipate, but with a rigidity they cannot loosen. Unable to de-jam the sluices, as the gates remain shut, water levels rise dangerously. In the final section of the novel, which is a Mosquito aside, we learn that the resisters had not planned on how error and chance could generate unforeseen outcomes. Inexorably, as the sluices thoroughly jam, the Kariba's walls heave to the weight of water—and yield. A massive flood envelops the town, the city, the region, and the country. Kariba—the dam connecting Zambia to Zimbabwe—is no more. National boundaries are submerged. Because it is a plateau, Lusaka survives.

We learn that with Kalingalinga as the capital, "a small community, egalitarian, humble" emerges: "People grow all the food they want to eat. There are a few clinics, and one or two schools. Beads are used for barter and voting. And in its midst our lone survivors, Naila's two lovers, now old. Haven't we told you? She died giving birth, but her son doesn't know who his father is."[113]

Conclusion

In *The Old Drift* the insistent search for origins, for ideological purity, for racial homogeneity, for stable history, for cultural monopoly, and for Manichean rigidity leads not to certainty and objectivity, not to uniform colonization and pristine empires, or stable postcolonial states, but to cross-racial and cultural hybridity, to the messiness of subaltern resistance and the disorderliness of decolonization. Whereas colonial history posits David Livingstone as "our father unwitting, our inadvertent pater muzungu,"[114] in the novel's postcolonial time of 2024, Naila's child does not know its father; it could be Joseph; it could be Jacob; it is a secret the mother does not reveal, nor do the mosquitoes. Just as Livingstone and empire cannot be wrenched out of Zambian history to reveal a glorious, innocent past, neither can Joseph nor Jacob be written out of the child's mother's life. Just as the colonial enterprise cannot be bracketed off as an epiphenomenon, the postcolonial state's subjugation of its subalterns cannot be written off as inconsequential. The child, like the survivors of the Kariba flood, is destined to live in the new post postcolonial world of Lusaka. Their stories of beginnings, of origins, their hopes for the future are waiting to be told. This is the old drift, the drift of postcolonial mediations, imprinted with violence, haunted by imperialism, crusted over with contingency, and re-narrated with subaltern agency.

The Old Drift's novelistic vision encompasses colonial and postcolonial histories; while exploring their uneven developments, it foregrounds the contingencies of life, of happenstance, of natural occurrences and biological organisms, as having significant influence over the exercise of colonial power and postcolonial resistance. In showing that the gendered dimensions of coloniality are perpetuated in stridently anti-colonial activities, the novel demonstrates the disjunctive continuity of colonialism in postcolonial time. Far from enabling people and the government to ameliorate economically and socially depressed conditions, the growth of Information Technologies in Zambia generates subaltern conditions that facilitate oligarchic exercises of power and illiberal policies of stifling dissent. In Zambia's networked society, micro drones become tools of subjugation and tools of resistance, but with a difference: the powerful ideologies of oppression and resistance are foregrounded in their materialist dimensions; that is, the efficacious operations of coloniality and postcoloniality depend in small or large measure on the unpredictability of natural occurrences, boundaries, topographies, and the inexplicability of mosquitoes, or biological life, interfering with human motivations. It is the complex, unpredictable interplay of ideology, place, nature, and biology that the novel seeks to grasp and render in narrative the rich possibilities for rethinking colonial legacies through postcolonial mediations.

Notes

1   Namwali Serpell, *The Old Drift* (New York: Hogarth, 2019).
2   Anne McClintock, "The Angel of Progress: Pitfalls of the Term Post-colonialism," *Colonial Discourse and Postcolonial Theory*. Edited by Patrick Williams and Laura Chrisman (New York: Columbia University Press, 1994), 66–111; Vijay Mishra and Bob Hodge, "What Is Post (-) Colonialism?" *Colonial Discourse and Postcolonial Theory*. Edited by Patrick Williams and Laura Chrisman (New York: Columbia University Press, 1994), 276–90; Bill Ashcroft, Gareth Griffiths, and Helen Tiffin, *Post-colonial Studies: The Key Concepts* (London: Routledge, 1998).
3   Rumina Sethi, *Politics of Postcolonialism: Empire, Nation, and Resistance* (London: Pluto Press, 2011).
4   McClinktock, "The Angel of Progress," 297.
5   Achille Mbembe, "African Modes of Self-Writing." *Identity, Culture and Politics* 2, no. 1 (2001): 1–39; Patience Mususa, "Who Is Setting Africa's Intellectual Agenda?" *CODESRIA Bulletin*, 1 & 2 (2017): 5–7; Adom Getachew, "Reimagining Decolonisation Today: A Review of Neither Settler Nor Native." *CODESRIA Bulletin Online*, 15, June (2021): 1–4.
6   Paul Zeleza and Paul T. "Historicizing the Posts: The View from African Studies," in *Postmodernism Postcoloniality, and African Studies*. Edited by Zine Magubane (New Jersey: Africa World Press), 1–38; Tejumola Olaniyan, "Postmodernity, Postcoloniality, and African Studies," in *Postmodernism Postcoloniality, and African Studies*. Edited by Zine Magubane (New Jersey: Africa World Press), 39–60.
7   Ania Loomba. *Colonialism/Postcolonialism* (Routledge, 1998); Larbi Kwaku, "Useless Provocation or Meaningful Challenge? The "Post" versus African Studies," *The Study of Africa, Vol 1: Disciplinary and Interdisciplinary Encounters*. Edited by Paul Tiyambe Zeleza, CODESRIA, vol. 1 (2006): 443–66; P. Yaeger, P. "Editor's Column: The End of Postcolonial Theory? A Roundtable with Sunil Agnani, Fernando Coronil, Gaurav Desai, Mamadou Diouf, Simon Gikandi, Susie Tharu, and Jennifer Wenzel." *PMLA/*

Publications of the Modern Language Association of America 122, no. 3 (2007): 633–51, doi:10.1632/pmla.2007.122.3.633; Robert Young, "Postcolonial Remains." *New Literary History* 43, no. 1 (2012): 19–42. Project MUSE, doi:10.1353/nlh.2012.0009.

8   Kwame Nkrumah, *Neo-Colonialism: The Last Stage of Imperialism* (New York: International Publishers, 1965), xi.
9   Ibid., 239.
10 Ibid., 243.
11 Ella Shoaht, Ella. "Notes on the "Post-Colonial, Face" *Social Text* 31/32 (1992): 106.
12 Ofunmilayo Arewa, "At the Crossroads of Digital Imperialism & Digital Development," Berkman Klein Center for Internet and Society, Harvard University, *youtube.com* May 24, 2021, https://youtube.com/watch?v=B1Yr9hwMm8s
13 David Pilling, "Are Tech Companies Africa's New Colonists?" *ft.com*. Financial Times. July 5, 2021, https://ft.com/content/4625d9b8-9c16-11e9-b8ce-8b459ed04726
14 Mirca Madianou, "Technocolonialism: Digital Innovation and Data Practices in the Humanitarian Response to Refugee Crises." *Social Media + Society* 5, no. 3 (2019): 7–8.
15 Bhakti Shringapure, "Africa and the Digital Savior Complex." *Journal of African Cultural tudies* 32, no. 2 (2020): 179.
16 Arewa, "At the Crossroads."
17 Frantz Fanon, *The Wretched of the Earth*. Trans. by Constance Farrington (New York: Grove Weidenfeld, 1963), 36.
18 Ibid., 35.
19 Ibid., 41.
20 Ibid., 38.
21 Jean-Paul Sarte, Preface. *The Wretched of the Earth*, by Frantz Fanon. Trans. by Constance Farrington (New York: Grove Weidenfeld, 1963): 15–16.
22 Fanon, *The Wretched of the Earth*, 93.
23 Andrew Sardanis, "Zambia: The First Fifty Years." *The Round Table: The Commonwealth Journal of International Affairs* 104, no. 1 (2015): 12, DOI: 10.1080/00358533.2015.1005355
24 Chris Dunton, 'Wherever the Bus Is Headed': Recent Developments in the African Novel." *Research in African Literatures* 50, no. 4 (2019): 4.
25 Namwali Serpell, "A Novelist and Critic Fictionalizing Zambian History," *newyorker.com*, interview by Isaac Chotiner, April 3, 2019, https://newyorker.com/news/q-and-a/a-novelist-and-critic-on-fictionalizing-zambian-history
26 Namwali Serpell, "Q&A With Namwali Serpell: Recipe for Revolution—Brief and Contingent Solidarity in 'The Old Drift.'"*zyzzvyz.com*, interview by Annah Omune Sidigu, 15 May, 2019, https://zyzzyva.org/contributor/annah-omune-sidigu/
27 Serpell, *The Old Drift*, 12.
28 Serpell, "Q&A."
29 W. E. B. DuBois, "The Souls of Black Folk," *Project Gutenberg*, eBook, January 1996, first published 1903, https://gutenberg.org/files/408/408-h/408-h.htm.
30 Andrew C. Ross, *David Livingstone: Mission and Empire* (London: Hambledon and London, 2002); Joanna Lewis, "Rivers of White: David Livingston and the 1955 Commemorations in the Lost Henley-Upon-Thames of Central Africa," *Living the End of Empire: Politics and Society in Late Colonial Zambia*. Edited by Jan-Bart Gewald, Marja Hinfelaar, and Giacomo Macola (Leiden: Brill, 2011): 160–205.
31 Ted Olsen, "One African Nation Under God." *Christianity Today*, 4 February 2002, 41.

32 US Department of State, Office of International Religious Freedom. Zambia 2020: International Religion Freedom Report, May 12, 2021, https://state.gov/reports/2020-report-on-international-religious-freedom/zambia/.
33 Olsen, "One African Nation," 38.
34 Miles Larmer, Mara Hinfelaar, Bizeck J. Phiri, Lyn Schumaker, and Morris Szeftel. "Introduction: Narratives of Nationhood," *Journal of Southern African Studies* 40, no. 5 (2014): 901.
35 John M. Mackenzie, "David Livingstone—Prophet or Patron Saint of Imperialism in Africa: Myths and Misconceptions." *Scottish Geographic Journal* 129, no. 3–4 (2013): 277–91; Sjoerd Rijpma, *David Livingstone and the Myth of African Poverty and Disease: A Close Examination of His Writing on Pre-Colonial Era* (Leiden: Brill, 2015); David Kilbride, "The Old South Confronts the Dilemma of David Livingstone." *Journal of Southern History*, 82, no. 4 (2016): 789–822.
36 Serpell, *The Old Drift*, 2.
37 Ibid., 2.
38 Serpell, "Q&A."
39 Namwali Serpell, "The Zambian 'Afronaut' Who Wanted to Join the Space Race." *newyorker.com* March 11, 2017, https://newyorker.com/culture/culture-desk/the-zambian-afronaut-who-wanted-to-join-the-space-race
40 Ibid., 163.
41 Ibid., 167.
42 Ibid., 200.
43 Ibid., 210.
44 Ibid., 211.
45 Ibid., 197.
46 Ibid., 206.
47 Ibid., 186–7.
48 Ibid., 193.
49 Ibid.
50 Ibid., 198.
51 Ibid., 210.
52 Ibid., emphasis in original, 198.
53 Ibid., 199.
54 Bizeck J. Phiri, "Gender and Politics: The Zambia National Women's Lobby Group in the 2001 Ripartite Elections." *One Zambia, Many Histories: Towards a History of Post-colonial Zambia*. Edited by Jan-Bart Gewald, Marja Hinfelaar, and Giacomo Macola (Leiden: Brill, 2008), 259–60.
55 Serpell, *The Old Drift*, 199.
56 Ibid., 240.
57 Ibid.
58 Ibid.
59 Homi Bhabha, "DissemiNation: Time, Narrative, and the Margins of the Modern Nation." *Nation and Narration*, edited by Homi Bhabha (New York: Routledge, 1990): 292.
60 David C. Mulford, *Zambia: The Politics of Independence 1957–1964* (Oxford: Oxford University Press, 1967); Timothy M. Shaw and Douglas G. Anglin. "Zambia: The Crises of Liberation." *Southern Africa: The Continuing Crisis*. Edited by Gwendolen M. Carter and Patrick O'Meara (Bloomington: Indiana University Press, 1979), 199–222; Marcia M. Burdette, *Zambia: Between Two Worlds* (Colorado: Westview Press,

1988); Miles Larmer, *Rethinking African Politics: A History of Opposition in Zambia*. ProQuest Ebook Central (London: Taylor and Francis, 2011).

61   Giacomo Macola, *Liberal Nationalism in Central Africa: A Biography of Harry Mwaanga Nkumbula* (New York: Palgrave Macmillan, 2010); Giacomo Macola, "Harry Mwaanga Nkumula and the Formation of ZANC/INIP: A Reinterpretation." *Living the End of Empire: Politics and Society in Late Colonial Zambia*. Edited by Jan-Bart Gewald, Marja Hinfelaar, and Giacomo Macola (Leiden: Brill, 2011): 27–65.

62   Harri Englund makes these points in reviewing several revisionary accounts of Zambian national history, in an essay that marks a critical intervention in highlighting a solid body of scholarship that includes Jan-Bart Gewald, Marja Hinfelaar, and Giacomo Macola, *One Zambia, Many Histories: Toward a History of Post-colonial Zambia* (Leiden: Brill 2008), and *Living the End of Empire: Politics and Society in Late-Colonial Zambia* (Leiden: Brill, 2011); David M. Gordon, *Invisible Agents: Spirits in a Central African History* (Ohio: Ohio University Press, 2012); Mile Larmer, *Rethinking African Politics: A History of Opposition in Zambia* (Farnham: Ashgate, 2011); Giacomo Macola, *Liberal Nationalism in Central Africa: A Biography of Harry Mwaanga Nkumbula* (New York: Palgrave, 2010); Bizeck Jube Phiri, *A Political History of Zambia: From the Colonial Period to the Third Republic* (New Jersey: Africa World Press. 2006). Many of these authors responded to Englund's review in "Debating 'The Rediscovery of Liberalism' in Zambia: Responses to Harri Englund," by David M. Gordon, Bizeck Jube Phiri, Giacomo Macola, and James Ferguson, *Africa: Journal of the International African Institute* 84, no. 4 (2014): 658–67.

63   Walima T. Kalusa, "Traditional Rulers, Nationalists and the Quest for Freedom in Northern Rhodesia in the 1950s." *Living the End of Empire: Politics and Society in Late Colonial Zambia*. Edited by Jan-Bart Gewald, Marja Hinfelaar, and Giacomo Macola (Leiden: Brill, 2011): 67–90.

64   Phiri, Bizeck J. *A Political History of Zambia: From Colonial Rule to the Third Republic, 1890–2001* (New Jersey: Africa World Press, 2006): 77.

65   Serpell, *The Old Drift*, 2.

66   Larmer et al., "Introduction: Narratives of Nationhood," 895.

67   Serpell, *"The Old Drift*," 473.

68   Statista, "Global Digital Population as of January 2021." *statista.com* January 2021, https://statista.com/topics/1145/internet-usage-worldwide/#topicOverview

69   Our World in Data. https://ourworldindata.org/grapher/number-of-mobile-cellular-subscriptions-by-country-1980-2013?country=~ZMB

70   J. Clement, "Share of Global Mobile Website Traffic 2015–2021." *statista.com* April 28, 2021, https://statista.com/statistics/277125/share-of-website-traffic-coming-from-mobile-devices/

71   Esteban, Ortiz-Ospian, "The Rise of Social Media." *ourworldindata* September 18, 2019, https://ourworldindata.org/rise-of-social-media

72   P. W. Singer, *Wired for War: The Robotics Revolution and Conflict in the 21st Century* (London:Penguin, 2009); Medea Benjamin, *Drone Warfare: Killing by Remote Control* (New York: Verso, 2013); John Muthyala, "Drones and Surveillance Cultures in a Global World." Digital Studies/La Champ Numérique, *digitalstudies.org*, September 27, 2019, https://digitalstudies.org/articles/10.16995/dscn.332/

73   Out of sight, out of mind. https://drones.pitchinteractive.com/

74 Eric Schmitt, "A Shadowy War's Newest Front: A Drone Base Rising from Saharan Dust." *nytimes.com*, 22 Apr. 2018, https://nytimes.com/2018/04/22/us/politics/drone-base-niger.html

75 Kerry Chávez and Ori Swed, "The Proliferation of Drones to Violent Nonstate Actors," *Defense Studies* 21, no. 1 (2021): 2.

76 David Rosen and Aaron Santesso, *The Watchman in Pieces: Surveillance, Literature, and Liberal Personhood* (Connecticut: Yale University Press, 2013).

77 Gregorie Chamayou, *A Theory of the Drone* (New York: New Press, 2015).

78 Matildah Kaliba, "Toward An Autonomous Civil Society: Rethinking State-Civil Society Relations in Zambia." *International Journal of Not-for-Profit-Law*, 16, no. 2 (2014): 7.

79 Serpell, *The Old Drift*, 523.

80 Thosam Streinz, "At the Crossroads of Digital Imperialism & Digital Development," Berkman Klein Center for Internet and Society, Harvard University, May 24, 2021 *youtube.com* May 2021 https://www.youtube.com/watch?v=B1Yr9hwMm8s

81 Todd C. Lopez, "National Geospatial-Intelligence Agency in Midst of Revolution." *DOD News*. 5 Dec, 2020, https://defense.gov/Explore/News/Article/Article/2447871/national-geospatial-intelligence-agency-in-midst-of-revolution/

82 Gayatri Spivak, "Can the Subaltern Speak?" *Colonial Discourse and Postcolonial Theory*. Edited by Patrick Williams and Laura Chrisman (Columbia University Press, 1994), 80.

83 Antonio Gramsci, *Subaltern Social Groups: A Critical Edition of Prison Notebook 25*. Edited and translated by Joseph A. Buttigieg and Marcus E. Green (New York: Columbia University Press, 2021), 19–20.

84 Ibid., 10.

85 Marcus Green, "Gramsci Cannot Speak: Presentations and Interpretations of Gramsci's Concept of the Subaltern." *Rethinking Marxism* 14, no. 3 (2002): 6.

86 Michael Edwards, *Civil Society* (Boston: Polity Press, 2009), 46–7.

87 Ibid., 63.

88 Ibid., 82.

89 Massimo Modonesi argues that social domination can be viewed in terms of social class and social group: "The class condition, with its material roots in the socioeconomic terrain, and subalternity as a sociopolitical situation" (37). Where Gramsci uses class, not groups, generally, is when stressing "situations with greater political density or class conciseness, or, alternatively, to emphasize its location strictly in the realm of production, of workers as instrumental classes" (39); social groups in relation to subalternity "must be understood as class fractions" (39). In this chapter, I use the terms subaltern/social groups as does Gramsci.

90 Serpell, *The Old Drift*, 528.

91 Amy S. Patterson, 'To Save the Community': Carework as Citizenship during Liberia's Ebola Outbreak and Zambia's AIDS Crisis." *Africa Today* 66, no. 2 (2019): 34.

92 UNICEF, Zambia. National HIV and AIDS Strategic Framework 2017–21. *unicef.org* (2017): 16 https://unicef.org/zambia/reports/national-aids-strategic-framework-2017-2021.

93 Serpell, *The Old Drift*, 364–5.

94 Ibid., 393.

95 Ibid., 306–7.

96 Ibid., 307.

97 Pádraig Carmody and Godfrey Hampwaye. "Inclusive or Exclusive Globalization." *Africa Today* 56, no. 3 (2010): 84–102.
98 Pramod K. Nayar, *Postcolonialism: A Guide for the Perplexed* (Bloomsbury, 2010), 193.
99 Rita Raley, "eEmpires," *Postcolonial Studies: An Anthology*. Edited by Pramod K. Nayar, ProQuest Ebook Central (New Jersey: Wiley Blackwell, 2016), 728.
100 Serpell, *The Old Drift*, 542–3.
101 Ibid., 549–50.
102 Ibid., 402.
103 Ibid., 483.
104 Mahwish Chisty, https://mahachishty.com/; James Bridle, https://jamesbridle.com/works/drone-shadow-001; Addie Wagenkecht, https://placesiveneverbeen.com/; Notabugsplat, https://notabugsplat.com/; Murmuration: A Festival of Drone Culture, https://murmurationfestival.tumblr.com/
105 Serpell, *The Old Drift*, 545–55.
106 Serpell, *The Old Drift*, 555.
107 Gayatri Spivak, "Can the Subaltern Speak?" *Colonial Discourse and Postcolonial Theory*. Edited by Patrick Williams and Laura Chrisman (New York: Columbia University Press, 1994), 66–7.
108 Spivak, "Can the Subaltern Speak?" 66.
109 Serpell, *The Old Drfit*, 535.
110 Yochai Benkler, "Networks of Power, Degrees of Freedom." *International Journal of Communication* 5 (2011): 723.
111 Darin Barney, Gabriella Coleman, Christine Ross, Jonathan Sterne, and Tamar Tembeck, eds. *The Participatory Condition in the Digital Age* (Minneapolis: University of Minnesota Press, 2016): vii.
112 Bill Wasik, "Welcome to the Age of Digital Imperialism." *nytimes.com* June 4, 2015, https://nytimes.com/2015/06/07/magazine/welcome-to-the-age-of-digital-imperialism.html
113 Serpell, *The Old Drift*, 563.
114 Ibid., 1.

5 THE NEW AESTHETIC: POST-DIGITALITY, EVERSION, AND DRONE CULTURES

In this chapter, I examine an aesthetic mood, the New Aesthetic, related to drones, and to grasp—in theory, concept, practice—the nature of human societies' immersion in worlds saturated with digital media. I am not offering a critical review of artistic digital production in the twenty-first century, an exhaustive accounting of a movement, a fad, a temporary hegemonic idea regarding the brave new world of fascinating technologies permeating our lives. The aim is to connect the New Aesthetic with drone aesthetics in a post-digital world.

The New Aesthetic can be understood as a loose assortment of creative orientations that use the drone and its affordances to signify or play on them, generating what Beryl Pong and Michael Richardson in *Drone Aesthetics: War, Culture, Ecology* call "drone aesthetics." Briefly, because drones are "both an object of aesthetic investigation and an instrument for aesthetic production," they foreground drone aesthetics as "visual culture and the arts; as the body and its relationships to the material environment; as the machine capacities for sensing and sensemaking that constitute drone systems themselves, and as the very foundation of how we understand politics and what makes politics possible—a question with increasing urgency, given the way drones erode boundaries between the military and the domestic."[1]

To Pong and Richardson's focus on sensemaking, visuality, and rethinking the political can be added other meanings of aesthetics about how creativity evokes, pleasurably or disturbingly, our senses; engages in defamiliarization, by reframing the common or obvious in new ways; foregrounds symmetry or harmony in unexpected places; generates affective responses of wonder, befuddlement, horror, shock, or surprise at the beautiful or disfigured. The attention to the formal elements of a work of art and their unique arrangements to thematize an idea, mood, event, or emotion are also part of drone aesthetics.

Pong and Richardson's point about the political nature of drone aesthetics can be linked to Thomas Stubblefield's insight in *Drone Art: The Everywhere War as Medium* that drone art's politics move beyond critique and rejection, beyond dismantling marginalizing tools and structures. Though "drone art" as a term risks coming across as a homogenous body of artistic productions in the book, Stubblefield's observation is important, because he points to a unique feature of drone art: deep immersion in the formal and technical affordances of the drone, not to artistically reject them with dismay but to use the creative impulse to defamiliarize them; that is, to playfully or seriously bring out the socially and psychologically alienating nature of drone apparatuses into full or partial view by artistically drawing on the sensemaking visual capacities of the drone.

Stubblefield notes that the different nature of political engagement in drone art is not only a shift in ideology to counter power but also a recognition that civilian and military networks and their cultures of communication are thoroughly imbricated. For instance, a digital device like a phone or "everyday media" have "a shared ground of operations that imbues everyday media such as the mobile device with an inconceivable simultaneity, such that the capacity to serve as both medium of civilian communication and drone targeting system is not only possible, but in fact comprises the very conditions of everyday mediality."[2] In such conditions, the politics of drone art turns into a "manifest criticality," a "second-order operation" that seeks "to redirect, reimagine, or otherwise introduce interferences from within these relations."[3] Stubblefield further argues:

> As a result, its reproduction of drone power is easily mistaken for the cool detachment of postmodern pastiche. However, as drone art is driven by a nonprogram rather than an antiprogram, its rejection of traditional modes of critique and resistance is not synonymous with the rejection of the political as a category or of the possibility of intervention. In fact, it is precisely by way of these relations of symmetry that this work seeks to amplify the internal contradictions and asymmetries of drone power, to harness the relations of becoming that inhabit this network in order to realize alternate iterations of its force.[4]

Similarly, Rob Coley and Dean Lockwood point out the asymmetries and paradoxical features of the drone that make it "weird," because "the drone is redacted, hidden in plain sight, present but opaque," as the "drone combines banality and mystique; as it withdraws, it magnetizes us to its hiddenness. It fascinates. Yet it is difficult to apprehend. There is, from the beginning, an aura of the hermetic about the drone. We are dealing with secret transmissions, recondite knowledge. The middleness of mediality of the drone that we have identified is inseparable from the question of the metaphysics of the drone, even the mysticism of the drone."[5] It is this weirdness, this fascination and mysticism of the drone, that drone art and culture represent; to apprehend the fasciation of drones with their extraordinary ability to become assassination machines, for instance, can evoke repugnance and curiosity, acceptance and rejection, the desire to distance from it and the desire to approximate it creatively.

While making visible the "internal contradictions and asymmetries of drone power" (Stubblefield's phrase) is a main feature of drone art, the New Aesthetic draws them into public view through an immersion in the protocols, processes, and material configurations of networked drones. Creators or artists seek out their dissonances; they play on, by refiguring or disfiguring, the silences and dissonances produced in these network ecologies; they use drone materialities, the numerous things that form their operational structures, and the discourses that legitimize them, to defamiliarize the familiar, and show, through new alignments and misalignments, the aesthetic nature of the drone: as art, idea, metaphor, language, culture, politics.

The New Aesthetic seeks out, not hesitatingly accept or cautiously reject, the gaps, glitches, disruptions, pixelizations, network lapses, visual oddities, ambient sounds, and material and psychosocial contexts that are part and parcel of digitalia. Where such elements are hidden or partially seen or publicly unacknowledged, the New Aesthetic seeks to make the hidden visible, the inaccessible available, and the unacknowledged acknowledged. We can now turn to the work of the British media artist James Bridle, which first registers the New Aesthetic as an emerging cultural mood.

James Bridle's New Aesthetic

In 2011, British technologist James Bridle posted bits of images, text, and video on Tumblr, which, taken together, were less about compelling media production and more about digital media captured in odd places, pixelated photos, snippets of code, Google map's visualization of places, and so on. Bridle creatively accumulated digital artifacts as products of the digitalization of daily life; they featured a view from space of patches of greenery embedded in rocky terrain; a Google satellite image of the building where bin Laden was killed; a pixelated umbrella; a Google image of a plane arrested momentarily in image processing; a map visualizing iPhone locations; a picture with multiple screens engaging in generating a view for the viewer, and so on.[6]

The public response, ranging from fascination to dismissal, was quick, eliciting strong reactions, because it seemed to speak to a growing mood, a sensibility, toward the increasing presence of digital media in many social spheres. A QR code, for instance, that was on a mesh near a building under construction, was not set up for use with a phone that would be directed to an online site; instead, "rather than being just badly applied, the code was being used purely as a decorative piece."[7] Will Wiles explains the emerging mood well: "In a sense, what the New Aesthetic truly represents is the eruption of a new kind of banality. It is the arrival of digital motifs, glitches and artifacts in the realm of the commonplace and the trivial, the advent of a world where it is thoroughly normal to see a Windows crash screen in place of an advertisement on the Underground, or for trading algorithms to cause a stock market to crash."[8]

The panel that Bridle led in 2012 at the South By Southwest conference (SXSW) was titled "The New Aesthetic: Seeing Like Digital Devices." SXSW's panel abstract, in part, reads as follows:

> We are becoming acquainted with new ways of seeing: the Gods-eye view of satellites, the Kinect's inside-out sense of the living room, the elevated car-sight of Google Street View, the facial obsessions of CCTV … As a result, these new styles and senses recur in our art, our designs, and our products. The pixelation of low-resolution images, the rough yet distinct edges of 3D printing, the shifting layers of digital maps. In this session, the participants will give examples of these effects, products and artworks, and discuss the ways in which ways of seeing are increasingly transforming ways of making and doing.[9]

Joining Bridle on the panel were digital artists, performers, and writers—Aaron Cope, Ben Terrett, Joanne McNeil, and Russell Davies.[10] Framing the discussion was Bridle's Tumblr post hesitatingly ruminating on a collection of digital artifacts exemplifying a new artistic mood, if not a movement. Bridle posted:

> For a while now, I've been collecting images and things that seem to approach a new aesthetic of the future, which sounds more portentous than I mean. What I mean is that we've got frustrated with the NASA extropianism space-future, the failure of jetpacks, and we need to see the technologies we actually have with a new wonder. Consider this a mood-board for unknown products. (Some of these things might have appeared here, or nearby, before. They are not necessarily new new, but I want to put them together.) For so long we've stared up at space in wonder, but with cheap satellite imagery and cameras on kites and RC helicopters, we're looking at the ground with new eyes, to see structures and infrastructures.[11]

Connections, Disconnections, Repositions

The New Aesthetic examines and immerses itself in the technological networks that connect, disconnect, and reposition us constantly. Bridle notes:

Since May 2011 I have been collecting material which points towards new ways of seeing the world, an echo of the society, technology, politics and people that co-produce them. The New Aesthetic is not a movement, it is not a thing which can be *done*. It is a series of artefacts of the heterogeneous network, which recognizes differences, the gaps in our distant but overlapping realities.[12]

Preferring to highlight "computation" or "computational" in referencing the digital, David M. Berry writes, "As computation has become spatial in its implementation, embedded within the environment, in the body and in society, it becomes part of the texture of life itself which can be walked around, touched, manipulated and interacted with in a number of ways ... Today the postdigital is hegemonic, and as such is entangled with everyday life and experience in a highly complex, messy and difficult to untangle way that is different from previous instantiations of the digital—indeed, the varieties of the digital should be treated as historical in this important sense."[13]

Marking a new turn in digitality, a core feature of the New Aesthetic is the nature of visualization, where what we often see and interact with is rendered in pixels and can be compressed and expanded digitally along nodes in the network in which multimedia content circulates. However, the pervasive spread of the digital also renders it as normal, as it becomes part and parcel of our routine lives; the tools we use, the screens we touch, the sounds we hear, the conversations we have, the images we see and respond to seem to happen naturally, as if the virtual manifests itself on its own. As Grant Bollmer points out in *Theorizing Digital Cultures*, all these are "an effect of the materiality of digital media," since material infrastructure refers to how "the screens, wires, servers, protocols, and software of digital media ... guide the global circulation of capital, communication, and transportation, underwritten by algorithms that sort, control, and mange bodies and commodities."[14] The New Aesthetic brings to the fore the partially or completely hidden or unknown aspects of such material infrastructure to offer new visualizations of digital culture in which virtuality and materiality are exaggerated, distorted, or rendered as part of the constructed environment.

Visualization—as digital product, material manifestation, and distributive process—generates "glitchy and pixelated imagery," producing "a way of seeing that seems to reveal a blurring between 'the real' and 'the digital,' the physical and the virtual, the human and the machine."[15] In the decade since the Tumblr post and SXSW panel, online posts, articles, interviews, videos, and talks involved suggestions that digital societies were creating a new mood or perception about the world and was emerging in digital societies and arguments that the New Aesthetic was a fad, a kitschy moment.

To assume that we have firm control over digital technologies and can discern and make choices that maintain a clear, stable distance from them contradicts the subtle and overt influence exerted by technologies over how thoughts and behavior. Autodesk, a program for architectural engineering, can sometimes produce a building whose materiality manifests Autodesk features. On seeing the building, one well-versed with the program can discern that it is designed by a particular software program. This means that far from simply being a complex tool that engineers use, the program's valence finds expression in the actions we take or things we produce with it.

Another example is the use of *lorem ipsum*, text used as temporary gap fillers in design and graphic interfaces using multimedia; *lorem ipsum* can influence the "real" textual content in format, shape, and style. The use of pixels on pillows, handbags, cupcake stands, shows, mannequins, installation art like the pixilized Orca by Douglas Copeland in Vancouver, Canada, the mirror that generates pixelized reflections to people by Hybe's Iris, and the pixels that represent the structure of local Wi-Fi local frequencies by Carina Ow show both the digital visualization of other objects and how such visualization is becoming a commonplace. The way we see and understand the world, the way we build environments, the way we locate ourselves and others in them, the way we interact with these environs and their life species: all are thoroughly digitally mediated.[16] Bruce Sterling views the New Aesthetic as "diffuse, crowdsourcey, and made of many small pieces loosely joined," adding that, in 2012, it had a "Wunderkammer" feel, like a "heap of eye-catching curiosities" missing a "compelling worldview."[17] In constantly juxtaposing "information visualization. Satellite views. Parametric architecture. Surveillance cameras. Digital image processing. Data-mashed video frames. Glitches and corruption artifacts," and so on, the New Aesthetic foregrounds the daily intrusion of the digital into all kinds of social, personal, and public spaces.[18] The New Aesthetic, then, is a sign of post-digitality, in that the digital has gone beyond its revolutionary impact in society to become a commonplace in daily life.[19]

The Digital Erupts in the Physical World

The New Aesthetic is about "making visible of something invisible and digital and using pixels to represent that … [It is] a making real of a digital artefact, something seen at low resolution and carried on out into the world as an aesthetic."[20] To Bridle, "the aesthetic of pixilisation" is an "instantiation of virtual things in the real world. This is how we imagine them coming into being."[21] These "eruptions of the digital into the physical world"[22] mark a new kind of societal integration of digital tools and systems and their related metaphors. As Teo Ballvé puts it, "The New Aesthetic is an assertive attempt to highlight the diffuse processes through which digitalia has seeped into and out of our everyday life."[23]

Such art embodies new ways of visualizing the world. Experimenting with robots for sexual gratification is another dimension of the new aesthetic where our sense of pleasure is strongly connected to our interaction with a technology, not to interact with another person, virtual or embodied, but as a means to interact with technology that stands in for the Other in a performance of sex. Such overlapping between the virtual and the real, between the fabricated and the actual, shows that "all our metaphors are broken. The network is not a space (notional, cyber or otherwise) and it's not time (while it is embedded in it at an odd angle), it is some other kind of dimension entirely."[24] About the New Aesthetic's interest in constantly collecting and juxtaposing its materials, its objects of fascination, Marius Watz points out, "NA [New Aesthetic] is part meme, part techno-ethnography and part Tumblr serendipity. Its art is juxtaposition: If we put this next to that and this other thing, surely a new understanding will emerge. And you know what? It works surprisingly well. Whether that success is the product of brilliant curation or the result of feverishly sign-deciphering minds scanning image after image for clues that might not be there is academic. If it works, it works."[25]

In *The New Aesthetic and Art: Constellations of The Postdigital*, Scott Contreras-Koterbay and Łukasz Mirocha observe that "the term is used to describe the increasing presence in the physical world of visual phenomena rooted in digital technology and the internet, in an effort to describe the increasing proliferation of visual language dependent on self-generative and computation structures rather than on natural language."[26] As "machine learning adaptive algorithms, big data and Internet of Things rapidly foster emergence of stand-along computation ecosystems and entities," the New Aesthetic foregrounds "glitches, compression and codec artifacts, satellite images."[27] But it does not seek to sort them or point out inadequacies for correction but to uncover, to reveal, to show in new modalities, the aesthetics of digitalia in moments of ruptures, overlaps, delays, noise, blurs, and processual unpredictability in computational systems designed to generate regularized operations. Crucially, these moments occur outside of individual or collective intention, because the machine, the digital itself, stands not for a human subject but operates with relative independence. It marks the moment when the digital "becomes a dominant force in contemporary society that is increasingly beyond the control of its users."[28]

Consider, for instance, the interdependency of drone technologies and nature, or how drone designs are based on animals, birds, and nature in general. To improve flying distance, maneuverability, payload delivery, efficiency, and safety, scientists and designers are studying how animals move, and birds and insects fly. Taking the box turtle as a design template, due to its concise, box-like shape that can protect the turtle, while it also projects itself out of the shell to move faster, they designed the GearQuad, a small drone whose wings fold inside the cage, which has a protective grid, when the drone finds humans in proximity, and expands out of the cage when flying at higher altitude. Using the pufferfish as a model, which gains its eponymous name due to its ability to puff up to deter threats, designers prototyped a drone with a "shield of plastic hoops" that can "expand in size from roughly 20 inches to 33 inches" to "prevent dangerous collisions."[29]

Similarly, another drone design is based on a study of pigeons, which fly confidently in different conditions because they change their wing shapes in flight. For instance, "morphing drones," so-called because they morph their wings in flight, the LisHawk, based on the goshawk, a bird, has three types of feathers in its wings, which can fold or expand to gain speed, slow down, glide, or maneuver a complex flight path.[30] The orinthoptors are "biologically inspired aircraft" that "fly by flapping their wings and may one day prove more versatile, safer and quieter than existing drones." Because they are very light and need less power than propellor drones, orinthoptors consume "40 percent less electrical power" than their counterpart.[31] Plants are also design models for drones; a drone has been designed based on the samara, a winged achene with a seed generated by maple, sycamore, and spruce trees, whose elongated shape makes it well suited for responding to wind shifts, moving up, sideways, or down lightly.[32]

Such developments are part of Bio-Inspired Robotics, which includes robotic bees, robotic fish, cheetah-inspired robots, and bird-inspired robots. This field "draws inspiration from biological systems and processes to design and develop robots ... This field is driven by the idea that nature has already provided elegant and efficient solutions to many challenges, and by emulating those solutions, robots can become more versatile, adaptive, and efficient in various applications."[33]

The point here is that drones are coming in many shapes and sizes, which make them more familiar to us, because their shapes and sizes and movements are drawn from nature, from birds, insects, fish, and animals; such nature-inspired drones create familiarity, making drones less strange and dread-inspiring, drones become domesticated, so to speak; they become part of the everyday world, as part of nature's engineered presence in built environments. Drones, their designs, functions, and uses, are becoming a commonplace.

We can say that the New Aesthetic is the banality of the digital in ordinary life, or, as Wiles puts it, "the eruption of a new kind of banality" that involves bringing to the fore what is taken for granted, like the cloud-like nature of the Internet, when in actuality, it's the deep interlinking of material products (hardware) and virtual ones (software) that form the armature of things digital.[34] Such attitudes typify the post-digital phase in societies where the digital has become ubiquitous.[35] Let's break down the term "post-digital" to understand the New Aesthetic as a feature of drone cultures.

The Post-digital Condition

The term "post-digital" denotes the scale and depth of digitalia's impact in all spheres of human activity. "The tendrils of digital technology," Kim Cascone points out, "have in some way touched everyone."[36] To Scott Contreras-Koterbay and Łukasz Mirocha, the "postdigital is therefore interested in assessing these consequences by locating, conceptualizing and critically examining manifestations of the postdigital condition in society, culture, economy etc."[37] Post-digital, argues Florian Cramer, describes a "contemporary disenchantment with the digital information systems and media gadgets," due to skepticism toward "techno-positivist innovation narratives."[38] Instead, the tendency is to accept and thrive in the "messy state of media, arts and design after their digitization."[39]

There is now "a deliberate choice of renouncing electronic technology, thereby calling into question the common assumption that computers, as meta-machines, represent obvious technological progress."[40] Carmer notes that checking out flea markets for vinyl records while listening to music on iPods, or using oil paint and photoshopping with the latest applications, shows a post-digital sensibility, one that seeks "the technology most suitable to the job, rather than automatically 'defaulting' to the latest 'new' media."[41]

What Cramer points to in post-digital culture can be viewed as a continuation of trends Henry Jenkins describes in *Convergence Culture: Where Old and New Media Collide*, which foregrounds the overlap of "media convergence, participatory culture, and collective intelligence" that facilitates "the flow of content across multiple media platforms, the cooperation between multiple media industries, and the migratory behavior of media audiences who will go almost anywhere in search of the kind of entertainment experiences they want."[42] It is a continuation of trends Rita Raley examines in *Tactical Media*, which highlights "tactical media" or artistic and popular "forms of intervention, dissent, and resistance" purposed toward "the temporary creation of a situation in which signs, messages, and narratives are set into play and critical thinking becomes possible ... Tactical media operates in the field of the symbolic, the site of power in the postindustrial society."[43]

Arguing for an expansive engagement with culture in surveillance studies, Anders Albrechtslund and Lynsey Dubbeld point to three trends: surveillance as a tool for state domination over peoples, comprising their rights and liberties; surveillance as method to protect and care for individual and peoples by the state and in private or personal settings; and surveillance used "to create surprising, innovative and sometimes even interactive entertainment."[44] The third point takes us to drones and surveillance in art and culture, which includes all three tendencies noted above, which embodies the New Aesthetic's impulse to bring the hidden to the fore, juxtapose the glitch with the perfectly rendered or balanced, the static with the smooth, the frazzled pixels with high-resolution, and so on. In culture, online or digital or crowdsourced games "do not seem to aim to criticize the legitimacy of surveillance practices. Instead, they are meant to do little else than produce excitement and diversion. The unilateral focus on fun is evident from the fact that surveillance as a theme is seldom, if at all, addressed, discussed or problematized in the games' descriptions and instructions."[45]

Eversion in the Everyware

The infusion into everyday life of the frazzled, blurred, pixelated, glitched, doubled, multiplied, composited, interactive, collaged, inter-medialized, frozen, static, delayed, broken, to Justin Hodgson, in *Post-Digital Rhetoric and the New Aesthetic*, "involves more than just the overt infusions of algorithmic media, mobile computing, data sensors, and the like into everyday life (unequally distributed as they may be). It also includes the slow-boil of a human-technology perspective that routinely imagines the materialities of the world as being/becoming digitally responsive and that increasingly situates human activity (and human bodies) as things to be tracked, targeted, and tabulated (data streams subject to computational manipulation)."[46]

Hodgson "points toward an increasingly human-technology-infused aesthetic (seeing and sensing patterns of perception germane to the assemblage itself."[47] Such orientations toward the built environment, such perceptions about human interaction with materiality point to a deep turning over, from the outside in and inside out, of digitalia. The material world and the digital world do not lose their difference to produce something entirely new, negating both categories, but are constantly interfacing to produce new experiences of living in a post-digital world: "In an everted culture the network no longer floats in the sky" but "exists down in the muck of everyday life."[48] Everyday life, in other words, becomes everted.

Steven Jones explains in *The Emergence of the Digital Humanities*, that in coining "cyberspace" in 1982–84 in a short story ("Burning Chrome") and novel (*Neuromancer*), William Gibson marks a shift to eversion as an emerging cultural environment in which the duality between the material and digital are not only blurred but, because they frequently imbricate, they influence what and how we make things and interact with them in altered environments. Gibson explains, "But cyberspace is everywhere now, having everted and colonized the world. It starts to sound kind of ridiculous to speak of cyberspace as being somewhere else."[49] He means that we can no longer immerse ourselves in cyberspace and get back to an analog world, despite their close connections. Cyberspace has moved past its status as a digital, other space seducing us into completed immersion, from which we can move in and out at will, a world that we can keep at bay, one distinguishable from the real or analog world; now cyberspace is becoming part and parcel of the built environment and of many facets of human interaction. Our material and psychosocial worlds are thoroughly mediated practices and have mediated forms.

As Odile, a character in Gibson's novel *Spook Country*, remarks to Hollis and Alberto, cyberspace "turns itself inside out ... it is everting."[50] Elaborating on Gibson, Jones says, "The metaphor of eversion is particularly resonant, particularly useful, because it articulates a widely experienced shift in our collective understanding of the network during the last decade: inside out, from a world apart to a part of the world, from a transcendent virtual reality to mundane experience, from a mysterious, invisible abstract world to a still mostly invisible (but real) data-grid that we move through every day in the physical world."[51]

Citing N. Katherine Hayles who underscored the early phase of cybernetics with disembodied forms and practices, which later morphed into hybrid realities as digitalia spread across social life, Jones notes, "what was once imagined as a realm apart is now discovered all around us in the physical world, as information and data are seen as complexly material phenomena, everywhere embodied."[52] Jones says that "as the augmented has displaced the virtual, and computing has gone mobile and locative ... [there is] the shift in attitude toward networked technology."[53] In the post-digital world, as data generation intensifies, they are becoming part of the lived spaces of daily life, such "that users will experience data (and data-enriched media) anywhere, everywhere, while moving through the world—and mobility is a key feature of the experience."[54]

What Gibson, Jones, and Hayles point to is nicely colloquialized by Adam Greenfield as "everyware." Nowadays, "the garment, the room and the street become sites of processing and mediation."[55] From "shower stalls" and "coffee pots" to "clothing, furniture, walls and doorways" Greenfield observes, "all the family rituals of daily life—things as fundamental as the way we wake up in the morning, get to work, or shop for our groceries—are remade as an intricate dance of information about ourselves, the state of the external world and the options available to us at any given moment."[56]

Everyware is "information processing dissolving in behavior";[57] it "isn't so much a particular kind of hardware or software as it is a situation";[58] it "acts at the scale of the body" by micro cameras, chips, and sensors that can take temperature, pulse, urine and stool analyses, and a host of other things, which turn the body into a site for ubiquitous surveillance, mapping, digitizing, and data generation for varied purposes.[59] As Greenfield notes, "The project of everyware is nothing less than the colonization of everyday life by information technology."[60] In the latter part of the 2000s, we see a major shift toward the post-digital condition, as My Space, Instagram, Google Books, Google Maps, iPhone, and other transformative innovations intensified the spread and depth of the digital's reach in society.[61]

Greenfield argues that "everyware must default to harmlessness," so that users are not unduly disadvantaged or harmed due to systemic failures or disruptions;[62] it must consider the user's "reputation and sense of dignity" and be "conservative of face";[63] it should be "conservative of time" in that users should not spend excessive time to do ordinary things because those things are everted or are permeated with digital technologies;[64] and it "must be deniable" by giving users the freedom to check out, to opt out, without undue burden.[65]

These principles are important to resist the allure of post-digitality as a given condition. When we are making the digital real, and the real digital, we are building our environments with the digital in mind, and vice versa. In creating a museum or event or, say, the décor of a plane's interior with an eye toward how their digital representation will play out, we live that moment of eversion, the turning of the inside to the outside and the outside turning inside—constantly, and to the extent where our early phase of enchantment with the digital has now become quotidian reality. The post-digital world, Hodgson avers, in its New Aesthetic dimension, marks "a transformation in which everything is susceptible to participating in/with the digital. The impact of this conditionality is that *working creatives now have to design as much for digital representation as for user experience.*"[66]

Hodgson offers the example of how producers of pastry toasters might focus on both the toaster and its aesthetics on Facebook, given the implied acceptance of the users' culture in which turning the material into digital modalities, including for sharing, creates a cultural ecology in which the value of form, function, and aesthetics play out variously. He also cites James Bridle's example of Access Agency proposing to Virgin Atlantic to build a plane's interior décor with an eye not only toward user comfort and taste but also to the potential for its digital shareableness, its aesthetic potential for being made into a digital artifact. "What matters with this shift," Hodgson explains, "is not any digital/real divide but rather the myriad ways in which people experience different configurations (and saturations) of mediation."[67] The New Aesthetic, then, as Hodgson explains well, "is the *making of things in a culture of eversion*," because it "offers an attunement to the making of things in an everted world."[68]

Critiquing the New Aesthetic

In ending this chapter, let me comment briefly on a few criticisms of the New Aesthetic and on how drones and surveillance are elemental to a new mode of seeing the world, and, more to the point, a new mode of understanding war and peace. About the New Aesthetic, two ideas need examination: the use of "aesthetic" and the self-reflective, self-referential posture adopted to unravel or unveil the network. The first issue: in "The New Aesthetic and its Politics," Bridle says he used "aesthetic" only as a general descriptor of the digitally networked society, "by which I meant simply, 'what it looks like'—I wasn't even really aware of how key the term aesthetics was to art historical and critical discourse. As a result of my use of this term, much of the critical reaction to it has only looked at the surface, and has—sometimes willfully it feels—failed to engage with the underlying concerns of the New Aesthetic, its own critique and politics."[69] This view of the New Aesthetic as an explanatory device to explain the elements of new phenomena involving digitality undercuts the term's immense affective and aesthetic meanings. In attempting to capture the energy or patterns of interactions that give shape and form to the power relations of network societies, the term often downplays the complex relation of art to society, the creative impulse to the political impulse. At times, art becomes politics through and through, resulting in politics swallowing up art, turning aesthetics and poetics into handmaids to politics.

Connecting Art to Society

The same concern is raised by Alan Liu in assessing the digital humanities as a knowledge field, a set of discourses and practices around the digital with a strong humanities focus. Liu writes:

> While digital humanists develop tools, data, and metadata critically, therefore (e.g., debating the "ordered hierarchy of content objects" principle; disputing whether computation is best used for truth finding or, as Lisa Samuels and Jerome McGann put it, "deformance"; and so on), rarely do they extend their critique to the full register of society, economics, politics, or culture. How the digital humanities advances, channels, or resists today's great postindustrial, neoliberal, corporate, and global flows of information-cum-capital is thus a question rarely heard in the digital humanities associations, conferences, journals, and projects with which I am familiar.[70]

I agree with Liu for a cultural analysis of all things digital to help us think "critically about the power, finance, and other governance protocols of the world."[71] Even as the New Aesthetic seeks to make visible the material networks that produce and manage virtual life, there is little extended exploration or systematic examination of the social and political contexts in which drone technologies and surveillance have become what they are in the twenty-first century: the continued desire to consolidate empire in the world. In my previous book *Dwelling in American: Dissent, Empire, and Globalization*, I addressed these issues in the context of rethinking globalization as an entanglement of empires and opposing, contradictory forces linking countries, nations, nationalisms, and other ideologies. This entanglement does not reduce globalization to Westernization or Americanization but examines the flows of power and influence along multiple social and economic networks in the world.[72]

In this book, the focus is on new forms of technology that are profoundly impacting our ideas of war and peace, good and evil, innocence and guilt, private worlds and public arenas. In focusing on the New Aesthetic as a cultural moment marked by the rise of drones, I am highlighting why art and politics do not disappear into each other but work through slippages and overlaps in form, meaning, articulation, reification, immanence: drones and surveillance have become integral elements of everyday culture in which ideas of beauty and form and aesthetic appreciation are produced and get entangled with ideas of national security, war on terrorism, national good, human rights, and global justice in and through these technologies and in the techno ecosystems they create.

Beyond Postmodernism

The second issue that needs reconsidering is the self-reflective, internally generated referential turn of the New Aesthetic when Bridle writes, "People are 'acting' in ways we may or may not understand, which may or may not have an effect in the real world, whether it's signing petitions, organising riots (on BBM), clicking, 'liking' KONY, whatever, the correct (maybe) response is not to have an opinion (default internet response, still) or a moral position, but to live inside the thing as it unfolds."[73] This passage puts into quotation marks—""—the entire enterprise of the New Aesthetic's objective to visibilize the power dynamics of drones and surveillance networks. Art becomes a purely self-referential performance that strains to make itself socially relevant, and what relevance it finds circumscribes the ambit created and maintained by the networks themselves. In more ways than one, this is a classic postmodern impulse: seek and thrive in immanence, claim no outside space beyond what one inhabits or can know through certain systems of epistemology, constantly blur distinctions of inside/outside, and so on. It comes dangerously close to turning artistic politics into political theater, where art can flourish while politics goes on as usual.

This is what troubles Bruce Sterling who, in "Essay on the New Aesthetic," observes, "'Aesthetics' are more than whatever gets splashed onto Cafe Press T-shirts this season. Aesthetics are by their nature metaphysical. Aesthetics are, by definition, how beauty is perceived and valued in a human sensorium. Aesthetics is therefore an issue of metaphysics. Perception, beauty, judgment and value are all metaphysical issues."[74] To Sterling, there is a hurried tone and style to the New Aesthetic, which is primarily associated with the work of technology-savvy creative groups in London, possessing an understandable generational perception of their work as marking a break from old or existing practices. The idea of computer detritus, glitch art, space images and satellite views of the earth and the cosmos, computational approaches to the sciences and the arts, digital media, and so on are not new, but the New Aesthetic tends to selectively focus on certain extreme or popular or unusual elements to herald a new mode of thinking about contemporary society.

The problem, points out Sterling, is that "a heap of eye-catching curiosities don't constitute a compelling worldview,"[75] a view shared by Ian Bogost in "The

New Aesthetic Needs to Get Weirder" when he notes, "In a century, art has evolved from caprice into bric-a-brac. The Futurists crashed cars; the New Aestheticians assemble scrapbooks."[76] There is too much announcing of new trends and fads and events: "The New Aesthetic is moving out of its original discovery phase, and into an evangelical, podium-pounding phase," avers Sterling.[77] When Sterling says, "It is generational. Most of the people in its network are too young to have been involved in postmodernity. The twentieth century's Modernist Project is like their Greco-Roman antiquity. They want something of their own to happen, to be built, and to be seen on their networks. If that has little or nothing to do with their dusty analog heritage, so much the better for them," he sharply underscores the flattening of history in the New Aesthetic, a disposition toward getting caught up with technological novelty, innovation, and fast-moving events without expending the energy to deepen understanding.[78]

Sterling's assessment is often on-target: the New Aesthetic presents compelling evidence that digital technologies are increasingly and invasively permeating daily life; it is not closely guarded but open to amateurs; it grew organically in response to prevailing cyber culture in London; its ideas and views are not place-bound in relevance but translate well where information technologies and cyber societies abound; it is less speculative and focused on abstracting principles out of phenomena, but more work-oriented with a deep-in-the-digital-trenches mentality. Nevertheless, Sterling cautions against viewing the New Aesthetic as a marked departure or attempting a radical mode of understanding, and against postulating about digital ephemera whose ruptures are not new. Like Sterling, Bogost acknowledges, "The New Aesthetic embraces an unusual creative technique: aggregation," but adds that "merely collecting things isn't aesthetics, it's just avarice."[79] Greg Borenstein disagrees, noting that the New Aesthetic has potential when linked to Object Oriented Ontology, which is a study of things as things, not only as we would like them to be. Studying the digital artifacts and how they affect us can be complemented by how they also interact with other artifacts we create:

> Moreover, as Object-Oriented thinkers, New Aestheticians are interested not just in the significance of face detection algorithms, surveillance drones, gesture recognition systems, image compression techniques, CCTV networks, book-scanning operations, satellite maps, and digital fabrication schemes for humans but they're also obsessed with how these new 21st century objects impact the things we design and cohabitate with. They want to know what CCTV means for social networks, what book scanning means for iOS apps, and what face detection means for fashion. And again these objects are not just interesting to each other as a set of constraints and affordances for the objects' human makers but for the hidden inner lives of the objects themselves throughout their existence.[80]

This approach, while signifying potential, comes with risks that are not adequately addressed, a point I earlier noted about the conflation of art with politics and politics with art to the point where full immersion in the New Aesthetic, despite the geographically and culturally variable effects of its objects of inquiry and tools of production and analysis, becomes its legitimating principle. Kyle McDonald, for instance, echoes Bridle's valuation of aesthetics: "The New Aesthetic observes the byproducts of functionally-driven design and appropriates the emergent aesthetic. Not because the machines 'picked' it, but because we see the common themes, and find them beautiful. We see the square pixels, the 8-bit color palettes, and we embrace them not for their function but for their beauty … a glitch isn't inherently 'New Aesthetic,' but it certainly becomes that when appropriated. Just like the voxel sculptures, glitch revels in the visual result of a functional system purely for its aesthetic merit."[81]

Here, art operates in rarefied contexts where form and function are examined "purely for [their] aesthetic merit," because we "find them beautiful." The object-oriented ontology of the New Aesthetic, also advocated by philosopher Ian Bogost, seeks to understand the machine *as* a machine, from within its own logics of operation, not as an entity having no relation to humans but as an object that has equal standing with everything else in the world, in the sense that an object's essence cannot be reduced to its relation to humans since it also relates to other things. Bogost explains it this way:

> Ontology is the philosophical study of existence. Object-oriented ontology ("OOO" for short) puts *things* at the center of this study. Its proponents contend that nothing has special status, but that everything exists equally—plumbers, cotton, bonobos, DVD players, and sandstone, for example. In contemporary thought, things are usually taken either as the aggregation of ever smaller bits (scientific naturalism) or as constructions of human behavior and society (social relativism). OOO steers a path between the two, drawing attention to things at all scales (from atoms to alpacas, bits to blinis), and pondering their nature and relations with one another as much with ourselves.[82]

The aim here is not to explain OOO or debate the merits of the New Aesthetic as a practice of OOO; rather, it is to point out that the critical reception of the New Aesthetic in McDonald and Bogost, who propose OOO as a key impulse of the New Aesthetic, dovetails well with Bridle's emphasis on immersion in the network to grasp its invisibility and make it visible, thus denting its political power. To quote him again, "People are 'acting' in ways we may or may not understand, which may or may not have an effect in the real world, whether it's signing petitions, organising riots (on BBM), clicking, 'liking' KONY, whatever, the correct (maybe) response is not to have an opinion (default internet response, still) or a moral position, but to live inside the thing as it unfolds."[83] But in laying bare the invisible workings of networks, algorithmic functions, face recognition, video and image mashing, surveillance systems, the New Aesthetic risks losing the ability to move or think outside itself and its creative spaces; it ends up, as it does in McDonald's formulation and Bridle's, eager to "live inside the thing as it unfolds,"[84] as a movement or practice or mood concerned with its own "aesthetic merit," to use McDonald's words.

Here, the New Aesthetic comes close to collapsing technology into social spaces devoid of the potential for radical breaks and disruptive fissures beyond its locational and systemic boundaries and limits. The differences in how tribal communities in Waziristan, Pakistan, deal with the deadly effects of drone strikes and how people in New York or London deal with the creative power of drones become redundant events whose dynamic relationship to technology becomes extraneous to the ethical and political systems that establish and support the networks. Or at best, they become supplementary differences in culture, attitude, and taste, differences of personal opinion, or subjective speculation.

New Aesthetic and the Surveillant Assemblage

The New Aesthetic's exploration of drone warfare and surveillance cultures stands out in Bridle's work. Extending the New Aesthetic into performance art, Bridle began drawing the outlines of armed drones in the streets of London, Istanbul, and Washington D.C. He uses Instagram, a social medium that allows users to post images online and to other media sites, to host *dronestagram*, a site Bridle created to post images from Google maps of places struck by drone missiles, and to document the scale and location of drone attacks not often given due coverage in the press or officials of the government and the military. By doing this, he seeks to publicly showcase how drones come with dispositions, that is, how they embody particular ways of understanding the role of technology in society. He writes:

> Drones—the armed, unmanned planes in action around the world—are dispositional. Their significance is not wholly in their appearance, but in how they transform the space around them.[85]

This new disposition reorients us to space and time. Here, politics and power do not operate outside of technology but are immanent in its form and presence:

> The drone also, for me, stands in part for the network itself: an invisible, inherently connected technology allowing sight and action at a distance. Us and

the digital, acting together, a medium and an exchange. But the non-human components of the network are not moral actors, and the same technology that permits civilian technological wonder, the wide-eyed futurism of the New Aesthetic and the unevenly-distributed joy of living *now*, also produces obscurantist "security" culture, ubiquitous surveillance, and robotic killing machines.[86]

Drones and surveillance cultures are interwoven into the fabric of our society today. There cannot be one without the other. Neither makes sense without the other. Drones, pixels, images, wireless connectivity, satellite imagery, and communication can be viewed not only as novel tools developed by decades of research, which in many ways they are, but also as systems in which "technology is the concretization, the instantiation of human politics and desires. It is deep and it is complex and it is hard to see the edges of it, but if you start to see a complete pattern you can kind of render it legible."[87] Moreover, "the network we've been building is a kind of framework to instantiate those desires."[88]

Drone warfare will not remain for long outside American national borders, but due to the immanent nature of their function and structure, their intertwined networks, optical and information inputs and outputs, and dataveillance protocols, drone warfare will, absent strong Congressional, juridical, and societal oversight, become part of American society and geography. Unchecked and unaccounted for, as the use of armed drones largely is, it will not be long before the elsewhere of Afghanistan, Yemen, Libya, and Pakistan where innocent people have lost lives, when we fight enemies whose imminent threat to us remains unclear, becomes the here and the now for America.

In this book, I have argued that the rise of drone warfare and surveillance in the United States are not coincidental developments but are tightly interwoven: they function as instruments to enhance government control over people and institutions abroad and at home. Furthermore, the state's power to govern hinges on controlling the terms in which peace and war can be deployed to serve not the interests of justice but the goals of exercising biopolitical control over vast territories, natural resources, and large demographics. As Bridle notes, "drones are designed to be hidden from view and their effects are kind of hidden from view as well."[89] And more to the point, "drones are prostheses, extensions of the network itself."[90] In "The New Aesthetic and Its Politics," Bridle elaborates on these ideas:

> Let us be clear: just as my work on the form of the book in the digital age was concerned not with the physical or digital object, but with people's understanding and emotions concerning literature; just as my drone works are not about the objects themselves, but about the systems—technological, spatial, legal and political—which permit, shape and produce them, and about

the wider implications of seeing and not seeing such technological, systematic, operations; so the New Aesthetic is concerned with everything that is not visible in these images and quotes, but that is inseparable from them, and without which they would not exist.[91]

Several questions arise in this context: How are digital technologies being integrated into organizational systems and structures and with what consequences for equity and democratic access? Where does individual and governmental responsibility lie? What are the modalities of interaction among businesses and corporations like Google, Yahoo, Facebook, Twitter, Skype, YouTube, and so on, and the National Security Agency, which store metadata of electronic communication and digital activity in massive data banks? How are privacy, personhood, and individuality being redefined and with what implications for social justice? What is the impact of digital technologies on international relations and military strategy? Such questions enable us to mark a cultural turn in the digital humanities. It is in this nexus of law, technology, foreign policy, new media, digital arts, and the humanities that I am grounding my analyses. To reiterate the main reason for focusing on the cultural turn in the digital humanities and the New Aesthetic: instead of viewing drones primarily as destructive weapons, we can understand them as products of a post-digital world in which innovative technologies that compress and expand space and time can be used creatively.

We must understand that drones weave networks of surveillance to become lethal weapons to execute a nation's foreign policy through military means, and that the same tools are being used by people to uncover the unseen, the hidden, the unacknowledged features of drone warfare and its surveillance cultures. The former generates states of exception to allow powerful nation-states to dominate populations and large territories, while the latter produces a New Aesthetic that creatively foregrounds the glitches, paradoxes, slippages, gaps, elisions, and layered effects of deadly weapons of destruction produced by the necropolitical surveillant assemblage. Whether this approach intervenes politically in the cultural realm, I take up in the next and final chapter of the book.

Notes

1   Beryl Pong and Michael Richardson, eds, "An Introduction: An Open Proposition," *Drone Aesthetics: War, Culture, Ecology* (London: Open Humanities Press, 2024), 9–10.
2   Thomas Stubblefield, *Drone Art: The Everywhere War as Medium* (California: University of California Press, 2020), 3.
3   Ibid., 5.
4   Ibid., 7.

5   Rob Conley and Dean Lockwood, "As Above, So Below: Triangulating Drone Culture," *culturemachine.net* vol. 16 (2015), https://culturemachine.net/vol-16-drone-cultures/as-above-so-below/
6   James Bridle, *The New Aesthetic*, May 6, 2011, https://web.archive.org/web/20111114184842/http://www.riglondon.com/blog/2011/05/06/the-new-aesthetic/
7   Will Wiles, "The Machine Gaze," *aeon.com*, September 17, 2012, https://aeon.co/essays/what-do-we-uncover-when-we-look-through-digital-eyes
8   Ibid.
9   "The New Aesthetic: Seeing Like Digital Devices." *South by South West* (SXSW), March 12, 2012, https://schedule.sxsw.com/2012/events/event_IAP11102
10 Joanne McNeil, https://joannemcneil.com/; Ben Terrett, https://noisydecentgraphics.typepad.com/design/2012/03/sxsw-the-new-aesthetic-and-commercial-visual-culture.html; Aaron Straup Cope, https://aaronland.info/weblog/2012/03/13/godhelpus/#sxaesthetic; and Russell Davies, https://russelldavies.typepad.com/planning/2012/03/sxsw-the-new-aesthetic-and-writing.html; Teo Ballvé, "The New Aesthetic Part II: Writing Like a Drone." *territorialmasquerades.com* October 26, 2012, https://territorialmasquerades.net/the-new-aesthetic-part-ii-writing-like-a-drone/
11 James Bridle, "The New Aesthetic," *riglondon.com* 2011, https://web.archive.org/web/20111114184842/http://www.riglondon.com/blog/2011/05/06/the-new-aesthetic/
12 Bridle, "The New Aesthetic." http://new-aesthetic.tumblr.com/about
13 David M. Berry, "The Postdigital Constellation," *Postdigital Aesthetic: Art, Computation and Design*. Edited by David M. Berry and Michael Dieter (New York: Palgrave, 2015), 50.
14 Grant Boller, *Theorizing Digital Cultures* (SAGE, 2018), 8.
15 James Bridle, "#xsaesthetic." Panel "The New Aesthetic: Seeing Like Digital Devices." South By Southwest Conference (SXSW). *booktwo.org* March 15, 2012, http://booktwo.org/notebook/sxaesthetic/
16 Douglas Coupland, *Digital Orca*, https://coupland.com/digital-orca/; Hybe, *Iris*, https://youtube.com/watch?v=qhdG7OltXnU&t=111s; Carina Ow, *Pixels Per Person*, https://architizer.com/projects/pixels-per-person/
17 Bruce Sterling, "An Essay on the New Aesthetic," *wired.com*, April 2, 2012, https://wired.com/2012/04/an-essay-on-the-new-aesthetic/. Also see The Creators Project Staff, "In Response to Bruce Sterling's 'Essay on the New Aesthetic,'" *vice.com*, April 6, 2012, https://vice.com/en/article/in-response-to-bruce-sterlings-essay-on-the-new-aesthetic/
18 Ibid.
19 These explorations, in the academic context, led to scholarly publications like David M. Berry et al., *New Aesthetic, New Anxieties* (V2 Publishing, 2012 https://v2.nl/archive/articles/new-aesthetic-new-anxieties); Scott Contreras-Koterbay and Łukasz Mirocha, *The New Aesthetic and Art: Constellations of The Postdigital* (Amsterdam: Institute of Network Cultures, 2016); Justin Hodgson, *Post-digital Rhetoric and the New Aesthetic* (Ohio: Ohio State University Press, 2019).
20 James Bridle, "James Bridle: Waving at the Machines." Transcript by Guy Leech. December 5, 2011, https://webdirections.org/resources/james-bridle-waving-at-the-machines/
21 Ibid.
22 Ibid.

23 Teo Ballvé, "The New Aesthetic Part II: Writing Like a Drone." *territorialmasquerades.com* October 26, 2012, https://territorialmasquerades.net/the-new-aesthetic-part-ii-writing-like-a-drone/
24 James Bridle, "#xsaesthetic." Panel "The New Aesthetic: Seeing like Digital Devices." South By Southwest Conference (SXSW). *booktwo.org* March 15, 2012, accessed May 19, 2014, http://booktwo.org/notebook/sxaesthetic/
25 Marius Watz, "The Problem with Perpetual Newness." *The Creator's Project*. April 6, 2012, http://thecreatorsproject.vice.com/blog/in-response-to-bruce-sterlings-essay-on-the-new-aesthetic
26 Scott Contreras-Koterbay and Łukasz Mirocha, *The New Aesthetic and Art: Constellations of the Postdigital* (Amsterdam: Institute of Network Cultures, 2016), 9.
27 Ibid., 9, 11.
28 Ibid., 24.
29 Charles Choi, "Mimicking Biology for Better Drones," *insideunmannedsystems.com* December 17, 2020, https://insideunmannedsystems.com/mimicking-biology-for-better-drones/
30 Ibid.
31 Ibid.
32 Akshata Shendge, "How Birds and Butterflies Are Inspiring Drone Design," *womenwhodrone.co* October 18, 2023, https://womenwhodrone.co/single-post/the-potential-of-bio-inspired-drones-nature-s-design-in-uav
33 Jagjit Singh Dhatterwal, Kuldeep Singh Kaswan, and Reenu Batra, *Nature Inspired Robotics* (New York: Taylor and Francis, 2024), 21.
34 Wiles, "The Machine Gaze."
35 In March 2011, James Bridle led a panel on The New Aesthetic at the South By Southwest conference (SXSW); panels members sharing their views included Joanne McNeil, Ben Terrett, Aaron Straup Cope, and Russell Davies. See "#sxaesthetic: Report from Austin, Texas, on the New Aesthetic Panel at SXSW," *booktwo.org*, March 15, 2012, http://booktwo.org/notebook/sxaesthetic/. Also see The Creators Project Staff, "In Response to Bruce Sterling.
36 Kim Cascone, "The Aesthetics of Failure: "Post-Digital" Tendencies in Contemporary Computer Music." *Computer Music Journal* 24, no. 4 (2000): 12. Failure in music composition, writes Cascone, has become essential to sound production, in that "it is from the 'failure' of digital technology that this new work has emerged: glitches, bugs, application error, system crashes, clipping, aliasing, distorting, quantization noise, and even the noise floor of computer sound cards are the raw materials composers seek to incorporate into their music" (13).
37 Scott Contreras-Koterbay and Łukasz Mirocha, *The New Aesthetic and Art: Constellations of the Postdigital* (Amsterdam: Institute of Network Cultures, 2016), 40.
38 Florian Cramer, "What Is 'post-digital'"? *APRJA* 3, no. 1 (2014): 12.
39 Ibid., 7.
40 Ibid., 11.
41 Ibid., 21.
42 Henry Jenkins, *Convergence Culture: Where Old and New Media Collide*. Proquest Ebook Central (New York: New York University Press, 2006), 2.
43 Rita Raley, *Tactical Media*. Proquest Ebook Central (Minneapolis: University of Minnesota Press, 2009), 6.

44 Anders Albrechtslund and Lynsey Dubbeld, "The Plays and Arts of Surveillance: Studying Surveillance as Entertainment," *Surveillance and Society* 3, no. 2–3 (2005): 218.
45 Albrechtslund and Dubbeld, "The Plays and Arts of Surveillance," 219. As examples of surveillance as entertainment, the authors cite computer games like *The Sentinel* (1986), *The Sims* (2000), the *Blair Watch Project* (2005), and *Monopoly Live* (2005). In the last two examples, people were encouraged to send pictures of Tony Blair and his entourage as they electioneered so that they could be posted on public websites to "assemble as many pictures of possible of handsome Tony and his elusive entourage" (219). (https://flickr.com/photos/blairwatchproject/) The company Hasbro Games launched Monopoly Live online as a game that extends the traditional game of purchasing or setting up real estate, but includes eighteen cabs in London, each with GPS systems that track how rent is collected. Buoyed by the popularity of the game, the company permitted players to play the game "for their own entertainment," separate from the game as brand in its marketing campaign (https://campaignlive.co.uk/article/taxis-monopoly-game-relaunch/510872)
46 Justin Hodgson, *Post-Digital Rhetoric and the New Aesthetic* (Columbus, Ohio: Ohio State University Press, 2019), 67.
47 Ibid., 69.
48 Ibid., 70.
49 William Gibson, "The Art of Fiction," interview with David Wallace-Wells, *Paris Review* 197, 2011 https://theparisreview.org/interviews/6089/the-art-of-fiction-no-211-william-gibson
50 William Gibson, *Spook Country* (New York: Putnam, 2007), 20.
51 Steven E. Jones, *The Emergence of the Digital Humanities* (New York: Routledge, 2014), 19.
52 Ibid., 23.
53 Ibid., 14.
54 Ibid.
55 Adam Greenfield, *Everyware: The Dawning Age of Ubiquitous Computing* (CA: New Riders, 2006), 1.
56 Ibid., 1, 19.
57 Ibid., 26.
58 Ibid., 31.
59 Ibid., 48.
60 Ibid., 33.
61 Jones, *The Emergence*, 20–3.
62 Greenfield, *Everyware*, 233.
63 Ibid., 239.
64 Ibid., 243.
65 Ibid., 246.
66 Hodgon, *Post-Digital Rhetoric*, emphasis in original, 80.
67 Ibid., 70.
68 Ibid., emphasis in original, 72.
69 James Bridle, "The New Aesthetic and its Politics." booktwo.org June 12, 2013, http://booktwo.org/notebook/new-aesthetic-politics/
70 Alan Liu, "Where Is Cultural Criticism in the Digital Humanities?" *Debates in the Digital Humanities*. Edited by Matthew K. Gold (Minneapolis: University of

Minnesota Press, 2013, Open Access Edition http://dhdebates.gc.cuny.edu/debates/text/20

71 Ibid.
72 John Muthyala, *Dwelling in American: Dissent, Empire, and Globalization* (Dartmouth: New England University Press, 2012).
73 James Bridle, "#sxaesthetic." *booktwo.org*. March 15, 2012, http://booktwo.org/notebook/sxaesthetic/
74 Bruce Sterling, "Essay on the New Aesthetic." *Wired.com* April 2, 2012, http://wired.com/2012/04/an-essay-on-the-new-aesthetic/
75 Sterling, "Essay."
76 Ian Bogost, "The New Aesthetic Needs to Get Weirder." *theatlantic.com* April 13, 2012, accessed May 21, 2014, http://theatlantic.com/technology/archive/2012/04/the-new-aesthetic-needs-to-get-weirder/255838/
77 Sterling, "Essay."
78 Ibid.
79 Bogost, "The New Aesthetic Needs to Get Weirder."
80 Greg Borenstein, "What It's Like to Be a 21st Century Thing?" *The Creator's Project*. April 6, 2012, http://thecreatorsproject.vice.com/blog/in-response-to-bruce-sterlings-essay-on-the-new-aesthetic
81 Kyle McDonald, "Personyfying Machines, Machining Persons." *The Creator's Project*. April 6, 2012, http://thecreatorsproject.vice.com/blog/in-response-to-bruce-sterlings-essay-on-the-new-aesthetic
82 Ian Bogost, "What Is Object Oriented Ontology? A Definition for Ordinary Folk." *Bogost.com*, December 8, 2009, http://bogost.com/blog/what_is_objectoriented_ontolog.shtml
83 Bridle, "#sxaesthetic."
84 Bridle, "The New Aesthetic and Its Politics."
85 James Bridle, "Drone Shadows and Dispositions." *booktwo.org*. May 16, 2013, http://booktwo.org/notebook/drone-shadows-dispositions/
86 James Bridle, "Under the Shadow of the Drone." *booktwo.org*. October 11, 2011, http://booktwo.org/notebook/drone-shadows/
87 James Bridle, "Naked Lunch." *booktwo.org*. The Conference, Malmö, Sweden, August 2013, http://booktwo.org/videos/
88 James Bridle, "The Future Symposium: Presentation by James Bridle." Film & Video Umbrella's 'Future' Symposium, CCA, Glasgow, June 2013, accessed May 21, 2014, http://booktwo.org/videos/
89 James Bridle, "Day of the Drones." Brisbane Writers Festival. *booktwo.org*. Video, September, 2013, http://booktwo.org/videos/
90 James Bridle, "A Quiet Disposition." Brighton Festival, Lighthouse, Brighton. *booktwo.org*. Video, May 2013, http://booktwo.org/videos/
91 James Bridle, "The New Aesthetic and Its Politics." *booktwo.org* June 12, 2013, http://booktwo.org/notebook/new-aesthetic-politics/; also see "The New Aesthetic."

6 DRONE DISPOSITIONS IN ART AND CULTURE

For more than a month starting in January 2014, the Ann Arbor Art Center in Michigan held a special gallery featuring drone art, explaining its choice of subject thus:

> Drones are the quintessential object of the 21st century. They are revolutionizing global warfare and domestic and foreign surveillance, galvanizing the creative impulse, and challenging democratic principles and personal values around the globe. They are changing the way we work, play, battle, and live in the 21st century.[1]

"Galvanizing the creative impulse" aptly characterizes the artistic and cultural activity about drones. Drones in cultural production raise questions about the relationships between art and life, artistic license and realistic representation, and creator's intention and viewer's response. These relationships are fraught with the paradoxes and frustrations of using drone art for personal expression, social communication, democratic dissent, commercial interests, group or collective hobbies, technological experimentation, education, research, or public safety. The authority of representation (who has the right to creatively represent drones?) and the politics of location (how does geography affect artistic production, circulation, and reception?) become knotty issues without easy resolutions. Arguing that we need to develop transnational social and political contexts to understand these developments, in this chapter I examine a range of multimedia art, music, graffiti, songs, and performances featuring drones to demonstrate elements of the New Aesthetic at play in them. They do, as a whole or individually, represent the New Aesthetic as such. I will describe specific aspects of the New Aesthetic as they relate to the use of drones, namely, glitches, pixelization, noise, automated performances, volumetric play, and so on, as noted in the previous chapter.

Drone as Disposition Matrix

Elaborating on the New Aesthetic feature of drone art, Bridle draws from the concept of "disposition matrix," which is used by the National Counterterrorism Center to explain the process by which intelligence about suspects is gathered and data mined to identify and dispose of targets. Bridle suggests viewing drones in terms of their "dispositions," their ability to project certain ways of understanding the role of technology in society. He writes:

> Drones—the armed, unmanned planes in action around the world—are dispositional. Their significance is not wholly in their appearance, but in how they transform the space around them; both physical space (the privileged view of the weaponised surveillance camera at 50,000 feet) and legal, national and diplomatic spaces that as a result permit new kinds of warfare and assassination. And the Disposition Matrix is an organizing principle: not a thing, not a technology, not an object, but an active form, a reorientation of intent into another dimension or mode of expression. In another sense, the Disposition Matrix is the network itself, the internet and us, an abstract machine, intangible but effective. Finally, the Disposition Matrix is an attitude and a performance.[2]

This disposition makes it difficult for us to grasp the dynamics of politics and power that operate outside of technology but are immanent to it. It increases the need to make visible what can technologically be invisible (drones fly at high altitudes while surveilling the terrain) and what governments want to be invisible (the presence or role of drones in a strike is not often announced but denied). To contest these two levels of invisibility, Bridle's drone art inscribes the shape of drones in public spaces and uses social media to circulate images of places targeted by drone missiles. By turning public spaces into theater, drone art engages with the politics of visibility and invisibility. The chalked or painted outlines of drones evoke the shadows they cast as they fly at variable altitudes.

"Drones," posits Bridle, "are just the latest in a long line of military technologies augmenting the process of death-dealing, but they are among the most efficient, the most distancing, the most invisible. These qualities allow them to do what they do unseen, and create the context for secret, unaccountable, endless wars."[3] The responsibility of the artist to society involves making the invisible visible and working with technologies of networks and open sourcing to infuse into the public commons subjects not often discussed, or even acknowledged. He, along with a small team of supporters, painted the shapes of drones on public streets and sidewalks, as he did of the Reaper and the Predator in London, Istanbul, and Washington, DC.

When his art was showcased at the Corcoran Gallery of Art in Washington DC, Bridle painted the shape of the armed drone Reaper right outside the steps to the building, not far from the White House. Most of such drawings are 1:1 representations in that he outlines the shape of a drone to represent the physical object's dimensions. It has a startling effect for two reasons: most people are largely unaware of drones as military tools, besides what they read or hear about in the media, which is often selective in its coverage, and the white outline of the drone cordons off, at least at first glance, an area that is off-limits because it appears as the site of a crime.[4] By using Instagram, a social medium that allows users to post images online and to other media sites, to host *dronestagram*, a site Bridle created to post images from Google maps of sites struck by drone missiles, he documents the scale and location of military activities that are not covered by the press and government officials.

Bridle pushes the envelope further in *Watching the Watchers*, as he began posting satellite images of drones in various parts of the world.[5] Because drones acquire their power through remote operations, distancing, and invisibility, showcasing drone images in hangars and classified locations, albeit some available online, turns them into objects for global viewing; that is, the watcher becomes the watched. Although it does not and cannot equalize power dynamics, the effort to watch the watchers performs a global act of "surveillance," in a manner of speaking, on the drone, its operations, and its effects. Jason Komada suggests that "by rendering them visible, people can eventually render their operation and politics legible, and thus open up this topic to intervention."[6]

By highlighting a site in ways commonly associated with places where extreme violence has taken place (gruesome accident, murder), such drone art evokes a *here that is an elsewhere*. The "here" of this drone art signifies an "elsewhere" of drone killings. The chalked or painted outlines of drones imply the possible criminality or illegality of drones. What Bridle says about drones as part of networks is worth noting:

> The drone also, for me, stands in part for the network itself: an invisible, inherently connected technology allowing sight and action at a distance. Us and the digital, acting together, a medium and an exchange. But the non-human components of the network are not moral actors, and the same technology that permits civilian technological wonder, the wide-eyed futurism of the New Aesthetic and the unevenly-distributed joy of living *now*, also produces obscurantist "security" culture, ubiquitous surveillance, and robotic killing machines.[7]

To the extent that it effects an intervention in public discourse about official discourse that downplays or silences discussions about drone warfare, the New Aesthetic reveals the invisible aesthetically: showing visualizations of sophisticated digital platforms that generate visual imagery and data about the surveilled. How the drone sees the world becomes part of how we see the world of drones.

Droning of Experience

Australian artist Kathryn Brimblecombe-Fox's war paintings represent new modes of seeing as drones and surveillance become commonplace. *Sky-Drone-Net* has an orange drone in the center of the canvas, with several straight lines emanating from it; the entire picture is backgrounded with a cloudy, blue sky. To peoples living in drone zones (Pakistan, Somalia, Afghanistan, etc.), the notion of an empty blue sky is difficult to imagine, because of the ever-present threat of drones loitering in the sky, surveilling them, and targeting them with missiles, all without notice.

Not a Game shows a drone with its surveillant radius in its front, and the satellite and reception tower locations and other data processing units located in various places on the canvas. It foregrounds the drone as a networked apparatus with a hidden infrastructure, but which, when represented against a variously colored blue sky, gains visual presence as a network of digital connections that facilitate drone surveillance and dominance. In *Swarm Surveillance*, a hive of mini drones swarm with surveillant activity, with each drone's eye of surveillance represented in straight lines, together forming a field of drone vision in which peoples, living things, and the topography are subjected to scrutiny. The drone hive radiates its surveillant gaze in all directions. These and other paintings in watercolor and gauche show drones in landscapes or dronescapes suggesting planetary motion and extreme distance; rendering detailed compositions of objects, peoples, contexts, situations, infostructure, missiles, and so on is not the focus. Brimblecombe-Fox comments:

> I call these landscapes cosmic landscapes. With the presence of the drone, they are also dronescapes. But, because they are cosmic there is the potential for numerous critical perspectives across time and space. The viewer is often unsure whether they are above, below, in front or behind the drone. I do this to trigger re-orientation towards an "everywhere" or universal/cosmic eye that can critically roam around and into the figure of the drone. The ability to imagine universal perspectives is outside a drone's capability—unfortunately, it is also difficult for some humans! That's why art is so important.[8]

As an artist, she apprehends the drone not as a complex militarized digital apparatus but as marking new modes of seeing the world and being in a world of drones: How does the sky appear to people living under the threat of drones? What enables the seemingly omnipresent drone appear and disappear, as it dispenses its version of justice? The drone vision, these paintings show, does not obtain clear pictures of suspects and protagonists; ethically and technologically, the drone's vision is dependent on data collection, distribution, algorithmic analysis, profile matching, and identity marking and geo-tagging. It's the "droned experience" that Brimblecombe-Fox artistically renders visually intelligible, what Mark Andrejevic describes as the "droning of experience"; his explanation deserves a full citation:

> The underlying claim here is that one of the reasons the figure of the drone has so rapidly captured the popular and media imagination is that, in addition to reviving what might be described as the ballistic imaginary once associated with technological gadgetry (in the Popular-Science vision of personal jet packs and rocket-ships), it encapsulates the emerging logic of portable, always-on, distributed, ubiquitous, and automated information capture: the droning of experience and response. The promise of the drone as hyper-efficient information technology is four-fold: it extends, multiplies, and automates the reach of the senses or the sensors, it saturates the time and space in which sensing takes place (entire cities can be photographed 24-hours a day), it automates the sense-making process, and it automates response. In this regard, the figure of the drone, generalised, stands for that of the indefinitely expandable and distributable probe that foregrounds the seemingly inevitable logic of algorithmic decision-making.[9]

Andrejevic nicely explains the powerful appeal of the drone in popular and military culture; indeed, the drone represents our post-digital condition's animating social energies, namely, portability, being constantly turned on, omnipresence, automated processes, and responses. Artistically rendering these energies in color and gauche is the critical task Brimblecombe-Fox sets up for herself, which explains why her paintings often have the mythical tree-of-life in varied sketches or small markings to suggest universal hope and regeneration, by "trigger[ing] questions about the future of life, humanity, and the planet."[10]

Notable in her work is the lack of bloody carnage, the literal result of drone strikes, which can be critiqued, notes Federica Caso, as a propensity to turn the drone into a fetish, an object devoiced of content except the artistic.[11] However, Caso argues, Brimblecombe-Fox's reluctance to render the human subject visible subverts the operational logic of the drone: what the drone wishes to identify, track, and immobilize cannot be identified, tracked, and immobilized in these creative works, which seek to provide alternate views of drones and surveillance. Not only does Brimblecombe-Fox render visible the invisible machinations of the drone but also vivifies, through her art, "the realm of affective cognition, that is, the knowledge derived from the emotive responses of the body in the encounter with the other, human and non-human. Affective cognition is an important yet understated component that participates in social and politics [*sic*] configurations. Art's currency is emotions, and therefore it is a crucial site of affective cognition."[12] By performing aspects of human behaviors, robotic artificial intelligence in drones, and networks and surveillance systems nudge us toward redrawing the boundaries separating humanity from artificiality, the real from the unreal, and a being in the world from an object in the world: they gesture towards a post-human future.

Humanizing Drone Wars

Operating Predator drones require new skill sets and a new mode of understanding terms such as "battlefield," "enemy," "emergency," and "collateral damage." Just twenty-one years old when he started working as a drone pilot, Brandon Bryant operated from the Ground Control Station Air Force base in Nellis, close to Las Vegas, Nevada. In discussing his experiences as a remote pilot operating MQ-1B Predators flying over Afghanistan, Bryant notes that his squadron made 1,626 strikes; in dealing with the aftermath of each strike, Bryant eventually sought therapy and was diagnosed with post-traumatic stress disorder. He realized that "the job made him numb: a 'zombie mode' he slipped into as easily as his flight suit." Reporter Matthew Power adds that Bryant "sometimes felt himself merging with the technology, imagining himself as a robot, a zombie, a drone itself. Such abstractions don't possess conscience or consciousness; drones don't care what they mean, but Bryant most certainly does."[13]

The role of human agency—an embodied sentient being feeling and thinking and deciding—becomes subordinated to the dynamics of data gathering, surveillance, and decision-making. Between the target and the drone pilot is a semi-autonomous digitally run system that generates vast gigabytes of data for surveillance, but as it multiplies its data and coordinates with a slew of other data structures and robotic systems to manage drone vehicles and pilot them, surveillance becomes dataveillance and the pilot and target merge into a vast digital superstructure where they become important nodes whose value and significance is internally assessed in relation to the purpose and viability of the military mission embodied in a global network of surveillance managed by the most powerful country on the earth. Ethics becomes immanent to the form and function of dataveillance, a situation in which external points of reference by which to pose questions about drone strikes become redundant. Ethics turns into assessing inputs and outputs, transmission protocols, evaluative criteria, collaboration among people analyzing varied data sets and military intelligence, readability of still and moving images, algorithmic machine learning to mine big data and generate patterns and trends to surveil, and targets to identify.

Put differently, human life is adiaphorized, Zygmunt Bauman's term that was discussed in the third chapter. To wit, adiaphorization refers to situations where "systems and processes become split off from any other consideration of morality... surveillance streamlines the process of doing things at a distance, of separating a person from the consequences of action."[14] An action becomes "neither good nor evil, measurable against technical (purpose-oriented or procedural) but not against moral criteria."[15] When drone pilots release missiles that rip apart or hollow out structures of steel, aluminum, iron, wood, earth, and human bodies, there is a splattering of things, and of blood and tissue; they call it "bug splat." They are "bugs" because humans appear as such on pixelated screens, and there is a "splat" because, when destroyed, there is human splatter. Bug splat: "collateral damage estimate methodology."[16]

Countering Adiaphorization

To counter the adiaphorization of human life in drone warfare, a collective of anonymous artists from America and Pakistan produced giant posters of victims of drone strikes and plastered them in the area where they were killed in the region of Khyber-Pakhtunkhwa in Pakistan. Featuring the photo of an innocent child whose parents were killed in a drone strike, the poster is enlarged enough to allow drone pilots see not a bug-like pixel on a screen but the face of a human being whose life is impacted by armed drones. Interestingly enough, a photo of this poster was taken by a small drone with cameras and posted online at #notabugsplat.com.[17]

In this public art installation, the aim to humanize victims re-orients the drone pilot's field of vision literally and conceptually. At the literal level, what is remote and bug-like becomes its actual representation in the artistic rendition of a poster photo of a victim's visage and body. The technology to zoom in on a subject to reveal its details comes up short in the drone video feeds, where the subject's human features are pixelated into non-human entities like bugs. Rather than covering the site or hiding it from drone operators, the artists explicitly foreground the killing site with enhanced pictures so that the literal field of vision of the drone pilot sees a different terrain, one re-mapped by human actors on the ground.

At the conceptual level, this enhancement of the subject, who is now dead or living through the trauma of being victimized in drone strikes, changes the logic of adiaphorization in dataveillance into one of human calculation. The giant poster shortens the literal distance by enhancing the subject's image to make it easier for the drone camera to locate it, and it shortens the psychological distance between the drone pilot and drone technology as it turns a datum into a human subject. The giant poster highlights the past (drone strikes killed innocent people) and foregrounds the present (local and other human agents register their views of the strike by signaling who was victimized), hoping that the future will be bereft of such strikes (drone pilots realize the human cost of drone wars and refrain from firing missiles).

Serving as a geo-tagger, the poster memorializes the victims while documenting history in local topography. Its geo-spatial and temporal coordinates are crisscrossed with the explicit purpose of countering the adiaphorization of drone warfare. By taking pictures of the giant poster with a mini drone attached with cameras and broadcasting them online for open access, these artists enact an artistic politics of adaptation and subversion: drone technology is used not to kill or maim or surveil but to relocate the drone that kills and maims and surveils within a re-mapped topography that explicitly foregrounds the ethically compromised effects of drone warfare. Where the US military cannot or does not (or does so surreptitiously) keep records of civilian casualties of drone strikes, the artists practice public history by both documenting the location and victim of strikes and publicizing them for the public and the drone pilot. The giant photo makes public what the drone operators would prefer remain private; the giant photo registers the innocent victims of drone wars where the drone operators see bug splats; the giant photo interrupts the drone's pilot's field of vision by serving as a constant signifier of the ethical dimension of drone warfare. The onus of drone strikes is placed on the shoulders of drone pilots.

Such a reorientation, to extend Lindsay C. Clark and Christian Enemark, can help us "regard care ethics as an added layer of morality."[18] Drawing on feminist discursive interventions in (Carol Gilligan, Ned Noddings, Sara Ruddick) in just war theories, Clark and Enemark affirm a feminist care ethic that moves beyond the valuation of abstraction and disembodiment to relational, embodied notions of human experience to respond to complex phenomena. It means that "when it comes to the exercise of drone violence by individual drone operators, the ambition of greater restraint would be pursued by augmenting *jus in bello* adherence with an ethics of care, and it would be founded on a thick conception of non-combatant harm ... that would require the avoidance of physical and non-physical harms to civilians."[19] *Notabugsplat*'s humanizing of drone violence is an attempt to infuse in the drone pilot's scopic vision a care ethic, inviting the pilot to act as a human agent using technologies to carry out military orders, not as a passive operator of a disembodied machine of war that surveils, targets, and kills. It is not a bug; it is not a splat. The poster reinserts what drone warfare, with all its sophistication, actively seeks to silence: the humanity of drone strike victims. This is art in the service of public history and public humanities.

Local Culture and the Drone as Aesthetic Object

Where *Notabugsplat* reinserts the human into a virtual war with deadly material results, Pakistani American artist Mahwish Chishty seeks to change the symbolic meaning of the drone from one associated with American empire and postmodern violence effected through virtual means to an object worthy of artistic curiosity. She pulls the drone from its militarized setting to turn it into a canvas where local Pakistani truck cultural practices can be painted so that the drone is delinked from foreign state violence and turned into a tool or site for creative experimentation with local culture. Featured at www.mahachishty.com/ are more than a dozen gouache paintings on paper, handmade paper, birch plywood, and Masonite boards. Drones are painted in many shapes, with the MQ-9 Reaper, a popular armed US drone, used as the prominent design. Chishty draws from the folk painting traditions of Pakistani trucking industries where carvings, bright colors, mirrors, calligraphy, and paint are used to adorn trucks, often at considerable cost to their owners.

Trucking in Pakistan is a major industry, as its roadways are used more than its waterways, railways, and airways for freight and public transportation. A total of 60 percent of its 258,000 kilometer road network is paved, and the Bedford Rocket, an iconic British-based truck brand, now shares popularity with Hino and Nissan models from Japan. Truck art, observes Jamal J. Elias in *On Wings of Diesel: Trucks, Identity, and Culture in Pakistan*, is "a function of visual culture as a window in the structure and politics of contemporary societies."[20] Truck drives are not the sole initiators of truck painting but are usually intermediaries between owners and painters with often different intentions for painting: the owners seek to make a business statement and establish uniqueness in the market, which also gives them a chance for personal expression as paintings can include specific requirements of subject and theme and color of the painters; the painters are part of a large circle of locally based small businesses run individually or in groups. Calligraphy in Urdu and English, for instance, signals the owner's familiarity with official or mainstream culture; on roads where top speeds are not feasible, decorative items like pinwheels are used inside trucks, since rough effects of road travel decrease the likelihood of wear and tear of the vehicle, which increases the longevity of art décor. (See Figure 6.1.)

Elias further notes, "The motifs on trucks display not just aesthetic considerations, but attempts to depict aspects of the religious, sentimental and emotional worldviews of the individuals employed in the truck industry. And since trucks represent the major means of transporting cargo throughout Pakistan, truck decoration might very well be this society's major form of representational art."[21] Elias distinguishes among five styles based on regions: Rawalpindi (stylized cowlings, appliqués of plastic), Sawat (wooden door carvings and metal hammered into shapes), Peshawar (a mix of the previous two styles that use carvings, metal, cowlings, paint), Baluch (chrome cowlings, complex, ornate designs patterned into mosaics), and Karachi (biggest truck center showcases all styles, with woodcuts and wide color spectrums). Subjects of decorative art include figures from religious, political, and everyday culture, women, personal art, or objects as talismans. (See Figure 6.2.)

FIGURE 6.1 Islamabad truck art, Pakistan. Baptiste Marcel, Wikimedia Commons.

Mahwish Chisty's Drone Art

Chishty uses many of these elements in painting drones, which are also represented in a variety of drone shapes: some are small, sharp, triangulations with boomerang shapes akin to X-47B; some have bulky, oval front-ends akin to Reaper and Predator drones; some are cast as twins joined at the back with two fronts facing opposite sides; some appear like thin butterflies in flight; and others have a burst of colorful missiles falling downwards from a flying drone. In an interview with Josh Harkinson of *Mother Jones* magazine, Chishty observes that her aim in painting drones this way was to make them "friendlier looking, instead of such hard-edged, metallic war machines." When asked if she were viewing militarized weapons idealistically, Chishty replies, "I don't know if I am glorifying it. I just want people to talk about it. At the same time, it has some kind of beauty to it. I am also looking at them as objects, and not as much as war machines."[22] To her, just as the truck drivers decorate their trucks ornately and with distinctive styles, which she views primarily as aesthetic expression, drone painting by using Pakistani folk art means using local culture to turn an object associated with death and war into an object of aesthetic contemplation.

FIGURE 6.2 Truck art in Pakistan. Riyan Chaudhary, Pexels.

In "By the Moonlight," a gouache painting on birch plywood, Chishty portrays the front underside of a wide-angled drone in green with decorative patterns of white appearing as conjoined shapes; the middle body is yellow and the tail-end is blue, with the wings rendered in darkened peach and around twelve semi-circular

DRONE DISPOSITIONS IN ART AND CULTURE 169

FIGURE 6.3 "By the Moonlight," by Mahwish Chisty.

shapes, their borders lined in blue and yellow and adorning each wing side. This colorful drone is placed at the center of what appears to be a modern street etched into plywood with tea stain. Several electric poles with wires line each side of the street with multistoried buildings. The contrast is sharp but not jarring. While the lack of color in the scene in which the drone is placed suggests its destructive force, it can also be viewed as an attempt to make the drone appear pleasant, colorful, and worthy of beautiful self-expression à la truck drivers styling their trucks. (See Figure 6.3.)

Put differently, Chishty is not practicing representational art in the general sense of using Pakistani truck art to depict realistic drone strikes or their repercussions on property, land, or humans; she is using local art to individually express her desire to counter the dominant perception of drones as objects of violence by turning them into colorful cultural artifacts. Many of them unambiguously titled after formal terms used in military jargon—RQ 170: the Beast of Kandahar, Hovering Reaper, Predator, Black Hawk, X-47B—the paintings evoke truck art in loud, pleasing colors, woodcuts, embroidered cloth, talismans, metal works, calligraphy, and religious and cultural symbols.

Meghan Neal calls such work a form of cultural repurposing: "Drone art can be seen as a form of reappropriation—taking back something that in the popular consciousness is so often a symbol of death and destruction and making it something beautifully provocative, even hilarious."[23] Along similar lines,

FIGURE 6.4 "Hellfire Missile" by Mahwish Chisty.

Anike in Muslim Media Watch of *Patheos.com* points out, "Chishty's drone art is reappropriation; it questions the popular image of the drone as an icon of death and destruction and thus in its own way protests this symbol by choosing to view drones as objects, not just as war machines."[24] (See Figure 6.4.)

However, while many online commenters support Chishty's views expressed in her interview with Josh Harkinson at *Mother Jones,* others voice strong disagreement about her choice of subject and her artistic work. One among them, Mariam Sabri, pointedly counters the supportive comments by noting, "I've been having discussions with a few artists, those who are involved with political advocacy through art, and an art teacher in Pakistan about this. We all feel collectively sickened after reading Mahwish Chishty's interview." Sabri calls such drone art "silly," "insensitive," and "deluded," because "she [Chishty] clearly seems to be depoliticizing drones." Sabri's criticism is not without merit given Chishty's observations in the interview: "I don't know if I am glorifying it. I just want people to talk about it. At the same time, it has some kind of beauty to it. I am also looking at them as objects, and not as much as war machines."[25]

The key question here, it seems to me, is not whether Chishty is getting it right or wrong about drones or if she is being insensitive, but whether the appreciation of beauty is possible for people who experience the horror of drone strikes and the constant unease of living under drone surveillance. Even if we grant that it is theoretically or experientially possible, the question is, to what extent? In other words, what are the politics of location in cultural production and reception? Does where we are located determine how we view art and culture? Evidently, yes. Speaking of truck art, Chishty says that truckers "spend so much time on it and they don't get any funding. This is something that they do, just a personal interest. It has no reason whatsoever other than just an aesthetic sense."[26]

To this view we can add Jamal Elias's anthropological analysis of truck art as not only personal artistic expression but also cultural and collective articulation of trucking culture: travails of truck drivers, the sense of home they create and evoke on the road, the geographic differences that influence their choice of themes, and so on. In other words, truck art is interwoven into Pakistani trucking culture. Chishty's approach draws on contemporary US-Pakistan politics about drones to highlight drones as aesthetic objects, which is a political act justified on the grounds of aesthetic autonomy. Chishty's appropriative stance on drone art can cut both ways: wanting people to talk about drones might well lead people to talk about drones primarily as works of art or only as tools of war. (See Figure 6.5.)

The risk here is that the political nature of the aesthetics of her creative work is that drone art, Pakistani truck culture and folk practices, gallery exhibitions, reviews, and interviews can become another charmed circle within which drones as art gain significance. There can be a dissonance among the intentions of the artist to rescue drones from military use, the political and social significance of drones, the experiential nature of drone strikes, the locational influences on people's responses to drone art, and the economy of the art culture industry. These risks notwithstanding, Chisty's work stages drone art as caught up with the quotidian realities of peoples whose responses to it are shaped by experiential, place-based histories. She boldly turns aesthetics into a mode of defamiliarization, turning the deadly armed drone into a subject for political inquiry that is also, at the same time, embodied in an aesthetic drive that apprehends the drone as generating the wonder of negotiating the limitations of space and time. (See Figure 6.6.)

Drones in Music and Tele-Dramas

The impulse to use drones aesthetically also finds expression in Pashto culture and literature. In "Impact of War on Terror on Pashto Literature and Art," published by the FATA (Federally Administered Tribal Areas) Research Center in Islamabad, Pakistan, the impact of war is generally divided between pre-9/11 and post-9/11 periods. Nature, romance, landscape, individual dreams, love, desire, and friendship are thematic concerns of the pre-9/11 period, and with the start of the war, changes become apparent as poets and artists began to shift focus to the devastating effects of war on small and big villages and semi-urban communities. Genres like the ghazal, nazm (Pashto poems), tappa, and jihadi tarana (anthem) all register this shift in focus. Popular and well-regarded artists who have engaged

FIGURE 6.5 Truck wheel art. Murtaza Imran Ali, Wikimedia Commons.

FIGURE 6.6 "Reaper Drone," by Mahwish Chisty.

with this shift include Salim ur Rehman Salim, Muqadar Shah Muqadar, Akbar Sayal, Ajmal, Bakht Sher Aseer, Shabab Ranizai, Roshan Bangash, Ata Muhammed Wardag, Rehmat Zalmai, and Syeda Haseena Gul, among many others.[27]

It would be a mistake, however, to romanticize the pre-9/11 period because the Soviet invasion in 1979, which lasted for more than a decade, saw noticeable effects on art and literature among Pashtuns, but what makes this periodizing important is the extent to which military themes of war, loss, devastation, enemies, invasion, destruction, and death and their associated symbols permeate creative activity. Responses to this war range from extreme anti-Americanism, where the West becomes the First Cause for war and, therefore, needs to be countered militarily, politically, and culturally, to broader explorations of how peoples living under the constant threat of military action or in militarized regions experience their effects on personal and public psyches.

In jihadi taranas, the Manichean dichotomy of the West and Afghani/Pashtun identity is explicit, and is generally oriented toward inciting readers to protest and rise up against the oppressive foreign powers. The output in this genre, however, is limited, while the political manifestation of this ideology in the political party of the Taliban and other such entities is undeniable.[28] This does not mean that pro-Taliban materials are not read widely. In Mohalla Jangi (Neighborhood of War), Peshwar, Pakistan, there are 2,000 printing presses, some of which regularly print materials supporting the Taliban, Islamic radicalism, and anti-Americanism.[29] In art, poems, ghazals and tappas, artists and writers view the landscape with less thrall because it is pockmarked with the effects of war; there is mourning and sadness in witnessing the changing landscape, which makes habitation increasingly difficult and associated with police actions and American military presence, on the one hand, and extremist, fundamentalist groups eager to subjugate and control society, on the other.

Dance of the Drone Gaze

Over the last few years, Pakistani Pasthto singer Sitara Younas's two songs received considerable attention on YouTube and in Pakistani regional popular culture. Her "Khud Kasha Dhamaka Yama" can be translated as "Don't chase me. I am an illusion. I am a suicide blast." Written by Pashto writer Rashid Johar and composed by Pashto musician Shakir Zeb, the song uses the ongoing US-Afghanistan and Pakistan military activities against terror groups as materials for song-writing and singing.[30] Its explicit analogizing of one smitten with amorous desire for another with the unexpected, shadowy power of a suicide bomber has drawn public attention, with journalists like Manzor Ali paraphrasing poet Farooq Fira, who says that "suicide attacks have left deep imprints on our society and that such songs are a result of overall negativity in society." Fira "proposes establishing a censor board—comprising of actors, writers and elders—to oversee and filter such content."³¹

We see here the lasting effects of wars, police, and military missions on people living in these societies. The intent of this song is not designed as propaganda to convince young people, especially disillusioned or frustrated with their lives, to become true believers in radical Islam and glorify the act of killing others through suicide; it is a registering of everyday life and the complex ways in which some people use the ideas and events they are familiar with to make sense of other aspects of their lives and infuse new symbols and analogies that dramatize the dynamics of young love, romance, heroism, risk, danger, and yearning, to wit, the stuff of which dreams are made in human societies.

Younas's second song pushes the envelope further in "Za Kaom Pa Stargo Stargo Drone Hamla," which translates as "My gaze is as fatal as a drone attack." Penned and given melody by Pashto director Maas Khan Wesal, the song was performed as an episode by actress Dua Qureshi in the television film "Da Khkulo Badshahi Da" produced by Khans Productions.³² Hidayat Khan publishes a translation of parts of the song thus:

> My gaze is as fatal as a drone attack/The touch of my lips sweeten words
> Intoxicating wine are my looks/My gaze is as fatal as a drone attack
> Coquettish stare is a snare of beauty/Smile fresh as early morning dew
> Ensnares lovers with amorous pangs/My gaze is as fatal as a drone attack
> O lovers! Go through a lover's agony/A leaping flame and a rose bud
> The clink of my bangles leaves one enchanted/My smile rustles desires in many a heart
> Tests lovers' courage/My gaze is as fatal as a drone attack
> My beauty and body/At its prime
> Leaves many going astray/My gaze is as fatal as a drone attack.³³

The singer recognizes the power that she, a woman, wields over a man; she is confident of her attractive looks as she croons that "the clink of my bangles leaves one enchanted" and "my smile rustles desires in many a heart." Her attractive features are so compelling that they heighten the desire of lovers to the point where their commitment to each is tested, because her "beauty and body at its prime, leaves many going astray." This woman knows she can "sweeten" her utterances and disorient others with her beauty to the point where they lose their senses. The force of these sentiments is echoed repeatedly in the refrain "My gaze is as fatal as a drone attack." The link between drones and fatality is certain. The power of the drone lies in its gaze that is fatal. In a neat stroke of lyricism, dance, and sentiment, the song captures the problematic nature of postmodern war: drones and surveillance cultures. It is the drone's unique, invisible ability to gaze at the other that makes the other succumb to the drone's missile. To counter the gaze of the seductive woman, the lover has to *resist her at the level of her gaze*; he has to turn that gaze around or ensure that he cannot be located in her field of vision. In other words, he has to contest the power of her surveillance that recognizes the disorienting effects she has on him. But that is what he cannot, thus the deadly accuracy of the woman's power: "My gaze is as fatal as a drone attack."

Unsurprisingly, disapproval followed quickly, when Gul Nazir Mangal, an artist from Waziristan, a region administered by Pakistan, said, "We should not be proud of these attacks, which are being carried out by foreigners on our land. This needs to be condemned instead of making songs and dancing on its tunes," because such songs are "not only harmful to culture and literature, but also create a sense of disunity amongst the people."[34] Officials should, suggests Mangal, set up a censor board to check cultural content before it's released to the public. Arshad Ali, another musician, reiterates this, saying, "It's not appropriate to incorporate drone attacks in music as it's a grave issue faced by our country. Each artist has a certain responsibility towards society."[35] But what is the nature of this responsibility when it comes to digital technologies, drones, surveillance, and networks?

Drone Art: Technology, Modernity, Culture

Pilobolus, a dance company in Connecticut, in collaboration with the MIT Distributed Robotics Laboratory, performed a dance titled "Seraph." Pilobolus describes the performance this way: "SERAPH explores the relationship between human and machine in a pastoral fable involving a girl and two flying robots. Set to a Schubert piano trio, the ten-minute work explores the expressive potential of the robots, presenting in the process a powerful commentary on the fundamental nature of movement."[36]

The setting—dark, blank, bleak—is bereft of the accouterments of modern society. A small drone (quad rotor model) glowing in blue, and a dancer (Matt del Rosario) with long hair and sporting only a dance belt, perform this dance at Joyce Theater in New York. The stage has a dark background, and the area in which the dancer moves is bathed in soft blue light, and the blue LED-paneled lights on the quad-rotor drone emit an ethereal glow and cast small shadows as it moves, bounces, swings, swooshes, lands, takes off, all while interacting with the dancer. When the dancer sits for a moment, the drone hovers downwards, almost touching the ground, and when the dancer stands up, it mimics the movement. The dance moves through several small stages starting from the initial sighting of the strange object, which appears to have a life of its own, to tentative explorations by the dancer of the strangeness of the wondrous being's responsive abilities, and to full-fledged interactions between dancer and drone. Soft, rendered in a piano trio, the music flows smoothly with the dancer and drone's movements.

At one point, having flashed a small light at the drone with curiosity and interacting with the drone awhile, the dancer achieves a moment of calmness. As the drone slowly settles into his outstretched hands, he touches it gingerly, having at last made first tangible contact. This is interrupted by the arrival of another drone with red lights and immediately all three actors, since now the drones, which have become actors with a modicum of agency, begin to asses themselves in relation to one another. The dancer shuffles around, doing somersaults, lunging, withdrawing, crawling, and bending, while keeping his eyes focused on the two strange objects, which have begun to interact with him less as objects and more as ethereal beings with the ability to sense, adapt, and move.

At one point, the first drone loses power or "life" and rests on the floor, and the dancer picks it up slowly and extends his hand to a string that the second drone hovers in front of him. After briefly touching the first drone with this string, the two drones start to move again and the dance resumes with more energy and movement. The MIT Computer Science Artificial Intelligence Laboratory explains the collaboration of dance and robotics by pointing to how machines used to surveil land and provide information can be used in aesthetic contexts: the dance is a "touching tale and exploration of the differences and similarities between humans and machines." To dance director Robby Barnett, "The idea that these (quad-rotors) could be made to indicate intelligence was intriguing. There is sort of a sensual consideration of speed and position in theatrical situations," and he adds that by "examining the way that humans physically react to one another, for example how they approach or retreat from each other, much can be learned about a personal relationship." The drones display "speed, agility and graceful hovering capabilities," just as do Pilobolus' dancers who "do these amazing acrobatic superhuman maneuvers," notes a producer. By using lights that blink, turn on and off, or emit glow in all or a few of the paneled LED lights, the drones are able to show an "emotional connection and communication between the robots and humans."[37] Reviewer Gia Kourlas observes, "As both inanimate robots become more fearless in their flying, they become more expressive—hardly a surprise— forming something of a bond with [the dancer]."[38]

Here, drones do not just have a utilitarian use for mapping lands or obtaining aerial footage; these are objects that can be represented aesthetically; it suggests drone are not lifeless, static objects, but things whose object-status can be changed through artificial intelligence. In the dance, the drones are symbolized not as creations of human beings but as extraterrestrial beings: they have a life of their own. What nature of life they have is a question that awaits exploration, but the drama in the dance is produced in the interaction between two beings, not between one human subject and a complex yet nonhuman artifact. The use of "seraph" as the title for the dance is telling: seraphs are heavenly beings that usually dwell with the Divine in cosmic, other-earthly settings. The dance, then, is seraphic, or otherworldly, suggesting many things: drones as beings are coming to earth, leading to a profound encounter between Humanity and Modernity. The dancer comes to symbolize Everyman, who represents not individuals, racial or cultural groups, and nations, but everyone: the dancer stands in for all of Humanity. The dance does not suggest that the drones were created by human beings who can take them apart and put them back together. Rather, the drones appear as other worldly beings who happen to encounter the human subject, and through interaction the dancer and drone begin to learn to anticipate one another's movements, and by extension, thought processes.

"Seraph" does not showcase artificial intelligence as an engineered product of human labor but as a new order of human experience where robots with artificial intelligence exhibit autonomous existence and autonomous agency. The separation between humanity and technology is not blurred but rendered obsolete: it presages a new age where one species is learning to interact with another species. And in the next example, the creative impulse pushes this idea further: the intersection of artificial intelligence and drones nudges the present into a post-human future.

Drone Dances

In "Dance with Drones" by *Elevenplay* and *Rhizomatiks*, which was performed in Spiral Hall, Tokyo, Japan, the interaction between humans and robots moves to a new threshold where the assumed equality of humans and machines in *Pilobolus'* "Seraph" is turned upside down as the drones ease human actors off the stage and assert primacy. Three dancers interact with three quadrotor drones with cone hats covering their tops, making them change the usual drone-like appearance. After a few moments where the dancers gingerly walk around the drones, they start to explore their nature by moving their hands slowly over them. Much to our astonishment, presumed, that is, the drones respond. In several graceful dance movements, the dancers stretch their bodies, raise their hands, and make wave-like motions—all of which the drones respond to similarly. The effect is one in which humans and drones are starting to merge not literally in a cyborg-like fashion but cognitively—drones are starting to think like the dancers; they are starting to anticipate human motions and respond appropriately. The music continues a persistent half-syncopated drum beat that mixes industrial sounds with New Age music, all harmonized to create an effect of integration: there are no moments of tension where drones and dancers assess and weigh each other. They recognize themselves as equals and dance together harmoniously as each seems in thrall of the other, a situation accentuated by the blue lighting on a stage that has a large screen at the back, and box-like units on the left and right. The audience can see the strobe lights at the bottom front of the stage, where computer-like monitors are also set. This differs starkly from "Seraph" where the performative space (literal spaces where actors and scenes are set on stage) was not part of the material stage, in the sense that the materiality of the stage was invisible.

In "Dance with Drones," there is no doubt that this is a stage, a site for the theater of dance. But this foregrounding of the setting is integrated into the performative space in such a way that they produce the ambience of a visible stage for the play of sound, movement, sight, and spectacle. Whereas in "Seraph," the otherworldly nature of the seemingly cosmic encounter between Humanity and Technology is explicitly foregrounded, in "Dance with Drones," the encounter is rendered not in heavenly vistas but in a technologically manufactured event horizon: that crucial point of no return where technology gains such dynamics that it starts to influence its environment beyond the expected and anticipated. The entity made by human labor and intelligence assumes autonomy, however hazily defined. The drone is no longer only a mass of wires and networks and screens and pixels: the drone has become an emergent subject produced in the interaction between human intelligence and technology.

Daito Manabe, found of *Rhozomaticks*, which collaborated with the dance company *Elevenplay*, makes several observations about this drone dance that are worth noting. To him, the performance is

> a system in which dancers can physically and more intuitively perceive the relationship between the body and data through computer-controlled drones has been developed. There are two kinds of drone movements: a motion produced by tracking a dancer's movements and an artificial motion operated on the software. At first, dancers had to be trained to interact with the drones because they could not predict how they would move, but eventually they were able to dance with the drones as closely as 10 cm away from them.[39]

What happens in the performance once this integration takes place, once relationships are established between dancers and data gathered through sensors, between motion-capturing cameras and software code that calculates at blinding speed the digital calibration of the dancer's movement and translates that data mining into data analysis in order to direct the drones to respond accordingly? This is the key question. And it is answered with drone-like ease: the human dancers are harassed into leaving the site of performance—the drones take center stage. As reviewer Jacob Kastrenakes points out, "By the end of the four-minute routine, however, the dancers vanish, leaving the drones as stars of the show."[40] To Chris Person, "The end result is a kind of hypnotic, futurist, Butoh dance; one where the humans eventually flee the stage to make way for an all-UAV, *Rez*-like performance."[41]

As the screen lights up with a projected image of crisscrossed horizontal and vertical lines, with three cubes moving across the screen in tandem with the drones that keep hovering on stage, the three dancers huddle together, hold their heads and bow down, only to be scrambled off the stage by the drones. When the dancers try to reenter the scene, the drones drive them out again, till no one remains on stage except the drones. The musical beat grows hard and insistent, the volume loud, and the blue ambience a pinkish-purple, as the projected images on screen interact with the drones on stage. Artificial intelligence has eased human intelligence and presence off the stage. It's a new world dawning. It's a world in which drones become part of everyday life.

Is drone technology primarily about the world losing its bearings and becoming totally subject to the whims and fancies of strange objects that compel us to do their bidding? Or are they going to become common, part of daily life, and thus lose their mystical power or deathly meaning? To artist Rajeev Basu, the answer emerges in the intersection of public interest in a new technology, commercial opportunities, and everyday culture, which is why he invited several artists to imagine what commercialization would entail for drones. Since the FAA is likely to issue official regulations for drone operations in non-military settings, as it anticipates 30,000 drones in use by 2020, it is not farfetched to imagine drones becoming common objects or tools.[42]

Urban Drones

Titled "Drones in New York City," the web project (the installation includes more) features a dozen or so colorfully and creatively rendered drones flying in various places in New York; they are painted like birds, covered with dots, given anthropomorphic symbols, and are represented primarily as products available to the public for personal or public use. Drones hover in Central Park, lead the Halloween Parade in New York Village, welcome visitors to Coney Island, advertise Coca-Cola at Times Square, escort people at Madison Avenue, or fly around 72nd Street where John Lennon was killed. Basu's artistic drones extend the idea of commercialization into drones as autonomous agents, when, for example, a drone is "spotted a long way from home" in places as far away as Brazil, or a "mystical spirit drone ventures out in the day," or when a "off-duty drone takes in some sights" by visiting a museum or stopping by a restaurant.[43]

There is a subtle integration of two types of drones into everyday life: one group of drones are represented as fascinating, fun tools that can be used for activities like patrolling a public park, escorting people, leading a parade, and memorializing a slain pop star's site of death, whereas the other group is represented as having a mind of its own and as beings that we spot here and there while they visit museums and restaurants. These drones, like the drones that displace human dancers in "Dance with Drones," act independently; they can leave "home" and go off to Brazil or take rest and chill out at a restaurant. Human beings become spectators of drones who do their own things. Drones have a life, just as we human beings do. This drone art imagines artificial intelligence as embodied in drones while partaking of commercial culture. They can be bought and sold and used in many ways, and they inhabit a world in which some drones also exhibit an ability to live in a world just as humans do. As they reorient us to public spaces by partaking of daily, ordinary practices, drones alter our ideas of space and place; they challenge us to examine the forms in which dissent against society, government, or people is expressed with a New Aesthetic dynamic that makes the digital tool and screen primary sites for transgressive politics.

Art and the Public Commons

In 2014, media artist KATSU presented "Drone Paintings" at the Silicon Valley Art Fair. These paintings are not about drones but *by* drones, in that the artist develops methods to control a drone that can carry and spray paint to create graffiti. The presentation offers a series of paintings created by using such drones; they have blotches, throw ups, or lines of paint that are sprayed onto the canvas by the drone that is remotely manipulated by the painter, KATSU; in this sense, the paintings "are very much part of a tendency in emerging art to engage with process driven abstraction; however in these works, the artist is not seeking to shirk responsibility by turning the composition over only to process; rather he is creating new opportunities of engagement, and their resulting difficulties and restrictions, through a challenging and pioneering process."[44] Producing graffiti and cleaning up graffiti generally involve two things: accessing the canvass or site for painting covertly, without being seen or subjected to formal permission processes, and using appropriate tools to remove graffiti, actions taken by those affected or concerned.

Drone Graffiti

Access to space and cleaning up graffiti involves technologies that allow participants to exercise a measure of control over the site or canvas. With drone technology, access to the site/canvas to tag or bomb surfaces (graffiti lingo for using paint in many areas of the surface) and to buff (use materials to remove graffiti) are raised to a new threshold because drones allow graffiti users to access sites as canvases that they cannot physically do like the sides of high-rise buildings or places from which they are locked out. With drones in KATSU's projects, the potential canvas is dramatically extended since drones combine movement, flexibility, and remote-controlled mechanisms into a single unit that can carry and use paint. To buff graffiti from places accessed by drones will likely involve the use of similar technology. Drones expand the space for spray painting and enlarge the canvas in the scopic field of the public or potential viewers. Because physical barriers or high walls, closed areas, restricted spaces are significantly overcome with drones, drone graffiti has the potential for new kinds of creative expression and social activism or transgression, depending on how it gets integrated, rejected, or marginalized in cultural and physical landscapes. To this view can be added another view: drone graffiti further extends the socially disruptive quality of graffiti while also inadvertently leading to an increased interest in and attempt at controlling material and social landscapes.

Because "graffiti unquestionably change the visual representation of a landscape, whether they are on public surfaces or private ones," local and governmental offices or individuals in general tend to control the landscape in order to maintain certain ideas of social order, normalcy, and stability, point out Terri Moreau and Derek H. Alderman in "Graffiti Hurts and the Eradication of Alternative Landscape Expression." When public spaces are tightly controlled, "landscape plays a major role in silencing some perspectives and giving voice to others."[45] When viewed solely as a symptom of social deviance, immoral acts, and illegal practices, graffiti is often misinterpreted as a threat to the social order and effectively marginalized or silenced. However, when viewed as a cultural practice designed to express a view or communicate alternate or unpopular ideas, graffiti "serve[s] as a tactic for challenging and offering alternative meanings for public space and for who belongs or whose ideas count within these spaces."[46]

Kidult, a graffiti activist, uses this form of communication to spread alternate meanings about global or consumer brands by recording the surreptitious ways in which he engages in his work and posting them online. To him, graffiti's aesthetics embody a struggle to claim public spaces for the expression of a variety of perspectives, not just those tolerated by organizations or people who can afford to exert control over a landscape because of their influence, wealth, or power.

In "Illegal World," which documents several of his taggings and bombings in different places, Kidult remains unidentifiable in a Halloween-like costume and speaks in a processed, disguised voice. Graffiti, he explains, "is like a weapon. It is the first form of revolt, whether it is inscriptions or drawings during wars, riots, or revolutions. The economy in which we live in is like cerebral dysfunction, and the people at the bottom of the ladder are starting. The Revolution will be the next step."[47] The use of digital technologies to record the process of graffiti and posting them online fundamentally changes earlier meanings of graffiti because the size of the audience increases a million-fold, and the literal site of graffiti becomes a digital canvas to which can be added voice-overs, music, and other multimedia. The physical and the digital canvases merge to produce a new representation of graffiti art. This doubling of canvases enables the artist to insert his or her perspectives regarding the process or the content of graffiti in ways unavailable without digital technology. Stephanie Keller captures this dynamic well when she says, "Since Kidult's work is "buffed" or cleaned away so quickly, the videos are the only documentation that the piece existed in the first place, backing up the point that the work is created solely so he can film it and make a video."[48]

In KATSU's video of his defacing Picasso's "Girl Before a Mirror" at the Museum of Modern Art, NY, a seemingly realistic account of tagging is produced, including loud voices of security personnel admonishing the artist. By digitally mixing canvases, KATSU carefully produces digital graffiti where the distinction between real and fake tagging is blurred, which nudges the question of politics and aesthetics into the complex realm of cultural symbolism. If, in fact, no graffiti was tagged on the actual work of art, Picasso's painting, nothing has been defaced and the painting remains as it was. But this view still has to account for how in the digital realm, the painting has been marked with graffiti, been defaced with tagging, to produce a realistic effect of artistic transgression of high culture. In digital aesthetics, graffiti, in KATSU and Kidult's work of blatantly transgressing brand or cultural symbols, is produced for audiences whose access to graffiti is mediated through digital tools; it "exist[s] purely digitally."[49]

It embodies the temporal schema expected of its social transgression: quick removal of the art. The impermanence of street art like graffiti is crucial to its structure and form, because it embodies the quick pace and rhythm of city life. Urban spaces, where graffiti has historically emerged and continues to play a major role, need constant upkeep, which means constant change or erasure of art. "The temporality of much street art," observes Anna Wacławek, "thus visually translates a city's experience of being part of the city's fabric," and points out that impermanence and illegality are contested notions in graffiti subcultures with some viewing both qualities as pivotal in animating the power of street art and others willing to extend its affects into mainstream culture.[50]

The turn to the digital in graffiti art reorients the artist, art, and art's potential viewers or responders to a different spatiotemporal canvas where the creative act is explicitly done for digital recording, which provides a pixelated blueprint that can be manipulated artistically. This new aesthetic seeks new audiences, new temporal phases, and new media integrations in which such social transgressions are enacted, documented, manipulated, and disseminated. The site where official control and governmental influence, and corporate influence have to be negotiated now includes the space of the digital and the aesthetic realms of the symbolic—it's the space of the digiscape. It is a space of and for multiple canvases. It's an assortment of spaces put together by the artist for performances whose completeness integrates the physical and the digital.

In digiscape, creative production registers both the spatiotemporal parameters of physical landscapes and the affordances of digital media where the creative or transgressive act is performed endlessly as viewers can choose to view art any number of times in any number of places; art in digiscapes can be recalibrated for new virtual performances for multiple audiences, while giving greater ability for artists to insert their own views directly and indirectly. Digiscape is a space not only of erasure and replacement but of juxtaposition and displacement of meanings and symbols, performances, and authorial intent. It involves a reorientation of space and time because it relocates artists and audiences, and the sites of cultural activity in multiple nonsequential physical and digital spaces where power can be contested, control deflected, influence thwarted, and aesthetics experimented.

Drone Cultures in Global Perspective

The state organized "Murmuration: a Festival of Drone Culture," whose aim is described as follows:

> The use and meaning of the drone is contested. The U.S. executive branch and other governments use this technology to fight wars in which the victims are all on one side, increasing states' power over civilians. But drones also have the potential to alter the balance of power. As DIY drones enter the hands of civilians, we can turn them around on our governments, police forces, and employers. We can hack the aggressive definition of the drone and rewrite it as something that could be liberating rather than oppressive. Drones can also be creatures of joy and play. They can make music and take aerial photos. Understanding and exploring the idea of the drone has never been more important.[51]

Organizers Olivia Rosane and Adam Rothstein further note that because "our understanding of the drones flying over Pakistan are informed as much by the science fiction of the past as they are by the Bureau of Investigative Journalism," a "drone is a literary character … Drones allow us re-image ourselves on both ends of the camera and on both ends of the geopolitical trigger."[52] The response, as evident in the selected pieces for the festival, shows a remarkable variety of thirty artistic projects in genres ranging from prose, poetry, music, video, stickers, paintings, and multimedia. Several pieces use mish-mash techniques where bits and pieces of information, images, sound bites, texts, and music are put together to extend a political view or creatively explore the topic. One music video is worth discussing here.

In "The Child and the Kite," media artist Ahmad Makia uses graphics, images, information, and other media fragments scoured from the internet to create a music video based on an adaptation of "The Child and the Kite," a song by Lebanese singer and folk artist Marcel Khalife. Released in the album "At the Border," the song, also known as "The Child and the Plane," narrates the dramatic experience of a child eager to fly a kite. While searching for a string, he spots a plane in the sky, and wonders that "its wings are bigger than the neighbor's house" and needs no string to fly. At this point in the music video, Makia uses a video feed of people being surveilled presumably through a drone hovering above. The boy's "heart fluttered and flew on the wings of the plane, and the whole sky told him its secrets." Skeletons with death-like grins dance up and down, presaging the deadly event to happen. The contrast between the innocence of the boy's rapturous delight in spotting a place and the impending missiles that we know will soon hit him from a drone underscore the tragedy of drone warfare; innocence about everyday occurrences like a plane flying in the sky, a boy prancing about and dreaming of kites and planes, eager to play with his friends, and the deliberate contrasting of images to show the profound irony of misstating the drone for a kite come across sharply when the screen shows a direct missile hit. When the "roar of the plane" drowns the "other voices," the suggestion is that alternate perspectives on drone wars are violently suppressed, namely, the perspectives of those living in a society haunted by American drones that sometimes kill innocent children and assess them as collateral damage.[53]

This video directly points to the many sources from which its media are taken in an Acknowledgments list used as a preface. The song, which was included in the album "At the Border," is about the civil war in Lebanon that ravaged the country from 1975 to 1990. Released in 1980, this song, and the album in general, can be viewed as a direct indictment of a country beginning to descend into social chaos. Makia adapts, not just borrows, Khalife's song, and uses contemporary contexts not so much to rewrite the song for a new era but to imply a continuity of struggles linking peoples whose lives are mangled by the Lebanese civil war, the context for Khalife's original release, and America's international war against terrorists, the context for Makia's re-narration of the song.

Instead of planes, Makia uses drones and images of drone strikes. Hearkening after the drone, the boy imagines it to be a symbol of freedom. He dreams of vistas of wonder opened up by the drone. Yet, as the video makes clear, it is the same object of wonder that becomes an agent of death. This is pivotal to understanding the New Aesthetic: drones are marvels of technology; they enable us to operate tools remotely; they reorient us to space and time. What remains common to the child in both narrations is the sense of wonder, which is why the idea of drone technology as a product of modernity, with its compelling aura and promise of technological exploration and exhilaration, comes across clearly. This notion of wonder at the marvelous and dread of the marvelous coexist in contemporary drone art and culture.

The imbalance of this coexistence is raised pointedly by Hamdan Azhar, who wonders if the nerdy immersion by young Americans in drone technologies risks making us indifferent to the ongoing use of armed drones to fight global terrorism and America's role in leading drone warfare. The rapid pace at which drone technology is becoming commercialized and extended beyond its military use is leading to an appreciation of drone technology, and to its creative uses in art and culture, a development that could normalize drone use. Rather than yielding to military hegemony, we can counter the power of the military by purposely wresting it away from their control and use it non-militarily, for business, exploration, humanitarianism, education, and pleasure,[54] a position also taken by Olivia Rosane and Adam Rothstein, organizers of the drone festival Murmuration, when they note that "we can hack the aggressive definition of the drone and rewrite it as something that could be liberating rather than oppressive."[55]

Artist Adam Harvey's work literally extends this critical impulse: his online store *Privacy Gift Shop* sells items to disguise digital communications in cryptography, covers for mobile phones to repel or detract signals of detection, and clothing, some as a burqa, hijab, and hoodie that can disguise itself from drone surveillance through infrared imaging.[56] Echoing Caribbean-American feminist Audre Lorde, Azar wonders if "the master's tools can help to dismantle the master's house." As Madiha Tahir tells him, "First, it mistakes technical problems for political problems. Second, the ideologies behind these technologies—even in their civilian uses—are ideologies of harm, surveillance, and risk ... The technical discussions ... are a way of masking the political issues. Drones exist in an institutional, economic, and power context."[57]

To better understand the significance of these perspectives, it will be helpful to step back and see the global context in which drone technology is being used as weapons of war *and* celebrated in conferences and festivals. What picture comes into focus when we take a geo-spatial view of drone cultures? It is not in Pakistan, Yemen, Somalia, Afghanistan, Libya, or Iraq that we see dancers exploring the aesthetic dimensions of drones. It is in America, the very country that uses drone warfare *against* these countries, that the entertainment and pleasurable nature of drones is in play; this fact foregrounds unequal relations of power in the international area, an idea persuasively argued for by Immanuel Wallerstein. In *World Systems Analysis*, Wallerstein identifies centers of capital accumulation and power that influence peripheral spaces in the world, which leads to center-periphery dynamics indicative of unequal power relations structuring international relations. Highly developed countries and cities tend to develop relationships with other countries and cities in ways that position the latter as sub-core regions that provide the core cities with resources and wealth. When grasped as a system, global trade and commerce show high unevenness and dependency among particular regions, conditions that are the result of political and historical factors, not just economics.[58]

The aesthetics of drone culture are shaped by geo-spatial power dynamics between America and other countries. To address these dynamics, Roopika Risam and Adeline Kohm note that "postcolonial digital humanities brings critiques of colonialism, imperialism, and globalization and their relationship to race, class, gender, sexuality and disability to bear on the digital humanities" which they see as "set of methodologies engaged by humanists to use, produce, teach, and analyze culture and technology."[59] Pace Risam and Koh, the question can be, how would we in America and the West conduct drone festivals and celebrate technology if armed drones from other countries strike at suspected terrorists in Seattle, Houston, or Boston, leading to the killing of innocent men, women, and children, and is rationalized by the instigating country as collateral damage?

Let me end with what I stated about the digital in Chapter 1: the conception, production, dissemination, and use of the digital are worldly endeavors, a series of innumerable acts and motivations profoundly and inescapably shaped by human interests, local pressures, national trends, and global flows. To engage with the worldliness of the digital is to grasp technological innovation as a social and cultural phenomenon that can rewrite, erase, redraw, or affirm the histories, cultures, and spaces of many peoples and living things in the world; it is to grasp the digital as affording new ways of conceiving of the world and our being in the world.

Notes

1. "Drones." *Ann Arbor Art Center,* accessed January 2, 2025, http://annarborartcenter.org/drones
2. James Bridle, "Drone Shadows and Dispositions," *booktwo.org* May 16, 2013 http://booktwo.org/notebook/drone-shadows-dispositions/
3. James Bridle, "Dronestagram: The Drone's-Eye View," *booktwo.org* November 8, 2012, http://booktwo.org/notebook/dronestagram-drones-eye-view/
4. Rebecca J. Rosen, "Drone Over Washington," *theatlantic.com* June 21, 2013, http://theatlantic.com/technology/archive/2013/06/drone-over-washington/277038/; James Bridle, "Drone Shadows and Dispositions." *booktwo.org* May 16, 2013, http://booktwo.org/notebook/drone-shadows-dispositions/; James Bridle, "Under the Shadow of the Drone." *booktwo.org* October 11, 2011, http://booktwo.org/notebook/drone-shadows/
5. James Bridle, *Watching the Watchers*, *jamesbridle.com* https://jamesbridle.com/works/watching-the-watchers
6. Jason Komoda, "Dronestagram," *digiart21.org* http://digiart21.org/art/dronestagram. Komoda's essay is part of a student-led project (University of Denver) titled "21st Century Digital Art: A Collaborative Survey of Digital Art Made since 2000."
7. James Bridle, "Under the Shadow of the Drone," *book.two.org* October 11, 2012 https://booktwo.org/notebook/drone-shadows/
8. Kathryn Brimblecombe-Fox, *Dronescapes*, accessed January 2, 2025, https://kathrynbrimblecombeart.blogspot.com/p/dronescapes.html
9. Mark Andrejevic, "The Droning of Experience," *The Fibreculture Journal* 25 (2015) http://twentyfive.fibreculturejournal.org/fcj-187-the-droning-of-experience/
10. Kathryn Brimblecombe-Fox, "Portfolio: Dronescapes by Kathryn Brimblecombe-Fox," interview with Maggie Barnett, *dronecetner.bard.edu* February 23, 2017, https://dronecenter.bard.edu/portfolio-dronescapes-by-kathryn-brimblecombe-fox/
11. Federica Caso, "Visualizing the Drone: War Art as Embodied Resistance," *E-International Relations* May 16, 2018, https://e-ir.info/2018/05/16/visualising-the-drone-war-art-as-embodied-resistance/

12 Caso, "Visualizing," May 16, 2028, https://e-ir.info/2018/05/16/visualising-the-drone-war-art-as-embodied-resistance/
13 Matthew Power, "Confessions of a Drone Warrior," GQ October 22, 2013, https://gq.com/story/drone-uav-pilot-assassination
14 Zyngmunt Bauman, *Liquid Surveillance*, line 140.
15 Bauman, *Postmodern Ethics* (Cambridge, MA: Blackwell, 1993), 125.
16 Micha Zenko, "Reforming US Drone Strike Policies," *Council on Foreign Relations*, Special Report 65, Publications Department: New York, 2013; "Bugsplat Predicts Bombs' Impact," *defensetech.org* February 22, 2003, https://military.com/defensetech/2003/02/22/bugsplat-predicts-bombs-impact
17 See http://notabugsplat.com/; "Pakistanis Target Drones with Giant Posters of Child Victims," *dawn.com*, April 8, 2014, http://dawn.com/news/1098351
18 Lindsay C. Clark and Christian Enemark, "Drone Warriors, Revealdn Humanitty, a Feminist Ethics of Care," *Ethics of Drone Strikes: Restraining Remote-Control Killing.* Edited by Christian Enemark (Edinburgh: Edinburgh University Press, 2021), 141.
19 Clark and Enemark, "Drone Warriors," 141.
20 Jamal J. Elias, *On Wings of Diesel: Trucks, Identity, and Culture in Pakistan* (Oxford: Oneworld Publications, 2011), 12.
21 Jamal J. Elias, "On Wings of Diesel: The Decorated Trucks of Pakistan," *Amherstmagazine*, Spring, 2005, https://amherst.edu/news/magazine/issue-archive/2005_spring/wings
22 Josh Harkinson, "Friendly Fire: Drones as Folk Art." Interview with Mahwish Chishty. *Motherjones.com* June 24, 2013, http://www.motherjones.com/media/2013/06/pakistani-drone-art-mahwish-chishty#disqus_thread
23 Meghan Neal, "Finally: a Drone for Dropping Rhymes, not Bombs." *Motherboard.vice.com* June 25, 2013, https://vice.com/en/article/poetry-drone-would-drop-rhymes-not-bombs/
24 Anike, "The Colorful Drones of Mahwish Chishty," *patheos.com* July 1, 2013, http://patheos.com/blogs/mmw/2013/07/the-colourful-drones-of-mahwish-chishty/
25 Harkinson, "Friendly Fire: Drones as Folk Art."
26 Ibid.
27 "Impact of War on Terror on Pashto Literature and Art," *FATA Research Center* Islamabad: Pakistan, 2014.
28 "Impact," pages 18, 19, 24.
29 Taha Siddiqui, "Taliban Jihad Literature: What's Read in Afghanistan Is Printed in Pakistan." *tribune.com.pk* August 12, 2012, http://tribune.com.pk/story/421356/taliban-jihad-literature-whats-read-in-afghanistan-is-printed-in-pakistan/
30 Manzoor Ali, "Khud Kasha Dhamaka Yama: The Song's a Blast." *tribune.com.pk* November 26, 2011, http://tribune.com.pk/story/298042/khud-kasha-dhamaka-yama-the-songs-a-blast/
31 Ali, "Khud Kasha."
32 Hidayat Khan, "My Gaze Is as Fatal as a Drone Attack," *tribune.com.pk* September 18, 2012, http://tribune.com.pk/story/438610/my-gaze-is-as-fatal-as-a-drone-attack/
33 Ibid.
34 Ibid.
35 Ibid.
36 "Seraph," *Pilobolus*. Washington Depot: Connecticut, 2011.
37 "Dancing Machines." *MIT Computer Science and Artificial Intelligence Laboratory*. November 14, 2011, http://csail.mit.edu/node/1640

38 Gia Kourlas, "Alone with Schubert and 2 MIT Flying Robots." *New York Times* July 19, 2011, http://nytimes.com/2011/07/20/arts/dance/piloboluss-seraph-at-joyce-theater-review.html?_r=0
39 Daito Manabe, "Dance with Drones," *daito.ws/en* March 2014, http://daito.ws/en/work/elevenplay_drones.html
40 Jacob Kastrenakes, "Drones Become Dancers in This Average Performance," *theaverage.com* May 22, 2014, http://theverge.com/2014/5/22/5742420/drones-join-dance-troupe-video
41 Chris Person, "A Drone Ballet Straight Out of the Cyberpuk Future," *kotaku.com* May 22, 2014, http://kotaku.com/a-drone-ballet-straight-out-of-the-cyberpunk-future-1580122943
42 Abdullah Saeed, "Rajeev Basu Wants to Sell You a Custom Painted Attack Drone." *The Creator's Project*. December 14, 2012. Accessed January 27, 2025. http://thecreatorsproject.vice.com/blog/rajeev-basu-wants-to-sell-you-a-custom-painted-attack-drone
43 Rajeev Basu, "Drones of New York." *rajeevbasu.com*, accessed January 27, 2025, https://www.rajeevbasu.com/projects/dronesofnewyork/
44 "KATSU Drone Paintings," *theholenyc.com* April 1, 2014, http://theholenyc.com/2014/04/01/katsu-drone-paintings/
45 Terri Moreau and Derek H. Alderman, "Graffiti Hurts and the Eradication of Alternative Landscape Expression," *The Geographical Review* 101, no.1 (2011): 106–124.
46 Ibid., 108.
47 KIDULT, "Illegal World." *kidultone.com*, accessed May 30, 2014, http://kidultone.com/?page_id=309
48 Stephanie Keller, ""How Graffiti Artists are Journeying from the Streets to the Computer Screen." *thecreatorsproject.vice.com* December 6, 2012,http://thecreatorsproject.vice.com/blog/how-graffiti-artists-are-journeying-from-the-streets-to-the-computer-screen
49 Ibid.
50 Anna Waclawek, *Graffiti and Street Art* (New York: Thames & Hudson, 2011), 91.
51 "Murmuration Festival." Mission Parameters, accessed January 2, 2025, http://murmurationfestival.tumblr.com/about
52 Ibid.
53 Ahmad Makia, "The Child and the Kite," *Murmuration: A Festival of Drone Culture*, accessed January 2, 2025, http://murmurationfestival.tumblr.com/ The lyrics of Marcel Khalife's song in "At the Border" released in 1980 is translated by Chris Gratien, a doctoral candidate at Georgetown University and specializing in Ottoman and Middle East History (*arabmusictranslation.com* April 28, 2007, accessed June 2, 2014, http://arabicmusictranslation.com/2007/04/marcel-khalifa-child-and-kite-el-tifl.html).

> There was once a little child
> Playing in the village, searching for a string to fly a kite.
> He looked around and said, "I don't know what that is shining."
> "Look, look the plane."
> "It's coming towards me."
> There was once a little child
> Playing in the village, searching for a string to fly a kite
> He looked around and said, "I don't know what that is shining"
> "Look, look the plane"

"It's coming towards me"
"It's a big plane (kite), I don't need a string"
"And its wings are bigger than the neighbors' house"
His heart fluttered and flew on the wings of the plane
And the whole sky told him its secrets
He stopped in the square and called to his friends
This roar of the plane was more powerful than all the voices
The boys gathered and stopped their game
And the country shook, a story like a lie
And the roar became a big cloud of smoke, I don't know what happened
The siren sounded
The plane carrying stories and poems
Set fire to the land and destroyed the home
It destroyed the home, destroyed the home
And flew off into to the borders
The borders that birthed me, lightning and thunder bombarded the world
The game flew away, and with it the story
And the boys became shards of the story
The story written on the village terraces
The timid village lit like a candle
And the candle shone bright, and the scream reverberated
Aaaaaah! Aaaaaah! Aaaaaah!

54 Hamdan Azhar, "Drones Are Not Dangerous: Normalization, New Journalism, and the New Drone Culture." *The State* December 18, 2013, https://web.archive.org/web/20160325125213/http://www.thestate.ae/drones-are-not-dangerous-normalisation-new-journalism-and-the-new-drone-culture/
55 Olivia Rosane and Adam Rothstein, "Concluding Thoughts." *Murmuration: A Festival of Drone Culture*, accessed January 2, 2025, https://murmurationfestival.tumblr.com/post/54350413114/concluding-thoughts
56 Adam Harvey. *Privacy Gift Shop*, accessed January 2, 2025, http://privacygiftshop.com/collections/
57 Azhar, "Drones Are Not Dangerous."
58 Immanuel Wallerstien, *World Systems Analysis: An Introduction* (Durham, NC: Duke University Press, 2004).
59 Roopika Risam and Adeline Koh, "Mission Statement," *Postcolonial Digital Humanities* January 21, 2014, https://slideshare.net/slideshow/theories-and-practices-of-postcolonial-digital-humanities-roopika-risam-and-adeline-koh/30663962

EPILOGUE
TRAGEDY OF THE COMMONS: DEMOCRACY AND THE PRACTICE OF FREEDOM

Drone warfare has led to the tragedy of the commons, undermining liberal democracy and the practice of freedom.
Let me explain.

Think of this scenario, urges American ecologist Garrett James Hardin: a pasture used by herdsmen, each with a ranch and cattle. Hoping to increase earnings, one day, one person adds an animal to his herd. Soon, others follow suit, and each gets his herd to graze on the common pasture, which is the "commons," because everyone uses and needs it. Each person acts independently, considering himself, first and foremost, a rational individual using reason and logic to increase earnings by adding to the herd and using the common pasture for grazing. But eventually, as each herdsman adds an animal to the ranch, the total number of animals grazing on the pasture dramatically increases, resulting in over-grazing and depletion of the pastures, or the commons. The result is that all herdsmen experience loss. That is the tragedy of the commons.

Each sought to use the commons according to a principle English philosopher Jeremy Bentham renders clearly: "It is the greatest happiness of the greatest number that is the measure of right and wrong."[1] Each person subscribed to a laissez-fare logic of the commons, which means giving autonomy to people to engage with the commons with little governmental control. The laissez-fare view holds that when people act out of self-interest, although it sounds contradictory, what actually happens is not mutual self-destruction but coexistence within the marketplace due to the power of the "invisible hand," Scottish economist Adam Smith's term, which balances out competing interests. Hardin says that such a hands-off approach and reliance on people's conscience to care for the commons will not prevent the destruction of the commons. Several things are at play here: individuals as independent actors; use of logic and reason by individuals to enrich property and pursue happiness; role of good intentions in increasing yield and producing something with assets and skills; and viewing the commons as available to all freely because it's in abundance or part of nature. But all these lead not to happiness but to conflict, environmental damage, and revenue loss. Common to all herdsmen, Hardin points out, is "the tendency to assume that decisions reached individually will, in fact, be the best decision for an entire society."[2] But when the commons is depleted, everyone suffers.

A good counterargument points out that the problem is not finite resources but inefficient social structures and organizations that do not allow for optimum use of space, skills, and knowledge—or science. Hardin rebuts this argument due to its reliance on technical solutions: "A technical solution may be defined as one that requires a change only in the techniques of the natural sciences, demanding little or nothing in the way of change in human values or ideas of morality."[3] Here, Hardin makes a strong case for the role of the humanities—literature, religion, philosophy, languages—because science alone will not help society progress and construct complex civilizations.

Published in 1968 and dealing with the impact of population growth on the environment, Hardin's essay is not dated but prescient: we have a better sense of the dramatic impact of technology around the world, and the scale and growth of global forces of large-scale migration, economic activity, travel, and communication. The impact of the choices we make about what tools to mass produce, use for recreation, education, surveillance, or war should not be left only to billions of people's individual consciences and millions of big and small businesses, assuming the invisible hand will eventually balance the odds and evens and prevent large-scale devastation of the commons.

Drone Warfare and the Global Commons

The analogy of farms and animals and ranchers can be transposed to UAVs, data links, and drone pilots, and to governments, big businesses, and public and private corporations. Current political orientations apply to Hardin's view: the left or Democrats favor governmental intervention and government-led and maintained public infrastructure or the commons, and the right or Republicans favor individual choice and economic dynamics that favor risk-taking and creativity and emphasize freedom of expression and constitutional governance. But this results in a skewed understanding of the challenges we face when dealing with the commons within global frameworks, where our territorial sovereignty cannot easily be obtained, because global forces make borders malleable and rigid in new ways *at the same time*.

Unless we grasp drones and digital technologies as systems and networks, digital artifacts and processes for military uses and civilian engagements, as instruments for aesthetic expression and political manipulation, and as tools that can help us wage war in secret, invade millions of peoples' privacy in secret, and subject them to nondemocratic surveillance even as we use them to explore our creative potential and push the boundaries of art and innovation, we will end up with the reductive choice that the national security state and Big Tech (technology companies with global reach) present to us: give up our private lives in exchange for public and personal security, and let consumer demand be the central criterion for creating drone economies.

As nations and groups vie with each other to create drones or acquire them in the international market, our commons—the air and the open spaces of the sky we assume are for us to see, feel, enjoy, care for, live with—will be depleted. Where the earth was the battlefield for old wars, the air will become the amorphous zone for new wars. Where the Cold War saw nuclear proliferation and horrifying disasters unfold in 1986 in Chernobyl, in the former USSR, and the gas leak in the Union Carbide factory in 1984 in Bhopal, India, the twenty-first century might well see a future in which we give other people, organizations, and businesses immense control over our privacy, our thought process, and our individuality. It won't be long before we will find ourselves condemned to live the pathetic life of always being watched, always being gazed at, and always turning that disciplining gaze against ourselves, our bodies, our lives, and against others. As this happens, we will face the stark prospect of not recognizing ourselves because we will have disfigured our humanity. We will become citizens of the Necropolitical State, managed by the rich and powerful, and sustained by the blood, sweat, and tears of the deplorables stripped to live bare lives.

Pivotal here is this: if we rely on the FAA, the Congress, the US Presidency, the UN, the EU, and other entities to care for the commons, we risk becoming subjected to their rules, whims, and fancies; if we leave it up to people in general and assume that capitalist and individualist enterprise will lead to a balancing of demand and supply and all will be well, we still will not be able to address (and restrict or stop) why drone wars and surveillance have gone global, why Americans are routinely subjected to unaccountable scrutiny without their consent or knowledge, and why the United States and many countries continue to engage in drone warfare without releasing relevant details of civilian deaths and ensuring appropriate recompense. Just as the proliferation of nuclear technology led to dangerous pursuits of power by several nation-states, the proliferation of drone technology is leading to a new form of warfare where Americans will also be subjected to its arbitrary exercise of surveillance and subjugation.

Reclaiming Privacy

The tragedy of the commons in this context is the tragedy of privacy becoming subjected to governmental edicts and secret policies, of information being collected to create electronic profiles, of large data sets being stored without our consent, and of surveilling peoples endlessly. Information thus obtained is used for political gain, media manipulation, international diplomacy, internally waging the political battles of other countries, and fighting a war on terrorism where the entire globe becomes wrapped up in networks of observation and evaluation according to metrics that are largely unknown to the people subjected to such practices. To talk about privacy in these contexts is difficult, because, for the most part, we have made a devil's bargain in the digital age: if governments, businesses, and other institutions give us services, access, security, and privileges to help us care for ourselves, work, provide, and live our lives as we wish, we are willing to part with privacy. To an extent, it is true that there is nothing pristine about privacy as if it is a sacrosanct petite self each human being carries in the soul or body.

Instead, we must think of privacy relationally, as social and personal spaces we create when interacting with others and the natural and built envoronments. In *The Ethics of Privacy and Surveillance*, Carissa Véliz offers useful conceptual handles to reimagine privacy. Territorial animal behavior involves privacy, whether for sustenance, reproduction, or survival. The desire to withhold information or prevent others from having it is driven by the need for privacy, something animals also exhibit. Privacy is desired to stare at or avoid being stared at, since staring can function as dominance. Functions of the body are also often regarded across culture as requiring privacy. Political institutions differentiate between public and private spaces, each accorded a different political and social value for exercising official power. When all private spaces are brought into the domain of state power, totalitarianism becomes the norm. Preventing it means distinguishing between private and public realms. Modernity's features of widespread literacy and scientific thinking lead to the necessity of working alone; its ontological corollary is about being alone, regardless of social or economic need, to be left to one's wishes for inner reflection. The history of architecture also shows the organization of space for privacy, which can range from keeping people separate due to sickness or to avoid subterfuge.

With the advent of digital technologies, however, Véliz notes that even these flexible boundaries between public and private have become not only more flexible but porous, each bleeding into the other, in some instances, almost erasing the very notion of private and public as predicates for social good. For instance, information circulated online can be viewed as public, irrespective of one's view of that information. When something enters the public domain, legal freedoms come into play, giving others the freedom to cite or use that information.

Véliz's argument that we should avoid pitting privacy as always antithetical to surveillance is worth highlighting, because surveillance, however defined, enables certain conditions of what we might call modernity: building trust systems, for instance, and establishing "trustworthiness";[4] seeking "accountability" and "safety";[5] making "informed decisions" and facilitating "research advancements" that can also involve "convenience" and "equality and justice."[6] She goes on to detail several meanings of privacy: the desire for "being left alone";[7] the need to "control information" and "control over being sensed by others";[8] the "need for 'control over intimate decisions';[9] the 'control over self-presentation';[10] the idea of 'privacy as keeping information safe';[11] ensuring 'privacy as limited access'; privacy as 'reductionism' which underscores its essential indeterminacy of meanings and inherent connection to other rights";[12] privacy as "contextual integrity" that enables one to control the circulation of information;[13] privacy as "resemblances," as a concept whose meanings emerge in clusters of other concepts and rights.[14]

Clearly, the many meanings of privacy and their entanglements with other obligations and rights demonstrate that privacy is better understood as a function of power and the biological and psychological nature of human life itself. The inflection moment, however, in technological history is the rise of the digital, and, in the context of this book, drones as weapons of war and surveillance and as tools for art and literature. When we move from analog to digital, we end up, whether we like it or not, with surveillance. Véliz says, "Digitization is a surveillance tool. There is no such thing as digitization without surveillance. The very act of turning what was not data into data is a form of surveillance. Digitizing involves creating a record where there was none before, making things taggable and searchable. To digitize is to make trackable that which was beyond reach. And to track just is to surveil."[15]

Perhaps surveillance is not an apt word here, because it is loaded with negative or concerning meanings. For instance, to observe something involves surveillance, but it does not mean, therefore, that observation is just another term for surveillance, or that drone flights over marked territory is observation. Surveillance carries it with a greater degree of intentionality, a desire to observe, with predetermined goals, something or someone. To surveil is to bring into play a series of associated meanings that are less suggestive of passive, neutral, or benign observation than hierarchical structures, unidirectional stares, and the risk of running afoul of social expectations or the law. We must work hard to ensure that privacy does not become a privilege given to us by an outside entity; instead, we can recognize that while surveillance brings significant modern benefits, we must actively engage in the many spheres of social life where privacy is constantly being negotiated so that we can pursue and affirm our humanity through creative endeavors, control the flow of information, and protect the spaces of the commons for democratic deliberation and participation.

Agency in the Commons

We the People—or, rather, the Multitude—can lay claim to what is ours, to what belongs to us, and to every other person on this precious earth—the air, the seas, space, the natural world: our commons. As Michael Hardt and Antonio Negri explain in *Multitude: War and Democracy in the Age of Empire*, unlike the People, which is tied to the nation-state, the masses, which combine differences into an undifferentiated whole, the crowd, which gathers together transiently without deliberation, and the mob, which exerts its will often without judicious restraint, the multitude seeks commonality and cooperation while continuing to be different. The multitude emerges in and through globalization; it emerges within the network itself: "the living alternative that grows within Empire."[16]

Two qualifications are in order. In Hardt and Negri's formulation, the multitude becomes too abstract, since differences continually remain differences as if collaboration and commonality mean that challenges and disruptions to differences do not emerge at all: "The multitude, however, although it remains multiple, is not fragmented, anarchical, or incoherent... . The multitude is the only social subject capable of realizing democracy, that is, the rule of everyone by everyone. The stakes, in other words, are extremely high."[17]

We do not have to view the multitude so abstractly, as devoid of the struggles through which differences emerge and continue. Instead, the multitude can denote the networked contingency of oppositional politics, and the fractured, yet mosaic, identities affirmed to create new solidarities. Here, contingency does not mean context-less pragmatism but the instability and incompleteness inherent in global systems of communication, politico-economic exchange, and cultural formation. The oppositional impulse here is not to do away with drones, armed or unarmed, but to launch a full-spectrum critical engagement—in the commons to affect public policy and public culture—with the manifold disruptions and wholesale transformations effected by drones and surveillance systems on our practices and ideas of privacy, individuality, free expression, creativity, and democracy.

Hardt and Negri also avoid "the commons" in favor of "the common,"[18] because, to them, the commons is predicated on the history of capitalism: the status of the world before and after capitalism, wherein, as we see in Hardin's essay, the pasture and the herdsmen change into individual entrepreneurs eager to multiply their potential by consuming common resources. Such a formulation of the commons ends up privileging a singular economic mode and history, as if without it, the commons are inconceivable, or that they are not subjected to perverse forms of control in non-capitalist, indigenous, or socialist societies. A more expansive approach is to extend the idea of the commons as continually produced through the networks that traverse our socius. We can—and must—create the commons as the space for the generative and regenerative impulses of liberal democracy to thrive in a world suffused with digital technologies.

Rule of Law and Liberal Democracy

The rise of AI is hurtling us into future where autonomous drones with AI can carry out intelligence, surveillance, or bombing operations on their own, without direct or indirect human supervision. That time will soon come. Instead of waiting anxiously for that time, we can learn from history, draw from traditions, and examine complex national, local, technological, and global dynamics to develop institutional systems and cultures that adhere to the rule of law and liberal democracy.

In *AI and the Rule of Law*, Paul Burgess differentiates between the Past Rule of Law and the Present Rule of Law. These thinkers' ideas—Aristotle, John Locke, A.V. Dicey, Friedrich August Von Hayek, Lon Luvois Fuller, and Joseph Raz— have influenced the Past Rule of Law. Fuller, for instance, prioritizes "generality, publicity, prospectivity, intelligibility, consistency practicability, stability, and congruence,"[19] while Raz stresses "prospectivity; stability; law-making guided by rules; judicial independence; natural justice; courts' review powers; accessible courts; and, [that] discretions should not pervert the law."[20] The critical focus in Past Rule of Law was to counter and bring accountability to the exercise of state power, including institutionalizing "predictability and procedural clarity."[21] The source of power was in the state, the official arms of governance, which, without checks and balances, would ride roughshod over the people, whose consent about the state and its activities is the bedrock of democracy.

The Present Rule of Law, gaining purchase in the second half of the twentieth century, focused on the arbitrary use of power beyond the state; that is, power in general, emanating from any source, anywhere: "Arbitrariness itself—in whatever sphere it arises—is seen as being able to be solved by the Rule of Law."[22] It is about the "exercise of arbitrary power *in general.*"[23] The second part of the Present Rule of Law extends the Past Rule of Law's emphasis on form and content of the Law to its outcomes, which are assessed in relation to law, as such. It changes the past's "ambivalence toward the outcome of the law-making process" to a social and legal commitment to examining actual and potential outcomes.[24] Another point relevant to our discussion of drones is AI and machine learning's three scenarios involving the human subject: "in the loop," "out the loop," and "over the loop," which means "decision-making being supported; without human intervention; or with human oversight."²⁵

If we are to (I think we should) apply these models to deal with drones and surveillance culture, we must, as individuals and members of social collectives, constantly insist on checking the power of the state and power in general. In addition to insisting on transparency, coherence, human rights, and accountability, we can consider the various levels at which our ability to impact drone cultures can happen when AI and drones support human activity, need human oversight, or are entirely autonomous. In the last instance, even when AI-driven autonomy is possible for drones, having clear connections to human subjects involved in producing such autonomy and subjecting them, their intentions and capacities, to critical and public examination and judgement will be crucial to avoid evacuating the human subject from general artificial intelligence, that condition when AI exhibits fully autonomous capabilities requiring neither human support nor oversight. The outcomes-based model of the Present Rule of Law will mean incorporating humanistic thinking and including scholars and thinkers from the arts and humanities in the industry's management structures.

Paul Scharre in *Four Battlegrounds: Power in the Age of Artificial Intelligence* highlights four areas for critical intervention: data, compute, talent, and institutions. Without relevant and vast data, AI's capacities are compromised; the hardware and software integration needed to store, archive, process, and retrieve data in response to the design and integration of algorithmic structures for machine and deep learning require extraordinary processing power; doing such work requires skilled researchers and scientists, but attracting top talent globally to the United States (or to any country seeking to invest in AI) must be prioritized; the institutional emphasis is about research generation in specialized settings, and its dissemination to impact public policy, and the formation of regulatory bodies accountable to the public to develop commonsense policies with an eye to future technological shifts. Scharre points out, "The creation and use of technology is an inherently political act. Technology can be used to repress human freedoms or bolster them, to elevate a message or suppress it, to strengthen one group or weaken another. How technology is used reflects the values, whether conscious or unconscious, of its creators and users."²⁶

As we hurtle to an AI future of robotic warfare and fully autonomous drones, we can extend the implications of Burgess and Scharre's models into secondary and postsecondary education, which can mean making AI literacies a requirement in general education and specialized programs of study; it can mean having students in the sciences and technology become conversant with traditions of humanistic thinking, those traditions that prioritize studying human languages, human cultures, and human behaviors. Such an approach can result in human-centered computational thinking and algorithmic designing, resulting not in an automatic reduction or absence of political and economic problems as AI moves toward general AI but in better equipping us to deal with them, because we would have been involved, from the get-go, in all critical processes of AI design and development, and in grounding those processes in the Past and Present Rule of Law.

We can, perhaps, end on this note: where drones and surveillance seek a biopolitical transformation of life itself, not only society, as they target and surveil entire populations in vast regions through complex networks, and remain invisible and visible at a time and in a manner of their own choosing, the peoples, citizens and noncitizens alike, and the multitude, emerging within these networks, can seek societal and cultural transformation. Our goals can be simple yet profound: retain, protect, and further the rights of association, expression, and public participation in the multiple spaces, real and virtual, of the commons, wherever they are found or created, and thereby affirm our common humanity.

Notes

1. Jeremey Bentham, *A Fragment on Government*, upload.wikipedia.org, edited by F. C. Montague (Clarendon Press, 1775, reis. 1891), accessed July 19, 2025, https://upload.wikimedia.org/wikipedia/commons/d/dc/Jeremy_Bentham%2C_A_Fragment_on_Government_%281891%29.pdf
2. Garrett James Harding, "The Tragedy of the Commons," *Science* 162, no. 3859 (1968): 1244.
3. Harding, "The Tragedy of the Commons," 1243.
4. Carissa Véliz, *The Ethics of Privacy and Surveillance* (Oxford: Oxford University Press, 2024), 113.
5. Ibid., 115.
6. Ibid., 117.
7. Ibid., 47.
8. Ibid., 51.
9. Ibid., 53.
10. Ibid., 59.
11. Ibid., 59.
12. Ibid., 65.
13. Ibid., 69.
14. Ibid., 70.
15. Ibid., 183.
16. Michael Hardt and Antonio Negri, *Multitude: War and Democracy in the Age of Empire* (New York: The Penguin Press, 2004), xiii.
17. Ibid., 99–100.
18. Ibid., xv.
19. Paul Burgess, *AI and the Rule of Law* (New York: Bloomsbury, 2024), 31.
20. Ibid., 35.
21. Ibid., 84.

22 Ibid., 43.
23 Ibid., 97, emphasis in original.
24 Ibid.
25 Ibid., 53.
26 Paul Scharre, *Four Battlegrounds: Power in the Age of Artificial Intelligence* (New York: W. W. Norton and Company, 2023), 302.

BIBLIOGRAPHY

Africa Goes Digital. *africagoesdigital.com*. Accessed December 27, 2024. http://afgoesdigital.com

Agamben, Giorgio. *Homo Sacer: Sovereign Power and Bare Life*. Translated by Daniel Heller-Roazen. California: Stanford University Press, California, 1998.

Agamben, Giorgio. "The Politicization of Life." In *Biopolitics: A Reader*, edited by Timothy Campbell and Adam Sitze, 145–51. Durham: Duke University Press, 2013.

Agamben, Giorgio. "The Invention of an Epidemic." *European Journal of Psychoanalysis*. February 26, 2020, https://journal-psychoanalysis.eu/articles/coronavirus-and-philosophers/

Agamben, Giorgio. "Clarifications." *European Journal of Psychoanalysis*. March 17, 2020. https://journal-psychoanalysis.eu/articles/coronavirus-and-philosophers/

Agamben, Giorgio. "Reflections on the Plague." Accessed December 5, 2024. https://journal-psychoanalysis.eu/articles/reflections-on-the-plague/

Ahmed, Albar. *The Thistle and the Drone: How America's War on Terror Became a Global War on Tribal Islam*. Washington, DC: Brookings Institution Press, 2013.

Ahmed, Sabeen. "From Threat to Walking Corpse: Spatial Disruption and the Phenomenology of 'Living under Drones.'" *Theory & Event* 21, no. 2 (2018): 382–410.

Air Force: Actions Needed to Strengthen Unamanned Aerial System Pilots," *United States Government Accountability Office*, April 2014: 23–5.

Airforce Technology. "Collaborative Combat Aircraft (CCA), USA." *airforce-technology.com* June 21, 2024, https://airforce-technology.com/projects/collaborative-combat-aircraft-cca-usa/?cf-view.

Airforce Technology. "Next Generation Air Dominance Programme." *airforce-technolology.com* March 8, 2024, https://airforce-technology.com/projects/next-generation-air-dominance-programme-us/?cf-view

Ajana, Btihaj. "Surveillance and Biopolitics." *Electronic Journal of Sociology* 7 (2005): 1–15.

Albrechtslund, Anders, and Lynsey Dubbeld. "The Plays and Arts of Surveillance: Studying Surveillance as Entertainment." *Surveillance and Society* 3, no. 2–3 (2005): 216–21.

Alex O'Hagan, Lauren, and Elisa Serafinelli. "Transhistoricizing the Drone: A Comparative Visual Semiotic Analysis of Pigeon and Domestic Drone Photography." *Photography and Culture* 15, no. 4 (2022): 327–51.

Alex O'Hagan, Lauren, and Elisa Serafinelli. "Rethinking Verticality through Top-Down Views in Drone Hobbyist Photography." *Visual Studies* 39, no. 4 (2023): 1–14.

Ali, Manzoor. "Khud Kasha Dhamaka Yama: The Song's a blast." *tribune.com.pk* November 26, 2011. http://tribune.com.pk/story/298042/khud-kasha-dhamaka-yama-the-songs-a-blast/

Allington, Daniel, Sarah Brouillette, and Davd Golumbia. "Neoliberal Tools (and Archives): A Political History of the Digital Humanities." *lareviewofbooks.org* May 1, 2016. https://lareviewofbooks.org/article/neoliberal-tools-archives-political-history-digital-humanities/

Amanda, Macias. "U.S. Sends 100 Killer Drones Called Switchblades to Ukraine." *cnbc.com* March 30, 2022, https://cnbc.com/2022/03/30/us-sends-100-killer-drones-called-switchblades-to-ukraine.html

Andrejevic, Mark. "The Droning of Experience." *The Fibreculture Journal* 25 (2015) http://twentyfive.fibreculturejournal.org/fcj-187-the-droning-of-experience/

Andrejevic, Mark. "Theorizing Drones and Droning Theory." In *Drones and Unmanned Aerial Systems: Legal and Social Implications for Security and Surveillance*, edited by Aleš Završnik, 21–43. Springer: 2016.

Anglin, Timothy M. Shaw, and Douglas G. Anglin. "Zambia: The Crises of Liberation." In *Southern Africa: The Continuing Crisis*, edited by Gwendolen M. Carter and Patrick O'Meara, 199–222. Bloomington: Indiana University Press, 1979.

Anike. "The Colorful Drones of Mahwish Chishty." *patheos.com* July 1, 2013. http://patheos.com/blogs/mmw/2013/07/the-colourful-drones-of-mahwish-chishty/

Ann Arbor Art Center. "Drones 2014." Accessed December 15, 2024, http://annarborartcenter.org/drones

Arewa, Ofunmilayo. "At the Crossroads of Digital Imperialism & Digital Development," Berkman Klein Center for Internet and Society, Harvard University, May 24, 2021, *youtube.com* May 2021, https://youtube.com/watch?v=B1Yr9hwMm8s

Ashcroft, Bill, Gareth Griffiths, and Helen Tiffin. *Post-colonial Studies: The Key Concepts*. Routledge, 1998.

Asrad, Peter. "The Labor of Ssurveillance and Bureaucratized Killing: New Subjectivities of Military Drone Operators." In *Life in the Age of Drone Warfare*, edited by Lisa Parks and Caren Kaplan, 282–314. Durham: Duke University Press, 2017.

Autonomous Systems and Robotics Group. "ChatGPT for Robotics: Design Principles and Model Abilities." *microsoft*, February 20, 2023, https://microsoft.com/enus/research/group/autonomous-systems-group-robotics/articles/chatgpt-for-robotics/

Azhar, Hamdan. "Drones Are Not Dangerous: Normalization, New Journalism, and the New Drone Culture." *The State. web.archive.org*. December 18, 2013. Accessed December 15, 2024. https://web.archive.org/web/20160325125213/http://thestate.ae/drones-are-not-dangerous-normalisation-new-journalism-and-the-new-drone-culture/

Ball, James. "NSA collects millions of text messages daily in 'untargeted' global sweep." *theguardian.com* January 16, 2014, http://theguardian.com/world/2014/jan/16/nsa-collects-millions-text-messages-daily-untargeted-global-sweep

Ballvé, Teo. "The New Aesthetic Part II: Writing Like a Drone." *territorialmasquerades.com* October 26, 2012, https://territorialmasquerades.net/the-new-aesthetic-part-ii-writing-like-a-drone/

Barnard-Wills, David. *Surveillance and Identity: Discourse, Subjectivity and the State*. Burlington, VT: Ashgate, 2012.

Barney, Darin, Gabriella Coleman, Christine Ross, Jonathan Sterne, and Tamar Tembeck, eds. *The Participatory Condition in the Digital Age*. Minneapolis: University of Minnesota Press, 2016.

Basu, Rajeev. "Drones of New York." *rajeevbasu.com*. Accessed January 27, 2025, https://rajeevbasu.com/projects/dronesofnewyork/

Bauman, Zygmunt. *Postmodern Ethics*. Cambridge, MA: Blackwell, 1993.

Bauman, Zygmunt. *Liquid Modernity*. Malden, MA: Polity Press, 2000.
Bauman, Zygmunt, and David Lyon. *Liquid Surveillance: A Conversation*. Kindle. Malden, MA: Polity Press, 2013.
Bhabha, Homi. "DissemiNation: Time, Narrative, and the Margins of the Modern nation." *Nation and Narration*, edited by Homi Bhabha, 290–322. New York: Routledge, 1990.
BBC. "Venezuela President Maduro Survives 'Drone Assassination Attempt." *bbc.com* August 5, 2018. https://bbc.com/news/world-latin-america-45073385
BBC, "India Covid: Anger as Twitter Ordered to Remove Critical Virus Posts." *bbc.com* April 26, 2021, https://bbc.com/news/world-asia-56883483
Becker, Jo, and Scott Shane. "A Measure of Change: Secret 'Kill List' Proves a Test of Obama's Principles and Will." *nytimes.com*. May 29, 2012, http://nytimes.com/2012/05/29/world/obamas-leadership-in-war-on-al-qaeda.html?pagewanted=1&_r=2&pagewanted=all&#p[TMATMA]
Benjamin, Medea. *Drone Warfare*. New York: Verso, 2013.
Benkler, Yochai. "Networks of Power, Degrees of Freedom." *International Journal of Communication* 5 (2011): 721–55.
Bentham, Jeremy. *A Fragment on Government*. Edited by F. C. Montague. upload.wikipedia.org. Clarendon Press, 1775, reis. 1891. Accessed July 20, 2025, https://upload.wikimedia.org/wikipedia/commons/d/dc/Jeremy_Bentham%2C_A_Fragment_on_Government_%281891%29.pdf
Bergakis, Brock. "US Launches Drone from Aircraft Carrier," *bigstory.ap.org* May 14, 2013, http://bigstory.ap.org/article/us-launches-drone-aircraft-carrier.
Bergen, Peter. "Drone Is Obama's Weapon of Choice," *CNN Opinion*. September 19, 2012, http://cnn.com/2012/09/05/opinion/bergen-obama-drone/index.html
Berry, David M. *Understanding the Digital Humanities*. New York: Palgrave Macmillan, 2012.
Berry, David M. "The Postdigital Constellation." In *Postdigital Aesthetic: Art, Computation and Design*, edited by David M. Berry and Michael Dieter, 44–57. New York: Palgrave, 2015.
Berry, David M., Michel van Dartel, Michael Dieter, Michelle Kasprzak, Nat Muller, Rachel O"Reilly, and José Luis de Vicente, *New Aesthetic, New Anxieties* V2 Publishing, 2012, https://v2.nl/archive/articles/new-aesthetic-new-anxieties
Bigo, Didier. "Globalized-In-Security: The Field and the Ban-Opticon." In *Translation, Biopolitics, Colonial Difference*, edited by Naoki Sakai and Jon Solomon, 109–56. Hong Kong: Hong Kong University Press, 2006.
Bole, Michael J. *The Drone Age: How Drone Technology Will Change War and Peace*. Oxford: Oxford University Press, 2020.
Boller, Grant. *Theorizing Digital Cultures*. New York: Sage, 2018.
Bogost, Ian. "What Is Object Oriented Ontology? A Definition for Ordinary Folk." *Bogost.com* December 8, 2009. http://bogost.com/blog/what_is_objectoriented_ontolog.shtml
Bogost, Ian. "The New Aesthetic Needs to Get Weirder." *theatlantic.com* April 13, 2012. http://theatlantic.com/technology/archive/2012/04/the-new-aesthetic-needs-to-get-weirder/255838/
Bond, Shannon. "Elon Musk Is Using the Twitter Files to Discredit Foes and Push Conspiracy Theories." *npr.org* December 14, 2022, https://npr.org/2022/12/14/1142666067/elon-musk-is-using-the-twitter-files-to-discredit-foes-and-push-conspiracy-theor
Borenstein, Greg. "What It Like To Be a 21st Century Thing?" *The Creator's Project*. April 6, 2012. http://thecreatorsproject.vice.com/blog/in-response-to-bruce-sterlings-essay-on-the-new-aesthetic

Bowden, Mark. "The Killing Machines: How to Think about Drones." *theatlantic.com* August 13, 2013. http://theatlantic.com/magazine/archive/2013/09/the-killing-machines-how-to-think-about-drones/309434/?single_page=true

Boyle, Matthew J. "Correspondence: Debating Drone Proliferation," *International Security* 42, no. 3 (2017): 178–80.

Brennan, Timothy. "The Digital-Humanities Bust." Chronicle of Higher Education. *chronicle.com* October 15, 2017, https://chronicle.com/article/The-Digital-Humanities-Bust/241424

Bridle, James. "James Bridle: Waving at the Machines." Transcript by Guy Leech. December 5, 2011, https://webdirections.org/resources/james-bridle-waving-at-the-machines/

Bridle, James. "The New Aesthetic." *riglondon.com*. The Really Interesting Group. May 6, 2011, http://riglondon.com/blog/2011/05/06/the-new-aesthetic/

Bridle, James. "The New Aesthetic," *riglondon.com*. May 6, 2011, https://web.archive.org/web/20111114184842/http://riglondon.com/blog/2011/05/06/the-new-aesthetic/

Bridle. James. *The New Aesthetic*, May 6, 2011, https://web.archive.org/web/20111114184842/http://riglondon.com/blog/2011/05/06/the-new-aesthetic/

Bridle James. "Under the Shadow of the Drone." *booktwo.org*. October 11, 2011, http://booktwo.org/notebook/drone-shadows/

Bridle, James. "Dronestagram: The Drone's-Eye View," *booktwo.org*. November 8, 2012, http://booktwo.org/notebook/dronestagram-drones-eye-view/

Bridle, James. "Four Greens." *booktwo.org* November 26, 2012, https://booktwo.org/notebook/four-greens/

Bridle, James. "The New Aesthetic: Seeing Like Digital Devices." *South by South West* (SXSW), March 12, 2012, https://schedule.sxsw.com/2012/events/event_IAP11102

Bridle, James. "#xsaesthetic." Panel "The New Aesthetic: Seeing Like Digital Devices." South By Southwest Conference (SXSW). *booktwo.org* March 15, 2012, http://booktwo.org/notebook/sxaesthetic/

Bridle, James. "Day of the Drones." Brisbane Writers Festival. *booktwo.org*. Video, September, 2013. http://booktwo.org/videos/

Bridle, James. "Drone Shadows and Dispositions." *booktwo.org*. May 16, 2013, http://booktwo.org/notebook/drone-shadows-dispositions/

Bridle, James. "The Future Symposium: Presentation by James Bridle." Film & Video Umbrella's 'Future' Symposium, CCA, Glasgow, June 2013, http://booktwo.org/videos/

Bridle, James. 'Naked Lunch." *booktwo.org*. The Conference, Malmö, Sweden, August 2013, http://booktwo.org/videos/

Bridle, James. "The New Aesthetic and Its Politics." *booktwo.org* June 12, 2013, http://booktwo.org/notebook/new-aesthetic-politics/

Bridle, James. "A Quiet Disposition." Brighton Festival, Lighthouse, Brighton. *booktwo.org*. Video, May 2013, http://booktwo.org/videos/

Bridle, James. "The New Aesthetic." Accessed December 10, 2024, http://new-aesthetic.tumblr.com/about

Bridle, James. "Watching the Watchers," jamesbridle.com. Accessed December 15, 2024, https://jamesbridle.com/works/watching-the-watchers

Brimblecombe-Fox, Kathryn. "Portfolio: Dronescapes by Kathryn Brimblecombe-Fox." Interview with Maggie Barnett, *dronecetner.bard.edu* February 23, 2017, https://dronecenter.bard.edu/portfolio-dronescapes-by-kathryn-brimblecombe-fox/

Brimblecombe-Fox, Kathryn. *Dronescapes*. Accessed December 15, 2024, https://kathrynbrimblecombeart.blogspot.com/p/dronescapes.html

Britannica. "Connectionism." *brittanica.com*. Accessed December 14, 2024, https://britannica.com/technology/connectionism-artificial-intelligence

Britannica. "Methods and goals in AI." *brittanica.com*. Accessed July 16, 2024, https://britannica.com/technology/top-down-approach

"Bugsplat Predicts Bombs' Impact," *defensetech.org* February 22, 2003. Accessed January 27, 2025, https://military.com/defensetech/2003/02/22/bugsplat-predicts-bombs-impact

Burdette, Marcia M. *Zambia: Between Two Worlds*. Colorado: Westview Press, 1988.

Burgess, Paul. *AI and the Rule of Law: The Necessary Evolution of a Concept*. New York: Bloomsbury, 2024.

Burghhart, Marjorie. "The Three Orders of Digital Humanities Imagined #dhiha5." *dhiha.hypotheses.org* April 28, 2013, http://dhiha.hypotheses.org/817

Carmody, Pádraig, and Godfrey Hampwaye. "Inclusive or Exclusive Globalization." *Africa Today* 56, no.3 (2010): 84–102.

Caso, Federica. "Visualizing the Drone: War Art as Embodied Resistance," *E-International Relations* May 16, 2018, https://e-ir.info/2018/05/16/visualising-the-drone-war-art-as-embodied-resistance/

Cascone, Kim. "The Aesthetics of Failure: "Post-Digital" Tendencies in Contemporary Computer Music." *Computer Music Journal* 24, no. 4 (2000): 12–18.

Caughill, Patrick. "Australia Is Deploying AI Drones to Help Prevent Shark Attacks." *futurism.com* August 8, 2017, https://futurism.com/australia-is-deploying-ai-drones-to-help-prevent-shark-attacks

Chamayou, Grégorie. *A Theory of the Drone*. New York: The New Press, 2015.

Chávez, Kerry, and Ori Swed. "Emulating Underdogs: Tactical Drones in the Russia-Ukraine War." *Contemporary Security Policy* 44, no. 2 (2023): 592–605.

Chisty, Mahwish. *mahachisty.com*. Accessed January 7, 2025, http://mahachishty.com/

Chivers, C. J. "How Suicides Drones Transformed the Front Lines in Ukraine." *nytimes.com* December 31, 2024, https://nytimes.com/2024/12/31/magazine/drones-weapons-ukraine-war.html

Choi, Charles. "Mimicking Biology for Better Drones." *insideunmannedsystems.com* December 17, 2020, https://insideunmannedsystems.com/mimicking-biology-for-better-drones/

Choi-Fitzpatrick, Austin. "Resist!: Resisting Technology and the Technology of Resistance." In *The Good Drone: How Social Movements Democratize Surveillance*, thegooddrone.mitpress.mitedu, July 20, 2020. Accessed December 28, 2024. https://thegooddrone.mitpress.mit.edu/pub/ttjs9hf3/release/1

Clark, Lindsay C. *Gender and Drone Warfare: A Hauntological Perspective*. London: Routledge, 2019.

Clark, Lindsay C., and Christian Enemark. "Drone Warriors, Revealed Humanity, and a Feminist Ethics of Care." In *Ethics of Drone Strikes: Restraining Remote-Control Killing*, edited by Christian Enemark, 130–40. Edinburgh: Edinburgh Scholarship Online, 2022. https://doi.org/10.3366/edinburgh/9781474483575.003.0008

Clarke, Roger A. "Information Technology and Dataveillance." *Communications of the ACM* 31, no. 5 (1988): 498–512.

Clement, J. "Share of Global Mobile Website Ttraffic 2015–2021." *statista.com*. April 28, 2021, https://statista.com/statistics/277125/share-of-website-traffic-coming-from-mobile-devices/

Conley, Rob, and Dean Lockwood. "As Above, So Below: Triangulating Drone Culture." *culturemachine.net* 16 (2015) https://culturemachine.net/vol-16-drone-cultures/as-above-so-below/

Contreras-Koterbay, Scott, and Łukasz Mirocha. *The New Aesthetic and Art: Constellations of the Postdigital*. Amsterdam: Institute of Network Cultures, 2016.

Cooper, Kindra. "OpenAI GPT-3: Everything You Need to Know [Updated]." *springboard.com* September 27, 2023, https://help.openai.com/en/articles/7842364-how-chat gpt-and-our-language-models-are-developed

Cope, Aaron Straup. *aaronland.info*. December 10, 2024, https://aaronland.info/web log/2012/03/13/godhelpus/#sxaesthetic

Coren, Anna, et al. "US Military Admits It Killed 10 Civilians and Targeted Wrong Vehicle in Kabul Strike." *cnn.com* September 17, 2021, https://cnn.com/2021/09/17/politics/kabul-drone-strike-us-military-intl-hnk/index.html

Coupland, Douglas. *Digital Orca*. January 7, 2009, https://coupland.com/digital-orca/

Cramer, Florian. "What Is 'Post-digital'"? *APRJA* 3, no. 1 (2014): 11–24.

Crawford, Neta C. "The U.S. Budgetary Costs of the Post-9/11 Wars." *Costs of War*. Watson Institute for International and Public Affairs. September 1, 2021, https://watson.brown.edu/costsofwar/files/cow/imce/papers/2021/Costs%20of%20War_U.S.%20Budgetary%20Costs%20of%20Post-9%2011%20Wars_9.1.21.pdf

Cropsey, Seth. "Drone Warfare in Ukraine: Historical Context and Implications for the Future." *hoover.org* March 14, 2024, https://hoover.org/research/drone-warfare-ukraine-historical-context-and-implications-future

Crumpler, William. "The Problem of Bias in Facial Recognition." *Center for Strategic and International Studies,* csis.org, May 1, 2020, https://csis.org/blogs/strategic-technologies-blog/problem-bias-facial-recognition

"Dancing Machines." *MIT Computer Science and Artificial Intelligence Laboratory*. November 14, 2011. Accessed May 28, 2014, http://csail.mit.edu/node/1640

Dandekar, Christopher. *Surveillance, Power, and Modernity: Bureaucracy and the Discipline from 1700 to the Present Day*. New York: St. Martin's Press, 1990.

Davies, Russell. *russelldavies.typepad.com*. Accessed December 10, 2024, https://russelldavies.typepad.com/planning/2012/03/sxsw-the-new-aesthetic-and-writing.html.

Dhatterwal, Jagjit Singh, Kuldeep Singh Kaswan, and Reenu Batra, *Nature Inspired Robotics*. Taylor and Francis, 2024.

Dean, Mitchell. *Governmentality: Power and Rule in Modern Society*. Thousand Oaks, CA: SAGE, 1999.

De Landa, Manuel. *War in the Age of Intelligent Machines*, New York: Zone Books, 1991.

DeLanda, Manuel. *Assemblage Theory*. Edinburgh Press, 2016.

Deleuze, Gilles, and Claire Parnet. *Dialogues*. Trans. by Hugh Tomlinson and Barbara Habberjam. New York: The Anthlone Press, 1977.

Deleuze, Giles, and Félix Guattari. *A Thousand Plateaus: Capitalism and Schizophrenia*. Trans. by Brian Massumi. Minneapolis: University of Minnesota Press, 1987.

Department of Defense, "The Army's Project Convergence." *Congressional Research Office* June 2, 2022, https://crsreports.congress.gov/product/pdf/IF/IF11654/6

DeVore, Marc R. "'No End of a Lesson': Observations from the First High-Intensity Drone War." *Defense & Security Analysis* 39, no. 2 (2023): 263–6.

DHS Program, Demographic and Health Survey, *US AID from the American People*. 2018. Accessed December 28, 2024, https://dhsprogram.com/pubs/pdf/FR361/FR361.pdf

Donavan, Joan. "Why the 'Twitter Files' Are Falling Flat," *politico.com* December 15, 2022, https://politico.com/news/magazine/2022/12/15/twitter-files-falling-flat- 00073979

Dowd, Alan W. "Drone Wars: Risks and Warning." *Parameters* 42 (4)/43 (1), Spring (2013): 7–16.

Drew, Christopher. "Drones Are Weapons of Choice in Fighting Qaeda," *nytimes.com* March 16, 2009, https://nytimes.com/2009/03/17/business/17uav.html

"Drones." *Ann Arbor Art Center*. Acessed January 2, 2025, http://annarborartcenter.org/drones

"Drone Strikes: Pakistan." *newamerica.org*. Accessed December 7, 2024, https://newamerica.org/in-depth/americas-counterterrorism-wars/pakistan/

"Drone Strikes: Yemen." *newamerica.org*. Accessed December 7, 2024, https://newamerica.org/in-depth/americas-counterterrorism-wars/us-targeted- killing-program-yemen/

DuBois, W. E. B. "The Souls of Black Folk," *Project Gutenberg*, eBook, Jan. 1996, first published 1903. Accessed December 28, 2024, https://gutenberg.org/files/408/408-h/408-h.htm

Dunton, Chris. "Wherever the Bus Is Headed": Recent Developments in the African Novel." *Research in African Literatures* 50, no. 4 (2019): 1–20.

Elliot, Carlene D. "Kid-Visible: Childhood Obesity, Body Surveillance, and the Techniques of Care." In *Surveillance: Power, Problems, and Politics*, edited by Sean P. Hier and Josh Greenberg, 33–45. Toronto: UBC Press, 2009.

Elias, Jamal J. "On Wings of Diesel: The Decorated Trucks of Pakistan," *Amherstmagazine*. 2005. Accessed July 20, 2025, https://amherst.edu/news/magazine/issue-archive/2005_spring/wings

Elias, Jamal J. *On Wings of Diesel: Trucks, Identity, and Culture in Pakistan*. Oxford, England: Oneworld, 2011.

Emmerson, Ben. "Promotion and Protection of Human Rights and Fundamental Freedom while Countering Terrorism." Report to the UN General Assembly. September 8, 2013. *Office of the High Commissioner for Human Rights*. A/68/389.

Englund, Harri. "Zambia at 50: The Rediscovery of Liberalism." *Africa: Journal of the International African Institute* 83, no. 4 (2013): 670–89.

Esposito, Roberto. "The Enigma of Biopolitics," *Biopolitics: A Reader*, edited by Timothy Campbell and Adam Sitze, 350–85. Durham: Duke University Press, 2013.

Esposito, Roberto. "Cured to the Biter End." In *Coronavirus, Psychoanalysis, and Philosophy; Conversations on Pandemics, Politics, and Society*, edited by Fernando Castrillón and Thomas Marchevesky, 28–9. Routledge, 2021.

Fanon, Frantz. *The Wretched of the Earth*. Translated by Constance Farrington, Grove Weidenfeld, 1963.

Farer, Tom, and Frederic Bernard. "Killing by Drone: Towards Uneasy Reconciliation with the Values of a Liberal State," *Human Rights Quarterly* 38 (2016): 108–33.

Fast, Omer. *5,000 Feet is Best*. Berlin, Germany: Sternberg Press, 2012.

Federal Aviation Administration. "DHS, FBI, FAA & DoD Joint Statement on Ongoing Response to Reported Drone Sightings." *faa.gov* December 17, 2024, https://faa.gov/newsroom/dhs-fbi-faa-dod-joint-statement-ongoing-response-reported-drone-sightings

Flying Labs, https://flyinglabs.org/. Accessed December 27, 2024.

Foucault, Michel. *Power/Knowledge*. Edited by Colin Gordon, and translated by Colin Jordan, Leo Marshall, John Mepham, and Kate Soper. New York: Pantheon Books, 1972.

Foucault, Michel. "Right of Death and Power over Life." *Foucault Reader*. Edited by Paul Rabinow, 258–72. New York: Pantheon Books, 1984.

Foucault. Michel. *Society Must Be Defended: Lectures at the Collége de France, 1975–76*. New York: Picador, 2003.

Foucault, Michel. *Security, Territory, Population: Lectures at the Collége de France, 1977–78*. New York: Palgrave Macmillan, 2007.

Ferrari, John. "Unleashing Innovation: The Case for a Drone Operator Branch in the US Army." *breakingdefense.com* June 3, 2024. https://breakingdefense.com/2024/06/unleashing-innovation-the-case-for-a-drone-operator-branch-in-the-us-army/

Frana, Philip F., and Michael J. Klein. *Encyclopedia of Artificial Intelligence: The Past, Present, and Future of AI*. California: ABC-CLIO, 2021.

France-Presse, Agence. "Russia, Ukraine Exchange Drone, Missile Attacks." *voanews.com* June 14, 2024, https://voanews.com/a/russia-ukraine-exchange-drone-missile-attacks/7655741.html

Galloway, Alexander. *Protocol: How Control Exists after Decentralization*. Boston: MIT, 2004.

Gertler, Jeremiah. "U.S Aerial Unmanned Systems." *Congressional Research Service*, U.S. Department of State. January 3, 2012, http://fpc.state.gov/c49126.htm

Getachew, Adom. "Reimagining Decolonisation Today: A Review of neither Settler nor Native." *CODESRIA Bulletin Online* 15 June 2021, 1–4.

Gibson, William. *Spook Country*. New York: Putnam, 2007.

Gibson, William. "The Art of Fiction." Interview with David Wallace-Wells, *Paris Review* 197. 2011. https://theparisreview.org/interviews/6089/the-art-of-fiction-no-211-william-gibson

Global Air Drone Academy. globalairdroneacademy.org. Accessed December 27, 2024. https://globalairdroneacademy.org/.

Gorman, Sibohan, and Jennifer Valentino-Devries. "New Details Show Broader NSA Surveillance Reach." *wsj.com* August 20, 2013, http://online.wsj.com/news/articles/SB10001424127887324108204579022874091732470

Government Accountability Office. "Drone Swarm Technologies." *GAO: Science, Technology Assessment, and Analytics*, September 2023, https://gao.gov/assets/gao-23-106930.pdf

Gramsci, Antonio. *Subaltern Social Groups: A Critical Edition of Prison Notebook 25*. Edited and translated by Joseph A. Buttigieg and Marcus E. Green. New York: Columbia University Press, 2021.

Green, Marcus. "Gramsci Cannot Speak: Presentations and Interpretations of Gramsci's Concept of the Subaltern." *Rethinking Marxism* 14, no. 3 (2002): 1–24.

Greenfield, Adam. *Everyware: The Dawning Age of Ubiquitous Computing*. CA: New Riders, 2006.

Greenwald, Glenn. *No Place to Hide: Edward Snowden, the N.S.A. and the U.S Surveillance State*. New York: Metropolitan Books, 2014.

Grižnić, Marina. "What Is the Aesthetics of Necropolitics?" In *The Aesthetics of Necropolitics*, edited by Natasha Lushetich, 17–36. Academic Search Complete, Ebook Central. London: Rowman and Littlefield, 2018.

Grižinić, Marina, and Šefik Tatlić. *Necropolitics, Racialization, and Global Capitalism: Historicization of Biopolitics and Forensics of Politics, Art, and Life*. New York: Lexington Books, 2014.

Guha, Ranajit. "On Some Aspects of the Historiography of Colonial India." In *Subaltern Studies I: Writings on South Asian History and Society*, edited by Ranajit Guha, 1–8. Delhi: Oxford University Press, 1982.

Gusterson, Hugh. *Drone: Remote Control Warfare*. Cambridge, MA: MIT Press, 2016.

Haggerty, Kevin D. "Tear Down the Walls: On Demolishing the Panopticon." In *Theorizing Surveillance: The Panopticon and Beyond*, edited by David Lyon, 23–45. Portland, OR: Willan, 2006.

Haggerty, Kevin D. "Foreword: Surveillance and Political Problems." In *Surveillance: Power, Problems, and Politics*, edited by Sean P. Hier and Josh Greenberg, ix–xviii. Toronto: UBC Press, 2009.

Haggerty, Kevin D. and Richard Ericson. "The surveillant assemblage." In *The Surveillance Studies Reader*, edited by Sean P. Hier and Joshua Greenberg, 104–16. New York: Open University Press, 2007.

Hall, Gary. "The Digital Humanities beyond Computing." *culturemachine.net*. 12, 2011, https://culturemachine.net/wp-content/uploads/2019/01/11-Digital-Humanities-441-894-1-PB.pdf

Hambling, David. "Special Forces Gigapixel Flying Spy See All." *Wired* February 12, 2009, https://wired.com/2009/02/gigapixel-flyin/

Hambling, David. "Ukraine's AI Drones Seek and Attack Russian Forces Without Human Oversight." *forbes.com* October 17, 2023, https://forbes.com/sites/davidhambling/2023/10/17/ukraines-ai-drones-seek-and-attack-russian-forces-without-human-oversight/?sh=2e0e6db66da6

Harding, Garrett James. "The Tragedy of the Commons." *Science* 162, no. 3859 (1968): 1243–48.

Harding, Luke. "Footage Released of Guardian Editors Destroying Snowden Hard Drives" *theguardian.com* January 31, 2014, http://theguardian.com/uk-news/2014/jan/31/footage-released-guardian-editors-snowden-hard-drives-gchq

Hardt, Michael, and Antonio Negri, *Multitude: War and Democracy in the Age of Empire*. New York: The Penguin Press, 2004.

Harkinson, Josh. "Friendly Fire: Drones as Folk Art." Interview with Mahwish Chishty. *Motherjones.com*, June 24, 2013, http://motherjones.com/media/2013/06/pakistani-drone-art-mahwish-chishty#disqus_thread

Harper, Jon. "Pentagon Gets $7.5 Billion for Unmanned Systems," *nationaldefensemagazine.org* May 27, 2021, https://nationaldefensemagazine.org/articles/2021/5/27/pentagon-gets-$7-5-billion-for-unmanned-systems

Hart-Davis, Guy. *Killer ChatGPT Prompts*. New Jersey: John Wiley and Sons, 2023.

Harvey, Adam. *Privacy Gift Shop*. Accessed December 15, 2024. http://privacygiftshop.com/collections/

Haque, Enamul. *The Ultimate Modern Guide to Artificial Intelligence*. London: Enel Publications, 2020.

Hazelton, Jacqueline L. "Drones: What Are They Good For?" *Parameters* 42, no. 4 (2013): 29–33.

Heaven, Will Douglass. "What Is AI?" *MIT Technology Review*, July 10, 2024. https://technologyreview.com/2024/07/10/1094475/what-is-artificial-intelligence-ai-definitiveguide/?truid=&utm_source=the_algorithm&utm_medium=email&utm_campaign=the_algorithm.unpaid.engagement&utm_content=07-15-2024

Hensley, Nathan. "Drone form: Mediation at the End of Empire." *Novel: A Forum on Fiction* 51, no. 2 (2018): 226–49.

Hernandez, Joe. "A Military Drone with a Mind of Its Own Was Used in Combat, U.N. Says," *npr.org* June 2021, https://npr.org/2021/06/01/1002196245/a-u-n-report-sugge sts-libya-saw-the-first-battlefield-killing-by-an-autonomous-d

Hier, Sean P., and Josh Greenberg, eds. "The Politics of Surveillance." *Surveillance: Power, Problems, and Politics*, 11–18. Toronto: UBC Press, 2007.

Hill, Mike. *On Posthuman War: Computation and Military Violence*. University of Minnesota Press, 2022.

Hindley, Meredith. "The Rise of the Machines." *Humanities: The Magazine for the National Endowment for the Humanities.*" 34, no. 4 (2013), http:// neh.gov/humanities/2013/julyaugust/feature/the-rise-the-machines

Hodgson, Justin. *Post-Digital Rhetoric and the New Aesthetic*. Ohio: Ohio State University Press, 2019.

Hoen, John R. "Joint All-Domain Command and Control (JADC2)," *Congressional Research Office, sgp.fas.org*. January 21, 2022. https://sgp.fas.org/crs/natsec/IF11493.pdf

Hurwitz, Elijah Solomon. "Drone Pilots: 'Overworked, Underpaid, Bored.' " *motherjones.com* June 18, 2013, http://motherjones.com/politics/2013/06/drone-pilots-rea per-photo-essay

Hybe, Irish. "Iris by HYBE." *youtube.com*. Accessed December 10, 2024. https://youtube.com/watch?v=qhdG7OltXnU&t=111s

IBM. "What Is Machine Learning (ML)?" *ibm.com*. Accessed July 20, 2025, https://ibm.com/topics/machine-learning

"Impact of War on Terror on Pashto Literature and Art." *FATA Research Center*. Islamabad: Pakistan, 2014.

Institute for Defense and Government Advancement. "Air Force Awards Contracts for Collaborative Combat Aircraft Development," *idga.com* April 25, 2024, https://idga.org/aviation/articles/air-force-awards-contracts-for-collaborative-combat-aircraft-program

International Drone Show, *internationaldroneshow.com*. Accessed December 7, 2024, https://internationaldroneshow.com/about/

International Human Rights and Conflict Resolution Clinic, Stanford Law School, and Global Justice Clinic, NYU School of Law, "Living Under Drones: Death, Injury, Trauma to Civilians From US Drone Practices in Pakistan." law.stanford.edu. September 2012. Accessed December 11, 2024, https://law.stanford.edu/wp-content/uploads/2015/07/Stanford-NYU-LIVING-UNDER-DRONES.pdf

Jacobsen, Mark. "Ukraine's Drone Strikes Are a Window into the Future of Warfare." *atlanticcouncil.org* September 14, 2023, https://atlanticcouncil.org/blogs/new- atlanticist/ukraines-drone-strikes-are-a-window-into-the-future-of-warfare/

Javelosa, June. "The First 'World Drone Prix' Is Being Held in Dubai." *futurism.com* March 11, 2016, https://futurism.com/world-first-world-drone-prix-held-dubai

Jeffrey Andrew Thorne Lupker. "Deep Learning," In *Encyclopedia of Artificial Intelligence: The Past, Present, and Future of AI*, edited by Philip F. Frana and Michael J, Klein, 112–14. California: ABC-CLIO, 2021.

Jenkins, Henry. *Convergence Culture: Where Old and New Media Collide*. Proquest Ebook Central. New York: New York University Press, 2006.

Jensen, Ole. "Thinking with the Drone–Visual Lessons in Aaerial and Volumetric Thinking." *Visual Studies* 35, no. 5 (2020): 417–28.

Jockers, Matthew. *Macroanalysis: Digital Methods and Literary History*. Chicago: University of Illinois Press, 2013.

Johnson, Khari. "Drone Racing League Launches $2 Million Autonomous Drone Competition." *venturebeat.com* September 5, 2018, https://venturebeat.com/ai/drone-racing-league- launches-2-million-autonomous-drone-competition/

Jones, Steven E. *The Emergence of the Digital Humanities*. New York: Routledge, 2014.

Kaliba, Matildah. "Toward an Autonomous Civil Society: Rethinking State-Civil Society Relations in Zambia." *International Journal of Not-for-Profit-Law* 16, no. 2 (2014): 5–15.

Kalusa, Walima T. "Traditional Rulers, Nationalists and the Quest for Freedom in Northern Rhodesia in the 1950s." *Living the End of Empire: Politics and Society in Late Colonial Zambi*a, edited by Jan-Bart Gewald, Marja Hinfelaar, and Giacomo Macola, 67–90. Leiden: Brill, 2011.

Kaplan, Amy. *The Anarchy of Empire*. Cambridge, MA: Harvard University Press, 2002.

Kaplan, Fred. "The World as Free Fire Zone," *MIT Technology Review*, June 7, 2013, https://technologyreview.com/2013/06/07/177754/the-world-as-free-fire-zone/

Kastrenakes, Jacob. "Drones Become Dancers in This Average Performance." *theaverage.com*. May 22, 2014, http://theverge.com/2014/5/22/5742420/drones-join-dance-troupe-video

"KATSU Drone Paintings." *theholenyc.com*. April 1, 2014. Accessed December 15, 2024, https://thehole.com/exhibitions/katsu-dot

Keating, Joshua. "What Happened to the Drone War?" *grid.com* February 2, 2022, https://grid.news/story/global/2022/02/02/what-happened-to-the-drone-war/

Keller, Stephanie. "How Graffiti Artists Are Journeying from the Streets to the Computer Screen." *thecreatorsproject.vice.com* December 6, 2012, http://thecreatorsproject.vice.com/blog/how-graffiti-artists-are-journeying-from-the-streets-to-the-computer-screen

Kennedy, Greg. "Drones: Legitimacy and Anti-Americanism." *Parameters* 42, no. 4/43, no. 1 (2013): 26–7.

Khan, Hidayat. "My Gaze Is as Fatal as a Drone Attack." *tribune.com.pk*. September 18, 2012, http://tribune.com.pk/story/438610/my-gaze-is-as-fatal-as-a-drone-attack/

KIDULT, "Illegal World." *kidultone.com*. Accessed May 30, 2014. http://kidultone.com/?page_id=309

Kilbride, Daniel. "The Old South Confronts the Dilemma of David Livingstone." *Journal of Southern History* 82, no. 4 (2016): 789–822.

Klar, Michael T. "The Future of AI Is War," *thenation.com* July 17, 2023, https://thenation.com/article/world/artificial-intelligence-us-military/

Komoda, Jason. "Dronestagram." *digiart21.org*. Accessed December 15, 2024, http://digiart21.org/art/dronestagram.

Korang, Kwaku Larbi. "Useless Provocation or Meaningful Challenge? The 'Post' versus African Studies." In *The Study of Africa, Vol 1: Disciplinary and Interdisciplinary Encounters*, edited by Paul Tiyambe Zeleza, 443–66. Vol. 1. Senegal: Codesria Book Series, 2006.

Kourlas, Gia. "Alone with Schubert and 2 MIT Flying Robots." *The New York Times*. July 19, 2011, http://nytimes.com/2011/07/20/arts/dance/piloboluss-seraph-at-joyce-theater-review.html?_r=0

Kreps, Sarah E. *Drones: What Everyone Needs to Know*. Oxford: Oxford University Press, 2016.

Kreps, Sarah, and John Kaag, "The Use of Unmanned Aerial Vehicles in Contemporary Conflict: A Legal and Ethical Analysis." *Polity* 44 (2012): 1–26.

Kumar, Govind. Introduction to ChatGPT and Open AI. Film. PACKT Publishing, 2023, https://video.alexanderstreet.com/watch/introduction-to-chatgpt-and-openai.

Landay, Jonathan S. "Obama's Drone War Kills 'Others,' Not Just al Qaida Leaders," *mcclatchydc.com* April 9, 2013. Updated June 17, 2015, https://mcclatchydc.com/news/nation-world/world/article24747826.html

Larmer, Miles. *Rethinking African Politics: A History of Opposition in Zambia*. ProQuest Ebook Central. Oxfordshire: Taylor and Francis, 2011.

Larmer, Miles, Mara Hinfelaar, Bizeck J. Phiri, Lyn Schumaker, and Morris Szeftel. "Introduction: Narratives of Nationhood," *Journal of Southern African Studies* 40, no. 5 (2014): 895–905.

Larsen, Mike, and Justin Piché. "Public Vigilance Campaigns and Participatory Surveillance after 11 September 2001." In *Surveillance: Power, Problems, and Politics*, edited by Sean P. Hier and Josh Greenberg, 187–202. Toronto: UBC Press, 2009.

Lawrence Livermore Laboratory, "The Birth of Artificial Intelligence (AI) Research." *st.llnl.gov*. Accessed December 14, 2024. https://st.llnl.gov/news/look-back/birth-artificial-intelligence-ai-research

Leaver, Tama, and Suzanne Srdarov, "ChatGPT Isn't Magic: The Hype and Hypocrisy of Generative Artificial Intelligence (AI) Rhetoric." *M/C Journal* 26, no. 5. 2023. https://doi.org/10.5204/mcj.3004

Lele, Ajay. "Defense Applications of Artificial Intelligence." *Artificial Intelligence, Ethics and the Future of Warfare*, edited by Kaushik Roy, 71–8. Taylor and Francis, 2024.

Lemke, Thomas. "A Zone of Indistinction: A Critique of Giorgio Agamben's Concept of Biopolotics." Outlines 1 (2005): 3–13.

Lewis, Joanna. "Rivers of White: David Livingston and the 1955 Commemorations in the Lost 'Henley-Upon-Thames of Central Africa.'" *Living the End of Empire: Politics and Society in Late Colonial Zambia*, edited by Jan-Bart Gewald, Marja Hinfelaar, and Giacomo Macola, 160–205. Leiden: Brill, 2011.

Liljefors, Max. "Omnivoyance and Blindness." In *War and Algorithm*, edited by Howard Caygill, Allen Feldman, and Sara Kendall, 127–64. New York: Rowman and Littlefield, 2019.

Litnarovych, Vlad. "Ukraine Launches over 54,000 Drone Strikes on Russian Targets in December, Half Using FPV Suicide Drones." *united24media.com* January 7, 2025 https://united24media.com/latest-news/ukraine-launches-over-54000-drone-strikes-on-russian-targets-in-december-half-using-fpv-suicide-drones-4920

Littlechild, Chris. "Why the U.S. Navy Decommissioned the Incredible X-47B Stealth Drone. *slashgear.com* April 29, 2023. https://slashgear.com/1272081/why-the-u-s-navy-decommissioned-the-incredible-x-47b-stealth-drone/

Liu, Alan. "Where Is Cultural Criticism in the Digital Humanities?" In *Debates in the Digital Humanities*, edited by Matthew K. Gold. Minneapolis: University of Minnesota Press, 2013. Open Access Edition. http://dhdebates.gc.cuny.edu/debates/text/20

Loomba, Ania. *Colonialism/Postcolonialism*, Routledge, 1998.

Lopez, Todd C. "National Geospatial-Intelligence Agency in Midst of Revolution." *DOD News*. December 5, 2020, https://defense.gov/Explore/News/Article/Article/2447871/national-geospatial-intelligence-agency-in-midst-of-revolution/

Lopez, Todd C. "Joint Staff Address Drones Over New Jersey Military Installations." *defense.gov* December 14, 2024, https://defense.gov/News/News-Stories/Article/Article/4002374/joint-staff-addresses-drones-over-new-jersey-military-installations/

Lupker, Jeffrey Andrew Thorne. "Deep Learning." *Encyclopedia of Artificial Intelligence: The Past, Present, and Future of AI*. Edited by Philip F. Frana and Michael J, Klein, 112. California: ABC-CLIO, 2021.

Lushenko, Paul. "Cult of the Drone: At the Two-Year Mark, UAVs Have Changed the Face of War in Ukraine—but Not Its Outcomes." *theconversation.com* February 26, 2024, https://theconversation.com/cult-of-the-drone-at-the-two-year-mark-uavs-have-changed-the-face-of-war-in-ukraine-but-not-outcomes-221397

Lyon, David. *Surveillance Studies: An Overview*. Malden, MA: Polity, 2007.

Mackenzie, John M. "David Livingstone—Prophet or Patron Saint of Imperialism in Africa: Myths and Misconceptions." *Scottish Geographic Journal* 129, no. 3–4 (2013): 277–91.

Macola, Giacomo. *Liberal Nationalism in Central Africa: A Biography of Harry Mwaanga Nkumbula*. New York: Palgrave Macmillan, 2010.

Macola, Giacomo. "Harry Mwaanga Nkumula and the Formation of ZANC/INIP: a Reinterpretation." *Living the End of Empire: Politics and Society in Late Colonial Zambia*, edited by Jan-Bart Gewald, Marja Hinfelaar, and Giacomo Macola, 27–65. Leiden: Brill, 2011.

Madianou, Mirca. "Technocolonialism: Digital Innovation and Data Practices in the Humanitarian Response to Refugee Crises." *Social Media + Society*. July-September (2019): 1–13.

Magnuson, Stew. "Changes in the Horizon for Special Operations Command as Force Grows," *nationaldefensemagazine.org* May 1, 2012. https://nationaldefensemagazine.org/articles/2012/5/1/2012may-changes-on-the-horizon-for-special-operations-command-as-force-grows

Makia, Ahmad. "The Child and the Kite." *Murmuration: A Festival of Drone Culture*. December 15, 2024, http://murmurationfestival.tumblr.com/

Malik, Kenan. "The Twitter Files Should Disturb Liberal Critics of Elon Musk—and Here's Why," *theguardian.com* January 1, 2023, https://theguardian.com/commentisfree/2023/jan/01/the-twitter-files-should-disturb-liberal-critics-of-elon-musk-and-heres-why

Manabe, Daito. "Dance with Drones." *daito.ws/en*. March 2014. Accessed December 15, 2024, http://daito.ws/en/work/elevenplay_drones.html

Mann, Steve. "Sousveillance: Inverse Surveillance in Multimedia Imaging," *Multimedia '04: Proceedings of the 12th Annual ACM International Conference on Multimedia*," 620–7. October 10, 2004.

Mann, Steve, Jason Nolan, and Barry Wellman, "Sousveillance: Inventing and Using Wearable Computing Devices for Data Collection in Surveillance Environments," *Surveillance and Society* 1, no. 3 (2003): 331–55.

Maurer, Kathrin. "Visual Power: The Scopic Regime of Military Drone Operations." *Media, War, and Conflict* 10, no. 2 (2026): 141–51.

Mbembe, Achille. *Necropolitics*. Durham: Duke University Press, Durham, 2019.

Mbembe, Achille. "African Modes of Self-Writing." *Identity, Culture and Politics*, 2, no. 1 (2001): 1–39.

McClintock, Anne. "The Angel of Progress: Pitfalls of the Term Post-colonialism." In *Colonial Discourse and Postcolonial Theory*, edited by Patrick Williams and Laura Chrisman, 66–111. Columbia University Press, 1994.

McDonald, Kyle. "Personyfying Machines, Machining Persons." *The Creator's Project*. April 6, 2012, http://thecreatorsproject.vice.com/blog/in-response-to-bruce-sterlings-essay-on-the-new-aesthetic

McNabb, Miriam. "Drone Attack on U.S. Power Grid Failed—This Time." *dronelife.com* 8 November 8, 2021, https://dronelife.com/2021/11/08/drone-attack-on-u-s-power-grid-failed-this- time/

McNeil, Joanne. *joannemcneil.com*. Accessed December 10, 2024. https://joannemcneil.com.

McPherson, Tara. "Why Are the Digital Humanities So White? Or Thinking the Histories of Race and Computation." In *Debates in the Digital Humanities*, edited by Matthew K. Gold. Open Access Edition. University of Minnesota Press, 2013. http://dhdebates.gc.cuny.edu/debates/text/29

Melville, Aja. "Drone Wars: Developments in Drone Swarm Technology." Defense Security and Monitor *dsm.forecasinternational.com* January 21, 2025, https://dsm.forecastinternational.com/2025/01/21/drone-wars-developments-in-drone-swarm-technology/

Mignolo, Walter. "Preface to the 2012 Edition," *Local Histories/Global Designs: Coloniality, Subaltern Knowledges, and Border Thinking*, ix–xiv. Princeton University Press, 2012.

Mishra, Vijay, and Bob Hodge. "What Is Post (-) Colonialism?" In *Colonial Discourse and Postcolonial Theory*, edited by Patrick Williams and Laura Chrisman, 276–90. New York: Columbia University Press, 1994.

MIT Computer Science and Artificial Intelligence Laboratory, "'*Seraph*' Featured in Robot Festival." *csail.mit.edu* July 5, 2012, http://csail.mit.edu/node/1771

Modonesi, Massimo. *The Antagonist Principle: Marxism and Political Action*. Leiden: Brill, 2019.

Moore, Jason H. "Automated Machine Learning." In *Encyclopedia of Artificial Intelligence: The Past, Present, and Future of AI*, edited by Philip F. Frana and Michael J, Klein, 20–2. California: ABC-CLIO, 2021.

Moreau, Terri, and Derek H. Alderman. "Graffiti Hurts and the Eradication of Alternative Landscape Expression." *The Geographical Review* 101, no. 1 (2011): 106–24.

Moretti, Franco. *Distant Reading*. New York: Verso, 2013.

Mulford, David C. *Zambia: The Politics of Independence 1957–1964*, Oxford University Press, 1967.

"Murmuration: A Festival of Drone Culture." Accessed December 15, 2024. http://murmurationfestival.tumblr.com/about

Mususa, Patience. "Who Is Setting Africa's Intellectual Agenda?" *CODESRIA Bulletin*, no. 1 & 2 (2017): 5–7.

Muthyala, John. *Dwelling in American: Dissent, Empire, and Globalization*. New England University Press, 2012.

Muthyala, John. "Drones and Surveillance Cultures in a Global World." Digital Studies/La Champ Numérique, *digitalstudies.org*. September 27, 2019, https://digitalstudies.org/articles/10.16995/dscn.332/

Nail, Thomas. "What Is an Assemblage?" *SubStance* 46, no. 1 (2017): 21–37.

Nancy, Jean-Luc. "A Viral Exception." In *Coronavirus, Psychoanalysis, and Philosophy; Conversati yesons on Pandemics, Politics, and Society*, edited by Fernando Castrillón, and Thomas Marchevesky, 27. New York: Routledge, 2021.

Natale, Simone. *Deceptive Media: Artificial Intelligence and Social Life after the Turing Test*. New York: Oxford University Press, 2021.

Nayar, Pramod K. *Postcolonialism: A Guide for the Perplexed*, Bloomsbury, 2010.

Neal, Meghan. "Finally: A Drone for Dropping Rhymes, not Bombs." *motherboard.vice.com*. June 25, 2013, https://vice.com/en/article/poetry-drone-would-drop-rhymes-not-bombs/

Negroponte, Nicholas P. *Being Digital*. New York: Vintage Books, 1996.

Newamerica.org. "Drone Strikes: Pakistan." https://newamerica.org/in-depth/americas-counterterrorism-wars/pakistan/

Newamerica.org. "Drone Strikes: Yemen." *newamerica.org* https://newamerica.org/in-depth/americas-counterterrorism-wars/us-targeted-killing-program-yemen/

"News from Brown," *brown.edu* September 1, 2021, https://watson.brown.edu/costsofwar/figures/2021/BudgetaryCosts

Nkrumah, Kwame. *Neo-Colonialism: The Last Stage of Imperialism*. New York: International Publishers, 1965.

Noori Farzan, Antonia. "Amid 'Heartbreaking' Coronavirus Surge in India, Government Orders Twitter to Remove Posts Critical of Response," *washingtonpost.com* April 26, 2021, https://washingtonpost.com/world/2021/04/26/twitter-india- coronavirus/

Norrholm, Seth Davin, Jessica L. Maples-Keller, Barbara O. Rothbaum, and Chad C. Tossell, "Remote Warfare with Intimate Consequences: Psychological Stress in Service Member and Veteran Remotely-Piloted Aircraft (RPA) Personnel," *Journal of Mental Health and Clinical Psychology*. mentalhealthjournal.org. December 21 (2023): 37–49.

Not a bug splat. https://notabugsplat.com/. Accessed December 27, 2024.

Office of Counter Terrorism. "Global Counter-Terrorism Programme on Autonomous and Remotely Operated Systems (AROS)." *United Nations*. Accessed January 3, 2025, https://un.org/counterterrorism/autonomous-and-remotely-operated-systems

Olaniyan, Tejumola. "Postmodernity, Postcoloniality, and African Studies." *Postmodernism Postcoloniality, and African Studies*, edited by Zine Magubane, 39–60. New Jersey: Africa World Press, 2003.

Olsen, Ted. "One African Nation Under God." *Christianity Today*, February 4, 2002, 36–43.

O'Keefe, Amanda K. "Turing, Alan (1912–1954)," in *Encyclopedia of Artificial Intelligence: The Past, Present, and Future of AI*, edited by Philip F. Frana and Michael J. Klein, 327. California: ABC-CLIO, 2021.

OpenAI, "How ChatGPT and Our Language Models Are Developed." *openai.com*. Accessed December 15, 2024, https://help.openai.com/en/articles/7842364-how-chatgpt-and-our-language-models-are-developed

Ortiz-Ospian, Esteban. "The Rise of Social Mmedia." *ourworldindata*. September 18, 2019, accessed June 18, 2021, https://ourworldindata.org/rise-of-social-media

Our World in Data. *ourworldindata.com*. Accessed December 27, 2024, https://ourworldindata.org/grapher/mobile-cellular-subscriptions-by-country.

Out of Sight, Out of Mind. *pitchinteractrive.com*. Accessed December 11, 2024, http://drones.pitchinteractive.com/

Ow, Carina. *Pixels Per Person*. Accessed December 10, 2024, https://architizer.com/projects/pixels-per-person/

"Pakistanis Target Drones with Giant Posters of Child Victims." *dawn.com*. April 8, 2014, http://dawn.com/news/1098351

Panel of Experts on Libya, United Nations. "Report Pursuant to Security Council Resolution 1973 2011." *documents.un.org* March 8, 2021, https://documents.un.org/doc/undoc/gen/n21/037/72/pdf/n2103772.pdf?token=0Hvd3Llb 46K04gLR8I&fe=true

Pannapacker, William A. "'Hacking' and 'Yacking' about the Digital Humanities." *Chronicle of Higher Education*. September 3, 2013, https://chronicle.com/article/hacking-and-yacking-about-the-digital-humanities/

Parks, Lisa. "Drones, Vertical Mediation, and the Targeted Class." *Feminist Studies* 42, no. 1 (2016): 227–35.

Parks, Lisa. "Vertical Mediation." In *Life in the Age of Drone Warfare*, edited by Lisa Parks, and Caren Kaplan, 134–57. Durham: Duke University Press, 2017.

PBS News Weekend. "How Militaries Are Using Artificial Intelligence on and off the Battlefield," *pbs.org* July 9, 1013, https://pbs.org/newshour/show/how-militaries-are-using-artificial-intelligence-on-and-off-the-battlefield

Person, Chris. "A Drone Ballet Straight Out of the Cyberpuk Future." *kotaku.com* May 22, 2014, http://kotaku.com/a-drone-ballet-straight-out-of-the-cyberpunk-future-1580122943

Phiri, Bizeck J. *A Political History of Zambia: From Colonial Rule to the Third Republic, 1890-2001*. New Jersey: Africa World Press, 2006.

Phiri, Bizeck J. "Gender and Politics: The Zambia National Women's Lobby Group in the 2001 Ripartite Elections." In *One Zambia, Many Histories: Towards a History of Postcolonial ambia*, edited by Jan-Bart Gewald, Marja Hinfelaar, and Giacomo Macola, 259–74. Leiden: Brill, 2008.

Pilling, David. "Are Tech Companies Africa's New Colonists?" *ft.com*. Financial Times. July 5, 2021, https://ft.com/content/4625d9b8-9c16-11e9-b8ce-8b459ed04726

Pincus, Walter. "Pentagon Has Far-Reaching Defense Spacecraft in Works." *Washington Post*. March 16, 2005, http://washingtonpost.com/wp-dyn/articles/A38272-2005Mar15.html.

Pincus, Walter. "Special Operations Wins in 2014 budget" *Washington Post*. April 11, 2013. https://washingtonpost.com/world/national-security/special-operations-wins-in-2014-budget/2013/04/10/80757bc0-a15c-11e2-be47-b44febada3a8_story.html

Plichta, Marcel. "Russia's Growing Kamikaze Drone Fleet Tests Ukraine's Limited Air Defenses." *atlanticcouncil.org* May 14, 2024, https://atlanticcouncil.org/blogs/ukraineal ert/russias-growing-kamikaze-drone- fleet-tests-ukraines-limited-air-defenses/

Pong, Beryl. "The Art of Drone Warfare," *Journal of War and Culture Studies* 15, no. 4 (2022): 377–87.

Pong, Beryl, and Michael Richardson, "An Introduction: An Open Proposition," in *Drone Aesthetics: War, Culture, Ecology*, edited by Beryl Pong and Michael Richardson, 9–29. London: Open Humanities Press, 2024.

Power, Matthew. "Confessions of a Drone Warrior." *GQ*. October 2013. http://gq.com/news-politics/big-issues/201311/drone-uav-pilot-assassination?currentPage=1

Presner, Todd, Jeffrey Schnapp, Peter Lunenfeld, et al. *Digital Humanities Manifesto 2.0*. 3. Web. February 2013, https://humanitiesblast.com/manifesto/Manifesto_V2.pdf

Presner, Todd. "Critical Theory and the Mangle of Digital Humanities." *toddpressner.com*. Accessed December 10, 2024. http://toddpresner.com/wpcontent/uploads/2012/09/Presner_2012_DH_FINAL.pdf

Raley, Rita. *Tactical Media*. University of Minnesota Press, 2009.

Raley, Rita. "eEmpires," *Postcolonial Studies: An Anthology*, edited by Pramod K. Nayar, 714–46. New Jersey: Wiley Blackwell, 2016.

Ramsay, Stephen. "Dh Types I and II." *stephenramsay.us* May 3, 2013. Accessed May 20, 2013, http://stephenramsay.us/2013/05/03/dh-one-and-two/

Reid, Alex. "digital nonhumanities … excerpt." alex-reid.net January 11, 2014, https://profalexreid.com/2014/01/11/digital-nonhumanities-excerpt/

Research, Expert Market. "Global Military Robots Market Outlook," *expertmarketresearch.com* 2022, https://expertmarketresearch.com/reports/military-robots-market

"Research Without Borders: Defining the Digital Humanities," *Center for Digital Research and Scholarship*, Columbia University. April 6, 2011, http://youtube.com/watch?v=Xu6Z1SoEZcc).

Rettberg, Jill Walker. *Machine Vision: How Algorithms Are Changing the Way We See the World*. Cambridge: Polity Press, 2023.

Rhee, Jennifer. *The Robotic Imaginary: The Human and the Price of Dehumanized Labor*. Minneapolis: University of Minnesota Press, 2018.

Richards, Neil M. "The Dangers of Surveillance." *Harvard Law Review* 126, no. 7 (2013): 1934–65.

Ricordeau, Gwenola. "Lethal Autonomous Weapons Systems." In *Encyclopedia of Artificial Intelligence: The Past, Present, and Future of AI*, edited by Philip F. Frana and Michael J. Klein, 207–9. California: ABC-CLIO, 2021.

Rijpma, Sjoerd. *David Livingstone and the Myth of African Poverty and Disease: A Close Examination of His Writing on Pre-colonial Era*, Brill Publishers, 2015.

Risam, Roopika, and Adeline Koh, "Mission Statement." *Postcolonial Digital Humanities*. Accessed June 2, 2014, http://dhpoco.org/mission-statement-postcolonial-digital-humanities/

Rogers, James. "The Second Drone Age: Defining War in the 2020s." *Defense and Security Analysis* 39, no. 2 (2023): 256–9.

Rosane, Olivia, and Adam Rothstein, "Concluding Thoughts." *Murmuration: A Festival of Drone Culture*. July 2013. Accessed December 15, 2024, https://murmurationfestival.tumblr.com/post/54350413114/concluding-thoughts

Rosen, Christine. *The Extinction of Human Experience: Being Human in a Disembodied World*. New York: W.W. Norton, 2024.

Rosen, David, and Aaron Santesso. *The Watchman in Pieces: Surveillance, Literature, and Liberal Personhood*. New Haven: Yale University Press, 2013.

Rosen, Rebecca J. "Drone over Washington." *theatlantic.com* June 21, 2013, http://theatlantic.com/technology/archive/2013/06/drone-over-washington/277038/

Ross, Andrew C. *David Livingstone: Mission and Empire*. Hambledon: Hambledon and London, 2002.

Roumeliotis, Konstantinos I., and Nikolaos D. Tselikas. "ChatGPT and Open-AI Models: A Preliminary Review." *Future Internet* 15, no. 6 (2023), 192, https://doi.org/10.3390/fi15060192

Rouvroy, Antoinette. "Algorithmic Governmentality and the Death of Politics." Interview by *Green European Journal, greeneuropeanjournal.eu* March 27, 2020, 1–5.

Rouvroy, Antoinette, and Thomas Berns. "Algorithmic Governmentality and Prospects of Emancipation." *Réseaux* 177 (2013): iii–xxxi.

Saeed, Abdullah. "Rajeev Basu Wants to Sell You a Custom Painted Attack Drone." *The Creator's Project*. December 14, 2012, http://thecreatorsproject.vice.com/blog/rajeev-basu-wants-to-sell-you-a-custom-painted-attack-drone

Said, Edward. *The World, the Text, and the Critic*. Cambridge: Harvard University Press, 1983.

Saini, Rajiv Kumar, MSVK Raju, and Amit Chail, "'Cry in the Sky' Psychological Impact on Drone Operators." *Industrial Psychiatry Journal* 30, no. 1 (2021): 15–19.

Santora, Mark, et al. "A Thousand Snipers in the Sky: The New War in Ukraine." *nytimes.com* March 3, 2025, https://nytimes.com/interactive/2025/03/03/world/europe/ukraine-russia-war-drones-deaths.html

Sardanis, Andrews. "Zambia: The First Fifty Years." *The Round Table: The Commonwealth Journal of International Affairs* 104, no. 1 (2015): 9–17, DOI: 10.1080/00358533.2015.1005355

Sarte, Jean-Paul. Preface. *The Wretched of the Earth*, by Frantz Fanon, translated by Constance Farrington, Grove Weidenfeld, 1963.

Savage, Charlie, Eric Schmitt, Azmat Khan, Evan Hill, and Christoph Koettl, "Newly Declassified Video Show U.S. Killing of 10 Civilians in Drone Strike." *nyt.com* January 19, 2022, https://nytimes.com/2022/01/19/us/politics/afghanistan-drone-strike-video.html

Savell, Stephanie. "United States Counterterrorism Operations 2018–2020." *watson.brown.edu* Watson Institute for International and Public Affairs. Brown University, 2021, https://watson.brown.edu/costsofwar/files/cow/imce/papers/2021/US%20Counterterrorism%20Operations%202018-2020%2C%20Costs%20of%20War.pdf

Scahill, Jeremey. *Dirty Wars: The World Is a Battlefield.* Nation Books, 2013.

Scharre, Paul. *Four Battlegrounds: Power in the Age of Artificial Intelligence.* New York: W.W. Norton and Company, 2023.

Schmitt, Eric. "A Shadowy War's Newest Front: A Drone Base Rising From Saharan Dust." *nytimes.com* April 4, 2018, https://nytimes.com/2018/04/22/us/politics/drone-base-niger.html

Schreck, Adam, and Samy Magdy, "A drone targets the Israeli prime minister's house during new barrages with Hezbollah," *apnews.com* October 18, 2024, https://apnews.com/article/israel-hamas-war-news-10-18-2024- c49911f11a40b7d81b21bc8568ecfe11

Schreibman, Susan, Ray Siemens, and John Unsworth, eds., *A Companion to Digital Humanities.* Oxford: Blackwell, 2009.

Sentient Digital, Inc. "Military Drone Swarm Intelligence Explained." *sdi.ai* 2024, https://sdi.ai/blog/military-drone-swarm-intelligence-explained/

"Seraph." *Pilobolus.* Washington Depot: Connecticut, 2011.

Serle, Jack, and Alice K. Ross, "May 2014 Update: US Covert Actions in Pakistan, Yemen, and Somalia." *Bureau of Investigate Journalism.* June 3, 2014. https://thebureauinvestigates.com/stories/2014-06-03/may-2014-update-us-covert-actions-in-pakistan-yemen-and-somalia/

Serpell, Namwali. "The Zambian 'Afronaut' Who Wanted To Join the Space Race." *newyorker.com* March 11, 2017, https://newyorker.com/culture/culture-desk/the-zambian-afronaut-who-wanted-to-join-the-space-race

Serpell, Namwali. *The Old Drift.* Hogarth, 2019.

Serpell, Namwali. "A Novelist and Critic Fictionalizing Zambian History." *newyorker.com.* Interview by Isaac Chotiner, April 3, 2019, https://newyorker.com/news/q-and-a/a-novelist-and-critic-on-fictionalizing-zambian-history

Serpell, Namwal. "Q&A with Namwali Serpell: Recipe for Revolution—Brief and Contingent Solidarity in 'The Old Drift.'" *zyzzvyz.com.* Interview by Annah Omune Sidigu, May 15, 2019, https://zyzzyva.org/contributor/annah-omune-sidigu/.

Sethi, Rumina. *Politics of Postcolonialism: Empire, Nation, and Resistance*, Pluto Press, 2011.

Shachtman, Noah. "Air Force to Unleash 'Gorgon Stare' on Squirting Insurgents," *Wired* February 19, 2009, https://wired.com/2009/02/gorgon-stare/

Shell, Elizabeth, and Vanessa Dennis. "11 'Leakers' Charged with Espionage." *pbsnewshour* August 21, 2013, http://pbs.org/newshour/spc/multimedia/espionage/

Shendge, Akshata. "How Birds and Butterflies Are Inspiring Drone Design." *womenwhodrone.co* October 18, 2023, https://womenwhodrone.co/single-post/the-potential-of-bio-inspired-drones-nature-s-design-in-uav

Shoaht, Ella. "Notes on the 'Post-Colonial.'" *Social Text* 31/32 (1992): 99–113.

Shringapure, Bhakti. "Africa and the Digital Savior Complex." *Journal of African Cultural Studies* 32, no. 2 (2020): 178–94.

Sidigu, Annah Omune, "Q&A with Namwali Serpell: Recipe for Revolution—Brief and Contingent Solidarity in 'The Old Drift.'" *Zyzzyva.org.* May 5, 2015, https://zyzzyva.org/2019/05/15/qa-with-namwali-serpell-recipe-for-revolution-brief- and-contingent-solidarity-in-the-old-drift/

Siddiqui, Taha. "Taliban Jihad Literature: What's Read in Afghanistan Is Printed in Pakistan." *tribune.com.pk*. August 12, 2012, http://tribune.com.pk/story/421356/taliban-jihad-literature-whats-read-in-afghanistan-is-printed-in-pakistan/

Sifton, John. "A Brief History of Drones." *The Nation* February 7, 2012, http://thenation.com/article/166124/brief-history-drones

Singer, Peter W. *Wired For War: The Robotic Revolution and Conflict in the 21st Century*. New York: Penguin Press, 2009.

Solove, Daniel J. *The Digital Person: Technology and Privacy in the Information Age*. New York: New York University Press, 2004.

Spivak, Gayatri. "Can the Subaltern Speak?" In *Colonial Discourse and Postcolonial Theory*, edited by Patrick Williams and Laura Chrisman, 66–111. Columbia University Press, 1994.

Stahl, Roger, and Sebastian Kaempf. "Sousveilling the 'Global War on Terror.'" *Australian Journal of International Affairs* 73, no. 4 (2019): 337–56.

Staples, William G. *Everyday Surveillance: Vigilance and Visibility in Postmodern Life*. New York: Rowman and Littlefield Publishers, Inc., 2000.

Statista. "Global digital population as of January 2021." *statista.com* January 2021, https://statista.com/statistics/617136/digital-population-worldwide/.

Stanford Law School, International Human Rights and Conflict Resolution Clinic at Stanford Law School and Global Justice Clinic at NYU School of Law. "Living Under Drones: Death, Injury and Trauma to Civilians from US Drones Practices in Pakistan 2012. https://law.stanford.edu/publications/living-under-drones-death-injury-and-trauma-to-civilians-from-us-drone-practices-in-pakistan/

Sterling, Bruce. "Essay on the New Aesthetic." *Wired.com* April 2, 2012, http://wired.com/2012/04/an-essay-on-the-new-aesthetic/

Strategic Futures Group, *Global Trends: The Future of the Battlefield*. dni.gov. National Intelligence Council, April 2021, https://dni.gov/files/images/globalTrends/GT2040/NIC-2021-02493--Future-of-the-Battlefield--Unsourced--14May21.pdf#page=6

Streinz, Thomas. "At the Crossroads of Digital Imperialism & Digital Development." Berkman Klein Center for Internet and Society, Harvard University. *youtube.com* May 2021, https://youtube.com/watch?v=B1Yr9hwMm8s

Stubblefield, Thomas. *Drone Art: The Everywhere War as Medium*. California: University of California Press, 2020.

The Creators Project Staff. "In Response to Bruce Sterling's 'Essay on the New Aesthetic.'" *vice.com*, April 6, 2012, https://vice.com/en/article/in-response-to-bruce-sterlings-essay-on-the-new-esthetic/

"The Drone War in Pakistan." *newamerica.org*. Accessed December 11, 2024. https://newamerica.org/in-depth/americas-counterterrorism-wars/pakistan/

The Intercept. "The Drone Papers," *theintercept*, accessed October 26, 2024, https://theintercept.com/drone-papers/

The Intercept. "The Drone Papers," *theintercept*. Accessed October 26, 2024, https://theintercept.com/drone-papers/

"The New Aesthetic: Seeing Like Digital Devices." *South by South West* (SXSW) March 12, 2012, https://schedule.sxsw.com/2012/events/event_IAP11102

"The War in Yemen." *newamerica.org*. Accessed September 22, 2025, https://newamerica.org/in-depth/americas-counterterrorism-wars/us-targeted-killing-program-yemen/

Terras, Melissa, Terras, Julianne Nyhan, and Edward Vanhoutte. *Defining Digital Humanities: A Reader.* New York, NY: Ashgate, 2013.

Terrett, Ben. *noisydecentgraphics.com.* Accessed December 10, 2024. https://noisydecentgraphics.typepad.com/design/2012/03/sxsw-the-new-aesthetic-and-commercial-visual-culture.html

Times of Isreal. "New details emerge of Sinwar's final moments," *theliveblog* October 17, 2024, https://timesofisrael.com/liveblog_entry/drone-catches-wounded- sinwars-final-moments-before-his-killing-by-idf

Turse, Nick. *The Changing Face of Empire: Special Ops. Drones, Spies, Proxy Fighters, Secret Bases, and Cyberwarfare.* Chicago: Haymarket Books, 2012.

Underwood, Ted. *Distant Horizons: Digital Evidence and Literary Change.* Chicago: University of Chicago Press, 2019.

UNICEF, Office of Innovation. *African Drone and Data Academy, unicef.org.* Accessed December 28, 2024, https://unicef.org/innovation/AfricanDroneAcademy

UNICEF, Zambia. National HIV and AIDS Strategic Framework 2017–2021. *unicef.org* Accessed December 28, 2024, https://unicef.org/zambia/reports/national-aids-strategic-framework-2017-2021

United Nations Human Rights Office. "UN Counter-Terrorism Expert to launch inquiry into the civilian impact of drones and other forms of targeted killing." *Office of the High Commissioner for Human Rights.* January 22, 2013, http://ohchr.org/EN/NewsEvents/Pages/DisplayNews.aspx?NewsID=12943&LangID=E

United Nations Human Rights Office. "Resolution Adopted by the Human Rights Council." *Office of the High Commissioner for Human Rights* A/HRC/RES/25/22. April 15, 2014, http://hrlibrary.umn.edu/hrcouncil_res25-22.pdf

United States Government Accountability Office. "Air Force: Actions Needed to Strengthen Unamanned Aerial System Pilots." April 10, 2014, https://gao.gov/products/gao-14-316

Unmanned Systems Technology. "Commercial Drones." Accessed December 31, 2024, https://unmannedsystemstechnology.com/expo/commercial-drones/#

"Unmanned aerial vehicle," *britannica.com.* Accessed December 11, 2024, https://britannica.com/technology/military-aircraft/Bombers

Vanderburg, Colin. "Drone Art." *Dissent.* 2016. Accessed December 15, 2024, https://dissentmagazine.org/article/drone-art-astro-noise-laura-poitras

Veliz, Carissa. *The Ethics of Privacy and Surveillance.* Oxford University Press, 2024.

Vergakis, Brock. "US Launches Drone From Aircraft Carrier." *pekintimes* May 15, 2013, https://pekintimes.com/story/news/2013/05/15/us-launches-drone-from-aircraft/47071520007/

Virilio, Paul. *The Vision Machine, Bloomington*: Indiana University Press, 1994.

Volpicelli, Gian, Veronika Melkozerova, and Laura Kayali. "'Our Oppenheimer moment'– In Ukraine, the robot wards have already begun." *politico.com* May 16, 2024, https://politico.eu/article/robots-coming-ukraine-testing-ground-ai-artificial-intelligence-powered-combat-war-russia/

Waclawek, Anna. *Graffiti and Street Art.* New York: Thames & Hudson, 2011.

Wagenknecht, Addie. https://placesiveneverbeen.com/, accessed June 19, 2021.

Wallerstien, Immanuel. *World Systems Analysis: An Introduction.* Durham, NC: Duke University Press, 2004.

Walzer, Michael. *Arguing about War.* New Haven: Yale University Press, 2004.

Wasik, Bill. "Welcome to the Age of Digital Imperialism." *nytimes.com* June 4, 2015, https://nytimes.com/2015/06/07/magazine/welcome-to-the-age-of-digital-imperialism.html

Watz, Marius. "The Problem with Perpetual Newness." *The Creator's Project*. April 6, 2012, http://thecreatorsproject.vice.com/blog/in-response-to-bruce-sterlings-essay-on-the-new-aesthetic

Weisgerber, Marcus. "'The Pentagon's New Algorithmic Warfare Cell Gets Its First Mission: Hunt ISIS," *defense.com*. May 14, 2017, https://defenseone.com/technology/2017/05/pentagons-new-algorithmic-warfare-cell-gets-its-first-mission-hunt-isis/137833/

Wiles, Will. "The Machine Gaze," *aeon.com*. September 17, 2012, https://aeon.co/essays/what-do-we-uncover-when-we-look-through-digital-eyes

Witt, Stephen. "The Weapon of Influence." *New Yorker*. May 16, 2022.

Wolfgang, Ben. "Trump Outpacing Obama in Drone Strikes; 80 in First Year: Report." *washingtontimes.com* June 7, 2018, https://washingtontimes.com/news/2018/jun/7/donald-trump-outpacing-barack-obama-drone-strikes-/

Wolfram, Stephen. *What Is ChatGPT Doing … and Why Does It Work?* Champaign: Wolfram Media, 2023.

Yaeger, P. "Editor's Column: The End of Postcolonial Theory? A Roundtable with Sunil Agnani, Fernando Coronil, Gaurav Desai, Mamadou Diouf, Simon Gikandi, Susie Tharu, and Jennifer Wenzel." *PMLA/Publications of the Modern Language Association of America* 122, no. 3 (2007): 633–51, doi:10.1632/pmla.2007.122.3.633.

Young, Robert JC. "Postcolonial Remains." *New Literary History* 43, no.1 (2012): 9–42.

Zambia Embassy. https://state.gov/wp-content/uploads/2020/05/ZAMBIA-2019-INTERNATIONAL-RELIGIOUS-FREEDOM-REPORT.pdf.

Zeleza, Paul T. "Historicizing the Posts: The View from African Studies." In *Postmodernism Postcoloniality, and African Studies*, edited by Zine Magubane,1–38. New Jersey: Africa World Press, 2004.

Zenko, Micah. "Reforming US Drone Strike Policies." *Council on Foreign Relations*. Special Report Number 65 (2013): 3–31.

Zuboff, Shoshana. *The Age of Surveillance Capitalism: The Fight for a Human Future at the New Frontier of Power*. New York: Hachette Book Group, Perseus Books, 2019.

1

INDEX

adiaphorization 69, 86, 87–9
   conceptual level 165
   countering 165–6
   defined 164–5
   geo-tagger 166
   of human life 165
   public art installation 165
   reorientation 166
AeroVironment 3
affective cognition 163–4
Afghanistan 10, 12, 14
Africa 35, 102, 103
African National Congress (ANC) 116
Agamben, Giorgio 61, 69–71, 74–6, 78–9, 96n3, 97n22
agencement 41
agency 107–8
Age of Surveillance Capitalism: The Fight for a Human Future at the New Frontier of Power, The (Zuboff) 73
Ahmad, Akbar 12, 13
Ahmed, Abiy 15
Ahmed, Sabeen 80, 98n54
AI (artificial intelligence) 25, 85, 93, 180
   drones and 50–3, 55–8
   face-recognition technology 92
AI and the Rule of Law (Burgess) 51
Ajana, Btihaj 75
Albrechtslund, Anders 143
algorithmic fog of drone warfare 85–7
algorithmic gaze 91–3
algorithmic governmentality 60
algorithms 52, 53

al-Muslimi, Farea 11
Al-Qaeda 5, 12
Altair 3
ambivalent legacies 108–11
Andrejevic, Mark 19, 31n89
Anduril 55
anti-Americanism 13
anticipatory anxiety 82
anxiety 88
AQM-34 Firebee 2
Arewa, Ofunmilayo 102, 103
Arguing about War (Walzer) 81
art 8, 17, 181
assemblages
   abstract machine 41, 42
   concept of 40–2
   concrete 41, 42
   personae 41, 42
   surveillant 40–4, 77, 95
Assemblage Theory (DeLanda) 41
automation 88
   of perception 26
Autonomous and Remotely Operated Systems (AROS) 5
Autonomous Real-Time Ground Ubiquitous Surveillance-Imaging Systems (ARGUS-IS) 77, 78
autonomous weapons systems 50

banal deception 93–6
Banda, Lionel 123
ban-opticon 47–9. *see also* panopticon
Barnard-Wills, David 38, 62n27

Barney, Darin 126
Bauman, Zygmunt 39, 40, 62n34, 69, 87, 88, 99n78, 164
Bayraktar TB-2 7, 15
beading system 120
Benkler, Yochai 126
Bentham, Jeremy 21–4
Bergen, Peter 82, 98n58
Bernard, Frederic 12, 29n38
Berns, Thomas 60, 67n167
Berry, David M. 139
Biden administration 8
Big Brother 46–7, 49
Big Data 36, 141
Bigo, Dieder 49, 63n83
bin Laden, Osama 12
Bio-Inspired Robotics 142
biometric measurements 21
biopolitics (biopolitical, biopower) 20, 61, 69, 70, 79
  drone warfare as 72–4
  problematizing 74–6
BLARNEY 35
blindness, forms of 25–6
Bluetooth technology 124
Bogost, Ian 150
Bollmer, Grant 139
BOUNDLESS INFORMANT 35
Boyle, Michael J. 12, 30n56, 83–4, 98n67
BRAVE 3000 50
Bridle, James 89, 99n96, 137–8, 146, 148, 152, 160, 161
Brimblecombe-Fox, Kathryn 162, 163
Britain 107
British South Africa Company (BSAC) 115–16
buffer zones 56
bureaucratized killing 83
Burgess, Paul 51, 53, 64n98
Bush, George W. 8, 9, 12
By the Moonlight 170

capitalism 76
Capricorn African Society 116
Carrier-Based Aerial Refueling Research System 6
Cascone, Kim 142
Caso, Federica 163
Cecil Rhodes 104, 109
centralized system 59
Chamayou, Gregorie 19, 20, 30n79
ChatGPT 53–5
ChatGPT-3 54–5
Chavez, Kerry 20, 31n92
China 105, 123
Chishty, Mahwish 166, 168, 170
Choi-Fitzpatrick, Austin 90, 99n97
civilian casualties 4, 5
civil society 20, 58–61
Civil War 1
Clarke, Roger A. 37, 38, 45, 62n22, 63n61, 81, 98n56
Clark, Lindsay C. 79, 80, 84, 92, 98n50, 100n107, 166
Clark, Percy M. 104, 107
Coley, Rob 136
Collaborative Combat Aircraft (CCA) 55
colonialism 105, 108
coloniality 104–5
colonial mentalities 102
compound annual growth rate (CAGR) 2
connectionism 51, 64n101
constant surveillance 24
Contreras-Koterbay, Scott 141, 142
Convergence Culture: Where Old and New Media Collide (Jenkins) 143
coronavirus 78, 79
counter-insurgency 4
counter-terrorism 4
Cramer, Florian 143
Crumpler, William 85, 98n73
culture 11
  American 13
  digital 16
  performative 24
cybernetics 145
cyberspace 144

Dandeker, Christopher 95, 100n118
data
   acquisition 25
   distribution 25
   flows 44–5
   fusion 19
   gathering 85
   'data doubles' 42, 43, 76
dataveillance 44–7, 61, 81. *see also* surveillance
Dean, Mitchell 58, 66n155
decentralized system 59
Deceptive Media: Artificial Intelligence and Social Life after the Turing Test (Natale) 93
decision-making 50
decolonization 105–7
deep learning (DL) 52, 53
DeLanda, Manuel 41, 42, 50, 63n45, 64n87
Deleuze, Gilles 40–3, 62n37
democracy 1
Department of Defense (DoD) 2, 56
depression 88
DeVore, Marc R. 15
Dialogues (Deleuze) 40
digital dossiers 44–6, 61
digitality 126
Digit-All Bead program 120
Digital Person: Technology and Privacy in the Information Age, The (Solove) 44
Digital Savior Complex 103
digital technologies 8, 16, 42
digitisation 60–1
"disappearance of disappearance" 44
Dishfire 35
disposition matrix 160–2
distributional shift 52
DIY (do-it-yourself) 15, 16
Domain Name System (DNS) 60
double consciousness 108
"double tap" strategy 82
drone (drones, drone warfare)
   Aesthetic object 166–7
   artificial intelligence (AI) and 50–3, 55–8
   benefits of 8, 12
   ChatGPT and 53–5
   command and control centers 7
   in cultural production 159
   dance of drone gaze 174–6
   dance with drones 178–80
   deployment 15
   disposition matrix 160–2
   ethics of drone wars 9–10
   flights 11
   formidable technologies 119
   imaginaries 16–18
   materialities 82–4
   in music and tele-dramas 172–4
   operation 9
   panoptic scopic power 21
   postcolonial mediations 124–7
   psychosocial impact of strikes 82
   rise of 1–3
   second drone age 14–16
   strikes 4, 5, 10–13
   theorizing 19–21
   urban drones 180–1
   visuals 16–17
   volumetric thinking 16–18
drone aesthetics 135, 136
Drone Aesthetics: War, Culture, Ecology (Richardson) 135
Drone Age: How Drone Technology Will Change War and Peace, The (Boyle) 12
drone art 136, 176–8
Drone Art: The Everywhere War as Medium (Stubblefield) 136
drone cultures 184–7
drone gaze 19, 20, 24, 25
droneopticon 25–7
Drone Paintings 181
drone power 137
Drone: Remote Control Warfare (Gusterson) 78
dronescapes 17
drone swarms 57
drone war 15, 20
droning 19

Dubbeld, Lynsey 143
DuBois, W. E. B. 104, 108

economic espionage 35
economic networks 103
electronic information 35
Elias, Jamal J. 167
Elliot, Charlene D. 21, 31n100
The Emergence of the Digital Humanities (Jones) 144
Emmerson, Ben 3–5, 28n19
Empire 6–8, 76
Encyclopedia of Artificial Intelligence: The Past, Present, and Future of AI (Frana & Klein) 49, 51
Enemark, Christian 79, 80, 92, 98n50, 100n107, 166
England 109
Enlightenment 21
equiveillance 89, 90
Ericson, Richard 42–4, 63n48, 95
Espionage Act (1917) 34
Esposito, Roberto 75, 79, 97n24
ethics 9–10
Europe 35
eversion 144–6
Everyday Surveillance (Staples) 47
Expert Market Research 2, 28n13
Extinction of Human Experience: Being Human in a Disembodied World, The (Rosen) 73
extremism 13

Facebook 35
FAIRVIEW 35
Fanon, Frantz 104, 105, 106
femininity 84
feminist ethic of care 91–3
Ferer, Tom 12, 29n38
file analysis 45
Firescout 3
First World War 1
Force Application and Launch Continental United States Program (Falcon) 77, 78

Foreign Intelligence Surveillance Court (FISC) 36
Forpost 15
Foucault, Michel 21–3, 25, 31n99, 43, 58, 60, 67n158, 69–72, 75, 76, 96n1
Frana, Philip F. 49, 51, 64n85, 64n100
friction 25
front-end audit 45
front-end verification 45

Galloway, Alexander 59, 60, 67n160
Gavuzzi, Pietro 107
gender 111–14
Gender and Drone Warfare: A Hauntological Perspective (Clark) 84
gendering of drone warfare 84–5
General Atomics 3, 55
Generative Pre-trained Transformer (GPT) 53
Ghana 102
Gibson, William 144, 145
Global Hawk 2–3
Global Information Grid 26
globalization 14, 16
Global North 103, 106
Global South 16, 73, 77, 103
goal displacement 12
Good Drone: How Social Movements Democratize Surveillance, The (Choi-Fitzpatrick) 90
Google Earth 83
Google satellite image 137
Gorgon Stare 77–81, 81
governance transparency 103
governmentality 58–61, 94
Governmentality: Power and Rule in Modern Society (Dean) 58, 66n155
GPT-2 52
GPT-3 52
Gramsci, Antonio 121
Greenberg, Josh 43, 44, 63n53
Greenfield, Adam 145
Greenwald, Glenn 36
No Place to Hide 34, 61n1
Grey Eagle 3

Grižinić, Marina 72, 73, 76, 96n15, 97n34
Guardian, The (newspaper) 34, 95
Guattari, Felix 41–3
Gusterson, Hugh 78, 97n41

habeas corpus (1679) 74
Haggerty, Kevin D. 23, 31n102, 37, 38, 42–4, 62n23, 63n48, 95
Hamilton, Booz Allen 34
Haqqani Network 12
Hardt, Michael 76
Harkinson, Josh 168, 171
Hayles, N. Katherine 145
Heaven, Will Douglass 51, 64n97
Hellfire Missile *171*
Hensley, Nathan K. 77, 97n40
Hernandez, Joe 51, 64n94
heroism 20
Hier, Sean P. 43, 44, 63n53
Hodgson, Justin 144, 146
Home Sacer: Sovereign Power and Bare Life (Agamben) 70
homo sacer 70, 71
Houthi Rebels 15
human agency 164
humanitarian initiatives 103
humanizing drone wars 164–5
human rights 4
Human Rights Council 4
human-technology-infused aesthetic 144
Hummingbird 3
hypervisibility 20

I-GNAT 3
Illegal World 182
immigrants 13
imminent threat 11, 13
India 107
In Dirty Wars: The World Is a Battlefield (Scahill) 10
influenza 79
information-processing technology 50
information technology globalization 101
intellectual privacy 48
intelligence analysis 50

international humanitarian law 9
Internet 33, 34, 60
Internet of Things 141
internet protocol (IP) 60
invisible trade, of financial loans 102
Iran 15
Iraq 10
ISIL 12
Islam 13
Italy 107

Jenkins, Henry 143
Jensen, Ole 16, 18, 30n69
Joint All-Domain Command and Control (JADC2) 56, 66n142
Jones, Steven 144, 145
Joseph K 46, 49
just war theory 9

Kaag, John 9, 29n42, 85, 98n75
Kaempf, Sebastian 72, 91, 100n101
Kafka, Franz 46
Kaplan, Fred 11, 12, 14, 30n51, 85, 98n76
Kariba Dam 104, 105
Kastrenakes, Jacob 179
Kennedy, Greg 10, 29n46
Khan, Hidayat 175
Klein, Michael J. 49, 51, 57, 64n85
Kreps, Sarah 9, 27n3, 29n42, 85, 98n75
Kunashankaran, Sumita 84

language modeling 54
large language models (LLMs) 53–5
Larmer, Miles 116
Larsen, Mike 22, 31n101
Leaver, Tama 55, 65n135
legitimacy 10
Lele, Ajay 50, 64n86
Lemke, Thomas 75, 76, 97n28
lethal autonomous weapons systems (LAWS) 51
Libya 86
Liljefors, Max 24–6, 31n112
Lina's action 107
Liquid Modernity (Bauman) 39

liquid modernity, surveillance in 39–40
Liu, Alan 147
LLMs *see* large language models (LLMs)
local culture 166–7
Local Histories/Global Designs (Mignolo) 75
Lockheed Martin 3
Lockwood, Dean 136
lorem ipsum 140
Lyon, David 37–9, 47, 62n19

machine intelligence 73
machine learning (ML) 52, 53, 92
machine translation 50
machine vision 40, 50
Machine Vision: How Algorithms Are Changing the Way We See the World (Rettberg) 40, 91
Madianou, Mirca 103
Makia, Ahmad 184
Manabe, Daito 179
Manichean paradigm 109
Mann, Steve 69, 89, 90, 91, 99n91
Mariner 3
masculinity 84
masked language modeling 54
Massachusetts Institute of Technology Review 51
mass surveillance 45
Maurer, Katherine 20
Mbembe, Achille 61, 69, 71–3, 75, 76, 96n14
McCarthy, John 51
McDonald, Kyle 150, 151
Melville, Aja 57, 66n150
Merkel, Angela 35
meticulous rituals of power 47–8
micro politics, of self-fashioning 114–15
Mignolo, Walter 75, 97n26
military robots 2
Mirocha, Lukasz 141, 143
ML *see* machine learning (ML)
mobile device 136
mobile eye of power 1–27

modern democracy 71
modernity 12, 13, 70
  as surveillance 38–9
  Western 72, 75
modern warfare 20
morphing drones 142
Mosi-oa-Tunya 107
MQ-1B Predator 4
MQ-9 Reaper 3, 77
MQ-25 Stingray drone 6
Multitude: War and Democracy in the Age of Empire (Hardt & Negri) 76

Nail, Thomas 41, 42
Nancy, Jean-Luc 78
Natale, Simone 93
nation 111–14
national security 22, 81
National Security Agency (NSA) 35, 36, 153
nation-states 8, 10, 14
necrocapitalism 73
necropolitics 61, 69, 71, 73, 76
Necropolitics, Racialization, and Global Capitalism (Grižinić & Tatlić) 72
Negri, Antonio 76
Negroponte, Nicholas 1, 27n1
neo-colonialism 102
Neo-Colonialism: The Last Stage of Imperialism (Nkrumah) 102
neoliberal capitalism 73
Neubronner, Julius 18
New Aesthetic 135, 137–8
  art to society 147–8
  banality 142
  connections and disconnections 138–40
  criticisms 146–7
  digital erupts 140–2
  digital technologies 139–40
  feature 139
  post-digital condition 142–3
  reposition 138–140
  surveillant assemblage 151–3
  visualization 139

The New Aesthetic and Art: Constellations of The Postdigital (Contreras-Koterbay) 141
Next Generation Air Dominance (NGAD) 55
Niger 119
Nkoloso, Edward Mukuka 104, 110, 111
Nkrumah, Kwame 102, 103
No Place to Hide (Greenwald) 34
Norrholm, Seth Davin 88, 99n89
Northern Rhodesia 116–17
Northrop Grumman 3
Notabugsplat 166–7
Not a Game 162

OAKSTAR 35
Obama, Barack 8, 12, 34, 118
    Overseas Contingency Operations 9–10
object-oriented ontology (OOO) 150
O'Hagan, Lauren Alex 17, 18, 20, 30n79
Old Drift, The (Serpell) 96, 101, 102, 104, 106, 108
Olsen, Ted 109
Omar, Mullah 12
omnivoyance 17, 24, 25
Operating Predator drones 164
Operation Anvil 1
Oppenheimer Moment 58
Orion 15
Ortiz-Ospina, Esteban 118
over-internet-protocol (VOIP) communications 123
Overseas Contingency Operations 9–10

Pakistan 4, 11, 12, 14
panopticon 21–23, 40, 42
paradoxical facticity 26
Parks, Lisa 10, 11, 29n48, 82–3, 98n63
participatory surveillance 22
Pena Nieto, Enrique 35
performative cartography 17
Phiri, Bizeck Jube 116
physical distance 14
Piche, Justin 22, 31n101
Pike, John E. 77

Pilling, David 103
pilobolus 176
plague 78–9
Poitras, Laura 34
political activism 113
political discourse 71
Pong, Beryl 135, 136
post-Cold War 14
postcolonialism 101
postcoloniality 104–5, 111–14
Post-Digital Rhetoric and the New Aesthetic (Hodgson) 144
Postmodern Ethics (Bauman) 87
postmodernism 148–51
postmodern violence 167
postmodern war 12
postpartum depression 112
posttraumatic stress disorder (PTSD) 88
power 59, 70
Predator 2–3
Predator C Avenger 3
PRISM 35
privacy 44
Project Convergence 56–7
Protocol: How Control Exists after Decentralization (Galloway) 59
PROWLER 50
Prowler II 3
psychological distance 14
Puma 3

Raley, Rita 90, 100n99
Raven 3
Raytheon 3
Reaper 2–3
reaper drone 173
reinforcement learning 52
religion 13
religious discourse 71
Replicator Program 57
Rettberg, Jill Walker 40, 77, 91, 92, 100n104
Rhee, Jennifer 77, 97n39
rhizome 43
Rhozomaticks 179
Richards, Neil 48, 63n77

Richardson, Michael 135, 136
Ricordeau, Gwenola 51, 64n95
robotics 88
Roff, Heather 84
Rogers, James 15
Rosen, Christine 73, 96n20
Rosen, David 23, 24, 31n111, 37, 38, 44, 62n21, 75
Rouseff, Dilma 35
Rouvroy, Antoinette 60, 61, 67n167
Russia-Ukraine war 5, 15, 20, 55

Santesso, Aaron 23, 24, 31n112, 37, 38, 44, 62n21, 75
Sardanis, Andrew 106
Sartre, Jean-Paul 106
Scahill, Jeremy 10, 29n45
Scan Eagle 3
Scharre, Paul 52, 53, 56
second drone age 14–16
Second World War 1, 50
self-censorship 48
self-fashioning, micro politics of 114–15
Sentinel 3
Serafinelli, Elisa 17, 18, 20
Seraph 178
Serpell, Namwali 96, 101, 104, 106, 107, 110
Shabab 12
Shirke 3
Shohat, Ella 102, 103
Shringarpure, Bhakti 103
Sidigu, Annah Omune 105
Singer, P. W. 87, 99n84
Sky-Drone-Net 162
slave trade 73
Snowden, Edward Joseph 34, 36
Snow, John 37
social institutions 102
social media 118
Solove, Daniel J. 44–5, 61, 63n65
Somalia 4, 12
sousveillance 69, 89–91
Special Operations Command 2
spectral suspects 83

Spivak, Gayatri 121, 126
Spook Country (Gibson) 144
Srdarov, Suzanne 55, 65n135
Stahl, Roger 72, 91, 100n101
Staples, William G. 47, 63n73
states of exception 70–2, 79
stereotype 22
STORMBREW 35
Stubblefield, Thomas 136
subaltern narratives 115–17
subaltern resistance 104
  civil society 121–2
  gesture 125
  homogeneity 121
  nationalist historiography 121
  social groups 121
Sum of the Parts, or state of the Planet (SOTP) 124, 126
supervised learning 52
surveillance 21–2, 77
  anarchy of 34–7
  assemblage 40–2
  capitalism 73
  constant 24
  defined 37
  digital surveillant assemblage 42–4
  elements 39
  of Internet 34
  knowledgeability 39
  in liquid modernity 39–40
  mass 45
  modernity as 38–9
  non-state agencies in 42
  performative self under 44
  persistent 19
  practices 24
  rationalization 39
  resistances to 91
  sorting 39
  technology 39
  urgency 39
  at work 39
Surveillance and Identity: Discourse, Subjectivity, and the State (Barnard-Wills) 38, 62n27

surveillance cultures 152
Surveillance, Power, and Modernity: Bureaucracy and Discipline from 1700 to the Present Day (Dandeker) 95
Surveillance Studies: An Overview (Lyon) 37, 62n19
Swarmer 56
swarm intelligence 57
Swarm Surveillance 162
Swed, Ori 20, 31n93
Switchblade 3
synoptic viewing 19
synthetic vision 26

Tactical Media (Raley) 90
"targeted killing" 5
Tatlić, Šefik 72, 76, 96n15, 97n34
technology 9
techno-neocolonialism 103, 104, 118–24
technovision 25
Tehrike-Taliban 12
terrorism 81
Theorizing Digital Cultures (Bollmer) 139
Theory of the Drone, A (Chamayou) 19
Thistle and the Drone: How America's War on Terror Became a Global War on Tribal Islam, The (Ahmad) 12
threats 8
    imminent 11, 13
thresholds of visibility 44
Tigray War 15
totalization of perspective 19
transformer 54
transmission control protocol (TCP) 60
Trial, The (Kafka) 46
tribes 12, 13
truck art
    anthropological analysis of 172
    in Pakistan *169*
truck wheel art *173*
Trump, Donald 8
Turing, Alan 51
Turing Test 51
Twitter 35

United National Independence Party (UNIP) 116
United Nations 3–5
United States
    Air Force 55
    communications infrastructure 35
    drones in 2
    drones strikes 86
    foreign policy 14
    Government Accountability Office 88
    military operations 36
    Replicator Program 57
    surveillance society in 14
Unmanned Aerial Vehicles (UAVs) 118
Unmanned Combat Air System Demonstration program 6
unmanned vehicles 1–2, 27n2
unsupervised learning 52
US national security policy 10
US Special Operations Command (SOCOM) 6

Vanderburg, Colin 8, 29n35, 83, 98n67
vertical mediation 10, 11
violence 105, 106
violent non-state actors (VNSA) 119
Virilio, Paul 26, 31n116
visibility (invisibility/invisible) 14, 17, 20, 21, 37
Vision Machine, The (Virilio) 26, 31n116
vision technologies 40
visual immersion 20
volumetric thinking 16–18

Walzer, Michael 9, 29n43
Walzer, Michal 81
warfare 4, 8, 20
War in the Age of Intelligent Machines (DeLanda) 50
Wasp III 3
Watchman in Pieces: Surveillance, Literature, and Liberal Personhood, The (Rosen & Santesso) 23
Western modernity 72, 75

Wilcox, Lauren B. 84
On Wings of Diesel: Trucks, Identity, and Culture in Pakistan (Elias) 167
Wired for War: The Robotics Revolution and Conflict in the 21st Century (Singer) 87
Wolfram, Stephen 54
The Wretched of the Earth (Fanon) 105

X-47B 6, 7
X-KEYSCORE 35

Yemen 10–12, 11, 14

Zambia 96, 101, 102, 105, 106, 107, 109
   AIDS crisis 117, 123
   rise of digital culture 117–18
   society 126
Zambia African National Congress (ZANC) 116
Zambia National Women's Lobby Group (ZNWLG) 113
Zambia Women Writers' Association (ZWWA) 113
Zenko, Micah 8, 9, 28n9
Zimbabwe 109
Zuboff, Shoshana 73, 96n21